SVRREY

The
North Downs

Box Hill has given delight to countless visitors over centuries and it recalls the 'not Swisserland' of Jane Austen's Emma Woodhouse in Emma *(1816), but John Brett's* The Stone Breaker *(1858) symbolises the poverty and hardship for persons who could gain no other employment amidst beauty, plenty and gaiety in the Vale of Mickleham.*

The North Downs

PETER BRANDON

Phillimore

2005

Published by
PHILLIMORE & CO. LTD
Shopwyke Manor Barn, Chichester, West Sussex, England
www.phillimore.co.uk

ISBN 1 86077 353 2

Printed and bound in Great Britain by
CAMBRIDGE PRINTING

Dedicated to my late Father who inspired me by repeatedly grinding his pedals through the Vale of Mickleham

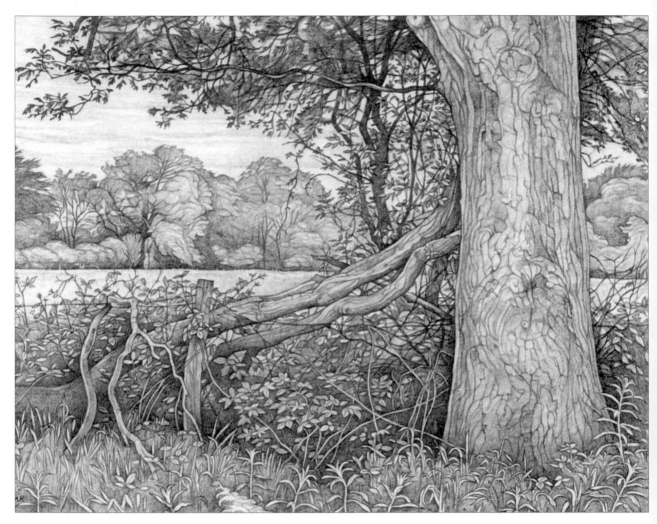

A.M. Parkin of Kemsing captures in exquisite detail the essence of the North Downs near his village — spreading oaks, small hedged fields, rich layers of wild plants and intimate woodland.

Contents

Kent, in the Commentaries Caesar writ,
Is term'd the civilis't place of all this Isle:
Sweet is the Country, because full of riches;
The People liberal, valiant, active, wealthy.

William Shakespeare

Farewell! – when youth, and health, and fortune spent,
Thou flys't for refuge to the Wilds of Kent …

Samuel Johnson, *London* (1738), 126/7

They [the North Downs] are the best chalk hills I know anywhere. The best wooded, and the most abounding in exquisite combes and bottoms.

Matthew Arnold, Letters, 29 July 1882

Surrey is entirely directed to serving urban man – in the Green Belt as much as anywhere else.

Ian Nairn in Nikolaus Pevsner,
The Buildings of England: Surrey (1977 edn)

List of Illustrations

Acknowledgements

I am greatly indebted to Ann Winser who compiled the index, read drafts with the greatest diligence, and made life-saving corrections. The support and unstinting help of Michael Wickham has also meant a great deal to me – and therefore to the book. I should like to thank Ann Money for introducing me to specific places and for her shrewd observations. Philippa Hewitt has been a most welcome guide to Kent. Alan Gillies generously loaned relevant material and pointed to sources. I also desire to express my cordial thanks to the staff of the Centre for Local Studies, Maidstone for their friendly help at all stages in the preparation of this book. I owe more than I can say to the staff of the London Library who have been unfailingly helpful especially during my illnesses. I am indebted to Elizabeth Rich, in charge of Bray manuscripts at Shere, for her willingness to unearth hitherto ignored primary material. Thanks are due to Tim Apsden of the Cartographic Unit, University of Southampton for the clear and accurate maps. I have also benefited from the help of so many persons who have assisted me in various ways. To the following, then, my most heartfelt thanks: the Rev. N. Ashworth, Douglas Bennett, John Biddulph, John and Mark Boyd, William Buck, Beryl Bush, Eileen Buxton, Graham Clarke, Mike Ebbs, Margaret Elston, Tony Gowers, David Hiscock, Gwen Hoad, Jack Hollands, Denver Hope, Paul Latham, Rob McGiven, Geoffrey Mead, Charlie Newington, Barbara Ogden, A.M. Parfitt, the Rev. S. Peal, Brian Philp, Dora Pilkington, Mary Price, Dr R.K. Quested, Alan Roberts, Chris Ross, Shepway District Council, Jill Skinner, the Countess Sondes, Martin Taylor, Clive Thomas and Alan Winser. As usual Noel Osborne and Nicola Willmot of Phillimore have given me every help and support.

The author is grateful to the following individuals and institutions for photographs and other illustrative material and for permission to reproduce them (photographs not listed were taken by the author):

Robert Berry, 11; Bristol's Museums, Galleries and Archives, 91; Robin J. Brooks, 134; Centre for Kentish Studies, 44, 49, 50, 72, 80, 133, IX; Graham Clarke, XX; Country Life, XXVIII; Dover District Council, 10, 13, 17, 138, 140, I; Field Studies Council, 21; Foundling Hospital Museum, XXI; Thomas Hooley, VIII; Francine Huin-Wah, 47; James Ingle from Eyes Wide Digital Ltd, XXIX; Imperial War Museum, XXVI; Juniper Hall Field Centre, 6, 8, 22, 33, 119, 131, XVI; Kent Downs AONB, III; Kent Messenger, 134-6; Lees Court Estate, XXVII; The London Transport Museum, XII, XXIII; The Ordnance Survey, 9. 10; Öster-reicheische Nationalbibliotek, Vienna, 103; Painted House Museum, IV; A.M.

Parkin, page vi, 129-30, XVII, XVIII; Brian Philp, 30, 31; The Photographic Survey and Record of Surrey, Woking, 98; Shell Archive and Chris Beetles, II; Ethel Wyn Shiel, XXIV; The Tate Gallery, 91, VI; Andy Williams, XI; Ann Winser, 18-19, 23, 38-9, 40-1, 42, 44, 45, 51, 53-4, 61, 62, 71, 74, 79, 82-4, 89, 93, 97, 99-102, 104-7, 110-11, 120-1, 123, IV, VII, XXV.

Preface

The double ridges of the North Downs and the bordering sandstone hills are the Londoner's own countryside. One-fifth of the population of the United Kingdom lives on or within easy reach of them on the 'fresh air side of the capital'. Generations have experienced enjoyment, inspiration and life-enhancement from their escape to peaceful downland and scenery of heather, bracken and pine, for there is a sense of space – the sky and its firmament, broad prospects, glimpses of horizon, beautiful buildings and contact with growing things.

This is the essence of the North Downs for centuries – their proximity to the capital city and the ways in which, by fencing people in from the world of worry, they have counteracted noise, congestion and polluted air for the Londoner who seeks a refuge from the inhibiting pressures of urban life within reasonable reach of the city. From the mid-19th century this most important of London's lungs became a residence, playground, sanatorium, health resort, field laboratory and open-air studio all thrown into one. The Downs attracted various types of person: wealthy *nouveaux riches* from London's villadom and railway lines, horrified at the disruption and ugliness brought into the new world of steam; the retired who wanted to live out their last days beyond the crowded precincts of the encroaching capital; the visitor seeking a day's excursion in air free of smoke and fog; the landscape artist, though born and bred in London, who fled from building sites for countryside which took on the character of an earthly paradise. They also enticed the misfits, rebels and 'escapists', some reacting like medievalists born out of their due time, who desperately longed, like languishing prisoners, to leave a London irrevocably committed to the gospel of the machine and in countryside to launch a counter-attack upon the materialism which they perceived was harming human values and religious experience. Thus the Downs and their adjacent hills have been the birthplace of ideas which were intended to make the world a better place and to give a respite to a town-weary society. It is this interaction between what was the world's largest city and its green girdle south of the Thames which is a major theme of this book.

The other is to recount the fascinating past before the early modern period of the rib of chalk culminating in the escarpment of the North Downs, the Vale of Holmesdale immediately to the south and the wonderfully diversified belt of sandstone hills which affords unforgettable panoramas of southern England from Leith Hill or Holmbury Hill in Surrey and from Boughton Monchelsea or Egerton in Kent. These landscapes comprise a tract of country about one hundred miles long of which the distinguished editors of the New Naturalist series of books remarked that it would be difficult to find anywhere in the world an area of comparable size which exhibits so perfectly the response of plant, animal and human life to this diversity.[1] It broadly coincides with the Surrey Hills and Kent Downs Areas of Outstanding Natural Beauty designated in 1958 and 1968 respectively. Despite the relentlessly expanding metropolis it is remarkable how so much of the ancient countryside survives. Formerly, powerful landowners kept the 'Wen' at bay and planning acts and Green Belt regulations now strive to keep the heritage green. The North Downs and their adjacent hills are a gift of history which is literally priceless, precious as well as vulnerable. On the threshold of the 21st century this complex of hills and vales is a cherished rarity which cries out for a prominent place in the present, tired, over-worked countryside of Britain.

This is the third volume on landscape and society in south-east England that I have written in an attempt to explain how it has become as it is, and to introduce some of the techniques for exploring it. Although the first, *The South Downs* (1998) is in the full sense a history, it was designed to lead up to a plea for their greater protection and possible restitution in a National Park. The second volume, *The Kent and Sussex Weald* (2003), was written from the perspective of the small family farmers, foresters, traders, artisans and farm labourers who were primarily responsible for the entrancing landscape of little fields and woods we have come to appreciate today. Both books were infused with my own interests and experiences, in part inherited, and these have really determined the kind of books they are. Many generations of the simple working people of my maternal forebears were shepherds, carters and foremen on farms in the South Downs. My joy at knowing that by origin I belonged to these serene and spacious hills was certainly not anything but deeply sincere. The Weald book is imbued with my father's small businessman's values with which I grew up and which have powerfully influenced my own dislike of the present disproportionate infatuation for the Big, the Bigger and the Biggest. The present volume draws its inspiration from my youth and early manhood when from Twickenham I cycled and walked over the Surrey Downs and first experienced their beguiling close-ups and unforgettable panoramas. Box Hill is richly layered in nostalgia for me, as it is for so many who have had a lifelong love-affair with it, partly because it was at Juniper Hall Field Centre, which still flourishes, that I was introduced to the techniques of geography by such gifted tutors as Professor S.W. Wooldridge and G.E. Hutchings, from which I gained a life-giving stimulus. Here, above all, I was taught the useful art of seeing things as they really are. Later, I learned how variously individuals perceive what they look at and how the writer and artist is able to invent in his own mind what he intends, imagines or dreams a place to be. Both these different strands are brought together in this book.

I

Introduction

It is remarkable how different, indeed radically different, the North Downs are from the South Downs, considering that both are basically pieces of chalk and diametrically opposed across the wooded Weald as the springs from an arch from which the keystone of a thick canopy of chalk has been entirely removed by denudation. The North Downs, though grazed by sheep, were too leafy to have had the extensive spreads of the short, springy turf which from the 17th century were accounted the chief glory of the South Downs. Entering the North Downs one is acutely conscious of entering another country. For persons unfamiliar with them, there is a special language to be learned and different landscapes to be appreciated. The eye is not set free along curves and hollows spread like an ocean without check as in the eastern part of the South Downs, because mantling the surface of the North Downs is a remarkable extent of woodland. The south-facing escarpment of the North Downs is not generally as spectacular and majestic as that of the South Downs and the greater part of the surface shows little sign of Kipling's 'blunt, bow-headed, whale-backed hills' coursing along the horizon. This results from a much less mature dissection by former streams and springs in the North Downs than in their southern counterpart, where huger quantities of chalk have been steadily sculpted to shape the muscular hills and hollow combes.[1]

The pre-war connoisseur of chalk hills tended to regard the North Downs as less glamorous than the South Downs, which were regarded as archetypal chalk country. With hindsight, the disparaging remarks about the North Downs struck depths of absurdity, as if apple trees should be reproved for not yielding peaches. A whole generation was taken in by this nonsense. There is no permanent element in landscape beauty. It is subject to fluctuations in the public taste of each successive generation, and changes are always taking place in a particular landscape over time. These evolutions of taste mean that a reigning favourite conforming to the taste of one generation may be displaced in favour of another demigod in the eyes of a later one. This fact can be applied to the case of the North and South Downs. Since the Second World War the latter have undergone a sea change which has been revolutionary, and for the worse. Beginning with war in 1940 and accelerating with post-war austerity, almost all the old chalk grassland (and nearly all the Southdown sheep) disappeared under arable agribusiness. The South Downs of Kipling and Belloc vanished at a touch, as it were. To older people the once-dazzling South Downs have lost freshness and seem like some strange other-world. The Downs' rolling ridges and wide skies still have the power to raise the spirit and lift the heart but the monoculture of the modern cornfield affords less refreshment for the soul than the more diverse landscapes of the past. Moreover, a generation ago Dutch elm disease wiped out most of the loveliest ornaments of their landscape. The South Downs still enjoy immortal fame but their former glamour has been tarnished; to some extent they are living on their past reputation and are now in need of restitution.

The North Downs have changed less than the South Downs in the post-war era and are now enjoying a vogue as strong as their previous obscurity was complete. They now appeal to a more recently learned and subtler emotion than that which responds to the beauty of the South Downs. The individual human scale of almost everything remains small. This mellow, habitable charm is good to look upon, feels instinctively right and comfortable and brings peace of mind with it. Because most of it is not intensively farmed, the 'wilder' landscape elements mix with the domestic garden-like character of the cultivated land, both types of landscape being present in turns and melting into one another. This admixture, an unusual element in the English landscape, was excoriated by agricultural 'improvers' of the 18th century, but, with the growth of London and other large cities and towns over the past one hundred years or so, it has come to be regarded as an unusual and delightful scenery where people can come into close contact with nature rich in human, plant and animal communities. This makes the landscape of the North Downs special as a vestige of a much older England which has largely disappeared elsewhere with industrial, urban and agricultural development since the 18th century.

The great glory of the North Downs is its escarpment which faces south into the sun, unlike the corresponding escarpment of the South Downs, and in consequence, a kind of 'inland riviera' prevails, where, sheltered by the undercliff, is the finest human habitat in southern England. Where it is free from encroaching scrub which has tended to invade it in recent times, it is also a matchless paradise of fauna and flora. In the comparative warmth continental species of plants thrive, whereas in the cooler, north-facing slopes of the South Downs the more oceanic species do better. The warmth imparted by the North Downs escarpment means that it is a good place for butterflies, such as the Adonis blue and the silver-spotted skipper which tend to fly only in sunshine in sheltered spots and thrive in sun-trapped warmth. The scarp at Oxted, where English Nature is encouraging wild plants and butterflies through scrub clearance, and the high concentrations on Kemsing Green Hill and on the undercliff at Wye are notable places for wildlife. Where chalk swards exist the miniature springy grass is sweet with marjoram and wild thyme and supports hosts of wild flowers and their attendant invertebrates. The naturalist Henry Salt has popularly described this haven of man, animal, plant and insect. He thought there was no diviner couch than the chalk greensward where 'the wandering flower-lover may revel in glowing sunshine, or take a siesta, if so minded, under that most friendly of trees, the whitebeam'. He was surprised to find that, although wild thyme has been so celebrated by poets and nature-writers, marjoram has by comparison gone unsung.[2]

1 *The bold escarpment of the North Downs near Reigate. Further east in the Kent Downs the steep slope is unwooded.*

From a human standpoint one can cite Titsey Place which lies in a sun-bathed combe etched into the face of the escarpment, sheltered from the wind and fringed in the 18th century with a backdrop of beech, the loveliest of all the trees that grow in England. This is the most perfect dwelling place imaginable. Nor is this seat of the Greshams before the Leveson-Gowers alone in this respect. It is evident that the affluent have had a similar idea of perfection and of ideal beauty and had a preference for living sheltered to the north and in sunlight all the year round, certainly for some two thousand years – witness the long line of Roman villas, medieval manor houses, and mansions mostly of Elizabethan or earlier origins that lie in the calm beauty of the rampart of the upper Downs. They are neither too close, nor too far away, whether for comfort and a sense of home-coming, or for hunting, or growing the prodigious crops on the home farm of an estate.

The overall impression of the North Downs is of the distinctive landscape known in Normandy as 'bocage'. This signifies land wrested from the wildwood in historical times but with a high proportion of woodland left, owing to un-rewarding soils and difficult topography. It is more characteristic of the heavy claylands of England, notably the Wealds of Kent, Surrey and Sussex.[3] The

2 The ploughshare running hard against the wood. A typical scene in the North Downs arising from woodland clearance and one stimulating literary and artistic imagination.

cause of its extension on to the North Downs is that their upper slopes and crest are largely masked by a thick coating of similar intractable soil mixed with flints, stones and gravel. Most of this mantle of deposits covering the chalk accumulated during the last Ice Age when a tundra-like climate prevailed. Under these conditions the chalk broke down into sludge-like masses which readily flowed down slopes in so-called solifluction flows. This ungrateful, stony ground has been the scourge of generations of farmers. Where this type of soil exists, the North Downs is surely one of the hardest places in Britain where human beings have tried to wrest a living. A good harvest was one for which a farmer scarcely dared to hope. For this reason much of the high ground has been a simple, self-sufficient countryside where nature has been used for centuries but not intensively exploited. The mantle of uncongenial stony soil was formerly denominated 'clay-with-flints' (in places it might be more appropriately called 'flints-with clay') but the deposits are of different geological ages and origins, though younger than the underlying chalk, and highly variable in depth and texture. At elevations of about 490-550 feet there is a flat, old sea floor, cut by waves in Late Tertiary (Pliocene) times and floored by sand and gravel layers. These marine deposits on Headley and Walton Heaths are sterile, but further east in Kent the Lenham beds of the same age have been ameliorated. On the highest parts, between approximately 600-690 feet in Surrey, is a coating of reddish and brown clayey material with large fractured flints in a deposit up to ten feet thick which is presumed to have been deposited by melt waters during thaws in the last glacial period. Immediately below, and also resting on the chalk itself is a layer of clayey material containing unbroken flints. This layer appears to have originated from the accumulation of impurities in the chalk resulting from the sub-surface solution in rainwater. On the Kent Downs these sticky reddish soils were evocatively known as 'cledge', a term which conveys the adhesive strength of the soil and the sucking and grinding sound that the ploughshare makes when driving deeply into heavy clay and flints. In east Kent and the Isle of Thanet most of the chalk is covered with fertile loess, a sandy silt loam which is considered to have been blown there by severe winds in the aftermath of the last glaciation.

Whatever its thickness, clay-with-flints produces a particular type of landscape and a particular type of agriculture. It has much the same properties as Weald Clay in the claylands below the chalk which Vita Sackville-West of Sissinghurst observed was the cause of such afflictions as back-strain and arthritis, of udder rash, worms and foot-rot in animals. It is the sort of curmudgeonly soil that 'turns health into sickness, youth into age and life, in due course, into death' which Roger Scruton has noted of his Wiltshire clayland: 'How unfriendly, how contemptuous of human need and comfort is that soil that passes from mud to brick and back again, with scarcely a day of benevolence in between!'.[4] Quite unlike the clean, drained chalky soil of the eastern South Downs the soil 'pulls like a hangman at the heels of his victim' and cracks and gapes in a dry summer. Generations of North Downs farmers have been locked in combat with this grudging soil and nothing has ever released them, although with modern machinery much of the back-breaking toil has been mitigated.

For centuries flints were picked off fields ploughed for autumn sowing. Traditionally it was the task of boys, women and children to pick up flints by the basketful from ploughed land and to carry the stones to the edge of a field for collection by horse and cart for building or road repairs. It was slow back-breaking work and cruel on the hands and ineffectual because seemingly the same number of flints remained, giving rise to the superstition amongst labourers that the land actually 'grew' flints – even where there were few flints on the surface, frost and rain would soon expose some more. It would seem that the labour of flint-picking might actually have reduced the productivity of the land because Arthur Young's experiment, conducted on the stony chalk of East Suffolk at the end of the 18th century, disclosed that the yield of crops from land cleared of flints was less than from that left untouched, presumably because the stones facilitated drainage.[5] Nevertheless, stone-picking continued because of its supposed benefits to the soil and for the little money it earned the farmer. As late as the 1920s mothers and children picked stones in buckets which filled a wooden box holding a square yard, the basis of payment.

Keeping the soil at bay was a special type of plough. This was the Kentish turn-wrest, universal in Kent and indeed in Surrey and Sussex, although William Marshall, the 18th-century agricultural writer, was probably correct in his surmise that it originated in the special conditions of the North Downs, for the massive turn-wrest alone was able to handle them.[6] The turn-wrest ploughed deeper and had a stronger pulverising action than ordinary medieval ploughs. Its large mouldboard which forced open the furrow was changed at the field's end to the opposite side of the plough for ploughing soil flat on a steep hillside. For 'landing up' heavy ground into ridges for sowing the mouldboard (the wrest or 'rice') was left unchanged and sods were thrown up on opposite sides of the furrow as the plough went back and forth. On very stony soils the plough-share underwent very heavy wear and tear and the winged or fin share was replaced with a sharp chisel-like one. The implement was enormous and needed four horses or more to pull it and Marshall was shocked that from force of habit it was used even on light soils in east Kent which could have been less expensively worked with fewer horses. He regarded the component parts as nearly equal in number to those of a ship. A North of England farmer would have called it a carriage, rather than a plough, and the mouldboard was attached to such a heavy beam that he might have been glad of it for a gate-post, and it had a pair of wheels as large as the fore-wheels of a moorland wagon. Today a trail of sparks in the wake of the plough in evening light or the noise of the share grinding against stones is a common experience.

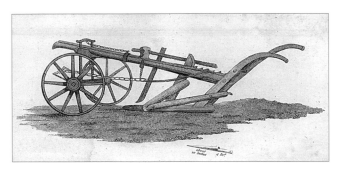

15 *The Kentish turn-wrest plough, universally used on the North Downs and in south-east England generally.*

The consequences of the terrible cover of clay-with-flints have been profound. Firstly, as we have noted, a special kind of landscape developed on it which is akin to that of the English claylands. Secondly, woodland clearance on the North Downs was a much more sporadic and lengthy process than on the South Downs, and this continued long into the historic period and was not fully completed. It would appear that the main assault on the woodland was in the later Anglo-Saxon period by which time the better land in the foothills had run out, but much woodland clearance had to be accomplished in the early Middle Ages. Tudor and Stuart 'improvers' renewed the onslaught on uncultivated wildness when population rose again after the 14th-century famines and pestilences, recovering, little by little, what had been previously lost since depopulation. This history implies that much of the Downs throughout history have been marginal, i.e. land cultivated close to the margin of profitability, the kind of land cultivated in times of high corn prices and population growth but abandoned to poor grass when bad times returned. From ridges, many valleys still look like woodland with farms in clearings as in some back-country. Much of the downland has been attached in various ways to the more fertile land 'below the hill'. The overall effect of this history is to leave a countryside on the Downs crowded with detail. There are dozens of scattered farms, scores of narrow, twisting lanes, countless little shaws and copses, several large stretches of woodland; in short a broken, parcelled, varied countryside thick with tiny settlements and ancient place-names. The Ordnance map covering Lyminge and Elham, for instance, has more than 170 settlements marked by name and another 50 names relate to woods and other topographical features. The comparison with the South Downs is vast (see opposite).

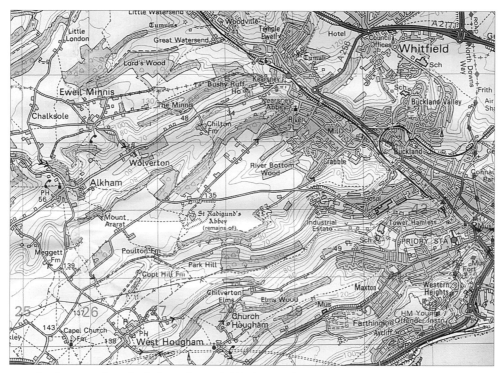

9 *An extract from the Ordnance Survey 1:50000 map, sheet 179, of part of the North Downs.*

10 *An extract from the Ordnance Survey 1:50000 map, sheet 197, of part of the South Downs.*

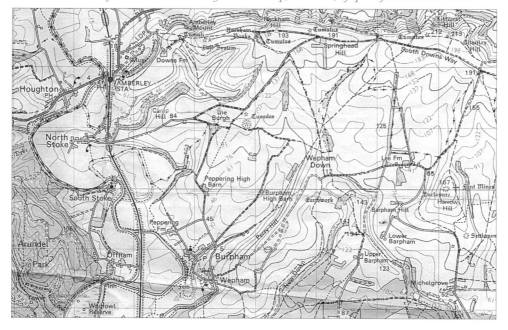

The stiff and stony downland soils were costly to cultivate. In favourable seasons they produced good crops of wheat from fields once in five years, to the amazement of strangers, but yields were subject to great variability on account of weather at times of fallowing, sowing and harvesting. The soil is most apt for grass, as in claylands, and farmers have tended to raise cattle and sheep, although at times of high corn prices, as in the mid-19th century, arable farming with average yields was possible. The farming society was distinctive, for the marginal land of the Downs was the home of the small family farmer who lived a hard life and had a deep knowledge of the soil and its qualities. He had to develop the special skills and virtues needed for laying hedges with bill-hook, clearing ditches by hand, logging in the woodland, coppicing with hatchets, planting covert, tilling, milking, herding and heaving contrary animals and heavy bales. The sheer ardour needed to cultivate the land was graphically described by James Malcolm.[7] Ploughing on hillsides and on stony and uneven fields needed great skill and only repeated ploughings produced the necessary tilth for sowing. There would be an unholy clatter all the time and in dry weather dust might cover the ploughman and temporarily blind him. Fallowing before wheat was deemed indispensable as much for resting the land as for controlling weeds. Much harrowing was also needed in advance of sowing, and rolling with a heavy roller was required to make the ground firm for plant growth. As farms had both pastures and arable fields and often assumed awkward shapes through the process of gavelkind inheritance, the plough and other heavy equipment would often go from one end of the farm to another, perhaps a long round-about journey across fields, through gates and along byways. Under-draining was carried out from the early 19th century on flattish ground. Unsurprisingly, many farming operations were conducted with flurry, haste and anxiety, and the management of a farm was a heavy responsibility. Nowadays much of the old farming routine is abandoned now that there is hardly a market for wood products and contractors are hired to do the basic farmwork. On the bare chalk surface of the South Downs it was the sheep which symbolised farming and its ways of life. In the North Downs, although sheep were important, the land would never have acquired its human population without cows.

The small farmers are responsible for the labyrinth of narrow lanes which characterise the Downs, for each wanted access to the common, the mill, the high road, the market town, the church and to droving roads down to the marshes. The remarkable tree-like network of minor ways which developed was even more intricate than at present since many have become obsolete and are no longer maintained, though they remain as bridle ways and footpaths. These unpaved green lanes are amongst the most beautiful features of the Downs with their flower-covered verges and ancient banks and ditches. To the pastoral economy which was the backbone of the small family farm for hundreds of years, with short interludes, is owed another landscape characteristic, the ubiquitous hedgerow. These ancient features are generally unusually wide and thick. Like Wealden hedges they are often unrestrained swathes of intertwined bramble and branch, the dense foliage of many species of shrubs and trees, supporting a lavish colony of wild flowers, mammals and song birds. They reveal their ancientness not only by their many species, their thickness and height, but by their crookedness which is due to the prolonged use of a four- or eight-ox team or its horse equivalent. Invariably the hedge is sending out brambles, nettles and shrubs on to the verge of the fields. In autumn the hedgerows are a riot of contrasting colours: the deep reds of berries of rowan, the vermilion guelder rose and hawthorn and the various yellows of leaves, for example, mingle with the purple sloes and blackberries amidst every shade of red, crimson, gold and auburn foliage.[8]

The friendliest and most fertile soil occurs in the Isle of Thanet and along the northern edge of the Downs between Chatham and Deal. Here the gentle chalk down swells are covered mostly by a rich loam of variable nature, usually known as brickearth from its suitability for the famed Kentish bricks and tiles. It is akin to loess on the continent, a deposit of wind-blown origin subsequently worked by streams. Other light soils include the water-worn pebbles around Wingham called 'sea-drift' by local farmers. Being light and well-drained 'garden mould' it was easy to cultivate, and thus inexpensive, nor was cultivation normally impeded by weather apart from frost. Moreover, no fences, furrows, ditches or drains were needed. The wide, open, hedgeless countryside was more wooded before the Conquest but has become treeless and exposed to the fury of wind in winter. The farms have tended to be of moderate size, some 2-300 acres or so, but have barns of an extraordinary size with a range of hovels or sheds on either

5 *The 'Happy Valley'. The chalk track up to the summit of Box Hill was a favourite walk of George Meredith.*

side, the same roof covering the whole, which gives a marked individuality to the scene. Where chalk comes close to the surface the land is not so productive.

Today, despite being smothered and over-built in places by suburban and industrial development, the Downs have a tranquillising and therapeutic serenity. They have the fresh winds to clear the air and keep changing the cloudscape, and deep country stillnesses which can almost be breathed. In places one feels a hundred miles from Charing Cross, such is the remoteness of the lonely farms, hamlets, isolated churches and the twisting narrow lanes. The Downs are also very changeable in mood, having high spirits or low, according to changes in weather, season or hour. There is never the same light, the same air, the same sky or the same sea. There is nothing special about much of the Downs – it is agricultural and wooded land, and cannot be described in terms of beauty spots – yet it is one of the loveliest regions in England and the ancient and delicate scenery must have looked much the same over the past six or seven centuries. One amongst so many who have praised them was the mountaineer Frank Smythe, whose earliest childhood recollections were of the Kent Downs and who retired to Haslemere. He was always as happy on low hills as on high hills and valuably pointed out that the actual matter of height counts for little because, whether the height be 500 or 5,000 feet, there is something precious that quickens life to a nobler rhythm, a sense of freedom, elation and triumph in an unobstructed view all round. This joy he called the 'spirit of the hills'.[9] A genius who shared this passion for a vantage point with wide prospects of ranges of hills was the landscape artist Samuel Palmer who, too poorly to work in the smoke of North Kensington any longer, took a house at Reigate from 1862, where from his parlour window he could look straight out on to the Brighton downs nearly thirty miles off, his side windows gave views of the magnificent range of Leith Hill, and by going a step or two outdoors he saw the range of chalk hills to the north – the complete panorama in southern England.[10]

Climatically, the Downs share the genial warmth of southern England and lie in the sunniest part of Britain. On the highest ground rainfall is considerably greater and temperatures a little cooler than in the lowlands. Winter can be harsh on high ground when easterly winds blow in from the continent and snow lingers longest on the summits. This bleakness in winter is reflected in the considerable number of place-names sprinkled over Ordnance Survey maps which signify coldness. Many of the hollows in the North Downs are frost pockets where warmth is slow in raising cold temperatures. One of the anomalies is the meteorological station at Redhill Airfield which, although in a relatively warm climatic region, regularly records some of the coldest winter temperatures in Britain because cold air is banked up against the local topography. In autumn and spring mist lingers on hill-tops and deep valleys but is dispersed quickly with rising temperatures. This imparts a mysterious, even mountainous quality to the hills and valleys of the kind captured in Chinese landscape paintings. Sunrises and sunsets between October and February are stunning. A notable element is the saltish breeze which acts like a tonic and 'blows the cobwebs from business world brains'. Wind, which has been increasing in strength over the past

7 *The North Downs Way near Westwell.*

twenty years or so, makes outdoor exercise exhilarating in autumn and winter. In tempestuous weather westerlies blow at up to gale force across the Downs, bending the trees and seeming to come from every angle at once. Meanwhile great waves are eroding the base of cliffs, resulting eventually in their toppling over into the sea. The wind also tears chalk fragments from the upper part of the cliffs and hurls them over the cliff top. In frosty weather particles of water freeze on cliff sides and force apart layers of chalk which fall in the thaw. Where severe erosion continues on the North and South Foreland the chalk face is kept white and steep from the constant fall of rock from the faces.

Associations

The leisure function of the Downs has had a long history. The London fringe of the Downs became one of the city's favourite hawking, hunting and coursing grounds before the Middle Ages. In the early 19th century the woodlands on the Kent side were immortalised by R.S. Surtees, whose 'smoke-dried cit', John Jorrocks, the grocer of Great Coram Street off Russell Square, was one of those tradesmen who flew from their shops to enjoy Saturday's shooting, racing and driving on the Downs. He made his debut as a true city sportsman with the Surrey Hunt and the Surrey Stag Hounds in the 1830s dressed in a huge antique red frock-coat with a dark collar and mother-of-pearl buttons and boots which looked as if they were made to tear up the very soil. Croydon was then the Londoner's favourite centre. The renowned West Kent Foxhounds, Mr Meager's

Harriers, the Sanderstead Harriers and the Surrey Stag Hounds met there. At an early hour 'grinning cits' were to be seen pouring in from the London side 'to the infinite gratification of troops of dirty-nosed urchins'. After a hearty breakfast at *The Greyhound*, bills were paid, pocket-pistols filled, sandwiches stowed away, horses accoutred and on they went 'now trotting gently over the flints – now softly ambling along the grassy ridge of some stupendous hill – now quietly following each other in long drawn files, like geese, through some close and deep ravine or interminable wood which re-echoes to their never-ceasing holloas – every man shouting in proportion to his subscription, until day is made horrible with their yelling'. Thus they made for Addington Heath, through the village and on up to the *Fox* at Keston. This was a hunting ground unequalled in southern England, a superiority arising from the nature of the soil and landscape, 'wretched starvation stuff most profusely studded with huge, sharp flints and the abundance of large woods, particularly on the Kent side of London'. These members of the Surrey Hunt were people who combined business with pleasure, 'even in the severest run' finding time to talk about the price of stocks or stockings. 'Yoof, wind him there, good dog, yoof wind him, Cottons is fell ... Hark! ... take your bill in three months.'[11]

Horse-racing in the special surroundings of the rolling downs between Banstead and Epsom, only 17 miles from London, was popular in the early Stuart years and during the fame of Epsom Spa. Although the resort fell into decline in the 18th century, annual horse races continued to be held on the springy turf and Lord Derby introduced the Derby Stakes in 1780 as a supreme test for three-year-olds on its downhill and uphill curves which led to the roistering Derby Day. In its heyday in the 1850s and 1860s this was a kind of national carnival, the institution attracting myriad crowds from the metropolis to the familiar scene of W.P. Frith's *Derby Day* (1858), where spectators waited for the magic moment when the words 'they're off' echoed round the Downs on the Surrey hilltop.

Earlier, in the 17th century, the fresh air of the Banstead Downs had been discovered by Restoration leisure-seekers, and Box Hill became a venue of the patrons of Epsom Spa. With the coming of railways and motor transport, few Cockneys could resist a Bank Holiday jaunt into this part of London's countryside on their doorstep to get some fresh air and exercise free of the London smoke. This Surrey part of the North Downs has also had an exceptionally rich association with people who became nationally prominent in public life. As William Cobbett put it with his usual extravagance, it was 'One of the finest places in the world for the breeding and rearing of Members of Parliament and Prime Ministers'.[12] Apart from politicians and statesmen, the Surrey Hills have for three hundred years also attracted philosophers, writers, landscape artists, architects and designers, in contrast to East Kent which has been primarily the preserve of bluff farmers and landed squires. Alfred, Lord Tennyson stayed at Boxley Park in 1842 and gave a graphic portrait of Sir Walter Vivian, who had given up his park for a great fête of the Mechanics Institute of Maidstone 'to let the people breathe', and who might be regarded as a model of the Kentish squires of his day:

8 *Box Hill from the south.*

No lily-handed baronet he,
A great broad shoulder'd genial Englishman,
A lord of fat-prize oxen and of sheep,
A raiser of huge melons and of pine,
A patron of some thirty charities,
A pamphleteer on guano and on grain,
A quarter-sessions chairman, abler none,
Fair-hair'd and redder than a windy morning …

Numerous commodities also made the North Downs famous. There was Alton ale, Farnham corn and hops, dainties like Dorking fowls and Banstead mutton; in Kent, walnuts and filberts for the rich man's table and enormous stores of faggots were supplied to London before coal was used in taverns and residences.

Continuing into the Kent Downs, which extend the range of the North Downs to the coast at Dover, we encounter an exciting historical arena with strong continental links through time, which has made its own notable contribution to the spiritual, economic and cultural making of early England and one of the most precociously developed parts of Europe. We can savour the growing skills of prehistoric navigators of the treacherous tides and currents of the English Channel from the Bronze Age, *c.*1500 BC. Julius Caesar graphically described the relatively opulent style of rural life in Kent compared with the British interior on his two landings in 55 and 54 BC. The Roman invasion of Britain in AD 43 is traditionally located at Richborough (though a counter-claim has been put forward for Fishbourne by Sussex archaeologists). In the early fifth century the former district was the legendary landing ground of Hengist and

9 *South Foreland lighthouse, St Mary's Bay.*

Horsa and a flourishing Jutish culture of the sixth and seventh centuries ensued. St Augustine in AD 597 landed at Richborough or Stonar from Rome and his mission inaugurated the conversion of England to Christianity. Commemorative statues to Ethelbert and Bertha, the king and queen of Kent who received St Augustine, are to be erected in Canterbury near their palace and church. Ethelbert's was the first English law code and the first surviving writing in the English language. In the ninth and 10th centuries Viking raiders pillaged the coastline. After the Norman Conquest, Canterbury became associated with the eminent abbots of the Abbey of Bec-Hellouin in Normandy, Lanfranc and St Anselm, the latter the greatest of the archbishops of Canterbury. Medieval pilgrims travelling to the shrine of St Thomas à Becket became so familiar with the edge of the Downs that Chaucer built their topography into his *Canterbury Tales* (p.215). Vast areas of the finest arable land were acquired by the Church who raised federated 'grain factories' in the Middle Ages to feed London and sustain national wealth. In these, and many other ways, east Kent was drawn into the mainstream of European civilisation. As we have noted, east Kent still fulfils this role. Canterbury has a resident population of only 70,000 but a further 800,000 live within five miles of it and up to eight million live within an hour's drive, including people in north-east France, via the Channel Tunnel. The scenic and wildlife value of the Kent Downs will become even greater as population in the metropolitan region grows and the needs of an urbanised society for fresh-air recreation intensify.

The White Cliffs of Dover and the Straits

It appears that from the 'White Cliffs of Dover' at the North and South Forelands Britain derived its earliest name of Albion, meaning 'white', bestowed on the island by the great Greek sea-captain Pytheas sailing from Marseilles in the fourth century BC and other early navigators who encountered these dangerous white cliffs in the narrow seas. It is not only the cliffs that are white. The shallow water offshore takes on a chalky whiteness from the eroding cliffs, and the luminous material seems to saturate the air, bleaching even the colour of the sky and the green of the short turf and the wild thyme on the cliff tops, so creating a special light and atmosphere.

For centuries the sea cliffs have been the reassuring image of home which greets native travellers on return, and for which departing travellers grieve when

10 *Dover Castle above the town.*

they lose sight of them. They have also been perceived as the island's main defence against her enemies. How true was Samuel Taylor Coleridge writing of his age when he wrote of England as Albion and his 'Mother Isle' and of the grassy uplands echoing to the bleat of flocks, which 'proudly ramparted with rocks', spoke safety 'to this Island child'. This part of the Channel coast has been the most closely-guarded coastline in Britain, as the Roman fortifications of Reculver, Richborough and Lympne, and the medieval and later castles of Walmer, Deal and Camber, together with the repeated strengthening of Dover Castle and other preparations against invasion, bear witness. Two hundred years ago Napoleon's camp at Boulogne threatened. In the First World War German cannons fired 'from where Gris-Nez winks' and drew a counterblast muzzle to muzzle across the Straits, and in the Second World War Dover was almost blown to smithereens by German guns from the same sites. Overhead were some of the most savage contests in the Battle of Britain, and in the Pas de Calais just across the Straits were built the launching pads of VI pilotless 'planes to blitz London in 1944. After the Dunkirk evacuation in the last war, the song '(There'll be Bluebirds over) the White Cliffs of Dover', made popular by Vera Lynn, helped to inspire the nation to take on the Nazis alone and by this stubbornness to help save the world.

The Kent historian Hasted described Dover as 'the lock and key of England'. This could not be more appropriate for, as well as barring foes, the Straits have been the main gateway for the comings and goings between England and the coast of France, and giving most people their first sight of mainland Europe, so making them one of the great cultural and economic highways of the world. France has been the Muse of successive generations of Englishmen, drawn by its allure and influence, and has seen over the centuries wandering scholars, pilgrims, those seeking enlightenment from the Grand Tour, and self-imposed exiles bound for the artistic and literary colonies of Paris, Florence and Rome. In the reverse direction have come the persecuted – Huguenots fugitives from the French Revolution, victims of the Nazis – cloth-and iron-workers seeking work in the Weald, and French and German admirers of English landscape design, architecture, agriculture and manufactures in the 18th and 19th centuries. The Straits remain the busiest shipping lane in the world and armed fleets have repeatedly fought there. As Kipling observed, if all the ships sunk over millennia were to be retrieved from its sea bed they would stretch round the globe. On the top of the cliffs are monuments to Captain Matthew Webb, the first man to swim the Channel in 1875, to Louis Blériot, marking the site where he landed after making the first cross-channel flight in an aeroplane in 1909, and to C.S. Rolls who made the first two-way flight across the Channel in 1910. In Dover Castle at 'Hell-fire Corner' is a statue to Vice-Admiral Ramsay who conducted the evacuation from Dunkirk.

Travellers in both directions had their eyes newly opened by the experience of crossing the Straits, the differences between the two sides being fresh enough in their minds to point the contrast. Horace Walpole, who travelled through Kent from the continent in 1741, stumbled to the realisation that much of its comfortable atmosphere was due to the littleness of its natural and man-made features, a quality lacking in the more coarse-grained and less-diversified landscape of northern France. By similar analogy and contrast he detected another notable omission across the Channel, the homely scale of the yeoman's hall.[13] When Byron crossed the Straits and sped along the new turnpikes of east Kent he discovered how smooth early 19th-century English roads were in comparison with France:

> On! On!
> Through meadows managed as a garden,
> A paradise of hops and high production.[14]

To the Elizabethan mind the cherry orchards, hop grounds, and beautiful multi-coloured fields of north-east Kent made it the Garden of England, and a presentable imitation of Eden unparalleled in beauty anywhere else in the world, a district already moulded by centuries of human use into the semblance of the then much admired *champion*, richly-cultivated open country. The 18th-century Duke of Nivernois, fresh from France, was so ravished by the sight of this garden-like cultivation along the Dover to London highway ('like the kitchen gardens of Choisy') that, although he loved France with the same demanding and complicated passion of his countrymen, he declared it to be 'the finest country in the universe, the most populous, the most animated, the most cultivated, the most varied in all kinds of produce'.[15] This pleasurable sense of farmscape, so well gardened that it resembled a work of art, entered into the consciousness of 18th-century Europe. Such a landscape, praised for its variety, suggestion of prosperous well-being, order and harmony, was in accordance with the

11 *Charlie Newington's* White Horse *at the entrance to the Channel Tunnel.*

literary visual disposition before the Romantic period for undulating countryside where the complete humanisation of nature had imparted many of the virtues conventionally ascribed to a garden where everything was available and useful, especially where the bordering Downs offered a contrast.

Charlie Newington's giant chalk figure of a white horse flying in the wind, cut recently on Cheriton Hill above Folkestone, is the first and last glimpse of England for users of the Channel Tunnel. This immense carving of the Folkestone Horse is reminiscent of one of Britain's most famous chalk figures, the Bronze-Age White Horse of Uffington which may have been created as long ago as 1400 BC and carries echoes of the worship of the ancient Celtic goddess Epona, a symbol of health, strength and fertility. The symbol of a horse is appropriate, for the name of the nearest village, Etchinghill, may be derived from the Celtic word 'each', meaning a horse, and a white horse has been the county symbol of Kent since Saxon times. The iconic image, approved by the government against the advice of its wildlife advisers on a sensitive habitat of chalk grassland, has been strongly supported by Folkestone as a spur towards its regeneration and will symbolise on this Rock of Ages to travellers how the very idea of Britain is now being de-constructed against its past.[16]

For various reasons these sheer walls of dazzling white chalk have come to embody a distinctive English quality which has been sung, written about and otherwise declaimed in praise of the 'White Cliffs', from the patriotic lyricism of poets to the bombast of politicians. Memorable is Shakespeare's evocation in *King Lear* of the height of the cliff now known as Shakespeare's Cliff:

> Come on, sir; here's the place: stand still. – How fearful
> And dizzy 'tis to cast one's eyes so low!
> The crows and choughs that wing the midway air
> Show scarce so gross as beetles; half-way down
> Hangs one that gathers samphire; dreadful trade!
> Methinks he seem no bigger than his head;
> The fishermen that walk upon the beach
> Appear like mice; and yon tall anchoring bark
> Diminished to her cock; at her cock a buoy
> Almost too small for sight; the murmuring surge,
> That on the unnumbered pebbles chafes,
> Cannot be heard so high: I'll look no more
> Lest my brain turn, and the deficient sight
> Topple down headlong … You are now within a foot
> Of the extreme verge; for all beneath the moon
> Would I not leap upright.

It was on Dover beach, upon a clear moonlit night on the Straits when Matthew Arnold saw the vast cliffs of England glimmering in the tranquil bay and looked across to a France which first gleamed and then went, that he listened to the

> … grating roar
> Of pebbles which the waves draw back, and fling,
> At their return, up the high strand,
> Begin, and cease, and then again begin,
> With tremendous cadence slow …

Which reminded him of Sophocles' sadness when listening to the same sound of the lapse and return of the Aegean Sea, but his own sadness was that of many other early and mid-Victorians who were worried about religion, immortality, sex, money and politics in the new environment of the Industrial Revolution, 'utterly new in the history of the race' and to whom it fell to begin to make a melancholy adjustment.

2

The Natural and Man-Made Setting

The North Downs extend from the 'White Cliffs of Dover' for nearly one hundred miles across Kent and Surrey in a great arm round the eastern and northern edges of the oval-shaped Weald. By long-standing convention they end, or have their beginning, at the gap cut through the chalk by the River Wey at Farnham. Nevertheless, much the same landscape prevails around Basingstoke and Alton and this can justifiably be considered part of the same range. At the other end of the Downs, on a clear day, when visibility is pencil sharp, Cap Blanc-Nez and Cap Gris-Nez, the counterpart of the North and South Forelands in England, are seen across the narrow Straits of Dover. They mark the former extension of the land bridge of the North Downs into the Boulonnais of northern France when Britain was part of the continental mainland before the Straits of Dover were cut, an event more important than any other in understanding Britain's history and culture. The separation of island and continent occurred when rivers filled and sea levels rose. Popularly, this is assumed to have happened relatively recently, at the end of the last Ice Age, *c*.10,000 BC, but archaeology suggests otherwise, although the date and manner of the separation are still matters of speculation. There are currently two opinions about the date of the breach. One is that it was due to the overflowing of an ice-dammed lake making the North Sea during the Anglian glaciation, *c*.480,000 years ago. The other maintains that the land bridge was still intact until *c*.250,000 years ago.[1]

Basically the North Downs are a piece of chalk, an unusually pure limestone, almost too soft to be called a rock. Tracing with a finger on a map the ribs of chalk hills that extend like a fan from the central node of Salisbury Plain, there is a seaward projection into the Dorset, Hampshire and South Downs. The North Downs extend as a continuous hill-range except where the rivers Wey, Mole, Darent, Medway and Stour have cut through the range. Yet another rib is the range of chalkland under the various names of the Berkshire Downs, the Chilterns, the East Anglian Heights and so on up to the Lincolnshire and Yorkshire Wolds. These chalk ridges have their own uniqueness because chalk rock is exceptionally rare (France excepted) and consequently the phrase 'chalk downland' is one of the most evocative in English topographical nomenclature; indeed, its scenery has come to be recognised as the most essentially English of the country's varied landscapes. Where the chalk is exposed in cliffs, as at Dover, it has assumed a symbol of Britain's defiance of her enemies. That the beautiful smooth swelling curves are some of the most perfect specimens of

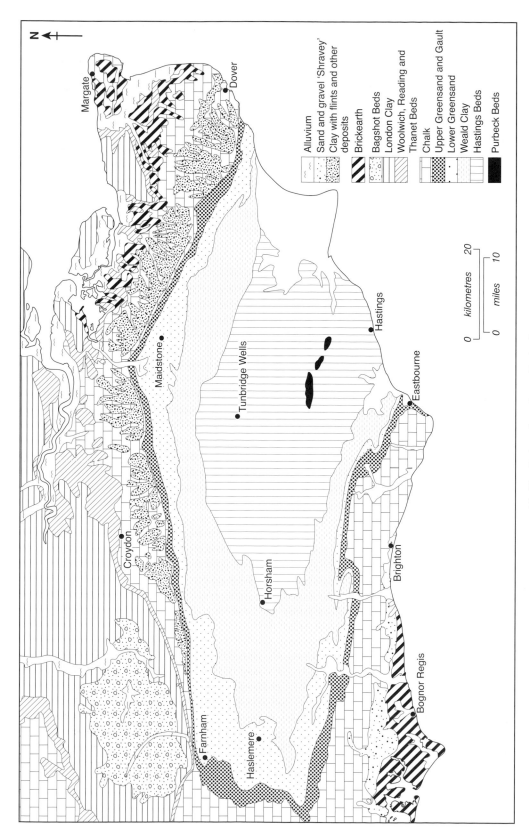

12 *The Geology of south-east England.*

Alluvium

Sand and gravel 'Shravey'

Clay with flints and other deposits

Brickearth

Bagshot Beds

London Clay

Woolwich, Reading and Thanet Beds

Chalk

Upper Greensand and Gault

Lower Greensand

Weald Clay

Hastings Beds

Purbeck Beds

Margate

Dover

Maidstone

Tunbridge Wells

Hastings

Eastbourne

Croydon

Horsham

Brighton

Farnham

Haslemere

Bognor Regis

kilometres

miles

0   20

0   10

graceful contours of any real, imagined or dreamt-of hills makes them jewels in England's crown. (Chalk is soluble in rainwater as well as friable, so that convex curves do not end abruptly as in other rocks, but continue as rounded hollows.) Moreover, being amongst the most anciently settled and farmed parts of England, chalkland was rightly regarded by novelist E.M. Forster (so closely identified with the Surrey Downs) as 'the heart of our island'.[2]

Geological history is the key to understanding the striking topography and local variety of the Downs and their adjacent hills and vales. This is due to sequential changes which took place during the Cretaceous epoch from 65 to 145 million years ago, a world much warmer than today, without icecaps, and with sea levels at times hundreds of feet higher than at present. Unique at that time was the accumulation of chalk in deep water far from land, composed of the calcareous remains of innumerable microscopic planktonic organisms. Earlier in the epoch, fossil ferns, mollusca and small crustaceans together with fish and reptiles are evidence of life on land in an environment of fresh or brackish water. In this phase the alternating sandstone and mudstone formations were laid down in the natural basin of the enormous Wealden lake, sea or delta.

Victorians consulted Gideon Mantell's *The Geology of South-East England* (1833) or Sir Charles Lyell's *Principles of Geology* (1830-3) which conveys the excitement of the discovery of sea-shells now stranded high above sea-level, the great rivers which flowed over the South-East and the arborescent ferns, palms, yuccas and the equisita and kindred plants which prevailed in the sweaty swamps, instead of oaks. They thrilled to the enormous reptiles bigger than elephants, such as the huge plant-eating iguanodon, the plesiosaurus and the megalosaurus, the crocodiles, turtles, flying reptiles and birds which inhabited the fens, rivers and the waters still teeming with ammonites, sea lizards and fishes. The diary of the rocks records important changes by the time dinosaurs had vanished from the earth. Deposits laid down in torrential streams record the wearing down of mountains no sooner than they had been heaved up above the plains when the Alps were elevated. The image of the Weald as a slowly changing entity with a fascinating history over geological time began to form in the public mind. The successive changes inspired Tennyson, for example. Box Hill, at the common boundary of the chalk and both later and earlier rocks, has been explored by field naturalists for at least three centuries. Ramsay's *Physical Geology and Geography of Great Britain* (1873) became the indispensable pocket guide for studying the Mole gorge and the beautiful shells and wild flowers of the chalk at the end of the 19th century.

A veritable mental leap is required to conceive of the unroofing of the great Wealden dome which occurred after the rocks were upraised in early Tertiary times. Victorians began to learn of this in the pages of Sir Charles Lyell's *Geology* but it was self-taught Benjamin Harrison of Ightham who captured their imagination by demonstrating that hitherto unsuspected humanly-worked flints were to be found in gravels laid down by rivers in the basins of the Strode, the Darent and the Leybourne stream, in localities on the plateaux up to a surprising several hundred feet above the present Darent and Medway valleys.

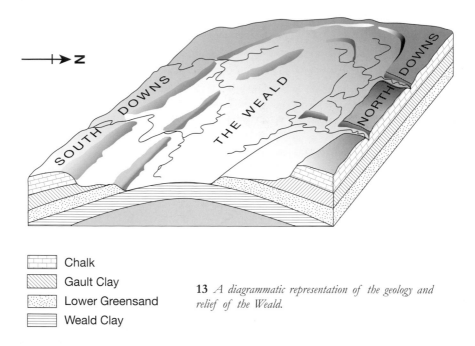

Chalk

Gault Clay

Lower Greensand

Weald Clay

13 *A diagrammatic representation of the geology and relief of the Weald.*

In so doing he not only revolutionised thought on the antiquity of man, but illustrated the enormous physical changes, such as the excavation of the present valleys through the chalk, which had happened since the presence of the earliest people on the Downs who were living on river banks more than 250 feet higher than they are now.[3]

The modern student is still as fascinated by the diverse geology. The various formations are intermittently traceable as a horse-shoe around the northern and eastern edges of the Weald, and several take their names from type sites on the Kent coast where they are exposed in cliffs. The Hythe Beds result from sandy detritus deposited by currents in shallow waters far from the shore. The limey Bargate Beds containing shelly cretaceous material, deposited in clear water, produce loams of great fertility and yielded good building stone used from Saxon times, whereas the succeeding Sandgate Beds originated from a muddier phase. The Folkestone Beds were rapidly deposited in shallow water when the adjoining land was uplifted and the invigorated streams brought down coarse sands and pebble in their swirling currents. Iron found in small quantities in several formations supported the local iron industry and small quantities of sand required for glass-making were locally obtainable.

Notable changes in the landscape arise from denudation processes, some of which still operate today.[4] After prolonged rainfall, sandstone may slip downward on lubricated clay beneath to form landslips or valley bulges, a process which has been operating from at least the cold climatic conditions in Pleistocene times.[5] Another process at work is the heaving and slipping of sandstone after a thaw following heavy frost. Where stream erosion undercuts a sandstone cliff, the

14 *Landslip at Coldharbour, near Dorking, after heavy rain in 2000.*

overhang eventually slumps forward. In the wet autumn of 2000 a minor road at Coldharbour at Leith Hill was rendered unusable through a landslip and the changed topography is still visible. In the same area earlier landslips are evident. Some of these are alluded to by John Evelyn in Gibson's edition of Camden's *Roman Britannia* (1695). The most spectacular of the landslips are on the slopes below Gibbet Hill on Hindhead and on the south-east slopes of Blackdown, both attributed to the free-thaw action of the cold period of the Pleistocene. Minor slips will be observed on steep slopes on many farms, recognisable from a vertical scar at the head of hummocky ground ending in a steep bank on the downward side. Such landslips appear to have first entered literature with Gervase Markham's early 17th-century comment that the area was 'hillish and sliding country'.

The Character of the North Downs

Although the North Downs are a unit for the purpose of geographical and historical study, they are a unity in diversity, for in reality they form a complex mosaic of numerous different little landscapes in which geology relief, micro-climate and soil had a decisive impact on ways of farming and human settlement.

One striking feature controlling the shape of the landscape is the changing dip of the chalk strata. We need to bear in mind the geological structure and evolution of the Weald region. Some 65 million years ago almost the whole of south-east England was a great sheet of chalk, originally a high tableland. In the great earth movements which produced the Alps and the Himalayas, the region was raised into a dome and in this process the chalk was violently twisted, rent asunder and wrenched about so that the original surface has many subsidiary folds and collapsings (faults), and was re-shaped according to the steepness of the dip of the rocks. Where the inclination is exceptionally steep, as along the Hog's Back, the width of the surface is correspondingly narrow; whereas where the extremely gentle dip occurs in the Canterbury district the Downs widen out to their greatest extent.[6]

On the high chalkland between Maidstone and Sittingbourne are the adjacent parishes of Stockbury, Hucking, Bredgar and Bicknor. To go to them is to plunge deeply into the Downs at their most secretive. There are no large villages: communities have been traditionally scattered widely in isolated farms and small hamlets in a maze of waterless valleys. Population has always been sparse. In 1982 Hucking had only 54 people, Bicknor 74, Bredgar 661 and Stockbury 768. Alan Everitt has noted that Bredgar and its surrounds developed as a typical agglomeration of scattered woodland farms in the outlying forest pastures of an estate centred on Milton.[7] It was initially used by herdsmen taking pigs to forage for acorns and beechmast in the autumn. They would have returned to Milton by the sunken lanes which functioned as droveways but probably from the later Saxon period some of the herdsmen began to settle in permanently and clear the land for farming. Those intimate with the district in the 1920s associated it with 'White Sunday' when the valleys were white with cherry blossom. Cottages then collected rain-water from their roofs or had wells. Sir Arthur Keith described the left-alone quality of Bredgar as 'an earthly paradise' when he saw it in the spring of 1900: 'The sun was shining, lambs were sporting in the greenest of grass under the cherry trees which were breaking into blossom, men were busy in the fields and in the hop gardens' (*Autobiography*, 1950, p.229). The orchards have now retreated to the foothills and the whiteness of winter when snow ploughs slowly cleared the by-ways is also in the past, as are the hop fields. The great wide spaces, bare and open, typical of the South Downs, are absent. Instead a multiplicity of small grass fields lie interspersed with woodland. Traditionally this is pasture country but most of the farmland was arable in the 1840s before cheap imports of food led to grass again. The farmhouses, mainly Georgian, make a special appeal to the sense of the beautiful. The glorious patchwork of ripening grain alternating here and there with grass and a brown fallow or a green root crop, which made the countryside beautiful to look upon, has now only a green sameness. Seedtime and harvest are not great events any more, a story, sadly, that is much the same over the more marginal areas of the North Downs.[8]

Hucking has a distinctive character. One climbs steeply up 'on to the hill' from the pretty village of Hollingbourne in the Vale of Holmesdale and enters a starved and bleak world in winter on the summit of the Downs. Here is a heavily wooded landscape on rolling slopes interspersed with small grass fields, originally called *groves*. Another local name which frequently occurs is *wald* 'woodland or forest', a name which also appears to have signified woodland pasture. The solitary inn is appropriately named after two woodman's tools, a hook and hatchet. The field patterns clearly indicate early medieval woodland clearance by the process of assarting (the piecemeal and sporadic assaults on the waste as a result of land hunger arising from population pressure). The landscape has the same appearance as that of the Weald of Kent but is more windswept. Nature here seems to have intended a wilderness, and as soon as the hand of man has been relaxed woodland has encroached. The present landscape retains its original woodland appearance. It abounds in trees standing – in hedgerows, copses, and small woodlands and often alone in the middle of fields which were once parklands. The return of the wild in the present-day scene is evident in these inhospitable uplands by the sight of hawthorn bushes dispersed amongst the grass, birches slipping from the woodland edge and yews and beech saplings climbing down hillsides. If present trends continue we shall witness the march of woodland down into the valleys imaginatively described by Lord Dunsany in his *Blessing of Pan* (1927), set in the Darent valley at Shoreham. Already, with the purchase of land for planting by The Woodland Trust, the landscape is taking on the character it had in the 13th century. Nearby at Oxen Hoath was Tom, the woodcutter, Denton Welch's evocation, probably the original of 'Jim' in *The Fire in the Wood* (included in the volume *Brave and Cruel*).

Edward Hasted, whose *History of Kent* was published between 1778 and 1791, and who had the tastes and prejudices of pre-Romantic Hanoverians, did not share present delight in the woodlands and a sense of the 'wild' was anathema to him. Of Hucking he wrote: 'It has a woody appearance throughout from wide hedgerows round the fields. The whole is an unpleasant dreary country, the soil very poor, being chalky and much covered with flint.' Bicknor was healthy but its soil was very poor, mostly infertile red earth with flints. Bredhurst was unfrequented, cold and bleak with frequent steep hills and lands poor and hungry. Bredgar was described as being largely dreary but with soils lately improved with coal ashes and flocks of sheep. Stockbury was more inviting than the other parishes and the soil was not as poor. He does not, of course, mention the rich flora and fauna which is so enticing at the present time. The carpet of bluebells and red campion was painted in realistic detail by Rosa Brett of Detling, a Pre-Raphaelite and no fewer than 320 of the 474 species of birds recorded in Great Britain are present in the four parishes under discussion.

The Elham valley, by contrast, is a pastoral paradise. Its stream, the Nailbourne, rises in springs near Lyminge and is a winterbourne, a seasonal stream which flows over ground only in wet winters. Its plants such as pond water-crowfoot and fool's water-cress are able to survive by resisting drought and colonising rapidly once water returns. The settlements are generally hamlets, probably originating in the Iron Age, if not earlier, and former markets existed at Elham and Lyminge. The base of the valley is good quality sheep-grazed pasture; higher up are good examples of old chalk grassland as on the Baldock Downs and a good deal of ancient woodland (woodland which existed on the same site since at least 1600) lies on the cappings of acid clay soil on the summits. The tiny village of Bishopsbourne, home of novelists Joseph Conrad and Jocelyn Brooke, has declined in population but has a splendid church, a smithy, a village inn and a cricket ground. Bekesbourne is another remote settlement at the convergence of a typical maze of narrow, winding lanes, almost empty of traffic during winter.

A world apart are the northern slopes of the Downs between Chatham and Canterbury and the chalk outlier of Thanet where a deposit of light soils and deep loams akin to wind-blown loess in continental Europe has given rise to sunny, wide-open fields intensively farmed and pervaded by the smell of the sea. This was one of the places which attracted the first agricultural populations in

15 *Samphire Hoe, a nature reserve successfully made from Channel Tunnel spoil.*

British prehistory because the ploughing was so easy and the soil has exceptional inherent natural fertility. This district has traditionally fed London since the Middle Ages, has supplied for generations the finest brewers' barley obtainable, and now grows as many vegetables in vast unhedged fields as the Fens. Its crop yields are as prodigious as the famed plateau of Beauce in the Paris Basin but its villages and towns, such as Wingham, Goodnestone and Minster, are so much more beautiful and historically interesting.

'For high drama the last few miles of the North Downs Way take some beating.' So wrote Charlie Pye-Smith of a landscape which until 1987 had hardly changed since Shakespearean times. Then came the building of the Channel Tunnel. Nine acres of land of great botanical interest were compulsorily acquired from the National Trust and a dual carriageway to Dover was constructed through the beautiful Farthingleo Valley, which the Trust opposed at the cost of £54,000. The cliffs are still as magnificent as ever but the valley is almost unrecognisable under a glistening ribbon of black tarmac. It sounds as bad as it looks, said James Cooper, the Trust's land agent for the property, 'the crows and choughs that wing the midway air are drowned by the thunderous roar of traffic'.[9]

It is not all a loss. Channel Tunnel spoil has been used to create a new coastline wilderness called Samphire Hoe. Seventy-five acres have been added between Folkestone and Dover comprising five million tons of chalky rubble dug out by Eurotunnel. Apart from the yellow-flowered rock samphire, it supports kidney vetch, wild cabbage and the early spider orchid. Ten years ago there were no animals to speak of and now there are 140 species of living creatures.

As for plants, 31 existed a decade ago and now there are 196. 'This place is a miracle', says the project officer, Paul Holt.

As different again are the rural areas protected by the Green Belt south of Croydon on the Kent-Surrey border. In 1971 Ian Nairn could write of Surrey: 'What is spoilt is utterly spoilt, what is left alone … is enchanting.'[10] It is only with reservations that this could be said of the east Surrey Downs in 2005. Climbing up the Roman road on Tilburstow Hill south of Godstone, the stone-built farmhouses, barns and outhouses on the sunny slopes of the sandstone ridge are all now the residences of well-to-do commuters and have the 'cared-for' look peculiar to Surrey. By contrast, the rural Downs wear a rather ragged coat and 'downy' chin. Farm buildings built during and immediately after the last war are hideously huge. Tillingdown Farm, near Warlingham, a former medieval manor, is a contractor's yard smothered with the flotsam and jetsam of the built-up area to the north. Hedges are straggly, commons scruffy. The land is passing from the old grassland agriculture in which cows and sheep were the main source of livelihood to one in which horses are kept by commuters. Cows needed to be confined by a properly laid hedge, armed with thorn, but horses are constrained by the flimsiest and ugliest of fences. Equestrian centres, saddleries, mobile farriers and golf courses are also proliferating. The quality of rural conservation has evidently declined in the past forty years. We seem to be living on capital here, destroying more than we create. Will it turn into a godforsaken country, propped up in a long agony between life and death in an encroaching urbanised world, or will steps be taken to reverse the downward trends in this tarnished landscape?

The bold south-facing escarpment of the North Downs in west Surrey includes some of the finest scenery in southern England. For generations the crest-line and range after range of wooded folds, 'composing themselves as

16 *View of the Surrey and Sussex Wealds from Holmbury House, near Holmbury St Mary.*

elegantly and harmoniously as a Claude landscape', have been admired from Newlands Corner. Although made easier for horses over the centuries, the crossing of the Downs' escarpment has remained dangerous to travellers to this day. The most distinguished victim of the descent to Crossways Farm was the Bishop of Winchester, Samuel Wilberforce, who was thrown from his horse and killed in 1873. He had ridden over the Downs from Burford Bridge and was intending to dine with the Leveson-Gowers at Holmbury House. A granite monument in Evershed's Rough marks this spot. A similar terror to travellers was the lane which descends into Shere from Colekitchen Farm down Combe Bottom. This is one of the most glorious spots in the North Downs range. With his customary bravado and delight in physical vigour, Wilfrid Scawen Blunt descended gloriously confident in a coach and four in 1894, his wife Judith wheeling round the sharp corners with a masterful grasp of the reins. He fancied that 'in all history no team of four horses was ever driven down that road', not even by Tommy Onslow of Clandon who adventurously drove a coach and six over his surrounding hills, and certainly not by a woman.[11]

The combes and valleys in this neighbourhood are deeply secluded in a tangle of trees. E.M. Forster, the successor to George Meredith on these downs, had a passionate feeling for them and struck firm roots into them: 'Wild, wild, wilder, than the genuine forests that survive in the south of Sweden,' he thought, when his path was blocked by trees in Honeysuckle Bottom, Abinger and he had a sense of something vaguely sinister around Blind Oak Gate, 'which would do harm if it could, but which cannot, this being Surrey'. This atmosphere of baffled malevolence, which has defeated the farmer through the ages, is a feature of the steeper slopes of the poor soils of the district. It is heightened by the dense yew woods, the junipers, holly and ash, and the wide stretches of scrub which in daytime can be thought eerie in filtering sunlight and terrifying at nightfall, haunted by Forrest Reid's ghosts. Yet, as Forster remarked, 'left to itself, there is not a safer place in England than Abinger' and the memory of this place is one of many people's keenest impressions and the loveliest.[12]

There are few places as strikingly beautiful in all English downland as the Vale of Mickleham, the spectacular tree-clad gap in the chalk cut by the River Mole. The corner bastion of Box Hill, clothed in box and yew, the glorious dry valleys cut into the backslopes (one felicitiously known as the Happy Valley), the precipitous river cliffs of the Whites with their scars of bare chalk and yew woods, the Cockshoot Woods in the Headley Valley and the beech hangers of Norbury Park on the opposite banks of the river, constitute a remarkable natural and man-made landscape of exquisite beauty. It is also a whole world of plant, animal and human life which is one of the best preserved and scientifically most significant in southern England. This is a special piece of country, a sentient landscape, if there is such a thing, which brims with historical and personal associations. The poet Keats walked up from Burford Bridge on a calm midnight and saw the prospect as being in its way as beautiful as Windermere or Rydal as a rival setting for his own poetry. Here, too, lived George Meredith for over thirty years.

17 *Ethelbert White's* Surrey Hills.

Up to this point the North Downs have been described and defined as if they were a separate autonomous region in south-east England. This has not, however, ever been the case. Although they have always retained their special identity and in certain respects their own peculiar character, e.g. in matters of farming and settlement (an example of what the French call a *pays*) they are embedded in a jigsaw of other landscapes adjoining them. In this 'coral reef' of other diverse little landscapes is the Vale of Holmesdale and the sandstone hills immediately beyond known as the Surrey Hills, and in Kent, variously as the Chart, Quarry or Red Hills which overlook the Weald. These are contrasting but eternally inter-connected with the North Downs culturally and economically, with a whole series of threads such as routeways and exchanges of crops, timber and building stones.

The Vale of Holmesdale

Go where you will, by car, horseback, or bicycle, or over even shorter distances on foot, sudden and unexpected differences will be encountered because this is a part of England where exceptionally varied rocks and corresponding variety of human use, wildlife and fauna occur. In his novel *Antic Hay* (1923) Aldous Huxley, never underplaying the extraordinary, conveys in ironic prose the excitement and emotion at discovering the exceptional diversity unfolded to the point of absurdity on the southern flank of the Hog's Back between Farnham and Guildford:

> Do you remember, Myra, that time we went down in the country – you remember, under the Hog's Back … How we liked the country …! All the world in a few square miles. Chalk pits and blue butterflies on the Hog's Back. And at the foot of the hill, suddenly, the sand; the hard, yellow sand with those queer caves … And the fine grey sand on which the heather of Puttenham Common grows

... And the enormous sloping meadows round Compton and the thick dark woods. And the lakes, and the heaths, the Scotch firs at Cutt Mill. The forests at Shackleford. There was everything. Do you remember how we enjoyed it all?'

Huxley is buried in Compton churchyard and to him it was a place to be always coming back to, the enchantment never dulled. Many others have found it as magical, and the urge to catch every detail as strong as ever over the years, as if the moment were to be their last. Huxley, indeed, was observing and expressing in the Vale of Holmesdale what every landscape historian should do in making a journey into the past – to look for divergences, breaks, contrasts and frontiers in order to identify places of an extraordinarily local character.

The Vale is a narrow corridor of great natural beauty extending throughout Surrey and Kent between the southern scarp of the North Downs and the rising slopes of the sandstone hills to the south. It has been aptly described by George Buckland as lying 'under the sunny side of the chalk hills like the forward border under the lee of a garden wall'. Although largely floored by intractable Gault Clay it has been ameliorated into fertility by downwash from the chalk and an admixture from the Lower Greensand formation on the sandstone hills. The warm southern slopes where springs gush out along the base of the Downs are lined with pretty villages, many of which are presumed to be on prehistoric sites. The springs have particular associations. Denton Welch tells of pure water at the bottom of a spring into which he cupped his hands on a long walk and which was so beguilingly clear that it had almost the look of 'old glass'.[13] Some of the springs were sacred and numerous churches exist as at Kemsing and Otford, which Everitt considers may have been sacred objects of veneration before the advent of Christianity. St Edith's Well at Kemsing was the centre of a monastery dedicated to St Edith who is said to have been born there. The parish church has been re-dedicated to this saint and a statue placed at her shrine.[14] On its margins, the natural routeway between Salisbury Plain and the Channel coast is threaded by two ancient trackways, the so-called Pilgrims' Way and the Greensand Way, both thought to be of prehistoric origin. It is also criss-crossed by ancient routes running north-south, intersecting the Downs, the sandstone ridge and the Weald. The present A25 trunk road which follows the Vale has been partially superseded by the M25/M20 motorways.

In this little tract of country is the Vale of Alton which William Cobbett considered to be 10 miles of the finest country in England.[15] Then follows the Vale of Albury, watered by the River Tillingbourne, almost enclosed by the chalk ridge of Newlands Corner. This Cobbett regarded as 'one of the choicest retreats of man' and few have since dissented from his judgement. It was here that Cobbett observed that the edges of the chalk and sandstone run so closely in parallel with each other that in many places one can actually have a chalk bank on one side and, at a distance of no more than fifty yards, a sandstone one on the other. His childhood links with Surrey enhance the vigour and clarity of his prose and his practice of illuminating one little landscape and comparing and contrasting it with another is a technique which will be used throughout this book.[16]

18 *Redundant triple oasts at Westwell Manor along the Pilgrims' Way.*

19 *View south of the Chart Country from Green Hill, Kemsing. The M25 has been discreetly landscaped, strongly influenced by local conservationists inspired by Samuel Palmer.*

Further east a magnificent view of the Vale is obtained from Green Hill above Kemsing. Here the beauty of the Vale is little damaged by the construction of the M25. Vocal champions to initial proposals, inspired by Samuel Palmer, who painted at nearby Shoreham in the 1820s, led to cleverly landscaped cutting. Rich grass fields with wide hedgerows and shaws are backed by continuous woodland on the summit of the sandstone ridge beyond. The eye can rove across the great sweep of the Downs towards Hythe in one direction and Leith Hill in the other or, by means of the Medway valley, can catch glimpses of the Weald. This was the arena of fierce dog-fights during the Battle of Britain in 1940. A wooden cross on the summit of Green Hill marks the spot where an airman was killed during the battle and older villagers possess copies of a photograph of 'planes engaged in dog-fights. A prominent feature is the springs of clear water which gush from the base of the chalk. Everitt has remarked that although the corridor is a narrow one it has had a profound influence on the history of Kent.[17] This remark can be applied to Surrey, for the Vale in the vicinity of Godalming and Guildford can be regarded as the cradle of the county.

The Sandstone Hills

Separated merely by the Vale of Holmesdale are the sandstone hills to the south, prominent round Petersfield, Haslemere, Midhurst, Sevenoaks and Maidstone. They were notable for ragstone and other building stones and for the copious springs of pure water used for fulling cloth and making paper in the Maidstone district, for the internationally famous hand-made paper with the Whatman water-mark, and also in the Tillingbourne valley of Surrey. Although some of the vantage points overlooking the Weald are well known to tourists, such as Blackdown, Hindhead, Leith Hill and Crockham Chart, most of the tract is one of the least known parts of southern England, yet it has been lavishly praised for its rare and distinguished beauty. The Devil's Punch Bowl at Hindhead is its most astounding natural object. Numerous springs welling up several hundred feet below the summit of Hindhead have undermined and washed away vast amounts of sand to form the Bowl, the bottom of which, called the Moor, is virtually an impassable swamp, a wild and lonesome district to be explored with caution.

All along the central hill range of Kent and east Surrey sandstones, the place-name 'chart' recurs from Limpsfield Chart to Brasted Chart, Seal Chart and, beyond the Medway, to Chart Sutton and Little Chart. Alan Everitt has noted that Saxon *ceart* is cognate with the Norwegian *kartr*, meaning 'rough, rocky, sterile ground'. Its poor stony and gravelly land can, however, be converted to fine fruit gardens once the stone has been quarried. Increasingly from the 16th century, its healthiness has made it delectable for residential purposes, one of the earliest migrants being William Lambarde, the first historian of Kent, who retired there from Lincoln's Inn. Heather and woods abound, and the long-distance path called the Greensand Way affords magnificent views over the Weald. The most famous quarry from a purely geological point of view is the

Iguanodon Quarry at Oakwood near Maidstone, so named after the discovery by Gideon Mantell in 1834 of the skeleton of a dinosaur. The centre of this district is Maidstone which lies in 'The Garden of England' at the base of the hills on soils enriched by limey downwash. The sandstones soak up rainwater like a sponge and hundreds of deliciously-clear springs break out more or less at the junction with the Atherfield Clay. It is this 'spring-line' which more than anything else created the line of settlements. The springs watered meadows and orchards, spread into teeming fishponds, provided pure water at no cost and were put to industrial use. At Loose, springs run down the village street to join the Loose stream, itself spring fed, and provided power for a sequence of industrial development which has only recently ceased. A visit to Mote Park in Maidstone adds a new perspective to the North Downs. Westwards from the wide embayment of the River Darent, approximately marking the boundary between Surrey and Kent, the steep face and summits of the Downs appear, if only an illusion, as one continuous woodland, akin to the hanging woods of the South Downs. Eastwards from the gap the corresponding features are largely treeless, shaven by the plough and stripped down for arable cultivation.

On the sandstones Blackdown has a summit of 919 feet, Hindhead (894) and Leith Hill, the highest of all, which rises to nearly 1,000 feet. This is owed to the resistance to erosion and weathering of the Hythe Beds. A bold escarpment is traceable eastwards from Hascombe Church, Hydon's Ball, Holmbury Hill to Leith Hill and Coldharbour. The headward erosion of springs at the base of the Weald Clay has chiselled a series of 'headlands and bays' into the escarpment which are unsurpassed for scenic beauty in the western Weald. Despite creeping suburbanisation, the Surrey Hills offer all the field naturalist could wish for in

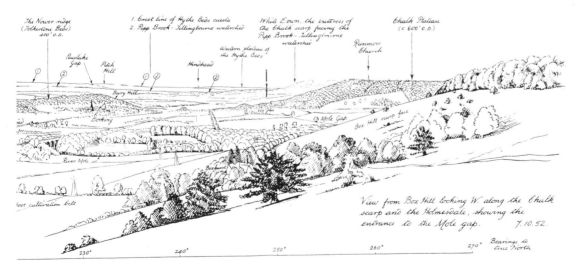

20 *A portion of one of G.E. Hutchings' field sketches designed to train students in the art of looking at country.*

the way of natural life – fur, fish and feather, to say nothing of the insect and floral wealth, and there are some of the loveliest views of woodland and heath that it is possible for anyone to look at. It has never figured much in agriculture, the soils being sterile, and rabbits swarmed down to the cultivated parts and simply devoured the crops.

21 *Geoffrey Hutchings.*

The sandstone hills which jostle on the Hampshire-Surrey-Sussex borders form comparatively unknown country outside Hindhead and Haslemere and have a particular individuality. They form a muddled, small-scale country of astonishing intimacy and variety, in which barns and farmhouses built of local stone are sprinkled in sticky clay, loam, sterile sandstone, wooded ridges, grassy hollows, heaths and tree-covered commons. The sound of running water fed by powerful springs, where permeable rocks meet impervious strata, enhances this landscape as does the remarkable profusion and luxuriance of the vegetation. Many observers have expressed the opinion that it is the most agreeable scenery they have ever experienced, including the political economist John Stuart Mill, Benjamin Disraeli and Dr Cyril Joad. It is such a landscape of miniatures that one can drive in half an hour across scenic diversity which in Germany might take two hours and, in the case of Russia and the United States, days. For one hundred years this diversity has provided a huge recreational value to walkers, cyclists, horse-riders, bird-watchers and botanists.

The exceptionally varied landscape of the chalk and sandstone country led to the early introduction of the technique of regional survey inspired by Patrick Geddes. The preparatory step to a regional synthesis of a land use survey, on the scale of six inches to one mile for 200 square miles centred on the Croydon district, was initiated by C.C. Fagg and completed by the local Natural History and Scientific Society in 1920. By 1923 numerous organisations all over the country had followed the example as a means of local research and Fagg, with G.E. Hutchings, wrote the first textbook on the subject.[18] The latter, a consummate observer, became the first warden of Juniper Hall Field Centre set up under the aegis of the Field Studies Council in the Vale of Mickleham, where he taught brilliantly the techniques of sensitive field observation to develop 'an eye for country'. Amongst these skills was the art of field sketching, for Hutchings considered that sitting down and making a drawing of the landscape was not merely for a record but a means of enabling the observer 'to see what he looks at'. Thus in many ways it was in the North Downs at Hutchings'

22 *Juniper Hall Field Centre, Mickleham, near Dorking. From 1793 this was the home of a distinguished group of French émigrés, including Madame de Staël, Talleyrand, General d'Arblay (who married Fanny Burney) and M. de Narbonne.*

earlier field centre at Stockbury near Chatham and in the Vale of Mickleham that generations of geographers, field naturalists and historians learned the craft of field observation.[19] Earlier at Downe near Orpington Charles Darwin had conducted his investigations of natural phenomena and the High Elms estate in the same neighbourhood was inherited in 1865 by Sir John William Lubbock, 1st Baron Avebury, the gifted writer on geology and the antiquity of man.[20] Another distinguished field scientist was Sir Joseph Prestwich who lived at Shoreham, and is commemorated in glass by Burne-Jones in Shoreham church.

3

Quarrying and Mining

The North Downs and the sandstone hills are a landscape seamed with stone, and working it by carving blocks from it with special tools was one of the most ancient traditions of the region. Stone quarrying also bred a deep sensitivity to the inherent qualities of the rock which was supplied to London, Middlesex, Essex and nearer places for some two thousand years.

Chalk and Flint

Chalk was generally too soft and lacking in durability to be suitable for building, at least for exteriors, but there are some more compact beds of chalk at the base of the escarpment which contain tiny fragments of shells and other impurities which produce a more gritty texture and are much more durable. At Farnham it was called 'Malmstone' but more generally 'clunch', a word strikingly redolent of its soft, yet dense and resistant quality. The best source of this stone was from the Melbourne Rock, a hard, lumpy material which intermittently occurs all along the range of the North Downs. At Selborne the stone gives the village an attractive character. This is enhanced by roofing with wide eaves which protected the walls from rain-bearing winds, and the sarsen or sandstone foundation course kept the chalk off the ground, for there was a local saying, 'Find chalk a good hat and shoe and it will serve you well'. The local use of hard chalk is also notable in the Sevenoaks and Maidstone districts where Melbourne Rock also occurs, e.g. between Wrotham and Chevening. Some chalk was worked near Guildford, possibly at Albury or Shalford, and used in the re-building of St Paul's Cathedral, presumably for interior carving as an alternative to Reigate Stone.

Much more generally used and accounting for much of the charm of downland villages is flintstone, the characteristic building stone of chalky country for the walls of churches, farmhouses, cottages, barns, stockyards, dovecotes and walls around orchards and paddocks. Alec Clifton-Taylor has remarked how strange flint is as a building material. It is quite unlike any other building stone, and, although readily portable, is not easy to handle. He thought it improbable that anyone would have chosen it if other stone had been available, but on downland there was no alterative to wood until the advent of brick.

The Surrey Greensands

Of greater commercial importance was the stone extracted from the Lower Greensand.[1] This formation yielded a predominantly siliceous, fine grained stone, variously known as firestone, hearthstone or Reigate, Merstham, Gatton or

Godstone. Stone quarries in Surrey in this formation are mentioned in Domesday Book and and a number of Surrey churches were built of this stone, including Stoke D'Abernon. Wren remarked that 'Reigate Stone' had been used by the Normans as a substitute for Caen stone in parts of Westminster Abbey. He did not regard this as a happy choice because it took in water and, when frozen, scaled off. Around Godalming a similar kind of stone from the Sandgate Beds was known as Bargate Stone. The largest workings were between Brockham and Merstham where the earliest mines were probably bell-pits. Later drift mines ran down the steep dip until the water-table was encountered. At Merstham adits were cut to drain the mines. Blocks of ashlar appear to have been dressed below ground. At Chaldon oxen were used for haulage. The mines were mostly on a small-scale, material being wheeled out in barrows or on make-shift sledges, and normally not more than 12 men or so were employed at each.

This stone was used in the construction of old London Bridge in 1176, at Westminster Palace and Windsor Castle in the late 13th century, at Eton College in 1443, at Hampton Court and Nonsuch in the early 16th century, and at the Whitgift Almshouses in Croydon in 1596, amongst many other buildings at different times from the early Middle Ages in London, Middlesex and Essex which had no building stone of their own, e.g. St Margaret's, Barking. The discovery of a Roman tile kiln at Reigate makes it now clear that the stone was used in London much earlier. With the growth of manufacturing in the 18th and 19th centuries, this stone was found to be ideal as refractory material for lining lime-kilns, ovens, furnaces, chimneys, etc., because it resisted the action of fire. Malcolm in 1805 regarded the stone from Bletchingley in the White Hills as the most superior stone for lining in Europe. This 'firestone' was particularly also the glassmaker's preference because it sustained the intense heat of manufacture without injury and large quantities were at that time exported by canal to Liverpool, the Midlands and the North. When stone doorsteps and window sills were introduced from c.1800, the soft calcareous sandstones embedded amongst the harder stones were used as 'hearthstone' as an abrasive to scour and whiten. The industry flourished when every maid-servant and housewife loved a newly-whitened doorstep and a clean hearth in the kitchen. The use of building stone greatly declined with brick making and the firestone trade was also diminished when railways were used to transport alternative supplies nearer the coalfields, whereas earlier the horse-driven Croydon, Merstham and Godstone Railway (1805) and the Croydon Canal (1809) enjoyed considerable business. No building stone has been quarried since 1961. Hearthstone quarrying, by contrast, grew rapidly from the 1840s, reached its peak between about 1880 and 1920 before becoming extinct only recently. In 1885, 62 men were recorded mining in Surrey, but this is certainly an under-estimate. Earlier the number of quarrymen would have been substantially more, and the places named should be considered ancient mining parishes. At Godstone some of the mines can still be entered.[2]

Further west this same stone was quarried at places such as Dorking and Hascombe. Massive carved fireplaces in the district remain a witness of this to this day. Bargate Stone from the Upper Greensand of west Surrey near Churt found its way to east Surrey churches in the Victorian period.

A vivid impression of the sources of different building stones needed in the construction of a great mansion comes from the accounts kept by Mr More of the purchases for the building of Loseley House near Godalming between 1561-9. He rented a quarry near Guildford for over six years for 'white stone', presumably for intricate carved work inside the house, e.g. for the fireplaces which remain as evidence of this, or for door frames and sills. From Halfpenny Lane at Shalford he obtained stone to make steps and quoins; Gatton and Merstham supplied small amounts of stone for paving, despite the cost of the overland journey, as did Hambledon (possibly refractory stone for the lining of chimneys). Hascombe Stone was supplied to make pillars and quoins and from Horsham stone was bought to cover his house. Additionally, second-hand stone was acquired from the ruins of Waverley Abbey and the Friary at Guildford.[3]

Ragstone

The most important source of building stone in the Lower Greensand was the 'ragstone' which outcrops at its widest near Maidstone in the south-facing escarpment of Chartland. This was so-named because it breaks in a rough or jagged fashion and so was not sawn but cut by process known as 'skiffling', performed with a heavy, double-pointed, hammer. This Kentish Rag was the only stone in the London area which could be conveyed by water. Ragstone was used, for example, for the foundations of a town house in Roman London in

23 *Former Ragstone quarry, Boughton Monchelsea. The warm sunny walls now shelter enchanting gardens.*

the second century and the Museum of London has on display part of a sailing barge wrecked at Blackfriars in the second century AD with part of its cargo of Kentish Rag intact. The stone was also used c.AD 85 for the triumphal arch at Rutupiae (Richborough Castle) and probably for the city walls of Rochester and London, the latter built c.AD 200. In medieval times the River Medway continued to be used for transporting stone for the walling of the White Tower of the Tower of London (late 11th century). This outlasted Caen and Quarr Stone used as quoins and doorway and window surrounds until replaced by Portland Stone in the 18th century. The Norman west doorway of Harrow church, Middlesex, has ragstone. It was also used at Westminster Abbey in the late 14th century and the Jewel Tower of Westminster Palace of the same period is a near-complete building in ragstone. Numerous City and Essex churches were also built of this material.[4] Until the 14th century ragstone was used principally for walling but it then became fashionable for window heads, moulded jambs, mullions, etc. to be carved in this stone, as in Bethersden, Headcorn and Great Chart churches. The 15th century was the heyday for the use of such high-quality Kentish Rag. The custom of buying stock moulding worked up at the quarry accounts for the lack of individuality in later Perpendicular churches. Charing church tower, 'among the most ambitious in Kent', was built between 1479 and 1537 of stone probably from Great and Little Chart. Its west and south walls are of evenly-sized blocks. Its north and east walls, less in public view, are comprised of smaller, more roughly finished blocks with slightly wider mortar joints. Ragstone also had a significant role in the armaments industry of the 15th century, cannon shot being supplied for the wars in France to the armoury at the Tower of London via Maidstone Hithe, a quay below the town. As a building stone it again became popular with Victorian architects during the Gothic Revival. Topley lists 33 London churches built with it in the mid-19th century. The local trade in stone was boosted by the Medway Navigation which was first improved in the 17th century. In Kent the stone is ubiquitous in 19th-century building of every kind.

The best ragstone was considered to be at Boughton Monchelsea which was also thought to be the most ancient of the workings. They are probably of Roman origin, though they are not recorded in Domesday Book, and were worked quasi-continuously until the 1960s, when only one person was said to practise the mason's craft. Although always primarily agricultural, mining was such an important activity that Boughton Monchelsea still retains the distinct personality of a former mining parish. Well-constructed dry walls climb the hillsides and rows of old quarrymen's cottages diversify the scene. One particularly notable range erected by John Braddick bears the injunction, 'With industry, economy, honesty, sobriety, civility and cleanliness a poor man may live happy and respectable'. Several 15th-century hall houses were once occupied by quarry owners. Brishing Court is an exceptionally important medieval hall-house. Most of the old extensive and deep quarries now furnish sheltered places for modern houses and converted barns which lie against the sheer walls. In their gardens, warmed by the reflected heat, flowering plants and fruit tees grow luxuriantly in limey soil. The springs issuing from the limestone encrust every substance. The surrounding fields are pock-marked with innumerable hollows, once dangerous to horses slipping in them when at work; some result from natural fissures, others marking the sites of small-scale medieval and later workings called 'quarry holes' or 'petts'. It appears that the larger quarries were then often in divided ownership.[5] For late medieval and the 16th century, documents record sales of parts of quarries as 'daywerks' to yeoman masons. In 1600 the royal purveyor ordered eight loads of stone for the building of the Tower Wharf in London from the 'quarreys of Thomas Fyssher and William Yoemanson in Boughton Quarry to the wharff of Thomas Parker in Maidstone'. Both the suppliers of stone lived beside their own quarry.[6] There was so much stone dug that many masons are mentioned in the parish registers.

The Boughton quarrymen recognised and put to use no fewer than 17 or 18 different strata they encountered in the ragstone quarries. Only some of the beds would bear a chisel; several were used for paving or squared stone, others for rough walls, road-making or for making lime. Interbedded between the strata were layers of rubbly limestone known as 'Hassock'; that above Great Rag was suitable for interior use, but most was rejected as waste or for hardcore and fill. The usual method of working was to undermine a portion of the face of the quarry which was supported by props until thrown down. The large fragments of rock were blasted into small pieces by gunpowder and then further broken up with sledges and other tools. The 'Quarriers' went to work in hob-nailed boots, their strong legs and arms swinging in easy rhythm as they walked.

Large-scale foreshore quarrying in the vicinity of Folkestone is evident not only in the Lower Greensand outcrop (worked for Kentish Rag) but also in that of the Folkestone Beds in the area which is now Dover Harbour. This stone was used, amongst other places, for Dover and Queenborough Castles. In the 16th century there are accounts of men wading into the water to load the boats. The construction of Dover Harbour in the same century entailed huge quantities of Folkestone Beds sandstone from the Folkestone foreshore. The transport of the huge stones *c.*1535 was accomplished by attaching them by chains to large barrels, which floated as the tide rose, and lifted the stones so that they could be towed by small boats to Dover. Henry VIII was so pleased with this device that he awarded a pension to the Dover fisherman who invented it.

Marl and Lime

Marl was the most important manure from Roman times to the 17th century when it was superseded by lime. The most sought after marl was a calcareous clay obtained from the Lower Chalk and the basal portion of the Middle Chalk, at or near the base of the chalk escarpment. A coating of calcareous marl was applied mostly to retentive clays to fields in rotation about once in 15 to 20 years.[7] Quarrying into the chalk escarpment for lime used in building or as manure made a great impact on the landscape eastwards from the Hog's Back from the late 18th century. Of great importance was the quarrying of chalk for mortar. Malcolm considered Dorking to be the best producer, its lime sought after by every mason and bricklayer in London who had work which was to be particularly neat, to set hard, or to resist water. The West India Docks had recently been built of it. At Denbies, lime was burnt in a big way by the largest producer with a famed six-kiln lime-burner which used coal for fuel from Kingston, wagons returning with grain. Conical brick kilns were specially designed to create intense heat for 20-30 hours and to be economical in fuel which was made costly by the land carriage. Extending eastwards along the chalk escarpment at Buckland, Betchworth and onwards to Reigate and Godstone, as well as westwards to Guildford, were chalk quarries producing agricultural lime. These had an enormous business from the late 18th century, for farmers southwards on the Greensands and on the Weald Clay used it as their main manure. Such prodigious quantities were being applied to fallows that when William Cobbett made one of his Rural Rides in 1823 he was astonished at the whiteness of fields being prepared for wheat,[7] and Arthur Young had earlier complained that farmers were spending as much on their manure as what the crop would earn them. The chalk was usually burnt with kiln faggots made of the tops of underwood or furze; some 7-800 of the former and about 1,200 of the latter would burn a kiln yielding four wagonloads of lime.

Until the late 18th century when large limeworks cheapened production, most farmers went annually to draw chalk from the quarries and burnt it in brick lime-kilns on their own farms near a convenient lane and generally against a natural or artificially constructed bank, so that the chalk and fuel might be thrown in from above. Each farm had its own kiln which was abandoned and allowed to fall into ruin when it became more convenient to purchase lime at the major limeworks but the remains may still be found at the present day in various stages of decay. Chalking land with up to 5-600 bushels of raw chalk to an acre was also widely practised on the tenacious clays in the Weald, on sandy soils and also on the sandy loams on the Downs, e.g. about Cheam, when by slow degrees the

24 *A typical limekiln supplying a farm. Most farms in need of lime worked one.*

chalk enriched and broke up soil into a better tilth. Raw chalk was particularly recommended for sour pasture that was to be brought into arable.

The Dover cliffs were repeatedly kept white in the 17th century by the quarrying of chalk for lime-burning. In 1649, for example, Ralph Bushkin of Otham and Edward Goodwin, a jurat of Dover, leased land 'lying and being under the cliff' to serve one lime kiln for a term of nine years. Bushkin with others also had another lease of land from the same year 'belonging to the pier and harbour Liberty' for quarrying chalk for lime-making, at the same annual rent of £5 6s. 8d. and one load of lime at two usual feasts in the year'. In yet another lease of the same year Bushkin and others leased a stretch of cliff 2,090 feet in length near Paradise Point for the same purpose. His rent was to be paid at the site of the manor house called the Priory of Dover together with a load of lime yearly. Bushkin had been in the lime-burning business at Dover as far back as 1617 when he was licensed to make chalk into agricultural or building lime from 6,080 yards of cliff near the sluices of Dover harbour. In 1705 Philip Papillon of Acrise near Folkestone, a member of the famous Huguenot family which played such a great part in the affairs of Kent, leased his land called the Cliffe at Dover for the purpose of lime-making for building or other purposes.[8]

The small-scale chalk diggings known as dene-holes have until recently escaped the attention of field workers. They are normally shallow depressions at the edge of a field which mark the site of a shaft dug through the superficial deposits to the chalk underneath. A number of chambers radiated from the shaft's base. The diggers climbed up and down the shaft by means of footholes cut into it. The chalk was winched up in leather or wooden barrels and applied to nearby land to render it more fertile. The chalk dug from underground apparently contained more unleached magnesium than that from the surface and was thus more effective as a fertiliser. The chalk was applied in winter so as not to dry out before the first frosts broke it up. Rather cruder chalk workings for lime in the 16th and 17th centuries are known as chalk-wells.[9]

In modern times the cement industry is the largest consumer of chalk, the principal location of manufacture being the Medway towns. Other natural resources were utilised. The Folkestone Beds are an important source of building sand, particularly around Farnham, between Redhill and Maidstone, and around Ashford. Works at these places also make from the sand paving blocks, roofing-tiles, wall-blocks and calcium silicate bricks. Specially fine sand from these sources is also used as an aggregate in hot-rolled asphalt. High-grade silica sand, also from the Folkestone Beds, has long been used between Buckland and Oxted in Surrey, and near Borough Green, West Malling and Aylesford in Kent. The Surrey areas yield sand especially suitable for glass-making. Carstone, a ferruginous sandstone occurring in thin veins in the Folkestone Beds and formerly used with other local stone in vernacular buildings, is now merely used as decorative stone in rockeries. Fuller's Earth, capable of absorbing oil, grease and colouring matter and therefore used from medieval times for cleaning ('fulling') woollen cloth, was produced near Redhill from Roman times and this area on the Sandgate

Beds is still the main centre of production today. Another source in the same beds near Maidstone supplied the cleansing material for the woollen industry centred on Cranbrook from the 14th to the 17th centuries.

The Kent Coalfield

In 1927 a rural area of great beauty, the corner of England that is east Kent, suddenly changed its character to fit it for a coalfield that had so far been associated only with places in the Midlands and North. The cause was the exciting underground deposit of coal under the coverlet of virgin white chalk. Buried deep beneath the chalk, sandstones and other younger rocks is the coal- and iron-bearing Palaeozoic floor. Geologists could dimly imagine the stupendous forces that had bent the carboniferous limestone hollow in which the coal lies and then sheared it off clean, thus removing it from that of South Wales and Northern France. Stranger still was a sharp wedge of Jurassic rock below the chalk which collects water from France; the chalk itself is saturated with water. The suggestion that bores should be sunk into these ancient rocks in an attempt to locate workable seams of coal was made as early as 1846 by Sir Henry de la Beche and in 1856 Godwin Austen inferred that the most likely success would be in the district which became the Kent Coalfield, where the ancient rocks were nearest the surface. It was not until 1890, however, that a two-foot seam of coal was confirmed at about 900 feet at the base of Shakespeare's Cliff on the site of the originally proposed Channel Tunnel. Professor Adshead remembered seeing the first shaft sunk and watched it almost with tears in his eyes, so fearful was he that Kent would be spoiled.

A colliery was opened here which proved unsuccessful and finally closed in 1915. Meanwhile, trial borings had been made in the vicinity between 1905 and 1910 to locate more workable seams; all of these were at deep levels and averaged only just over three feet in thickness. A number of collieries were abandoned by 1914 without producing coal, such as Stonehall and Wingham, but Snowdown Colliery which produced coal from 1912, Tilmanstone from 1913, Chislet from 1914, and Betteshanger from 1921 were in production until the Kent Coalfield was closed down entirely between 1969 and 1986. The causes were primarily geological: the costs of obtaining relatively thin seams of coal beneath a great thickness of water-bearing strata proved too great an impediment. The envisaged annual production of about 10 million tons was never realised, one reason being the failure to attract coal-using industries to the area such as the planned iron-smelting works at Dover and ancillary chemical plants.

One important development did happen, the creation of a new industrial community. Owing to the absence of mining expertise, families from the North-East, South Wales and the Midlands had to be imported into the area. These families settled down remarkably well in the new surroundings and their descendants have tended to remain, having found alternative employment, at the Channel Tunnel for example, since the closure of the collieries. There is a remarkably strong community spirit amongst this group which is evident in the

25 *George Scharf's drawing of limekilns near Betchworth, 1823.*

liveliness of sporting, social and cultural activities and the crime rate is lower than in urban areas of Kent generally.

A great deal of the credit for this is due to (Sir) Patrick Abercrombie who was responsible for the survey of the East Kent Region in 1928 which had the over-riding aim of a Special Advisory Committee emanating from a conference convened by the Archbishop of Canterbury to minimise change to the face of the countryside and to provide healthy conditions for the migrants amidst industrial change produced by coal and, possibly, by iron.[10] It was a situation fraught with danger but full of possibilities. Every attempt was made to avoid the scarring and squalor familiar in Lancashire and elsewhere in the North. Abercrombie was himself a good choice of planning consultant in that he and Professor Adshead had previously designed Dormanstown for Messrs Pearson and Dorman Long Ltd (who owned two of the Kent collieries), which was accounted 'second to none in the kingdom'. As Abercrombie remarked, 'the smutch-faced collier, indeed like a smoke-laden atmosphere and straggling houses is symbolic of the palaeotechnic age of industry'. Although the first consideration in developing the new coalfield was an economic one, Abercrombie was particularly concerned to avoid indiscriminate scattered buildings and ribbon development along the main roads, then the scourge of England. He was also against anything that would destroy the existing assets of the region, the ring of seaside towns between Whitstable and Folkestone and the rural landscape of great charm which was used increasingly by summer visitors as a contrast to the unmitigated sea-coast delights. Except in the neighbourhood of Folkestone this was not the bare chalk down country of Sussex or Woldingham but a rolling cultivated terrain with unfenced roads between richly-wooded settlements, whether villages, farm-houses or noble parks in the sheltered hollows.

A particular problem that was addressed, when it was decided to locate housing deliberately on limited amounts of land, was whether a single new town with quick means of transport from and to all the pits should be planned or whether creating villages and towns for several pits should be the policy. The latter arrangement was preferred. Chislet was designed by the architect G.J. Skipper for 1,000 houses. A village green was provided with a church, institute, rectory, library, school, banks, hospital, shops and inn surrounding it. Elvington was expanded from a small group of houses built in the early days of the Tilmanstone Pit. The old house with its walled kitchen garden and noble trees was turned into a Miners' Hostel. Pixhill was planned as a hillside town near the village of Little Mongeham.[11]

Aylesham, in the heart of the coalfield, was designed by Abercrombie and his assistants on a *tabula rasa* as a self-contained town of ultimately 15,000 people to serve the nearby Snowdown Pit and another which was aborted. The site selected was a fold in the chalk hills backed by an extensive beechwood, so the town is sheltered from the fierce winter winds that beat upon this little peninsula of England. A main broad avenue follows the fold and leads to the market square. Sites for churches and schools were reserved at focal points, an encircling boulevard was provided and the town was extremely well furnished with open spaces. An attempt was made to give each street its own character, but the severe financial limitations of the time meant that houses were of a basic design, though each had a bathroom, and the 'faint Flemish flavour which is so characteristic of the local work of the late 17th and 18th centuries' could not be attempted. Another cost-cutting exercise which was regretted was the import of bricks and tiles from abroad, although Kent had traditionally made the finest in England. The ultimate size of the new towns ranged from one the size of Ramsgate, others of the size of Canterbury and the smallest about the size of Deal.

Owing to the recession in the 1930s only 500 of Abercrombie's houses in his original vision for Aylesham were built and the other new towns were cut back proportionately.[11] The pitheads which had nothing but electric winding gear and some low roofs were not conspicuous in the landscape. Abercrombie in 1927 thought that in two years' time it would be interesting to visit east Kent: 'We hope that by then the coal will be raised, houses lived in, and that some of the wounds we are at the moment inflicting upon the garden of England will have been healed.' In actuality the iron-works and ancillary industries did not develop and the performance of the coalfield was disappointing even during the Second World War, owing mainly to geological conditions. Since the colliery closures a regeneration and expansion programme for the former coalfield has been launched.[12] Further reclamation of colliery and tip sites and other despoiled land is under way, together with the construction of new work places and homes whilst acknowledging the cultural heritage which the mining industry brought in the last century. Aylesham is now to be expanded with 1,000 more houses.[13]

4

Early Man

Our knowledge of pre-history and the Roman period has increased by leaps and bounds since the 1970s with the use of aerial photography, the techniques of environmental archaeology and excavation in advance of motorway construction and other big development projects. The miles of countryside sliced through by Motorways 2, 20 and 25, the expansion of Dover and other major works, such as oil and water pipe lines has resulted in Kent being in the vanguard of many new discoveries. Apart from spectacular ones, the many lesser finds have begun to fill in a picture of human occupation at different periods that was unrealisable a generation ago. The later Iron Age (*c.*100 BC-AD 43), for example, then only known fragmentarily, is now represented by 20 sites in west Kent and another 20 are suspected from aerial photography. The very many new sites show how many more have yet to be found. The Kent Archaeological Rescue Unit, led by Brian Philp, has built up a great reputation for highly skilled excavations and speedily-produced reports.

Much new information has also been gleaned from archaeological excavations in the wake of the high-speed railway to London together with the construction of the Channel Tunnel. This transect through Kent has revealed numerous Bronze- and Iron-Age settlements with field systems on or at the foot of the North Downs. Another Neolithic longhouse was also found in the vicinity of the Medway megaliths. At the site of the Roman villa at Thurnham, near Detling, a continuous sequence of occupation ranging from the late Iron Age through to the fourth century AD was discovered and at Pepper Hill there was evidently a substantial settlement marked by a Romano-British cemetery containing 326 inhumations and 235 cremations. Altogether, the transect has yielded evidence of considerable early settlement on the Downs.[1]

Meanwhile, a splendid example of what can be achieved by metal detectionists and archaeologists working together, is at Ringlemere Farm, Woodnesborough near Sandwich. Here a detectionist discovered in 2001 a Bronze-Age gold cup on the site of a round barrow which had been ploughed flat. This led to field walking and to repeated excavations at the site led by Keith Parfitt of the Canterbury Archaeological Trust in conjunction with the British Museum and other organisations which have yielded evidence of a large early Bronze-Age cemetery site on ploughed-out barrows and underlying Neolithic occupations which produced a fine example of one of the earliest pots made in Britain.

Another method which is yielding immense new knowledge is the intensive study of aerial photographs and field surveys. This can be illustrated by recent work on the Isle of Thanet. A general impression had been formed that it was sparsely populated in the Roman period and functioned primarily as a granary for the Saxon shore forts of Richborough and Reculver. The new picture which has emerged after 25 years' research is of a populous island landscape liberally sprinkled with villas and farming settlement. No fewer than 83 sites have been recorded, including 23 villas and other substantial buildings. It seems evident that Thanet's corn-growing properties were established in antiquity but it is uncertain, owing to the lack of dating evidence, how many of these buildings co-existed at any particular time.[2] Other areas, not yet surveyed intensively, may have the same potential.

Emerging as a significant part of the rich treasure-house of buried archaeology which is being discovered are the river valleys cut through the Downs. In its 10 miles from Otford to Darenth, the Darent valley, for example, is apparently abounding in buried archaeology. It has been called a multi-period landscape including a concentrated assemblage of Mesolithic flints, Bronze- and Iron-Age remains, very important Roman features, two certain and two probable Saxon *grübenhausen* and a major fifth-century Saxon cemetery. Almost all has been discovered in advance of recent pipe-laying operations. Also relatively densely populated was the brickearth on a chalk base in north-east Kent which has been so intensively farmed for centuries that little trace is observable above ground. It is likely that Kent, which in Caesar's day was populous and precociously advanced, was similarly relatively well developed at earlier periods.

A sign of this is the inherited skills manifest in the construction of the Dover Bronze-Age boat, discovered in 1992, which was navigating the English Channel *c.*1550 BC, the oldest surviving sea-going vessel in Europe. This was an oak plank-built boat propelled by paddles which was buried under 19 feet of mud in a former creek of the Dour River. After being cut in sections, soaked in a liquid wax solution and freeze-dried, the vessel is superbly preserved in Dover Museum. The replica section of the boat was made with tools similar to those thought to have been used by the boat builders. It has been suggested that some fifty persons probably built the boat with tools which included bronze axes hafted on to wooden handles which proved more effective than expected and that the builders had previous experience of boat-building. With a crew of perhaps 16 paddlers and three or four bailers, a crossing of the Channel with up to three tons of cargo would have been made in about five hours.[3]

Before the Wildwood and the Earliest Human Occupation

A remarkable chapter in the history of flint-using people in Kent was contributed by Benjamin Harrison, the village shopkeeper of Ightham who demonstrated that hitherto unsuspected Palaeolithic flint implements were to be found in high-level gravel beds on the elevated plateau of the North Downs and the surrounding hills, as at Oldbury, now a classic site of very early man. Here hunters used the protection of rock-shelters and caves in a dreary world totally unlike the lush wooded aspect of today.[4] Harrison's discoveries were received in many quarters with great scepticism, although championed by Professor Joseph Prestwich of Shoreham, but evidence that people were hunting on the North Downs some 450-500,000 years ago was dramatically confirmed at the world-famous site of the Swanscombe human skull near Rochester.[5] 'Swanscombe Man' crafted hand tools from the flint on the chalk to butcher wild horses, deer and other meat and his life was based on the hunting of such wild animals in a comparatively warm phase during the last glacial period. Perhaps our view of his lowly culture should be revised because Mark Roberts, who has interpreted the human and animal remains of similar age found at Boxgrove, Sussex, has demonstrated that hunters were not opportunist scavengers but resourceful people in total command of their patch.[6] It would appear, however, as J.J. Wymer has suggested, that his culture may mark a phase of consolidation because successive Palaeolithic hunters transmitted the same hunting culture from one generation to the next over the enormous span of something like half a million years.[7]

This long and static civilisation was played out against the rigours of a cold, cheerless and inclement tundra climate similar to that of northern Scandinavia today, lasting many thousands of years, ameliorated during warmer phases. In the coldest phases it is likely that no one ventured into this hostile landscape, even in summer. During intermittent warmer phases humans entered Britain across the land bridge then connecting the island to the continent.

The best known evidence for hunting groups succeeding 'Swanscombe Man' is on the classic flight of river terraces at Farnham.[8] The oldest humanly-struck flints (palaeoliths) are found on the highest terrace. They are of disputed age, but possibly 400,000 years old and represent human activity after the River Thames had been pushed by glaciation from a former course through the Vale of St Albans to one north of Heathrow Airport. As the river and its tributaries eroded the land it spread sediments on lower terraces. On intermediate terraces flint axes are believed to have come from the long geological period known as the Wolstonian, existing from c.305,000 to 120,000 years ago. Implements on a lower terrace have been identified by J.J. Wymer with the Devensian period some 70,000-13,000 years ago, when the Wey and Blackwater rivers were diverted into their present valleys. Another group of very early palaeoliths exists on the high plateaux of the North Downs, e.g. at Walton and Banstead Heaths, which may be of the same age as those of a high terrace at Farnham. It would appear that hunters bivouacked and used the flint boulders scattered so freely on this high ground for their tools. Ancient worked flints have frequently been found on the edge of the scarp of the North Downs above Folkestone and Cheriton, suggesting fairly widespread human activity.[9]

The Wildwood

The sward of sheep-cropped grassland was the downland habitat first singled out for praise and it is so peculiar to chalk and its best-known and loved feature that the old view was that turf was natural to chalkland and that the earliest inhabitants moved freely over open, bare chalk, free of woodland, and that they were attracted to it for this reason. This is a myth which has not been entirely eradicated. In their otherwise delightful book *Downland Life* (1992), Burton and Davis write of chalk ridges as 'natural walkways'.[10] True, it would have been *easier* for early peoples to have traversed downland than the denser woodland on clay, but we must continually bear in mind that large areas of the summit plateaux of the North Downs are plastered with cold, heavy soils, the natural habitat of woodland. There is now general acceptance that chalk grassland is a product of human and animal clearance of the lighter cover of deciduous woodland that with gradual climatic warming colonised the chalk from *c*.10,000 BC, replacing the juniper, hazel and birch of the colder period.

Such a change in vegetation to the Wildwood has been detected by the new technique of environmental archaeology. Cores of silt deposit (colluvium) found in dry valleys or combes are analysed to discover what they contain of fossil insects, molluscs and tree and plant pollen that was blowing in the wind. This data, which tends to vary according to the depth below the present surface, helps considerably to build up a picture of which trees, plants and animals were living at particular times in the past and changes over time. An important section through the silts of a dry combe in the Kent Downs has shown changes in habitat from woodland *c*.8000 BC, through to open pasture in the Middle Ages. In the lower deposits were shells of snails that once lived in woodland while in the overlying deposits snail shells were more typical of an open grassland environment. By dating the deposits it has been possible to speculate that the changes from woodland to more open downland began when Neolithic farmers began clearing the woodland, taking advantage of light soil conditions (where they pertained), which presented opportunities for its early clearance. This episode is now recognised as one of the most significant in the history of the Downs.

The possibility that some grassy patches might have persisted throughout the period of the Wildwood is not discounted and this is the view held at the present time by Dr Francis Rose.[11] The Dutch ecologist F.W.M. Vera has recently challenged the purely anthropogenetic origin of grassland on the continent of Europe and has stressed the effect of grazing over long periods of prehistoric and historic time by larger herbivores such as deer, wild pigs, wild horses, wild cattle, together with domestic animals. This process he suggests resulted in a park-like landscape before the introduction of agriculture, comprising a mosaic of grassland, scrub, solitary trees, groves and more extensive woodland.[12]

Mesolithic Hunters and Gatherers and the First Farmers

It was not until the warming after the last glaciation that hunter-gatherers were able to begin the continuous occupation of the Downs which has remained unbroken to the present. There is more evidence of these nomads on the Surrey Hills than in any other district of south-east England, and the Surrey scene, through the work of Dr Wilfrid Hooper, Graham Clarke and W.F. Rankine, established the Mesolithic as a distinctive culture in Britain. These people made

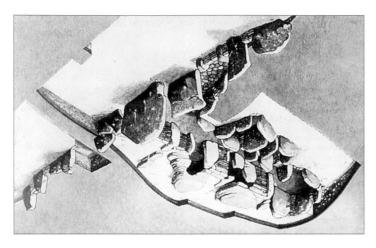

26 *Diagrammatic impression of the chambers in a Neolithic long barrow.*

distinctive hollowed flint points (microliths) and their characteristic legacy is the chipping floor where flint derived from the Downs was prepared by flaking into flint-points for arrow shafts, knives, saws, gauges and scrapers. The many thousands of such implements and 'wasters' is evidence of intense hunting activity on the free-draining sands and gravels in a period when, with climatic warming, birch and pine were being succeeded by broad-leaved deciduous woodland. It has been noted that most of the hunting occupation on the sands and sandstones is in the first half of the Mesolithic period, say to about 6000 BC. Abandonment of the hunting grounds may have arisen from the intentional burning of woodland to create open pasture for the attraction of game which eventually resulted in a degraded soil structure changing from a forest brown earth when colonised by trees to a podsolised barren heath. This implication that British lowland heaths on poor soils are not natural but man-made is now generally accepted, but that it could be as early as the Mesolithic will have to be determined by later research. Dwellings in summer were probably basically huts or tents, possibly of light timber construction clothed with turf or bracken, which have left no trace. The Abinger Manor Farm site, excavated by Dr L.S.B. Leakey and deemed to be the oldest humanly-made dwelling preserved in Britain, is now regarded as of a later origin, and even its use as a dwelling is disputed. The most convincing examples of 'pit-dwellings' are in Weston Wood at Albury, where traces of stake holes with a wider gap at the entrance were found in shallow pits.

The onset of the first farmer-herders in the Neolithic period from *c.*4000 BC, who adopted the inventions of agriculture and the art of pottery, flint-mining and barter or trade, is poorly represented in Surrey in the current state of knowledge. Few worked flints have been recorded from the chalk west of the Mole gap, though numerous scatters have been traced around Headley and Banstead, in the Coulsdon and Sanderstead area, and at the foot of the Downs dip-slope between Croydon and Ewell. There are large concentrations on the sandstone around Limpsfield and in the Elstead, Tilford, Abinger and Peaslake areas. It is

27 *Kit's Coty House, a remnant of a Neolithic long barrow.*

in the Neolithic that the dual North Downs trackway probably first came into use. This lay on the flanks of the Vale of Holmesdale and provided access between the more desirable habitation sites of early man on the chalklands of Wiltshire and those on the channel coast of Kent. Known as the Harrow Way in Hampshire and the Pilgrims' Way in Surrey and Kent, it forms a continuous trackway at the foot of the chalk escarpment. The lower route is duplicated by a ridgeway which would have afforded easier going in summer when the heavy mire had dried out. Yet another ridgeway was the track that runs along the line of the sandstone hills between St Martha's and Maidstone.

The best-known of the Neolithic sites in Kent are the splendid remains of megaliths, or chambered tombs (long barrows), of the Medway valley. These were built of sarsen stones, silicified sand from the Eocene era, which is a dense, hard, durable rock found widely on the upper reaches of Blue Bell Hill and the backslopes of the Kent Downs. Some of the megaliths are more impressive than their counterparts in Wiltshire and Berkshire and are particularly numerous in the Cobham neighbourhood. Concentrations of stone cleared from the fields are thought to have been collapsed tombs and Everitt has remarked that 'stone' place-names in Kent may denote former sarsen stone and even vanished megalithic monuments. When first built, the Medway long barrows extended up to 200 feet in length and were divided into chambers, the entrances blocked by a portal stone. The best-known example is Kit's Coty, a mere remnant, with only three upright stones capped by a fourth large stone which was originally part of a chambered long barrow. It is the survivor of a group of nine stone-built long barrows in the vicinity. These include the Addington long barrow where a detailed survey in 1981 revealed that a burial mound about 60 yards long had been bordered by 25 equally-spaced stones on all four sides of the structure. The excavation of the barrow at the Chestnuts, Addington, disclosed the cremated remains of at least nine people and objects of late Neolithic or Bronze-Age date. The exceptionally large numbers of barrows suggests that the Addington-Aylesford district had special qualities for Neolithic society. It has been suggested that an intrusive group at the end of the Neolithic period came in from the Thames estuary and established a powerful community in the mid-Kent area between *c*.2300 and 1700 BC.

In east Kent is a Stour valley group of earthen (i.e. non-megalithic) long barrows on the North Downs between Canterbury and Ashford. Julliberries Grave is well-known but two others nearby have recently been recorded. They clearly indicate prehistoric settlement in a wooded district which had been regarded as largely unoccupied before Saxon times.[13]

The Bronze and Iron Ages

The Bronze Age, marked by the discovery and use of bronze, a mix or 'alloy' of tin and copper, finally reached Britain *c*.2300 BC. Stone tools and flint arrowheads were still used, but not as widely as in earlier ages. Pottery survives usually as cremation urns in round barrows. Gold jewellery, such as the gold bracelet found at East Wear Bay near Folkestone, is also found, mainly at burial sites. Bronze-Age people tended to live in small farming communities with few buildings, some used for specific functions such as weaving, grinding corn or keeping animals. Cattle, pigs, sheep and goats were reared and at some point the horse was domesticated. The land was worked in small squarish or rectangular fields by a type of plough called an ard which drew a furrow for sowing wheat and barley but did not turn the sod as does a modern plough. Oxen were probably used for traction. The dwelling took the form of a thatched roundhouse of wood supported by rings of wooden posts, with walls of wattle hurdles, daubed with clay or mud and dung. By the middle Bronze Age cremation was common. The ashes were placed in cremation urns, often under or in barrows. Most of these were ploughed flat in the more intensive agricultural district of east Kent and it is only recently that grave-goods have been recovered from such sites.

Clearly the hinterland of Dover was an important Bronze-Age settlement area where perhaps as many as 50 people could have been involved in building the Dover Bronze-Age boat. The cluster of sites recently discovered in Surrey has made habitation in the Thames valley much clearer than it was 20 years ago, but on the chalk the earliest substantial evidence at present is of Bronze-Age metalwork finds Ewell, Beddington, Wallington and Carshalton. The latter site is a circular enclosure which is interpreted as a 'central place' in the distribution of metals and a power base, though nothing is known of the farming settlement around it. On the Greensand there is a substantial group of middle Bronze-Age settlements in the Blackheath-Farley Heath district.

One of the most significant insights into Bronze-Age farming on the chalk from excavation in advance of the Channel Tunnel is the effect of soil erosion following clearance of the natural forest cover to establish fields for crops and pastures for domesticated animals. This apparently occasioned massive soil loss. Soil erosion was usually initiated when the bare ground surface was exposed to heavy rain, which carved rills and gullies in the topsoil and carried it away. Along the foot of the North Downs in the Channel Tunnel area various periods of

28 *Soay sheep, not normally as biddable as in this photograph.*

erosion and deposition have been identified dating back over 3,800 years to the early Bronze Age, with later evidence of further soil losses in the Iron-Age and Anglo-Saxon periods. At Holywell Combe, an early Bronze-Age settlement was found to have been buried, through time, by a thick carpet of migrated soil. A number of other Bronze-Age habitations have since been found under hill-wash in the same area. These discoveries vividly illustrate the way in which prehistoric agricultural operations exhausted land fertility and caused a cycle of erosion and deposition which would have forced the occupants to exploit new areas of the Downs. The implications of the new information for the investigation of the prehistoric occupancy of early farmers on other chalklands is obvious.

In Surrey the Iron Age on the North Downs and Greensand ridges is not well understood at present.[14] An important group of more than 40 round houses has been discovered around Tongham and Runfold, east of Farnham. Iron-Age farms were at Hawks Hill, Leatherhead, and at West Clandon, and ever-increasing lists of discoveries suggest that a chain of such farms lay on the Downs most free of superficial deposits east of the Mole gap and that a line of them existed along the edge of the dip-slope at the spring-line. At Leatherhead the farmstead was of the classic Little Woodbury type. The main dwellings would have been large round houses; pits and post-holes have been interpreted as grain-storage pits or raised granaries or corn-drying racks. At Farthing Down, Coulsdon, is a rare example in Surrey of the small squarish field systems divided by lynchets which are such a feature of the chalk in Wiltshire, Dorset and Sussex. Other sites are known from aerial photography but yet to be dated. 'Banjo'-shaped enclosures at Tadworth and Effingham are thought to have been used for livestock. Iron-Age settlement on the Downs between the rivers Wey and Mole is sparse despite investigations since 1987. This may be the consequence of extensive clay-with-flints. Curiously, with only one exception (War Coppice at Caterham) the hillforts of Surrey are grouped to north or south of the Downs, not on the chalk itself. The two temple sites at Wanborough had a special religious sanctity in the Roman period. Others were at Titsey and Farley Heath. Hascombe, Holmbury and Anstiebury form an important group of promontory hillforts of the Iron Age along a range of the sandstone hills. None has been fully investigated and their precise function is still debatable. They are too small to be reckoned embryonic towns and they were possibly refuges for use in emergency and the headquarters of lordships containing many scattered farms thereabouts. At Felday, nearby, an enclosure has feeble defences and may have been used for impounding livestock, possibly driven along long-distance droveways in the course of transhumance.[15]

In Kent the Farningham late Iron-Age farmstead on a steep chalk hillside above the River Darent (found during motorway construction in 1975) has become a type site of Iron-Age occupation in the country for the period *c.*50 BC-AD 50. A circular hut lay in small ditched enclosures. Sixteen pits were probably underground storage silos for grain. Surviving bones indicate that cattle were the main source of meat. It was probably a small farm representing a single family unit. A large number of fire-cracked stones were found on the site, suggesting that hearths were built to dry grain. It seems likely that the middle slopes of hillsides with a south-facing aspect were most favoured for dwelling sites and for arable cultivation, the hill pastures lying above on the ridges, as in the South Downs.[16]

Much new knowledge of the Iron Age has also been acquired from the Channel Tunnel excavations. To the east of Dolland's Moor has been uncovered the greatest concentration of early to mid-Iron-Age settlement found in Kent. A system of square fields probably existed. Pottery from the site has continental parallels in the Low Countries and northern France and it is tempting to suggest links between communities on either side of the Channel at this period. The origin of Canterbury is traditionally associated with the abandonment of the settlement at the nearby Bigbury hillfort *c.*15 BC. This was probably the work of a folk movement of Belgic settlers whom Caesar tells us had come to south-east England some fifty years before his invasions. Significant quantities of Iron-Age pottery are buried in hill-wash, indicating that intensive agriculture caused further erosion at the foot of the Downs. Further evidence of late Iron-Age occupation is also to be found in Caesar's *Commentaries* made after his military campaigns in 55 and 54 BC. He describes east Kent as being thickly studded with farmsteads and that the people enjoyed an advanced economy. The density of sites now being uncovered supports his testimony. He adds that Kent was known as Cantium, but was not a unified territory, being ruled by four kings.

Einkorn, one of the first cereals cultivated for food by Neolithic farmers, is thought to have originated in the upper area of the Fertile Crescent of the Tigris-Euphrates region. Yields were probably substantially lower than that for Emmer wheat, also from the Fertile Crescent, which superseded einkorn in the late Bronze Age. In turn Emmer was displaced by spelt, a wheat found wild either in Iran or in south-eastern Europe which was widely distributed in Europe as civilisation migrated westwards. It was widely sown in the Roman Empire and can be assumed to have been the basic wheat in Britain during the late Iron Age and Romano-British period.

Dr Peter Reynolds' unique project of studying the agricultural and domestic economy of the late Iron Age at Chalton in Hampshire and the environmental consequences has resulted in the construction of a working farm as it would have been *c*.300 BC, with livestock crops and equipment. This has greatly illuminated our knowledge of conditions in the North Downs. Among the many questions the project seeks to answer are: what happens to an Iron-Age house over the years from rising damp, rain, wind and snow; its function in the economy of the farmstead; the level of agricultural productivity; and what effect ploughing and earthworks had on the land surface. The sheer quantity of rods and stakes

29 *Emmer wheat appears to have supplanted einkorn as the principal wheat of the Roman Empire. The plant is very productive and sustained a larger population in Roman Britain than hitherto had been believed.*

required for building and fencing an Iron-Age farm implies that woodland was coppiced for the purpose. At Chalton ploughing is done with the simple ard, and crops are grown in distinct rows allowing the hoeing of weeds and beans sown in the crop rotation, so adding nitrogen to the soil in advance of wheat sowing, as there is evidence for adoption of these actual practices. Research since 1972 has indicated that crop yields were remarkably high under different treatments, averaging one ton an acre (modern yields are many times higher). Altogether, ongoing research at Ancient Farm Chalton is deepening our knowledge of the considerable achievements of Iron-Age peoples. This is unlikely to remain purely in the academic sphere because prehistoric wheats when milled and made into flour are higher in protein than modern flour made from winter wheat, are tastier, and have a higher concentration of vitamins. A gene extracted from the threshing and storage areas of Danebury hillfort shows that it might be feasible to improve modern corn crops with genetic material from ancient varieties.[17]

The Roman Town and Countryside

Roman Surrey has recently been re-assessed by D.G. Bird. It is likely that the eastern part of 'Surrey' fell within the tribal territory of the Cantiaci, whose capital was Canterbury, and the remainder lay in that of the Atrebates governed from *Calleva Atrebatum* (Silchester). The most important event affecting 'Surrey' was the founding of London by the Romans as a great centre of communication by land and sea and with a large population providing an important market for food and consumer goods. Villa sites on the Downs seem to have been confined to the area east of the River Mole. They include the villa at Chelsham, a group of three villas at Headley, Walton on the Hill and Walton Heath and possible villa sites at Woodcote and Banstead. At the scarp-foot of the Downs or further south on the Greensands were villas at Titsey, Bletchingley, Abinger, Compton, Brinscombe near Godalming, and Puttenham. We have a general picture of well-organised villa life at Ashtead and a brickworks there, with what appears to have been a manager's house and bath building abandoned *c.*AD 200. Bird suggests that there are many more villas to find and that there is clearly the need for much more fieldwork.[17] A Romano-British village existed in Park Lane Ashtead. Another Roman building was so close to the site of the parish church that Normans used Roman materials in the fabric. Apart from Ashtead, which was clearly an important Romano-British settlement, a string of London outposts which began as posting-stations on the new roads, such as Ewell, have been identified. A number of important pottery and tile works have been found, probably serving a London market.

The largest Roman villa in Kent is at Darenth in the Darent valley. It comprised 71 rooms or buildings, mostly grouped in long ranges around two large courtyards. A bathhouse lay adjacent. In scale it corresponds to the largest villas in Britain, such as Bignor or Brading in the Isle of Wight, and developed over some two centuries between the second and fourth centuries AD.[18] Another villa in the valley was at Farningham where all the walls were apparently plastered and decorated with painted designs. Yet another in the vicinity was at Lullingstone, one of the most rewarding places in Britain, which is discussed on p.93. At Thurnham farm labourers discovered a Roman building in 1833. Further excavation in advance of the M20 revealed it to be almost certainly an important Roman villa and nearby a continuous sequence of occupation ranging from the Iron Age through to the fourth century AD was discovered. The Crofton Roman villa at Orpington has the remains of 10 rooms under a later building. At Pepper Hill (TQ 6190 7210) is a Romano-British cemetery containing 326 inhumations and 235 cremations. Many of the burials were in wooded coffins, marked mainly by metal fittings and wood stains. Finds also indicate a substantial settlement from Neolithic times onwards.[19]

The civitas capital, Canterbury (*Durovernum Cantiacorum*) was supplied with a forum and basilica complex, a

30 *Lullingstone Roman Villa, notable for its Christian connections.*

temple, baths and theatre, etc. Excavations have suggested that up to *c*.AD 70 the Iron-Age pattern largely remained unaltered but re-development then began, resulting in the disappearance of circular post-built houses. Surrounding it are few villas. Andrews has suggested that this is the result of a military occupation of a strategic district. Stray finds imply that population was high but that the land was being exploited by native landowners rather than in Roman-style villas decorated with mosaics and wall paintings. A key site in this regard is Westhawk Farm near Ashford, excavated in 1998-9. The site was abandoned about the middle of the third century, but had circular structures which appear to have been thatched, and not the expected rectangular romanised buildings. The decline of the iron industry with the departure of the Dover squadron of the *Classis Britannica* may explain the abandonment of the site. This continuance of 'Iron-Age style' settlement well into the Romano-British period throws doubt on the depth of romanisation in Kent, which on circumstantial evidence would have been expected to have more than a veneer.[20]

The Roman Painted House at Dover, *c*.AD 200, was partially demolished and buried under rubble when the Saxon Shore fort was built *c*.AD 270. The thick walls are built of chalk, flint and brick. Remarkably preserved under the rubble is the largest area of wall painting found in Britain. This has motifs dedicated to Bacchus, the god of wine, and is framed by broad panels in bright colours. An elaborate system of underfloor heating was provided. The house was probably used as a *mansio*, a transit hotel by leading officials such as the Governor and his staff when travelling between Britain and Gaul. A Saxon *grübenhaus* was dug into the soil above the Painted House *c*.800. This was without comfort and refinement and the occupiers were totally unaware of the civilised surroundings beneath. The presentation of the surviving buildings at the Painted House Museum at Dover has won national acclaim.[21]

31 *Discovering the Roman Painted House, Dover, possibly a Governor's residence, and general view showing painted plaster.*

5

The Anglo-Saxons

The Coming of the English

It has been rightly observed that to study the two hundred years after the departure of the Romans 'is to venture into a quagmire'.[1] This is because our knowledge of the consequences of the arrival of Jutish settlers in the north-east coastlands of Kent some 1,565 years ago and that of Saxons from the North Sea coastlands into Surrey at about the same time is fragmentary in the extreme. As John Gillingham has noted, this is, of course, the period's excitement. It is a matter of taking bold, speculative leaps. The old questions receive new answers, and each new answer only raises more questions.[2]

From the third century AD Roman Britain became prey to attack from outside which accelerated when the army and fleet left the province unprotected at the beginning of the fifth century. A long drawn-out period of violence, raiding and settlement then ensued which ultimately brought about the total collapse of the Romano-British economy. This period is known as the Dark Ages because a whole civilisation, at least nominally Christian, was destroyed by pagan barbarians: dark, also, because our knowledge of what actually took place is so obscure.

It is still very uncertain, for example, what actually happened to Romano-Britons in general and what form the new rural landscape took. Were the Britons exterminated? One must bear in mind that the recent discovery of more and more Romano-British settlement sites has led archaeologists to revise upwards their estimates of the population of Roman Britain in the fourth century, to as high as four or even six million and not as formerly thought between one and two million. This compares with the Domesday (1086) estimate of about two million. The view of 19th-century historians was that the English wiped out or drove away the native inhabitants and made a fresh start with farming and settlement in an emptied landscape. It was envisaged that the invaders immediately introduced a new rural pattern based on large manors with the nucleated villages still existing in the present landscape at the scarp- or dip-foot of the Downs in the Vale of Holmesdale or below the southern scarp of the sandstone hills.

Some fifty years or so ago this cataclysmic theory was replaced by one favouring more continuity in some respects. It is true that utter devastation seems to have occurred. Towns such as Canterbury were totally deserted during the early fifth century, villas were similarly abandoned, well-made pottery disappeared along with Latin and literacy, coins were no longer used, masonry building ceased and Christianity was swept away. It is clear that romanisation was stripped off the landscape which became littered with the fragments of Rome. There is also good evidence of mass migration to the continent in the fifth century. Yet the English actually settling in Kent and Surrey seem to have been modest in number and the British population must surely have been too great to have been massacred or driven away entirely. Attention is now given to the less romanised population of the countryside who had continued to live through the Roman occupation much as they had done in the late Iron Age. There is no doubt that catastrophe occurred but there is the possibility that it took a different form from that earlier envisaged, such as the pandemic of bubonic plague which struck Europe in recurring visitations from the 540s onwards.

The most careful and comprehensive study of the evolution of settlement from the end of the Romano-British period is that by Alan Everitt.[3] He specifically attempted to identify where continuity of occupation with the Roman period seemed likely and found substantial evidence of this amongst the lands settled by the Jutes at the end of the fifth century. That the invaders of Kent should have retained the Celtic name of Cantium for their kingdom (unlike the English in Essex and Sussex, for example), and the fact that place-names like Thanet, the rivers such as Medway, Darent, Cray and Dour and a substantial number of its oldest settlements are derived from primitive Celtic roots suggests continuity between British life and that of the invaders. Also to be borne in mind is the origin of the Jutes themselves. The great eighth-century historian Bede implied that they came directly from Jutland, as their name might suggest, but archaeology has demonstrated conclusively that their jewellery and other grave goods show a variety of influences, but chiefly Frankish. Moreover, there were strong Roman elements in their law which appears to have arisen from their

32 *Modern reconstruction of Saxon* grübenhausen.

contact with Roman rule in the middle Rhineland. A significant Roman influence appears to be the adoption of the lathe as an administrative and judicial division in Kent and of 'jugation' as a system of tax assessment possibly introduced into the area by the Romans. The rectangularity of medieval land division at Gillingham and neighbouring districts, for example, and the parallel nature of the road pattern, may be evidence of the survival of Roman centuriation. What is indisputable is that the early migrants soon developed close dynastic and commercial links with Merovingian Franks across the Channel and rapidly created one of the most cosmopolitan, prosperous and influential kingdoms of the early English. It is worth speculating that this was in part due to the continued economic activities of the conquered.[4]

There are important parts of Kent, notably the northern side of the Downs and the coast between the Downs and Romney Marsh, which still bear the imprint of the Roman world more obviously than most. The name Lyminge has a Celtic root and its parish church, one of the earliest in Kent, was a minster founded on the site of a Roman temple and within a mile of an early Jutish burial ground. Nearby is Lympne, another place-name with a Celtic root. It is derived from the old name of the River Rother, or Limen, and means 'the territory of the Limen people'. Darent is also a significant Celtic river name. There is a pagan burial site in the vicinity of Darenth itself and the neighbouring Roman villa and the Roman brickwork in its church all point to a continuity with Romano-British Kent. Indeed, the whole of the Darent valley and its estate (which included Westerham, so named because it was the most westerly of the Darent settlements), is recognised as one of the earliest cradles of English settlement in Kent, but we must not assume that it was wholly English. The Vale of Holmesdale has a special significance. Everitt has suggested that the Vale, which had potential arable land for the English to exploit, was one of the most important of the original primary settlements of the Jutes and that subsequent colonisation proceeded up on to the wooded Downs and southwards to the wooded Chart Hills. All the settlements had summer pastures in the Weald and some on the Downs as well. In this district, and in the valleys cut through the Downs, it is likely that the Jutes intermingled with the surviving Romano-Britons rather than invading catastrophically. A number of early settlements became centres of a dependent territory or estate comprising as much as 20,000 or more acres. Most of these early centres were sited on rivers cutting through the Downs. For example, an old estate based on the Cray valley has six place-names bearing the Celtic name of the river. Dover, deriving its name from the River Dour, another Celtic name, also had a subsidiary settlement in the downland combes.

Everitt has also demonstrated the remarkable extent to which the Church was built upon Roman foundations.[5] Most of the early minster churches appear to have been established in Romano-British communities and Roman brickwork and parts of Roman structures are incorporated perhaps in more parish churches in Kent than in any other county. It is suggestive, for example, that King Wihtred's grant of privileges to the churches of Kent (AD 696-716) lists eight minster churches, including Reculver, Dover, Folkestone and Lyminge, where continuity with the Romano-British population seems marked. Moreover, the 15 minsters in Kent recorded in the Domesday Monachorum and other sources by the end of the 11th century were established in areas where Romano-British continuity is especially apparent. 'It seems clear', writes Everitt, 'that the Kentish minsters were as a rule deliberately established in former Romano-British communities.' David Bird has recently reviewed the place-name evidence in Surrey for continuity in the transition from Roman Britain to Saxon England.[6] Such names were not, of course, recorded until later in Saxon times, but some are held to be early on philological grounds. Names that include the Saxon word for Britons, *wealh*, including Wallington, Walton-on-Thames and a lost Walton in Old Windsor; possibly Walton-on-the-Hill should be added because the parish has two Roman villa sites. Kingston had a *Waleport* on Kingston Hill and a *Walehulle* nearby. Chertsey's Saxon charter refers to *Wealas Hythe* ('landing place of the British') and Chertsey's name is British.

Leatherhead and Merrow are also held to be wholly British names, while Coulsdon, Limpsfield, Caterham, Crutchfield near Reigate, Creek Coppice in Bramley and Crooksbury Hill have names which are partly Celtic. The names of the three main rivers, the Thames, the Wey and the Mole (its old name being Emen), are also Brittonic. Additionally, the name of Croydon should be cited. Margaret Gelling suggests that this probably means 'saffron valley', incorporating the words *croh* and *denu*, the first element being derived from the Latin *crocus*, which had various uses in the Roman world. Addiscombe includes *camp*, from the Latin *campus*, which often denotes the presence of a Roman villa. This word also is found at Merstham and there is a Great and Little Comp in Godalming (and there is a cluster of related names in and around the Darent valley). Bird points out that such names must indicate some degree of contact between Saxon and Briton, even in the area of earliest English settlement. He believes that other parts of the county may have remained more wholly British, becoming more 'Saxon' by a long-continued process of cultural assimilation during which the surviving Britons adopted the styles of pottery and metalwork of the incomers. This could well have been the case in the Surrey Downs where early Saxon cemeteries are few in comparison with the gravels to the north.

According to the folk-memory version of the event in the Anglo-Saxon Chronicle, Hengist and Horsa landed with their army at Ebbsfleet in AD 449. The presence of these initial and succeeding early migrants is mainly represented by cemetery sites well known for the quality of their grave goods, particularly jewellery. The early habitation sites of a later stage have largely eluded archaeologists, but at Folkestone on the site of the Channel Tunnel terminal four separate sites of both early and late Saxon occupation have been recovered. Two sunken-floored buildings associated with an isolated household had axial post-holes for stout timbers supporting the roof-ridge and posts for the structural corners were lined with small stakes which once retained horizontally planked walls. Distinctive grass-tempered pottery, loom weights and animal bones were recovered from the backfill of the huts. Another sunken-floored hut, also probably that of a subsistence farmer or shepherd, was cut deeply into the ground surface. Substantial structural posts survived at the four corners, and small stake-holes lining the internal edge of the house indicated wattle walls covered with dung or clay. This hut was buried under downwash caused by an attempt to cultivate the higher slopes of the Downs. The pottery, sea shells and animal bones suggest a frugal life of an impoverished family.

Cemeteries in Surrey with their origins in the fifth and early sixth centuries include those at Guildown on high ground above Guildford and lower down in the Mount Street area, Ewell, Hawk's Hill, Leatherhead, where it overlies the Roman site, Ashtead, Headley Drive, Banstead, Farthing Down, Coulsdon, Galley Hills, and Tadworth. Several of these sites have barrows which may commemorate military leaders and others of a high social status. Most of the other pagan sites lie northwards on the gravels towards the Thames. In Kent pagan cemeteries lie in the river valleys cut through the chalk and along the Vale of Holmesdale. The Anglo-Saxon cemetery on an elevated site in the Darent valley near Polhill, Sevenoaks, yielded 182 graves dated from c.AD 650-750. The cemetery is likely to have gone out of use when Christian graveyards and villages were being formed on lower ground. Sonia Hawkes suggested that as

33 *Coppiced beech near Reigate.*

prestigious long-swords and high-class jewellery were absent, the burials were probably of the 'Ceorl' class, freemen and smaller landholders, the backbone of Saxon England. The large size of the cemetery suggests a community of 70-90 people. A study of the skeletons indicates that over 30 per cent of the population died before the age of 20 years, another 35 per cent between the ages of 21 and 40 and 20 per cent after the age of forty. None reached the age of 60 and infant mortality was probably high.[7]

The Polhill cemetery in Kent and sites in Surrey also on high ground raise the question of when the present nucleated villages at the foot of the Downs and sandstone hills, which are such an attractive feature of the present-day scene, were created. A systematic campaign of intensive fieldwork and excavation, which has yet to be done in Surrey and Kent, may be able to throw light on this matter. Meanwhile, Barry Cunliffe's archaeological excavations and hypotheses relating to a block of chalk downland around Chalton in Hampshire may provide a model which can be applied to movements of population for the North Downs and sandstone hills. Cunliffe walked the fields after the ploughed land had been washed by rain and searched systematically for grass-tempered pottery. This technique yielded a number of new early Saxon sites, including substantial villages of early occupation on hill-top sites. He deduced that a number of high ground locations were abandoned from the ninth century when valley villages came to be occupied at the same time. Cunliffe has argued that such places, being more convenient for farming, gradually eclipsed the mother settlements and drew off their populations to the spring-line villages which grew in size to about 1,300 people. These places had peasant farmhouses lining the main street and, in Surrey, expanding common fields. Although the location of specific villages was controlled essentially by a convenient, sometimes sanctified spring, the virtually equidistant spacing of many of the scarp-foot villages suggests that the boundaries of their parishes may have been inherited from the bounds of Romanised villa estates. It is unlikely that their sites were former wastelands. More likely they had been occupied by isolated Romano-British farms until the downward migration.

Saxon Dover is now better understood through the excavations of Brian Philp and his team between 1970 and the present day. It appears that the Roman defensive walls of the shore fort of Dubris constructed *c.*AD 270 remained upstanding during the seventh to the 11th centuries and that within this framework the Saxon settlement, starting in the sixth century, originated. In addition to the spread of sunken-floored buildings, including a large weaving hut, was a stone-floored hall, and an entirely wood-built single-cell church dating from the seventh century. This was successively rebuilt as a monastic establishment before being replaced by the Norman stone church of St Martin-le-Grand. The location of this early church within a Roman fort of the Saxon Shore is replicated by St Mary's church at Reculver (AD 669) and also St Peter's-on-the-Wall at Bradwell, Essex (AD 654). From this evidence it seems clear that there was a deliberate policy of siting many monastic sites within ruined Roman fortified sites which served as useful quarries, and gave protection and splendid isolation. St Martin's church was probably founded for canons by King Eadbald of Kent who died in 640. In 716 it is listed as one of the seven major churches in Kent. There is clear archaeological evidence of fires at Saxon Dover in the seventh, ninth and 10th centuries and it is recorded that the town was destroyed by fire in 1066.[8] Dover, with Fordwich, Hythe and Sandwich, was one of the lesser towns recorded in Domesday Book (see p.67).

The Agrarian Ground Plan

To a remarkable degree it is possible to discern traces of the Saxon agrarian ground plan in the present landscape. The rambler who comes to enjoy the best of Surrey walking on the woods and heaths in the lovely country within the Guildford, Dorking and Horsham triangle, invariably finds himself traversing tracks trending roughly north-south. These first sharply descend the North Downs escarpment in a way still testing to driving skills and then proceed into little villages in the Vale of Holmesdale before heading upwards on the sandstone hills and then dropping as sharply as before from superb viewpoints on to the clays of the Surrey Weald before losing themselves around Cranleigh, Ewhurst and Forest Green. The long stretches of these ruts which are still unmetalled can be explored on horseback, foot or cycle and constitute an unrivalled recreational heritage in Surrey. An example is the trackway from Wotton church which sharply climbs up the sandstones as an unmetalled hollow way (the Greensand Way) to make for a col near Leith Hill before dropping down to Oakwood church in the clayland of the Surrey Weald. A parallel trackway from Westcott Heath makes for Anstiebury hillfort to drop down to the bottomless clayland at Ockley. Similarly Critten Lane, a 'C' class road from Effingham, tumbles down the edge of the North Downs scarp to Crossways Farm and then across the sandstone hills through Abinger, Sutton and Holmbury St Mary where it becomes a walker's paradise, dropping down as a metalled track by Holmbury hillfort and losing its identity in the Surrey Weald around Smoke Jack brickworks in Somersbury and Wallis Woods. A third example is to the west, where a minor road from Ripley uses Combe Bottom to reach Shere and makes its way via Pitch Hill to the site of the Roman villa near Ewhurst and has a spur to Cranleigh. The metalled stretches formerly had many lengths which remain bridleways and footpaths which have been well-used by London ramblers for more than one hundred years.

The rambler who has some historical background can make some sense of these routeways and derive much extra enjoyment from his walking forays. The broad north-south pattern results from the territorial links between earlier and later settlements in Surrey. Initially they were droveways between manors to the north on the periphery of the forested Weald and their outliers in the south in the oakwoods of the Surrey Weald functioning in summer as wood pasture for cattle and pigs. Thus the manor of Dorking held land at Capel (Old French, *capelle*, a chapel), where a subordinate chapel was erected for local use, hence its name. Wotton manor held outlying land at Oakwood where another chapel of ease, now a church in its own right, was built; Shere manor held land at a distance in Cranleigh, and so on. As John Blair has shown, the system of Saxon landholding with dependent outliers in the Weald from their headquarters was general, and especially true of the extensive royal and episcopal manors of Farnham, Godalming, Woking, Kingston, Reigate and Wallington. Later, the religious organisation of Surrey was largely based on this manorial system, minster churches and leading parish churches in the then more developed parts of Surrey having subordinate chapels attached to them in the newly settled districts of the late Saxon period and early Middle Ages. It is also significant how many churches are sited on, or near, the ancient droveways. In the district we are considering, they include East and West Clandon, East and West Horsley, Effingham, Fetcham, Great Bookham, Westcott, Wotton, Gomshall, Shere and Albury. Moreover, it is plain that some of the trackways were focused on Iron-

1 *The whiteness of the White Cliffs of Dover is one of the most expressive icons of England and it has always been identified with the defence of the island against the enemy.*

II *S.R. Badmin evocatively captures the essence of the 'Evelyn Country' near Dorking for the* Shell Shilling Guide to Surrey, *1963. Between the bold chalk escarpment of the North Downs and the wooded sandstone hills lies the Vale of Holmesdale. Dorking and Westcott churches are visible.*

III *The Devil's Kneadingtrough in the Kent Downs near Wye is one of the most spectacular dry valley coombes etched into the escarpment. The inspirational wooded Weald stretches southwards to the South Downs.*

IV *The gardens of Titsey Place, sheltered by the escarpment, are one of the gems of the North Downs.*

V *The Bronze-Age Boat, exhibited at Dover Museum, is one of the oldest surviving sea-going vessels in the world.*

VI *George Lambert's* View of Box Hill, Surrey *(1733) is one of the earliest naturalistic paintings of England.*

VII *A narrow, winding lane lined with cow parsley in May leads to the Hucking Estate Woodland near Maidstone.*

34 *Ruins of St Augustine's Abbey.*

Age hillforts and possibly on Roman and earlier settlements in the Weald. For these reasons there is a probability that the pattern of routes which so dominates the present-day geography was laid down, at least in part, before the Saxon era. We are in fact examining the road pattern of a number of ancient self-sufficing communities, a conscious design related to the three main resources of each Saxon manor and earlier administrative units: the arable and meadow on the richer soils around headquarter settlements; the sheep pastures on the turf and heaths of the Downs; and the swine pastures, timber, ore and fuel resources of the Weald. This also explains the striking symmetrical distribution of rural settlement at the foot of the Chalk escarpment and also the edge of the Lower Greensand formation, for here the best soils were to be exploited. The remarkable pattern of strip parishes, exceptionally long and narrow, which is such a conspicuous feature of each settlement in a scarp-land location, was itself the product of communities with predominantly north-south axes and not east-west linkages throughout most of their history. The latter links were useful for access to markets but they were of limited practical use for primitive communities for they would have been in touch with commodities they produced themselves. Looking east of our present district, Newdigate was designed as a subordinate chapel, presumably of Reigate; much of Burstow parish was originally part of the archbishops' manor of Wimbledon; Thunderfield in Horley was a detached swine pasture of Sutton manor; much of Charlwood lay within the manor of Merstham to the north, owned by the monks of Christchurch Canterbury; Horne was a detached part of Bletchingley before becoming a parish in its own right in the reign of Queen Anne.

In Kent similar territorial links are discernible between the more anciently developed parts of Jutish, Roman, or earlier origins and the countryside which remained undeveloped until the late Saxon or medieval period. An assured guide is K.P. Witney's *The Jutish Forest* (1976) and there is a brilliant monograph *Pre-Feudal England: The Jutes* (1933) by J.E.A. Jolliffe. The latter's conclusion – that the roots of Kentish institutions and civilisation can be traced in the settlement of the Jutes in Kent towards the close of the fifth century and during the period when Kent was an independent kingdom until the eighth century – has been upheld by later scholars, although more recent discussion has been steadily modifying his theories and giving greater weight to evolution. The extensive network of routes woven by men travelling to and from the principal centres of manors and their numerous outlying summer pastures is one of the most conspicuous characteristics of the modern road map. Witney has demonstrated how the close network of by-ways and obsolete greenways tends to be oriented crab-wise around the oval-shaped Weald. Tracing the old droving roads involves linking up the present intermittent paths and bridleways into former continuous trackways. By way of illustration, the droveways of the manor of Wye can be cited. Wye was a huge royal manor dating from AD 762, which also had jurisdiction in its lathe covering about one-fifth of Kent. Two main droveways from Wye crossed the Great Stour and made for the swine pastures in the Weald in the Cranbrook and Hawkhurst areas respectively.

The Domesday Survey, 1086

This can be regarded as a summing-up of the wealth and development that accrued under the Saxons. Kent and Surrey are revealed as a land of very large, complex, fragmented and composite manors, variously called federal, discrete and multiple by scholars. Studied in the clearer light of the 13th century they emerge centred upon a head village, normally bearing the name of the whole manor, containing the principal church, the lord's hall and court, the demesne (home farm) and tenants' lands, the lowliest of whom performed work services on the lord's demesne. Numerous dependent hamlets, separately named, were also dispersed over the manor. In Surrey peasants cultivated common fields and commons; both wood-grazings and sheep downs, interspersed between settlements were more important for farming than in Kent. Some of these manors, especially the royal and episcopal ones, were huge in extent and already considerable in population. Unfortunately, Domesday was never intended to differentiate each individual settlement that was a dependency of the manorial headquarters, and thus the villages of the North Downs and the Greensands do not figure clearly in the Survey. It was Maitland who first showed that numerous villages and hamlets were grouped together in one entry. He pointed out that the bishop of Winchester's manor of Farnham comprised Farnham, Frensham and some other villages and that the simple phrase '*episcopus tenet farnham*' disposed of 25,000 acres of land.[9]

Within these limitations the regional geography of Surrey and Kent in 1086 can be explored. The region of great prosperity in 11th-century Surrey appears to have been the settlements on the gravel terraces along the River Thames. On the

North Downs were numerous small Domesday vills and along the northern edge of the dip-slope, well endowed with springs, was a line of larger and wealthier villages. Below the chalk escarpment was a line of villages with substantial numbers of people, ploughs and water-mills. The Lower Greensand outcrop further south was largely sterile heathland with small and few settlements. By contrast, the River Wey basin in the neighbourhood of Guildford and Godalming had rich, light soils and a number of prosperous villages. This area, as previously mentioned (p.32), had a profound influence on the county and it can be regarded as the cradle of Surrey. The Weald was sparsely populated. The information on Guildford is fragmentary; a minimum of 81 dwellings is implied which would suggest a total population of about 750, but this estimate is guesswork. An examination of the town plan by O'Connell and Poulton has demonstrated that Guildford was created largely by a single act of late Saxon town planning, but that the area near the late Saxon church of St Mary was notably older. Godalming had a mint before the Norman Conquest, indicating an important economic status.[10]

In Kent the Downs themselves were sparsely populated as were the Chart Hills. Conversely the dip-slope and scarp-foot were lined with prosperous villages. The river valleys cut through the chalk by the Cray, the Darent, the Medway and the Stour were also thriving places and the loamy soils of the north-east around Sandwich were crowded with a farming population. Vineyards are recorded at Chart Sutton, Chislet and Leeds. Deer parks are mentioned specifically at only two places, Chart Sutton and Wickhambreaux. Faversham had a prosperous market. Surrey had only two urban centres, Southwark and Guildford, but Kent had eight boroughs – Dover, Canterbury, Fordwich, Hythe, Rochester, Romney, Sandwich and Seasalter. Dover supplied King Edward the Confesssor with 20 ships for 15 days a year and in each ship were 21 men. Charges were made for crossing the Channel. Although the town was destroyed by fire in 1066 it had expanded its activities and had a guildhall, four churches and tide-mill. It appears that there were at least 231 burgesses in Hythe, which suggests a total population of 1,000 people. Canterbury had probably 438 burgesses and other categories of people which implies a total population of 2,500. This made the ecclesiastical centre of England the biggest town in Kent and of the very first rank in the country. It was larger than places such as Exeter and York, although smaller than the largest provincial cities such as Norwich. There are references in a contemporary document, the *Excerpta*, to cobblers, drapers, a porter and to the making of bread and beer. Canterbury had been a place of trade from a remote date. It had a market as early as 762 and was called 'port' in the ninth century.[11]

6

Living on the Land in the Early Middle Ages (1100-1348)

This period saw a dramatic alteration in the state of the economy. Population growth fuelled much economic development, innovation and change, including the intensification of agriculture and the rise of towns and industries, but the Great Famine of the early 14th century and the Black Death (1348-9) caused severe mortality and consequent disruption which was only arrested by population growth again from the early 16th century. Most people worked on the land and the patchwork of local landscapes we are considering evolved in rather different ways and with different farming objectives. Settlement patterns also developed in different ways so that travellers even then would have been acutely aware of different types of countryside.

Kent Agriculture

Kent continued its growth and prosperity, far outstripping Surrey in its economic contribution to England's development. The extensive estates held by the Church, richly endowed with demesne and with parts occupied by knightly families or rented out to yeoman farmers, were significant factors in this economic growth. Du Boulay has perceptively remarked of the Lordship of Canterbury that 'the finger which traces the route from the Channel north-westwards along the ancient arable lowlands on either side of the North Downs and thus to London will never stray far from archiepiscopal property'.[1] The archbishop was the largest landowner in Kent for a millennium and one of the greatest in medieval England. In east Kent the archbishops' landed possessions were particularly thickly spread. In Canterbury itself, the archbishops had their Norman palace, their monastic home and substantial property. The largest of their estates, the immense manor of Wingham, on some of the most fertile land five miles to the east, was on the road to the port of Sandwich which the archbishops also owned. Characteristically for this region, this manor was composed of a number of villages and 34 hamlets as well as demesne. It extended over 20 square miles and was interspersed with land belonging to other lordships. The archbishops also held the large tracts of woodland which still extend to the west and north of the cathedral city. On the downland south of Canterbury, and extending into Romney Marsh, was a second major complex centred on Aldington, which was later to be the richest bailiwick of all. A third and more scattered group of manors lay across mid-Kent and included Boughton-under-Blean, Charing,

Teynham, Gillingham and Maidstone. In north Kent was a well-defined group of manors centred on Otford, which included Crayford, Bexley, Darenth, Wrotham and Sundridge. The Surrey manors including Croydon gave access to political life at Westminster.

A remarkable social characteristic of Wingham was the settlement of more than thirty of the archbishops' knights. One of the manors, Walterstone, was granted to Ordericus Vitalis, immortalised on the Bayeux tapestry as the man who went forward for Duke William to reconnoitre the English army at the Battle of Hastings in 1066. So content were his direct descendants that a number of them were still resident there a century or more later. When their estates emerge into clearer light in the 13th century they are revealed as intensively farmed properties with little fallow, rich marsh pastures, meadows, orchards, large gardens and a farm staff consisting almost entirely of hired labourers working under the supervision of a sergeant. Their owners handed them down to 15th- and 16th-century people of the same class who often then became country gentlemen who gentrified their rural seats.

The Benedictine institutions of Christ Church Priory, St Augustine's Abbey and Canterbury Cathedral Priory also became prominent arable farmers par excellence. On such church estates of the 13th and 14th centuries can be traced the hallmarks of high farming – rising production, big capital investment, technical improvements and flexible rotations of crops. Among the most famous of high farming churchmen was Prior Eastry of Christ Church who acquired much property, made improvements to farm buildings, and invested heavily in water- and windmills, land drainage, marsh reclamation and soil improvement.[2]

35 *The Great Barn, Lenham.*

With their continuity of administration over so long a period, the leading Church institutions were a permanent element in the medieval countryside. In the present landscape some of the buildings erected to store the expanding produce still exist, notably in north-east Kent, where huge aisled barns reflect the productivity of landed estates in that district, such as the barn 210 feet long at Frindsbury on a demesne of St Andrew's, Rochester, with its 13 bays and structure suggesting a building of c.1300. Littlebourne (172 feet) and Godmersham Court Lodge barn on a demesne of Christ Church Priory are also magnificent. Until recent fires, a gigantic barn existed at Chislet Court and Lenham, also on former demesnes of St Augustine's, has lost one of its barns.[3] They are a fitting memorial to the entrepreneurial efficiency and foresight which established a farming regime unmatched generally in England until 300 and more years later.

What of the peasants? With hindsight, perhaps, they could be called kulaks, upwardly mobile, economically successful with few feudal restraints, desperate to buy the status to which they thought their standing entitled them. What of the knights and yeomen? It seems that they were also free of cropping restraints and were engaged in selling substantial amounts of surplus corn.

Until recently medieval farmers were scarcely thought of as profit maximisers or even as rational decision makers. Agriculture within feudalism was seen as technologically stagnant and constraints on economic growth were determined by Malthusian demographic forces. There was little room in this view for the liberalising effects of the market, the cash nexus and its effect on the adoption of crop rotations, on regional specialisation and the disappearance of serfdom in the most advanced areas of economic development. More or less uniform systems of husbandry were assumed to exist over 14th-century England, so that the Hampshire estates of the bishops of Winchester, which were particularly well documented, could be deemed representative of the whole of English farming.

North and East Kent

There is now a more flexible view of medieval society and an increased awareness of its local and regional complexity and achievements. North and east Kent afford clear evidence of advanced farming techniques. By the third quarter of the 13th century, when documents become available, both north and east Kent and coastal Sussex were amongst the leading legume producers of medieval England. By means of legumes (peas, beans and vetch) in crop rotations, nitrogen was added organically to the soil which acted as a primary fertilising and conditioning agent. On manors of Canterbury Cathedral Priory in 1291, 29 per cent of the total sown acreage was put under legumes at Monkton, 23 per cent at Eastry, 32 per cent at Ickham and 24 per cent at Adisham.[4] On the most fertile soils fallowing was replaced or greatly reduced. The more intensive husbandry increased organic matter in the topsoil and there is a possibility that legume husbandry reduced the incidence of cereal disease because long-continued experiments at Rothamsted have demonstrated that fallow is less effective than a break crop like legumes in the reduction of diseases transmitted by cereals. A further improvement in physical soil properties would have resulted from heavy marling (a practice largely absent on the bishop of Winchester's estates) which quite apart from its effect in counteracting acidity would have had a beneficial effect on tilth. If these advantages of legume husbandry are broadly correct on estates where legumes could account for 20-25 per cent of the total crops sown, one can postulate a cycle of more fodder (mainly legumes), leading to more livestock, which in turn produced more manure and hence higher yields.

The significance of this legume husbandry on the arable productivity of medieval England has only lately been recognised. The virtual elimination of fallowing so general in most parts of England in the Middle Ages was first recognised by H. Gray when he drew attention to the evidence of continuous cultivation on the extents attached to *Inquisitiones Post Mortem* of 1338. These specifically stated that all acres on the demesne could be sown yearly – *possunt seminari quolibet anno* – and the high valuation of 12d. an acre reflected this.[5] Such annual tillage of the entire or at least the best parts of the demesnes has since proven not to be exceptional in north-east Kent. In each case the intensive cultivation is associated with exceptionally high valuations per acre. Gray was of the opinion that annual tillage was seldom to be met with outside Kent, but similar evidence has since come to light for the Sussex coastal plain and the foot of the South Downs and B.M.S. Campbell has recently demonstrated that 'islands' of intensive arable occurred in a national context elsewhere, notably in eastern England.[6] The medieval historian has learned that Hampshire is not England, just as England is not the world.

A high level of productivity by medieval standards was reached in north-east Kent, partly from the adoption of thicker sowings than the anonymous author of *Hosebondrie* recommended.[7] In east Kent at the end of the 13th century the monks of Canterbury Cathedral Priory, during a flush of 'high farming' during the priorate of Henry of Eastry, were sowing four bushels per acre for wheat, six for spring barley and six for spring oats, nearly three times the seed of their French peasant counterparts on the same unit of land. The *Hosebondrie* author proposed to sow wheat at 2½ bushels per acre, and barley and oats at four bushels. On the manors of the bishops of Winchester, using data provided by Titow, the usual sowing rates for cereals during the period 1325-49 were very similar to those advocated by him. In terms of net yields wheat considerably exceeded the 11 bushels per acre which was deemed a proper return and which so few demesnes of the bishops of Winchester attained. The same superiority was reached in oats and barley. Ann Smith has recorded yields per bushel sown on the manors of Canterbury Cathedral Priory for 1291. A fuller examination covering a sufficient number of successive years would be necessary to obtain a better picture of yields. Joan Thirsk has suggested that there is little reason to suppose that on the estates studied by Ann Smith the return on the archbishop's demesnes would have been very different from the bishop of Winchester's. This would not appear to be correct. The ratio of seed to yield is certainly similar, but the thicker sowings on the Kent estates than the bishop's produced substantially larger crops per acre than on the Winchester estates and this was a great advantage when it was vain to hope for plenty when a third of a standard-sized crop elsewhere would be reserved for seed.[8]

The present author has argued that the denser sowings were adopted on inherently fertile land by lords aiming to produce a substantial surplus of grain for the coastwise trade. In the coastal districts of north and east Kent both growing and marketing conditions for grain reached their optimum in medieval England. The great church institutions, whose financial needs were met by market profits rather than by money rents in the late 13th and 14th centuries, took advantage of this to engage in the coastwise export of corn. Thicker sowings were also apparently required to counteract the various hazards of the time, such as the need to smother weeds in the absence of fallowing and to offset the large amount of broadcast seed lost to birds or which failed to germinate in the rougher seed-beds produced by the rudimentary equipment available. Only with the quicker and more efficient tillage of the 19th century did thinner sowings become practical in commercial agriculture.

Another characteristic of north and east Kent was the skill of its cultivators in the protracted care of the soil. The preparation for wheat, an operation expressively called a 'season', involved three ploughings and often more, using a yoke of eight oxen, or exceptionally four oxen and four horses, which was quicker and more efficient.

Specialised production for market was also a characteristic of east and north Kent farming from at least the end of the 13th century. The manors of Canterbury Cathedral Priory in the coastal fringe specialised in barley for export, presumably for malting (as did manors in north Norfolk). Fertility was sustained by legumes, by the use of seaweed as manure, by marling and by the judicious use of the sheep-fold which consolidated the light chalk soil which would not otherwise have been suitable for intensive tillage; as a method of dunging it was unsurpassed for cheapness and efficiency. The adaptability of the sheep-fold may well have contributed to the early development of flexible rotations. It was very properly regarded as the basis of corn production and manorial custumals testify to its importance by specifying the regulations to be observed in its use.

Manorial Organisation in Kent

The background to this intensive husbandry is the manorial system of medieval Kent. In the Vale of Holmesdale, the valleys of the Darent, Medway and Stour, and on the lower dip-slopes of the Downs much land was held in open fields subdivided into unenclosed parcels in intermixed ownership or occupation. These were not, however, the common fields found extensively in England for they were not generally either cultivated or grazed in common. The lands of individual holdings tended to be concentrated in one part of the open field and not dispersed throughout it. Such open fields were generally associated with hamlets and isolated farmsteads, a pattern strongly influenced by the custom

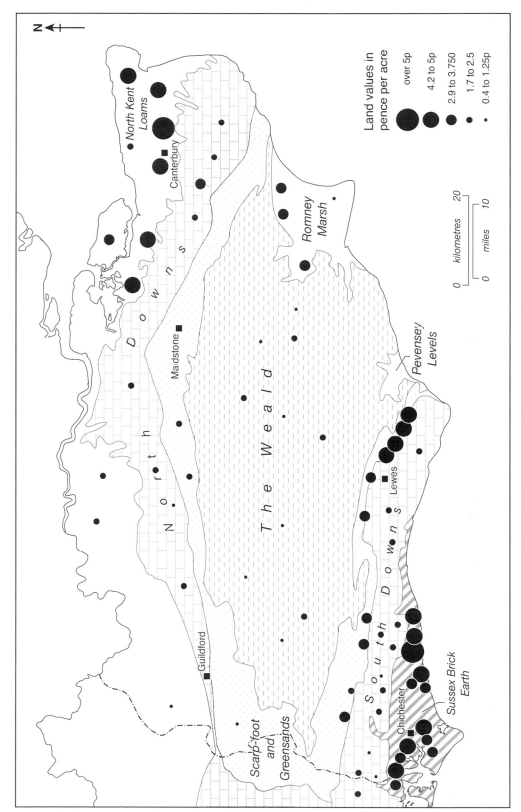

Land values in
pence per acre

over 5p

4.2 to 5p

2.9 to 3.750

1.7 to 2.5

0.4 to 1.25p

N

North Kent
Loams

Canterbury

Romney
Marsh

N
o
r
t
h

D
o
w
n
s

Maidstone

The Weald

Pevensey
Levels

Lewes

S
o
u
t
h

D
o
w
n
s

Guildford

Scarp-foot
and
Greensands

Chichester

Sussex Brick
Earth

0   kilometres   20

0   miles   10

36 *Land Values, south-east England, in the early 14th century.*

of gavelkind whereby an inheritance was divided among male co-heirs who sometimes built their own homestead on their portion. The yoke (*iugum*) may initially have been a unit of tenure which had a physical relation to the lay-out of fields but by the 13th century it had become a notional division of land into a fiscal unity for the assessment of rents and services. A tenant in gavelkind could freely give, sell or let his land to whom he wished during his lifetime, provided that the old rents and services were properly secured to the lord. This custom would have led in some cases to the extreme fragmentation and small size of holdings in the 13th century but Du Boulay concluded that, although the physical portioning of landholdings was a normal practice of gavelkind tenure, it never went ridiculously far enough for us to imagine 'a world dominated by restless smallholders living below subsistence level'.[9] The number of eligible children was seldom so large that the custom became impracticable and the free alienation of land in the market by sale, lease or exchange, was another counter-balance. Excessive parcellation could also be mitigated in various ways. One or more heirs to a holding can be seen to waive their claim to part of it, in return for a money payment or rent. More enterprising and prosperous tenants augmented their holdings by purchase or lease and rose socially into the ranks of the yeomanry or gentry, fields being consolidated in the process.

The demesnes of manors in Kent in the 13th century did not lie intermingled in strips with those of the tenants, as was often the case with demesnes in the Midlands or Surrey, but were situated in blocks, sometimes within larger fields and cultivated in severalty, even if not always separated off by permanent physical barriers from other men's crops. When demesne fields were directly cultivated by manorial officials they were frequently sown in sections with more than one kind of crop in any given year and cultivated quite independently of tenants' lands. In the Vale of Holmesdale and on the manors of Christ Church Priory there was a nucleus of more or less permanent arable, which T.A.M. Bishop called 'infield' while other fields on the 'outfield', less accessible to the plough and more irregularly dunged, were cropped at longer intervals.[10] On some Kent manors, as at Wrotham, tenants were required to fold their sheep on the lord's demesne for the sake of the dung and on others any enclosures were taken down after harvest so that the lord's beasts could graze collectively with the beasts of those tenants who had helped him to plough and of any others who had arranged terms with him. Heavily wooded land on relatively poor soils which was cleared and colonised in the early Middle Ages was enclosed directly into individually held small fields.

The medieval manor of Wye also throws much light on manorial organisation in Kent.[11] Wye became a royal manor before AD 725, when Kent was still an independent kingdom. After the Norman Conquest, King William granted it to Battle Abbey, which he founded, when it became the abbey's most valuable possession. Like other great manors of Kent it was of huge extent, spread over a great area of country with its lands interspersed with those of other manors, a federative rather than a unitary manor, as J.E.A. Jolliffe has termed it. Included within it were Kingsnorth, *Wachindene* and the sheep pastures at Dengemarsh

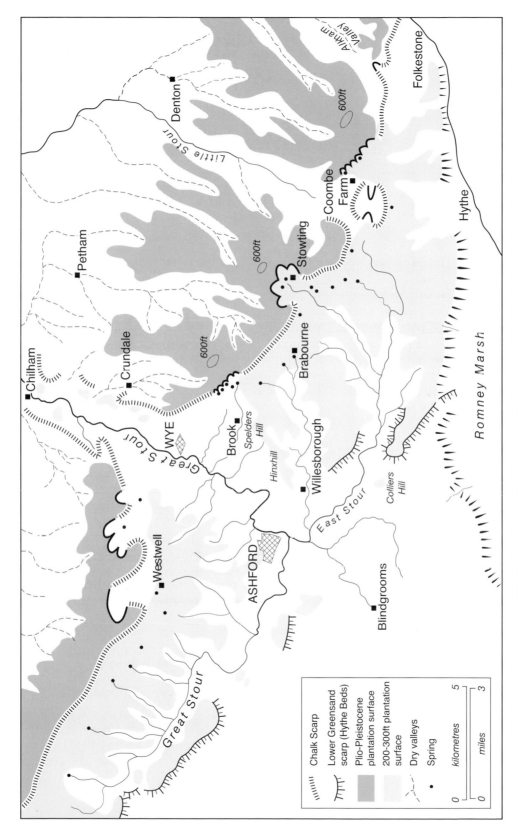

37 The hinterland of Wye, an inspiring landscape of scarp, vale and deep combes.

Map labels:

Folkestone

Alkham Valley

Denton

600ft

Little Stour

Coombe Farm

Hythe

Petham

600ft

Stowting

Chilham

Crundale

600ft

Brabourne

Romney Marsh

WYE

Great Stour

Brook

Spelders Hill

Hinxhill

Willesborough

Colliers Hill

East Stour

Westwell

ASHFORD

Blindgrooms

Great Stour

Legend:

- Chalk Scarp
- Lower Greensand scarp (Hythe Beds)
- Plio-Pleistocene plantation surface
- 200-300ft plantation surface
- Dry valleys
- Spring

0 5 kilometres
0 3 miles

in Romney Marsh which eventually were managed independently; an extensive demesne and tenant holdings at Wye itself; other arable holdings from Bilting to Orlestone; and 12 denns scattered in Hawkhurst and adjoining parishes in the Weald more than 15 miles away. Typical of the range in size of manorial denns were the seven Wye denns in Hawkhurst parish which alone covered more than 2,000 acres. These denns, again typical of Kent, were located along a droveway connecting the intensively farmed lands at and around Wye with the wooded pastures originally used in summer to fatten swine. The great division in this agrarian estate was between the arable lands in the river valley of the Great Stour, the coastal grazings in Romney Marsh and the *weo-were-weald*, i.e. 'commons of the men of Wye', as the wooded denns of Wye were called in their earliest mention in a charter of 724 when the countryside was still undeveloped. This vast estate formed a discrete territory of between 40,000 and 50,000 acres. Wye was not only the headquarters of a great medieval manor; it was also the centre of its lathe, one of the primary divisions of Kent which had judicial and administrative functions.

A survey of the manor in the early 13th century helps to clarify the manorial organisation illustrating the typical system of medieval Kent. The heart of the manor was the lord's demesne in the Vale of Holmesdale and at Wye itself. In the 13th and 14th centuries this was directly farmed by the Abbey through the steward. Land divisions were known, as in Kent generally, as yokes. Wye contained 60½ yokes, each containing four virgates, themselves apparently artificial units of assessment for taxation purposes. Half of the yokes were *juga libera*, free yokes, and the other half *juga servilia*, or unfree yokes. The 'servile' yokes lay on the 'inland' which was held by tenants owing specific services to the lord, such as ploughing, sowing, harvesting, carting and droving. Provisioning the abbey at Battle was an important function of unfree tenants who had the arduous and dangerous task of carting foodstuffs along tracks through the Weald almost impassable in winter and wet weather. On the 'outland' were the 39 landholders who were freemen, liable for military service. The services required of them were light or virtually non-existent and tenure was by gavelkind.

Some of the yokes and their associated fields have been identified by means of place-names inherited by present-day farms. For example the servile yokes of *Broke* (Brook in Kennington), *Orgar* and *Baker* (Agmond's and Baker's Withersdane), *Chelcheborne* (Chelsbourne Farm near Brook) and Henwode (Henwood) are readily identified on the ground. Free yokes include *Olynteghe* (Olantigh), a holding which later became gentrified as the home of the Kempes and the birthplace of Archbishop Kempe, *Nacholte* (Naccolt) and John Reynolds' holding (Raymond's Farm). The yoke of *Amminge* can possibly be identified with Amage Farm, now part of the Wye College estate. The farmhouse dates from an aisled hall-house of the 15th century with two-storey wings jettied at either end. The yokes lay in spacious named fields around the manor, perhaps originally divided by marker stones but as the lands became fragmented subdivisions may have been separated by earth banks on which hedges had been created. When field or yoke boundaries cross sloping ground, retaining banks, or lynchets, were formed by the down-slope movement of soil by cultivation and the surface run-off of water. The best examples are on Godmersham Down and less well developed ones occur on the Wye College estate. Sheep folds to ensure the efficient use of dung entailed the use of temporary hurdles, a practice continuing in Kent until relatively recently. Until overtaken by Ashford as a market and regional centre from the 16th century, Wye was a successful medieval town whose importance as a place for spiritual worship (originally signified by its place-name derived from Old English 'wig' and 'weoh', meaning a sacred place or heathen temple) was enhanced by Archbishop Kempe's foundation of a secular college for priests in 1447.

A.R.H. Baker has made a case study of Gillingham in north Kent in 1447 which is also illuminating.[12] Most of the holdings were very small. One quarter of the 98 holdings were only two acres or less; two-thirds were of 10 acres or less; one in seven more than 50 acres. This suggests an active market in land and the effects of partible inheritance. Of freeholds, the most highly rented were on the fertile loams, whilst those on the chalk and the clay-with-flints were the lowest. There was a nucleation of settlement around the church but farmhouses were mainly dispersed in twos and threes or as isolated buildings. In the late 13th century the situation was not so very different, though parcels of an individual holding were less dispersed than in 1447 and there were more smaller holdings. The settlement pattern at Gillingham is reproduced on the lower dip-slope of the Downs and in the valleys of the Darent, Medway, and Great Stour. For example, at Wrotham, many dwellings were nucleated around the church at the foot of the escarpment, but numerous farmsteads were dispersed throughout the township, although a survey of 1494 reveals that few farmhouses had been erected on the heavily wooded clay-with-flints country on the high downs. A similar pattern of settlement prevailed in 1285.

38 *Old Soar, Plaxtol, stone-built, dating to 1290, one of the oldest houses in Kent.*

Baker's studies and those of others have sustained and illuminated discussion which has steadily modified, developed and occasionally overturned some of the older assumptions and theories about the origin and arrangement of the heterodox land system of Kent. As a result Kent is less of an agrarian puzzle than it was, but some unsettled issues are sufficiently ambiguous to leave room for doubt. The strong sense of individualism and freedom which pervades Kentish civilisation at the latest by the early 13th century, the gavelkind tenure permitting the free selling of land, the brisk leasing and social mobility (doubtless all stimulated by the free circulation of money along the main route between England and the continent) were at variance with the severe restraints imposed on collective farming practised in Surrey and in other parts of England. The absence in the landscape of the large centralised villages as in much of Kent has often been held to be evidence against a common-field system originally but this argument has been greatly weakened by the subsequent discovery of hamlet-type common-field systems in western Britain. The presence of residual common fields on the dry, stony soils of the North Downs near Canterbury, such as at Paddlesworth and Stelling Minnis, may indicate that, at least on poorer localities where soil management required smallholders to share a sheep fold in order to manure their soils, some form of common fields was earlier adopted in Kent.[13]

The Kentish Knight

The Kentish knight and yeoman shared a great deal of the prosperity of Kent and their standard of living was higher than that of the average English farmer, perhaps rather like Chaucer's idea of how the franklin lived, as told in robust, earthy idiom:

> Withoute bake mete was never his hous,
> Of fish and flesh, and that so plenteous,
> It snewed in his house of mete and drinke,
> Of alle dyntees that men coude thinke,
> After the sundry seasons of the yeer,
> So changed he his mete and his soper,
> Ful many a fat partriche hadde he in mewe,
> And many a breem and many a luce in stewe.
> Wo was heis cook, but if his sauce were
> Poynaunt and sharp, and redy at his gere'
> His table dormant n his halle always
> Stood ready covered all the longe day

So very comfortable was the life of a Kentish knight that, apparently, most wanted simply to manage their estates and provide for their children, with only the pastime of hunting to break the monotony of the daily round or occasional service on some local commission. They were at their happiest as plain country gentlemen busy about their stables and kennels. A remarkable example of armigerous families who kept out of politics but produced farmers, clergy and scholars were the various branches of the Boys family (pronounced 'Boyce') who in some respects are unique. They were descended from two Norman knights of the same name who fought at Hastings, Richard and William de Bois (de Bosco). Both secured estates in east Kent and their prolific successors distinguished themselves in the district as well as migrating to Surrey, Sussex, Buckinghamshire and other places. It is difficult to go into any church between Canterbury and the coast without finding memorials to branches of the family because they had lands at Betteshanger, Sandwich, Fredville in Bonnington, Uffington, Hythe, Deal and Merston in Willesborough, for example. The Boys Memorial volume traces the families living under 37 kings up to modern times. Eighteenth- and early 19th-century John and Henry Boys of Betteshanger and Mailmans Farm are encountered on page 138.[14]

38 *Roof over solar, Old Soar.*

Exceptionally a knight broke with this modest status and gradually, generally through training in law, rose to higher rank in public service in the day-to-day administration of the county on behalf of the king. An excellent example is the Cobham family of Cobham near Chatham and their branch at Starborough near Lingfield in Surrey. The first Henry Cobham (d. 1230) and his sons acted as justices itinerant. The family later rose to become keepers of castles, sheriffs, conservators of the peace, assessors, collectors of taxes (including the Ninth of 1340) and commissioners of every kind. John Cobham 'the elder', in the role of sheriff, sent orders to arrest all ships of a certain size in the Cinque Ports for the king's service.[15] The Cobham custody of Rochester Castle was almost hereditary in the 13th and 14th centuries, and other important custodies entrusted to the family included the Cinque Ports together with Dover Castle, the islands of Guernsey and Jersey, the city of Calais in 1354-5, confiscated lands of the Templars and lands of rebels. Reginald Cobham received Eleanor, wife of Prince Edward when she landed at Dover in 1255, entertained her at Dover Castle, and escorted her to London. A large proportion of the family's work was judicial. After the Peasants' Revolt, John, Lord Cobham, served on the commission for the peace of Kent as did Reginald, Lord Cobham of Starborough for Surrey. When taxes had to be collected and levies arrayed when war appeared imminent, the Cobhams were inevitably involved. Thus in 1335, in the Scottish campaign, John, 2nd Lord Cobham, was acting as one of two admirals of the king's fleet guarding the English coast. War against France was declared in 1337 and John collected the 10th and 15th in Kent. In 1369 the 3rd baron Cobham was commissioned 'to survey the coasts of the Isle of Thanet and to have all places which ships and boats can put in, defended by walls and dykes, where possible, and all other necessary measures taken for the defence of the island'. The Cobhams were required from time to time to select a specified quota of men for military service, shares being allotted to the administrative divisions, e.g. hundreds, townships and liberties. Constables or bailiffs, of the hundreds, under the Cobhams' direction, summoned able-bodied men and selected the strongest and most vigorous of them for the king's service. This was an onerous task, the arrayers, either singly or jointly, or by proxy, having to pass between the 62 hundreds of Kent and from township to township, organising the whole. Occasionally a Cobham investigated problems outside Kent, as in 1258, when there was a complaint that lime burnt with sea-coal in London and Southwark caused polluting smoke. Despite all the dangers and inconvenience of public service the Cobhams seemed willing, and even eager, to take part in it. Apart from financial gain, it conferred prestige and power.[16]

Surrey Agriculture

The lord's demesne in Surrey was generally consolidated and farmed separately from the peasants' lands which were dispersed in strips in common fields. The enclosure of the common fields began early in the 15th century and, when the earliest estate maps become available in the late 16th and 17th centuries, only fragmentary common fields systems survived. The reason for the early enclosure was probably the necessity for flexible farming systems on soils equally suited to arable and grass. Common fields survived longest, where the soils were light enough for sheep folding.

The manors between Leatherhead and Epsom can usefully serve as examples of the field system which prevailed on the Surrey Downs. Three broad belts of land use can be detected before the enclosures from the 17th century. On the highest part of the Downs was the sheepwalk, grazed in common. On the lower slopes of the chalk were common fields in which the lord's demesne and the tenants' lands were generally intermingled. To the north of that, on the clays, were small fields which had been enclosed directly from the waste in the early Middle Ages and had never been part of a common field system. Residual common land survived this process into the 19th century. The proportions of these three belts contrasted with Midland manors. Whereas in the latter, proportions of the three categories of open, enclosed land and 'waste' might be 50:30:20, on Surrey manors it was more like 25:45:30. The larger amount of

40 *Church House, Loose, in the old quarrying and paper-making district of Maidstone.*

enclosed land reflects the heavy soil, either tenacious clay mantled on the chalk or that of younger deposits to the north, where place- and field-names indicate that this largely enclosed character had existed throughout post-Conquest time and even earlier.

In Surrey hereditary servile status was normal. An interesting feature of early Surrey society is the large number of slaves (*servi*) recorded in Domesday Book. It is possible to envisage a process in which slaves were being placed in outlying woodland swine pastures for the task of clearing woodland and cultivating demesnes before the practice began of encouraging freeholders to do the same work. Overall, the tenurial conditions in Surrey were very variable and represent a picture of free tenure due to assarting in the 12th and 13th centuries alongside the heavy villein services of more ancient origin on highly organised estates. That these different conditions could exist within a few miles of each other would have added considerably to tensions in the countryside and contributed to the early enclosure of the common fields.

For the Surrey and Kent Downs 13th- and 14th-century valuations made for taxation purposes upon land in *Inquisitiones Post Mortem* provide illuminating information as to the intensity of land use. Used with caution they show how practically minded farmers responded to environmental difficulties and opportunities. If we accept that the maximum efficiency of most of English agriculture was probably reached under a three-course rotation of wheat, barley and oats, thus leaving one-third of the farmland idle under fallow in any given year, it is significant that Surrey in general failed to reach this level of land use. On the stony intractable 'clay-with-flints' on the Downs and on the lean, hungry sandy soils

41 *Boughton Monchelsea Place on the summit of the Chart Hills.*

of the Greensands, only half or less of the cultivable acreage was cropped in any one year. It was only near London, where good market conditions prevailed, and in the Vale of Holmesdale below the chalk escarpment in the middle of the county that manors achieved something like two-thirds or more use of arable land. It is not only mediocre soils which accounts for this; manors far from navigable water lacked facilities for the carriage of produce to market. Everywhere in England the difficulties and expense of land carriage were an insuperable barrier to economic development. The contrast with the agriculture of north and east Kent is brought out on p.75.

Woodland Management

An important element in the manorial economy was the management of woodland. The most distinctive form of tree-farming to emerge was enclosing woods managed as 'coppice-with-standards' for three specific purposes, wood fuel, timber for shipbuilding and construction, and for the manufacture of wood products from the spring of hazel and hornbeam, e.g. the whippy young stems provided material for hurdles and barrels; older growths made stakes, thatching spurs, wattles to be covered with clay in house building; and, later, a big market in hop poles and pit props. Coppicing was a highly sustainable method of exploiting fast-growing shoots from the stump (stool) which may reach four feet in the first year after cutting and continuing this enormous regeneration for centuries without the need to re-plant. Downland manors were evidently coppicing in the 11th century because *silva minuta* is referred to in the Kent Domesday Book, but the principle of cyclical cutting of underwood on a rotation of 14-20 years, depending on species, the condition of soil and thickness of timber required, was apparently understood and practised in England two thousand and more years earlier.

The practice of growing 'standards' (mainly oak, ash and beech trees) above the lower storey of coppice in the same wood, so producing the highest possible yield of timber, was another thread of woodmanship on the North Downs, although it is unclear when this was fully established. Practice sometimes fell short of precept. In 1312 the coppices of Wye were of little value because of their deterioration through neglect of systematic rotation.[17] In contrast, on the Merton College estate at Farleigh, Surrey, in 1377, we catch a glimpse of well-managed 'coppice-with-standards'. The college sold a parcel of underwood for charcoal and other purposes, and forty to fifty large trees growing above it, and instructed woodmen to fell all trees before their hands on one side of the wood and not 'fell one here and another there as it suits them'. The college agreed to enclose the wood at its own cost, presumably by means of hurdles or by an earth bank intended to keep cattle and deer from grazing the young shoots until they were tall enough to withstand damage. In such documents the college is shown to have been attentive to efficient woodland management which was not basically different from modern practice.

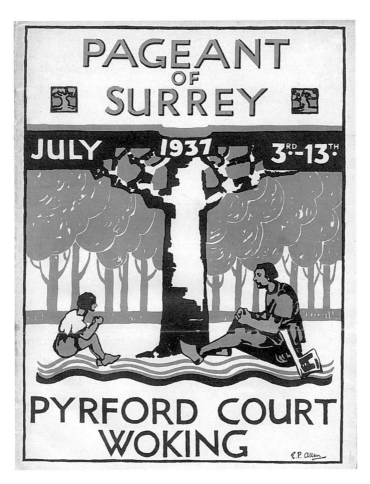

42 *The narrators, the Woodman and his Son, at the Pyrford Pageant, 1937.*

7

The Later Middle Ages
(1348-1520)

It was assumed until recently that the downturn in the agrarian economy of England generally took place after the appalling mortality of the Black Death in 1348-9 in which it is estimated that more than one third of the population died. The tax returns for a Ninth in 1340 (which do not survive for Kent and Surrey), however, provide evidence of a considerable contraction in arable land between 1292 and 1340. A main cause of this appears to have been the deluge of two years' almost incessant rain during 1315-16 which involved extensive flooding and severe hardship. On the Sussex Downs, for example, 32 parishes reported lands untilled in 1340 which had been cultivated in the period before 1292.[1] There were several explanations for the decline. Some parishes reported exhausted soil (*debil*); floods occasioned by tempestuous seas and heavy rain from inland were quoted; the poverty and 'impotence' of peasants is mentioned, together with the lack of tenants, imparking by the aristocracy and devastation of landholdings near warrens by escaped rabbits. The Nonae Returns seem to indicate that the clear and undisputed age of expansion in the English economy which characterises the 12th and 13th centuries was over, so that some lands, usually the most marginal, had been taken out of production. Symptoms of this malaise include deserted and shrunken settlements and shortened and rudely repaired churches.

Although we lack the Nonae Returns for Kent and Surrey, there is every reason to believe that these counties experienced the same terrible losses as other parts of England arising from the Great Famine of 1315-17. Moreover, they shared the run down in the economy arising from the pandemic of the Black Death and recurrent pestilences until population again began to rise substantially in the early Tudor period. The effects of this were dramatic. The persistent deforestation of the North Downs over several preceding centuries came to an abrupt end, for there were no more men to clear and occupy them. Numerous properties lacked tenants; villages shrank and some settlements were abandoned. It would seem that much of the 15th-century countryside would have had the air of dereliction imparted in times of crisis and recession. Disorder and dilapidation would have been everywhere. Farmhouses and gardens would have had an untidy look: gates broken down, hedges and fences carelessly repaired, the husbandry slatternly – in short the neatness and rustic elegance of the surroundings of the well-to-do farmer would almost certainly have been absent.

An example of the manorial economy on the North Downs between 1325-71 is Tillingdown, situated south of Croydon near their highest point, Botley

Hill (877 ft). At Domesday the manor comprised four ploughs in demesne and four-and-a-half plough-teams, five villeins and eight slaves. There was a church and woodland pasture for 390 pigs. After Domesday it was held of Richard de Clare of Tonbridge Castle with Portley, Marden, Caterham, Farleigh and Woldingham. Crops included wheat, barley, oats and also legumes, together with fodder crops of *sorug* (a mixture of barley and oats) and *haras* (a pulse for animal feed). The impression is of a mixed farm with a very modest output. The manors of Portley, Marden and Woldingham had very little arable in the later 14th century and the chalk downland was presumably used for sheep and cattle pasture. At Marden was a rabbit warren, first mentioned in 1358, but this appears to have been short-lived.[2]

The economic conditions in east and north Kent were considerably better. Although in England generally the raising of beef cattle for sale dominated over arable farming in the 15th century, arable farming continued apparently prosperously in the rich grain-growing lands. The Christ Church manors, for example, continued to produce extensive supplies of grain, and the tithes they received did not diminish. Nor is there any evidence that local peasants had abandoned arable for pasture farming. Moreover, a slump in the demand for pasture that had begun in the 1430s continued in the 1440s and 1450s, as at Wye, where pasture had to be let at reduced rents. Similarly at Otford the high rents for pasture in 1402 had to be halved in 1427/8 and in 1440 lay vacant for lack of a renter.[3] The fall in rents for pasture is presumably related to the end of the Hundred Years War. In the early years of the century farmers produced stock for markets supplying the armies abroad. As population contracted and wars wound down there was a reduced demand for horses and cattle.

Du Boulay examined the trends in demesne farming at Otford in the 15th century which was kept in hand until 1444.[4] From the mid-14th century the arable was increasingly under-exploited. The sown acreage declined from a maximum of 315½ acres in 1315-16 to only 168½ in 1391-2 and 149½ in 1443-4. The six ploughs kept up to 1393 were reduced to four and efforts were made to curb the rising costs of labour. The demesne cultivation appears to have been kept going to supply the archbishop's household, rather than for purely commercial reasons. Small parts of the demesne were let to various persons at 8d. an acre. Other parts brought in nothing owing to the lack of a *conductor* and were occupied by the lord's sheep. 1437-8 was a bad year when only 23 acres of the demesne at Shoreham could be leased. Finally, in 1444 the whole of the Otford demesne was let to Richard Clerk, clerk, for eight years at £15 6s. 8d. per annum, the

43 *Medieval sower.*

archbishop being responsible for the maintenance of buildings. Clerk also farmed the manor of Filston in Shoreham and subsequently acted as coadjutor bishop in the Canterbury diocese. It is noteworthy that some other local families were evidently prosperous and had some financial standing. Rather earlier, the then serjeant, Thomas Brounswayn, had taken part of the demesne but by 1418 it had passed to a well-to-do member of the established Dorkynghole family. Another renting family was the Multons, who first appear in 1439 and were still farming the whole demesne a century later. The then lessee, George Multon, was styled 'gentleman', and was the father-in-law of the Kent historian William Lambarde. Several of the 15th-century lessees are perpetuated by place-names on the O.S. one-inch map.

Despite the decline in the economy, for the ordinary man the 15th century might well have represented a peak in living conditions which worsened in the Tudor period. Paradoxically, it appears that each individual of a declining population had a larger share of the smaller economy. Sir John Clapham noted that between 1300 and 1450 the price of cereals and oxen remained much the same and that in the same period wages rose by 100 per cent. The general prosperity is reflected in the substantial amount of church building in the 15th century. The ancient market of Sevenoaks is an example of a town which was expanding in the late Middle Ages. The more prosperous lesser gentry and yeomen were building substantial hall houses, the distribution of which was densest near Maidstone.[5]

At Wrotham the cropped arable dropped from 184 acres in 1310 to about 150 at the end of the 14th century. For the 15th century a series of ministers' accounts for the archbishop's manor of Wrotham permits a closer examination of the letting of the demesne which in the first half was normally let at £12 16s. per annum but in 1448-9, 1454-5 and 1468-9 it appears to have been vacant. At times only a portion of the demesne was let: in 1428-9 it raised only £4 6s. 8d., in 1429-30 £7 and in 1441-2 merely 56s. 8d.[6] In the 1450s, '60s and '70s tenants were similarly unwilling to take up the whole demesne but there was a marked improvement during the last twenty years of the 15th century.[7] Pannage receipts dropped off, probably because of difficulties in collecting tolls. On the other hand the list of vacant lands and premises (the *decasus*) does not lengthen and the shops in the market place increased from six to eight by means of the conversion of part of the stable block. The archbishop's two parks were extended by the inclusion of small tenements which could not be let.

It was in the later Middle Ages that north-west Kent and the nearer parts of Surrey began noticeably to have a closer relationship with London. Du Boulay has tentatively suggested that the whole of west Kent was being developed for the London market. Moreover, many of the growing numbers of rich gentry, who had connections with south-east England and who principally lived in the capital, periodically escaped from pressures of the city and recurrent plagues by investing in a tranquil residence out of town which could be realised, at will, into a liquid asset. The Lay Subsidy Roll for London in 1436 shows that, of the 358 men with high assessments, 17 are also specified as holding land in Kent,

33 in Essex and 35 in Middlesex, while 17 had property in Surrey. The tenurial system of Kent was particularly favourable to settling there. Most of the land was held by gavelkind tenure and was freely negotiable on the open market. It could be alienated at will without reference to the lord and could be bought in a series of small parcels, so gradually building up into a largish estate.

It becomes noticeable how fashionable was this movement into the country from London.[8] John de Pulteney, draper and Lord Mayor of London no fewer than four times, bought the whole manor of Penshurst and in 1340 constructed the fine beamed hall. John Peche, a rich clothier and alderman in the City, bought Lullingstone manor in 1360 and created the deer park. His son Sir William Peche held it until his death in 1411. His descendants became Sheriffs of Kent and famous and powerful at Court. On the death of the last Sir John Peche in 1522, Lullingstone passed to his nephew, Sir Percival Hart. The manor remained in the hands of the Hart family until 1738, when the marriage of the heir of Lullingstone, Anne Hart, took the estate to Sir Thomas Dyke, whose descendants still own this tract of the Darent valley. William Newport of London acquired the manors of Clayton and Rous, as well as the castle of Lullingstone, before 1391. Rich merchants were not the only persons investing in property. Administrative officials were also doing the same, e.g. Robert Belknap, the Chief Justice at the time of the Great Revolt in 1381, was amassing property in flamboyant style. In 1365 he acquired the manor of Shawstead in the parishes of Chatham and Gillingham and in 1381 he bought the enormous manor of Sandling which lay in Orpington, Chislehurst, St Mary Cray and St Paul's Cray. A number of Chaucer's friends lived in the Cray valley on the edge of the North Downs. The impression is that from the early 14th century north-west Kent was becoming as much a residential area as a mixed farming countryside. From the 16th century places further afield, such as Westerham, became more practicable and popular amongst the London wealthy.

A result of the fall in population was the lord's problem of maintaining services from unfree tenants at a time in the late 14th century when their relative scarcity led them into a spirit of disobedience. Archbishop Islip's Register tells of the ruin of Wrotham manor in 1352 through the pestilence and widespread decay of property for lack of money to maintain it. It became difficult to obtain agricultural labour at the price a great estate organisation could afford.[9] In 1381 on the Isle of Thanet rebels raised the cry that no tenant should do service or custom to the lordships as they had done hitherto, and books and rolls were burnt. At Wingham in 1390 there was truculence amongst peasants, and further signs of it on the archbishop's estates at Sevenoaks in 1461 and Northfleet in the 1450s, 1460s and 1478. Archbishop Courtenay was an aristocrat and a lord of the old school who viewed refractory tenants as sinners and punished them in a humiliating way. In 1390 he summoned six customary tenants from Wingham for failing to perform their service of driving cartloads of hay and litter to his palace at Canterbury. The service was not arduous and could have been performed without hardship by proxy. What offended the archbishop was that the work had been done secretly on foot and not with carts so that the men, ashamed of their obligation, were refusing to acknowledge it openly. The sentence of his tribunal at Saltwood was that the offenders should parade with slow steps like penitents round Wingham churchyard, each carrying on his shoulders a sack of hay and straw.

There is much to be said for the view that peasant revolt broke out in places where and when the English countryman was 'anything but sunk in misery', but felt himself confident and strong enough to protest against obsolete restraints or novel impositions. This seems true of the prevailing anti-clericalism of the Peasants' Revolt which broke out in 1381 and led to damage at the archbishop's residences. Malcontents of Otford and Shoreham, for example, destroyed the gates into the park, attacked the Palace of Otford and burnt manor rolls and other registers. Some customary services from peasants had been commuted on the archbishop's estates even before 1284, and in 1381 after the assassination of Archbishop Sudbury a royal commission was appointed to compel the tenants of Otford to do their reaping services.[10]

Lawlessness and rebellion reached their climax in Jack Cade's resistance to Henry VI's corrupt government dominated by William de la Pole and the unpopular extortioner Lord Saye and Sele (who was murdered by rebels at the Tower of London). Cade's well-organised Kentishmen assembled on Blackheath in 1450 and occupied London but his men alienated the citizens who threw them out. An offer of a royal pardon led to the collapse of the rebellion. The list of pardoned rebels contains numerous men from Wrotham, Seal, Ightham, Chipstead, Penshurst and Sundridge.

A feature of the reduction in population in the later Middle Ages is the deserted or shrunken village, although neither in Surrey nor Kent is the phenomenon as marked as in the Midland counties. In some cases in Surrey a solitary church suggests vanished homesteads, as at Tatsfield, Chelsham and Wotton. Many single farms may also be the only surviving descendants of once prosperous hamlets or villages: Tillingdown, Chivington, West Humble.[11] In Kent, the medieval site of Little Farleigh appears to be a deserted settlement and another is probably at Chapel Wood at Hartley. Ridley Dode and Stansted are further examples.[12]

A prominent feature of the later Middle Ages was the growth of the cloth trade. For four hundred years from the 13th to the 17th centuries clothmaking was one of the staple industries of Surrey. Almost every village had inhabitants engaged in one or more stages in the production of woollen cloth. Caterham, Nutfield and West Horsley, by way of example, each had their shearmen and weavers. The villages of Gomshall and Shere were outstanding as weaving centres. In 1380 they had between them 14 weavers and 42 spinners, besides pelterers, shearers, dyers, fullers and so on. Drapers were mentioned in Shere, Gomshall and neighbouring villages in 1436, and in Henry VIII's reign Shere is mentioned in a list of places at which long cloths of 20, 22 and 24 yards were made. In Shere village many of the houses of clothmakers are still identifiable with their central balconied room and wider windows. The most important centre of cloth manufacture was Guildford, followed by Godalming and Farnham. Both

44 *Dode church has been unused since the 14th century. Norman wall benches remain in the nave. The interior has been adapted for weddings.*

Guildford and Godalming possess coats of arms featuring wool-packs. Much new building is attributable to the cloth trade. For example, at least eight timber-framed houses at Shere were built originally as medieval open halls. Throughout the clothmaking districts water mills on the fast-flowing River Wey and its many tumbling tributaries, notably the River Tillingbourne, were used for fulling cloth. A similar picture presented itself in the Maidstone district where convenient water power existed on the Rivers Loose and Len.[13]

The Archbishop's Palaces

The archbishops' records throw much light on their life style and the functions of the archiepiscopal residence of the later Middle Ages. The medieval part of the archbishop's palace at Charing, dating from the late 13th and early 14th centuries, is unusually well preserved and Sarah Pearson has drawn from the documentary evidence a vivid picture of it.[14] The manor of Charing was recorded as a possession of the see of Canterbury from the eighth century. It lies, like many manors of this part of Kent, on the spring line below the scarp of the North Downs and in common with many of the other archiepiscopal residences, e.g. Croydon and Maidstone, the buildings were placed directly next to the parish

45 *The former Archbishop's Palace, Charing. The buildings were converted to a farmhouse in the 16th century. The former Hall is still used as a barn and the barbican survives.*

church. In the Middle Ages the main road from Maidstone to Ashford passed directly in front of the archbishop's gate where a market grew up. This was replaced gradually from the 15th century by permanent shops in the village street just west of the residence.

The surviving buildings are ranged round a courtyard entered by means of a gatehouse from the market place. The south range contained the lodgings. The great hall and entrance porch lay along the east side of the courtyard and beyond it is evidence of another service court, now destroyed. The north side of the main court comprised the private apartments, including two chamber ranges and a chapel. The archbishops had 17 residences in constant use in Kent, seven in Sussex and three in Surrey. The registers of Archbishop Pecham (1279-92) show that he was endlessly on the move. In his time as archbishop the manors were being directly exploited but from the 11th to the early 13th centuries they were leased out to local farmers, who tended to be important local men, e.g. Adam of Charing, the archbishop's steward in 1188. He had succeeded his father Ivo and was to be followed by his son. The lease contained a clause requiring the farmer to provide for the archbishop and his household for two weeks each year. The Pecham survey shows that certain tenants were responsible for maintaining part of the roof over the private treasury or chamber and part of the hay barn. Other buildings they had to maintain included the corn barn. Wealden tenants had to provide timber. The great chamber, one of the largest unaisled halls in England, was evidently built after Archbishop Kilwardby's time. Details of corbels and tracery suggest *c.*1300-10. The gateway is of this period and has two wings used as lodgings.

By the mid-14th century the palace was a large complex. An expense account of Archbishop Stratford dating *c.*1348 reveals that hay was needed for 80 horses when the archbishop visited and that his servants consisted of four valets, 15 pages and 58 other boys. Six hundred herrings were bought for Lent and on two occasions 428 loaves of bread were baked and 15 gallons of wine and 160 gallons of beer laid on. Archbishop Morton (1486-1500) is noted by Leland the antiquary as 'making great building at Charing'. The brickwork on the top storey of the surviving chamber ranges, with diamond patterns of black headers set in red brick with stone quoins, is very similar to brickwork on the gatehouse of Lambeth Palace, or that of the west façade of the range at Croydon, both of which were built in Morton's time.

Archbishop Islip had part of the Palace at Wrotham pulled down and he used the materials for his residence at Maidstone but much of the ragstone building survived and the east wing has recently been restored using stone from the derelict church in Tovil and a house near Leeds. Archbishop Morton almost re-built the manor house at Ford in Wrotham in brick in 1493. It appears to have been held by John Clerk in the reign of Henry V, who was steward of the archbishop's household in 1460-2, and previously bailiff at Aldington, another archiepiscopal manor. The ruined hall range is the earliest building on the site, probably dating from the 14th century. It is of stone, one of the group of surviving medieval stone houses in this part of west Kent which includes Old Soar Manor of the 13th century, Ightham Mote and Yaldham Manor of the 14th and Starkey Castle of the 15th century.

It is appropriate at this point to compare change in the distribution of regional wealth and population in previous centuries with that of the early 16th century.[15] Insofar as this can be measured from taxation evidence, three cross-sections in time are available: the Domesday Survey of 1086, the 1334 Lay Subsidy return (particularly valuable as it enables us to see the situation on the eve of the Black Death) and that of 1524-5. Domesday Surrey reveals relatively dense distributions of plough-teams and population along the spring-lines at the foot of the escarpment in the Vale of Holmesdale and dip-slope of the North Downs to the north. The Downs themselves were more thinly peopled in the 11th century but a considerable number of

46 *Otford Palace.*

small vills extended on to the chalk, notably in east Surrey which usually had mills, meadow and wood (p.113).

The 1334 subsidy records the relative prosperity of north and east Kent compared with the rest of the North Downs in Kent and Surrey and that of the Weald. The highest taxed districts in the 1524-5 subsidy are identified with the production, preparation and marketing of cloth in the Guildford-Godalming district and the milling sites used for fulling cloth on the headwaters of the Medway and its tributaries, the Teise, Beult, and Loose stream in the Maidstone district. The rich agricultural area of north and east Kent also emerges as one of the wealthiest districts in England.

8

Early Churches and Religious Houses

Broadly, the development of churches in the Downs and Hills was comparable with that of England at large. A number of churches have Saxon fabric but most were completely re-built, and a late 11th- or early 12th-century nave with one or two aisles added during the period of population growth (13th to early 14th centuries) is characteristic. A small Norman sanctuary was almost invariably replaced by a larger chancel in the 13th century and this was often flanked by one or two separate side chapels. There are often signs in the churches of the depopulation in the later 14th and 15th centuries in the churches. Fine 15th-century western towers are less common than in the Weald. Rood screens and lofts were inserted in most churches in *c.*1500.[1]

The story of Kent's churches begins two centuries earlier than St Augustine's mission in 597, for the history of Christian worship in the Darent valley has been practically continuous from the fourth century during the Roman occupation to the present day. Excavation of the Roman villa at Lullingstone beginning in 1949 revealed wall plaster which on patient restoration was found to depict Christians at prayer. The figures are thought to have represented the family who embraced Christianity *c.*350. There was, in effect, a chapel incorporated into the villa, the earliest known in lowland Britain. The evidence of coins suggests that the chapel was in use from *c.*383 to the first decade or two of the fifth century.

47 *Ruins of Reculver Abbey, founded in the late seventh century by King Egbert of Wessex.*

Another Christian church of this period may have existed at Otford where the inscription *chi rho* has been found in a Roman context. The supposition is that many inhabitants of Darent valley villas may have embraced Christianity.

The collapse of Roman authority required the re-introduction of Christianity by St Augustine in 597. Yet it appears that Christianity had not been entirely wiped out.[2] Even at the time of Augustine's arrival the faith almost certainly persisted in some places. One of these is St Martin's church, Canterbury.[3] Here, as a condition of her marriage to Ethelbert, King of Kent, his Frankish queen remained a Christian. She had been brought up near Tours where St Martin had been bishop two centuries earlier. St Augustine's mission had its first base at St Martin's whilst the cathedral and monastery were being built, and tradition has it that Ethelbert was baptised there. The king evidently restored a Roman building, possibly a Christian church, which survives as the western part of the chancel of the present church. St Martin's later became a parish church, the oldest in England, and has rightly been described as the cradle of English Christianity. The presence of the Christian Bertha helps to explain Pope Gregory's choice of Kent for conversion. St Augustine's landing-place on the Isle of Thanet is thought to have been at Ebbsfleet, a spur of land projecting into the Wantsum channel, marked with a stone cross since 1884. Ethelbert gave land adjoining a former Roman burial ground near St Martin's as a site for a monastery.

There are other places where Christianity was practised in Roman times and probably persisted into the pagan period of the Germanic invasions.[4] Churches were built in the Darent valley where fords crossed the river and these sites are remarkably close to Roman sites. It is considered likely that the villa estate boundaries can be equated with those delimiting Christian parishes. Alan Everitt has remarked that most of the early minster churches were established in former Romano-British communities and that Roman brickwork and parts of Roman structures were incorporated, perhaps in more parish churches in Kent than in any other county. Of the specifically Christian place-names in Kent, that of Eccles is the most interesting. This was a great Roman villa in the Medway valley which evidently became an early Christian centre, for it is the only example in south-east England of a place-name for a Christian community or church. In Surrey, Ashtead church, lying within a triangular earthwork incorporating Roman work, may be connected with a Roman villa. Norman builders quarried tiles from the adjacent Roman building.

Blair has elucidated the system of Saxon landholding in Surrey based largely on districts focused on royal or episcopal estates, viz., those of Godalming, Woking, Kingston, Reigate, Wallington and Farnham, and thrown great light on the early religious organisation which was founded on this basis.[5] He has identified the earliest churches as minster churches founded by kings or bishops at important administrative centres, typically comprising five to 15 modern parishes, each minster having priests who had a responsibility for the whole area served by the minster. These minster churches were Chertsey, the oldest of all, Bermondsey, Farnham, Woking, Kingston, Croydon, Godalming, Lambeth, Leatherhead, Southwark and Stoke near Guildford. Some 60 to 70 per cent of parochial churches had been established by Domesday, mainly on manors of wealthy ecclesiastics or lay persons and the flood continued in the 11th and 12th centuries which owed much to land clearance and new settlement.

The humble Saxon and early medieval church is as characteristic of the North Downs and of the sandstone hills as it is in the South Downs. When their churches were built, numerous downland and heathland communities were poor and unimportant and remained so for centuries. This poverty and small population is the background to the modest little Kentish churches with their simple, austere interiors; for example, the unrestored Badlesmere, lonely one-cell Hawkinge and tiny Paddlesworth which lies in a field. In Surrey fewer of these simple churches exist owing to Victorian re-building and restoration, but originally they were plentiful. The small estates on the relatively inhospitable downland of east Surrey, for example, were surprisingly well endowed with tiny churches in the 11th and early 12th centuries. Domesday Book lists them as Banstead, Chaldon, Chelsham, Coulsdon, Waddington, Woodmansterne and Caterham. Farleigh and Headley are likely to have been only shortly afterwards. Apparently the holder of each independent estate aimed to provide his tenants with their own little church, or they may have originally been built primarily for household use. Banstead has no fewer than four medieval churches or chapels serving what were then separate manors, three of which have disappeared. Chaldon survives as a small chapel in a fold of the Downs famed for its grimly realistic wall-painting, finely preserved of c.1200, representing the Ladder of Salvation rising out of Purgatory. Farleigh is a remarkable survival of a simple

48 *St Agatha's, Woldingham was replaced as the parish church by a new building in 1934.*

Norman village church of *c*.1100 which has Norman nave windows, a Norman west door and nothing later than *c*.1250, which has only been gently restored.

Woldingham is another example of a minute settlement on the North Downs which lasted for hundreds of years. When John Evelyn the diarist in 1677 visited the estate of Marden he found the parish of Woldingham, now covered with houses, totally remote among hills and, although only 16 miles from London, accessible only by winding and intricate ways and supporting no more than four or five dwellings on downs 'so full of wild thyme, marjoram and other sweet plants, that it cannot be overstocked by bees'. Evelyn urged the new owner of Marden Park to repair the 'old desolate dilapidated church' which stood on the hill above the house but this appears not to have been done until 1832 when the church was rebuilt – and further restored in 1889.[6] The original church had only one tiny room, divided into two parts by a wooden screen, and was without tower, spire or bell. The new church is described by Pevsner as 'the meanest little village church in Surrey'. It was superseded as the parish church by St Paul's, built in 1934 when Woldingham was becoming a dormitory settlement sprawling all over its once beautiful valleys and ridges.

Wanborough is another of the smallest places of worship in Surrey. It is a single-cell 13th-century chapel, disused in the 17th century, but sensitively restored in 1861. A screen of Spanish chestnut divides sanctuary and nave. Before Victorian restoration, Elstead possessed the humble timber and plaster screen that served as a division between nave and chancel in poorer churches, as also at the hilltop churches of Chelsham and Warlingham. Pyrford and Wisley are also comparatively unaltered churches. Blair has noted that Hascombe, a daughter church of Shalford, is one of four churches in south-west Surrey which are standard two-cell churches built virtually on an identical ground plan to common dimensions in the late 11th century. From detailed observations, the famous architect G.E. Street considered that the Surrey churches of St Mary, Merstham, St Margaret, Chipstead and St Helen, Cliffe at Hoo in Kent were designed by the same man in the 13th century and he detected traces of the same person's work in St Mary, Merton, St Martin, Brasted, Kent and St Martin, Gatton, Surrey.[7]

Even small archaeological excavations can demonstrate that, in addition to an observable evidence of some Saxon work in the exterior of many existing churches, there is also a strong Saxon element underlying or influencing present structures dating from after the Norman Conquest. An example of Saxon church building which still awaits full discovery is St John's Wotton, which stands magnificently on a spur overlooking the stretch of the North Downs extending to Box Hill. Until a limited excavation was made to correct rising damp in 1975, the earliest parts of the church were reckoned Norman, but the massively thick walls of a former church were found, oriented on a north-south axis, which had been destroyed by fire. This is attributed to the middle-late Saxon period. A small church with rubble walls in line with the present tower was then built. The tower was later heightened, the nave re-floored and the chancel extended outwards as population grew.

VIII *St Martin's church, Canterbury. In the foreground is Queen Bertha's chapel. The nave is considered to be the work of St Augustine.*

IX *An 18th-century print of Barfreston church.*

X *Canterbury: an aerial view.*

XI *The legendary valley of the Mole at Mickleham near Dorking.*

XII *Edward McKnight Kauffer's poster, The North Downs, 1915.*

XIII *Dover Castle, the 'lock and key to England'.*

XIV *Surrey woodmen traditionally making fencing poles and hurdles.*

XV *The interior of Gatton church, furnished by Lord Monson in the 1840s with medieval and 16th-century 'cast-offs' from continental religious institutions. The family pew was equipped with a fireplace and comfortable chairs.*

XVI *Wotton church: evening.*

On the other hand unwarranted antiquity to both church and yew tree in the graveyard has been attributed to Tandridge.[8] It was claimed that the foundations of a Saxon church were aligned to avoid the roots of the even then ancient yew which now has a circumference of about 32 feet some three feet above the ground. However, neither the resident priest who did much research into the origins of the church some years ago nor Gerald Walkdin who has studied the matter recently, has found any evidence of Anglo-Saxon foundations. The earliest part of the existing church appears to date from c.1100. The priest's door on the north side of the chancel, with a small window beside it, is the earliest surviving part of the present building. The yew tree with the largest girth in England is reputed to be that at Ulcombe churchyard in Kent which is 35 feet.

For Kent, Alan Everitt has demonstrated the early development of churches.[9] As we have seen, the original churches were mainly minsters. Forty-one downland and chartland churches, in woodland regions initially, were daughter churches of 19 mother-churches strung out along the Vale of Holmesdale. These relatively late and subordinate churches include Boughton Malherbe of Lenham; Pluckley of Charing; Leeds and Hucking of Hollingbourne; Sevenoaks of Shoreham; Otham and Linton of Maidstone; Hythe of Lympne. Churches in east Kent which similarly hived off later churches include Wingham, which had Ashby-Sandwich as a daughter church; Reculver which had St Nicholas-at-Wade; Milton Regis, Rodmersham; and Minster, which had Woodchurch near Tenterden. Significantly, Everitt drew attention to the fact that most of the dedications of subsidiary churches were not represented in the mother-churches in the Vale of Holmesdale. Although fashion has something to do with this, Everitt noted that dedications tended to revert to the early saints of the Christian church, like St John the Baptist, pre-eminently the saint of the wilderness; St Michael who slaughtered the Beast in the 'Book of Revelation' and is connected with the remote hill-top churches of Hawkinge and Chart Sutton; and St Leonard, St Blaise, St Anthony and St Damian, each of whom was connected with regions of unreclaimed woodland. Everitt has remarked: 'What we probably see is the characteristic response of a pastoral people to the reclamation of a wooded, inhospitable, countryside. As the summer shielings of the herdsmen developed into permanent farms, churches and chapels began to appear along the old droveways, and it was but natural that they should be placed under the patronage of those saints who seemed most able to protect them in a hostile environment.' Thus, church dedications throw much light on the evolution of settlement as well as the development of the Church. The relatively late clearing of the wood on downland and chartland is vividly brought out by this approach.

For Surrey it is perhaps significant that the parish church of Chelsham, high on the remote Downs, is dedicated to St Leonard; Betchworth and Mickleham to St Michael; Capel, Croydon, Oakwood, Puttenham and Wonersh to St John the Baptist; Caterham and Effingham to St Lawrence; Charlwood, Compton, Cranleigh, Godstone, Great Bookham, Peper Harrow and Pyrford to St Nicholas; Crowhurst to St George. All these appear to have been originally subsidiary to mother-churches and most were settled relatively late in woodland clearings.

49 *Moulded porch, Patrixbourne church.*

Originally a number of pre-Conquest churches were built of stone as opposed to timber. Patrixbourne was possibly one of these, for there is evidence of an earlier building in roughly laid herring-bone masonry visible on the west wall, and the narrow south aisle is thought to have been part of the floor of an earlier church. After the Conquest the manor was held by the ancient and wealthy Patrick family of La Lane-Patry, near Flers in the Calvados region of Normandy, and its subsequent history is of exceptional interest. A two-cell church, characteristic of east Kent, was erected in the 12th century, though the position of the tower midway along the south aisle is unusual. Of exceptional interest is the wealth of Romanesque decoration round the south door and at the east end, which is similar to that round the south door of Barfreston and the west door of Rochester Cathedral. It has been suggested that a 'school' of craftsmen in the third quarter of the 12th century worked at Rochester and Canterbury Cathedrals, and possibly at Faversham, and that the elaborate decorative styles of Patrixbourne and Barfreston are examples of this school of design. Mary Berg, however, has stressed that the work at Patrixbourne appears to have been initiated by the Patrick family themselves. Patrixbourne also shares with Barfreston a 15th-century wheel window with eight decorated 'spokes' strikingly similar in detail.[10]

A number of Surrey churches are distinguished by the amount of wood used in their construction, appropriate in a county of good timber and thinly populated in the past. Hascombe and Hambledon have a wooden steeple from the centre of the nave, Tandridge has a bell turret with a shingled spire on the west gable dating from *c.*1300. The tower is supported by four corner oak posts measuring 14½ inches square. The shingles were originally oak but they have now been replaced by Canadian cedar. Compton possesses the oldest wooden screen in England, a Norman example, and other beautiful medieval screens still survive at Gatton, West Horsley, Leatherhead, Nutfield, Reigate and Shere.

Westerham parish church on the Kent-Surrey border is a classic example of a church which had to be successively enlarged to accommodate the increased congregation, sustain changes in liturgy and to maintain its intimate connection with the daily life of the community. The name 'Westerham' implies that the

medieval manor, which probably exceeded 30,000 acres in area, anciently
grew from the cradle of English settlement in the Darent valley. It became an
important royal estate in the seventh
century and later one of the earliest
markets in Kent. A church was built
near a springhead venerated probably
from at least the Roman period and
a dependent chapelry was founded at
Edenbridge when the woodland was
being colonised. The present church
largely dates from the 15th century, the
tower being older. This has an interesting spiral wooden staircase, basically
medieval, turning in an anti-clockwise
direction. The most visible part of
the roof is of Horsham stone which
has been recently relaid and re-set in
concrete.

Religious Houses

As the ecclesiastical capital of England, Canterbury had an immense
stake in the medieval church – two
vast Benedictine abbeys, a priory, a

50 *Barfreston church, the most decorated early medieval church in England.*

nunnery, three friaries, five ancient almshouses and a score of parish churches.
The extant rentals of Christ Church are remarkably complete and give precise
locations of some 400 properties in the city from *c*.1200. Between 1198 and
1223-4 an apparently rapid expansion of the city caused a remarkable rise in
income from houses and shops and a further five-fold increase in rents occurred
in the 13th century, reflecting the considerable growth of the city. By about
1300 Canterbury had some 200 shops and numerous markets. A merchant guild
was founded in the late 11th or early 12th century and craft guilds emerged
in the early 13th century. Cloth-making, leather, victualling and building trades,
goldsmiths, moneyers, priests, shopkeepers, Jews and aliens all contributed to
Canterbury's regional importance. Its mint was the only one in the country to
survive the centralisation of 1218. The ground plan of medieval Canterbury has
survived largely unaltered to this day so that it has been possible to reconstruct
the ground plots of citizens of 750 years ago.[11]
   It was principally in the great buildings of Caen and Canterbury under the
rule of Lanfranc that the Anglo-Norman High Romanesque emerged. Lanfranc
adopted the style of his abbey church of Saint Etienne for the new metropolitan church in Canterbury *c*.1070. Contemporaneously, the important abbey of

51 *The Sondes family memorials in Throwley church.*

St Augustine was being constructed, so making Canterbury the fountainhead of English Romanesque architecture. These two major churches, together with Caen, epitomise the great Norman 11th-century church with the high altar and shrine set in an eastern apse, a long choir for the community of clergy celebrating the new liturgy, the lantern tower and flanking transepts and a long nave forming almost a distinct building at the western end of the church. Great cathedral churches in this style spread across southern England, notably to Rochester and Chichester, the grander parish churches of east Kent and to new towns, such as New Shoreham in Sussex, where the magnificent church bears witness of the decorative work of Canterbury masons. Such Romanesque buildings were amongst the most daring in Europe and led directly towards the development of Gothic.[12]

This is evident in the decisive impact of Canterbury Cathedral, rebuilt after the fire in 1174. The new style was closely related to contemporary practice in north-west France, because the reconstructions were entrusted to William of Sens, who brought with him sculptors and glaziers from that district. In its pointed arches, delicate rib vaulting and detached shafts, its large aisle windows, rich capitals and the use of marble, the nearest counterparts were Notre Dame in Paris, St Remi at Rheims, and the cathedrals of Laon, Arras and Valenciennes. During the next 70 years most of the greater churches of England had their eastern ends rebuilt in Purbeck marble with lavish decoration. The spectacular shrine erected in 1220 to display the relics of the martyred Archbishop Thomas à Becket, which was the visual and liturgical focus of the cathedral, was destroyed at the Reformation.

In Kent the three largest and richest monastic houses were the Benedictine Christ Church Priory, St Augustine's Abbey, both at Canterbury, and St Andrew's Priory at Rochester. At Christ Church, Lanfranc's dormitory in the crypt housed up to 150 monks, and under Anselm the cathedral which had arisen on the Anglo-Saxon site was greatly expanded and new priory buildings were erected. A hall, the largest in England after Westminster; and the frater range and other buildings were completely re-built in the early 13th century. In his long priorate, Henry of Eastry (1285-1331), put the priory finances in order and did much to develop the landed estate. A new start on the rebuilding of the nave occurred in 1379 and Prior Chillenden, 'the greatest building of a Prior that ever was in Christes Church', according to Leland, rebuilt the great cloister, chapter house, guest house and other buildings. At the Dissolution Christ Church had a gross annual income of nearly £3,000, and was the third richest ecclesiastical house in England after Westminster and Glastonbury. St Augustine's Abbey also developed into a huge monastery in the Norman period, probably completed by Abbot Hugh (d. 1124). The middle and later 13th century was another great period of rebuilding and expansion under Abbot Fyndon, culminating in the licence to crenellate the Great Gate in 1308. The very late 14th and early 15th centuries was also a period of active building, as at Christ Church.

The excavation of the site of St Pancras church in 1900, one of the three churches of St Augustine's, revealed the earliest type of Saxon church which was probably built in the time of King Ethelbert in the

52 *Part of the cathedral service commemorating the martyrdom of Thomas à Becket in the 13th century. Each stanza has five alexandrines all ending with the same rhyme, an adaptation for easy chanting (BL Galba 1:4).*

early seventh century, with walls constructed entirely of regularly laid Roman bricks. The lower part of one of the chancel arches, set in a 13th-century wall, is classically moulded, another indication that Roman styles were being revived three centuries after the departure of the Romans. Numerous burials were interred but no definite evidence was found of St Augustine himself. In 1843 A.J. Beresford-Hope, the ecclesiologist, purchased these and adjacent ruins of the Abbey. They were then encumbered with sheds; the gateway was a brewery, part a dance hall, the Great Hall, Chapel and Infirmary had vanished, the dormitories were in ruins, the great tower had fallen down and one of the walls of the Abbey church served as a fives court. Beresford-Hope founded St Augustine's College, which, as in medieval times, became a missionary centre. The gateway was restored. Before the Dissolution it had been occupied by many guests of the old abbots and afterwards served as a bedchamber to Queen Elizabeth, to Charles I, who spent part of his honeymoon with the Princess Henrietta Maria there, and to Charles II, who slept in it on his triumphal progress to London at the Restoration.

53 *(left) 'Candle beam', Challock church. The church contains modern frescoes.*

54 *(right) Rood screen, Molash (brought from Eastwell church).*

St Mary's Abbey, West Malling was founded by Gundulf, bishop of Rochester in the late 11th century as an abbey for Benedictine nuns. It has a magnificent west front. The Abbey was dissolved in 1534 and the present Anglican community of Benedictine nuns dates from 1916. Waverley Abbey holds a position of great importance in church history as the first Cistercian house in England, founded in 1128 by William Giffard, bishop of Winchester, with monks from L'Aumone in Normandy. The Cistercians practised the strict rule of not building monasteries in cities, or near castles or villages, and devoted their lives to meditation and scholarship. Their abbey was beautifully sited on the banks of the River Wey, two miles south of Farnham, on a sandy waste. The church was almost completely destroyed at the Dissolution of the Monasteries. Excavation has revealed a modest aisle-less structure contrasting vividly with those of Rievaulx and Fountains in Yorkshire and it may thus reflect an older, short-lived, tradition of the order. Bestowed on Waverley were numerous endowments of land, much of it virgin wasteland, some of which the monks reclaimed and became the economic basis of the monks' life. Distant properties were exploited as sub-stations called granges, such as Leigh, Tongham, Neatham near Alton, and Wanborough, none of which were particularly large or prosperous. Boxley in Kent was founded by William de Ypres, son of the Count of Flanders, in 1143. It became the second Cistercian abbey in England directly affiliated to Clairvaux. Partly on account of its site near the London-Canterbury highway, its abbots played a prominent part in England's political affairs in the late 12th century.[13]

9

The Late Sixteenth to the Mid-Eighteenth Centuries (c.1560-1750)

It was in this period that the Surrey Downs first acquired their reputation among the wealthier classes as a health resort and place of recreation. Banstead's medical fame was evidently brief, for by John Aubrey's day, *c.*1680, London physicians no longer prescribed its 'wholesome air', but referred patients to the newly opened spa at Epsom or to Cotmandean near Dorking, where Defoe noted that some 'learned physicians have singled out as the best air of England'. Banstead, however, continued to hold the affections of wealthy tourists as a sporting centre because it had abundant facilities for physical exercise. With ever-growing indulgence post-Restoration London flocked to enjoy riding, hunting, hare-coursing and horse-racing on its sheep-cropped downs. Fashionable attention was still heaped on Banstead Downs as the most delightful spot of that kind in Britain in the 1720s when Defoe rhapsodised about them for being so near to London and surrounded by pleasant villages on ground so smooth, level and dry (even after a few hours of rain) that was perfect for outdoor pursuits. He noted the gentlemen and citizens of London who thronged the race-course

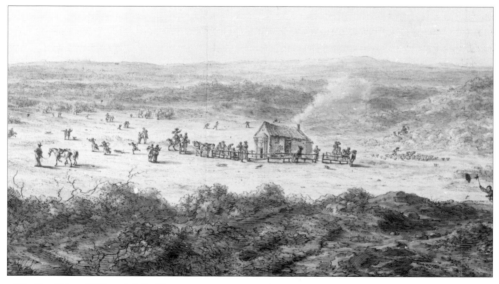

55 *Detail from William Schellink's* Epsom Common and Wells, *1662. The small building housed the wells. People can be seen taking the waters behind the railings. Note the horse-racing, the main leisure activity.*

to see 'Racers, flying over the course, as if they either touch'd not the ground they pass upon …'.[1]

John Aubrey writes a little earlier of local people riding to Epsom with the choicest fruits, herbs, roots and flowers, with all sorts of wild fowl, the rarest kinds of fish and venison, and with every kind of butcher's meat, among which Banstead mutton was accounted a most relishing dainty.[2] From John Macky, also writing at about the same time, we learn of the 'discovery' of Box Hill. Some visitors would have taken the air and walked over the turf and the box woods but he also tells of people making love in the labyrinths which had turned into a 'Palace of Venus'.[3] Defoe mentions a great beech tree which grew on the summit above a cave or vault much visited by coach parties from Epsom in summer. The innkeeper of the *King's Arms* in Dorking made the venue so popular and raucous on Sunday nights that some people in the town blew up the vault with gunpowder and stopped these rowdy sessions on the Sabbath. Is this one of the earliest recorded incidents in the conflict between tourism and traditional rural life?[4]

Samuel Pepys' Visit to the Surrey Downs

One visitor to whom we are grateful was Samuel Pepys, whose account of a little episode in his diary not only adds a nice local touch to the geography of the North Downs at this period but throws light on his perception of the rural, indeed rustic world, contrasting with his cosmopolitan existence at the Admiralty in London.[5] By dint of a very early start (although delayed by his wife's dressing), his party were at Epsom in a coach-and-four by eight a.m. on 14 July 1667. The waters drunk, and stools made, they called at the *King's Arms* in Epsom for a meal and then went on to church. After a nap Pepys, who was a good walker, took some of his party to see his cousin Pepys' house at Ashtead and then led them into a familiar coppice bordered by the green turf of the common and to a common arable field of the village where Mrs Turner gathered one of the prettiest nosegays he had ever seen. Pepys then made for a flock of sheep on the commonland and saw a most pleasant and innocent sight. A shepherd and his little boy were reading the Bible together 'far from any house or sight of people'. Pepys congratulated the old man 'most like one of the old Patriarchs that I ever saw' on his son's reading and took notice of his woollen stockings of mixed colours and of his shoes shod with iron at toe and heel with great nails in the soles. On inquiry about this, the shepherd replied, 'Why the Downs, you see, are full of stones, and we are fair to shoe ourselves thus' and, he continued, 'I will make the stones fly till they sing before me.' Pepys noted how he valued his dog, which turned the flock of 18 score sheep any way he wanted, and got them into the fold at night and that all he earned was 4s. a week all the year round.

Pepys' party set off for home at seven p.m. and arrived home at eleven, after searching for glow-worms in the dark. Pepys was so moved by the experience that he noted that it brought into his mind thoughts of an Old World for several days afterwards. He was as much a Londoner as Samuel Johnson was one hundred years later and, like him, Pepys needed short breaks in London's countryside to refresh himself from the daily smoke and bustle of the City and valued the contrast in the surroundings of his daily life.

Pepys' description of Ashtead is only a snapshot, as it were, but, with patient research, the local scene and its immediate surroundings can be reconstructed from early maps and documents. Let us work backwards in time (always a good technique of the historian and historical geographer because information is usually fuller at later than earlier dates), using the map of 1817 engraved for the use of travellers by coach between London and Brighton. A section takes in the Downs between Dorking and Epsom and depicts the setting of the beautifully diversified scene from Jane Austen's *Emma*; extensive commons at Epsom, Chessington, Ranmore, Headley, Mitcham and at Walton, Kingsham and Banstead; the common downs of Fetcham, Betchworth, Leatherhead and Walton, Epsom with its race-course; the commonable heaths of Headley and Ashcombe; the common fields in each of the parishes of Ashtead, Leatherhead and Bookham. All this diversity was thickly beset with gentlemen's country houses and parks, including Norbury Park, Churt Park, Denbies, the Deepdene,

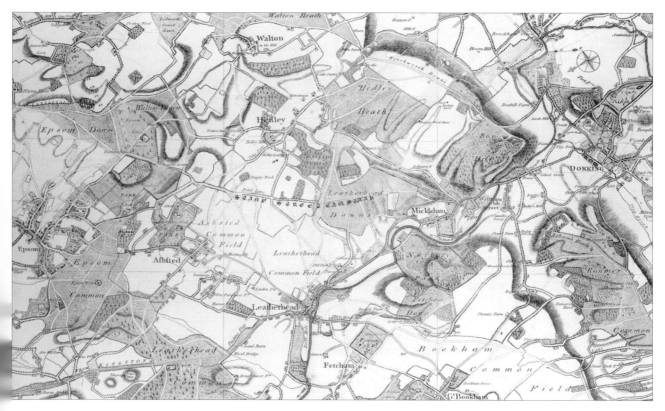

56 *Map of Leatherhead and District, 1817.*

ASHTEAD IN 1638.

BASED ON THE SURVEY, BY
JOHN LAWRENCE, OF THAT DATE.

A.W.G.L., 1950.

57 *Map illustrating Pepys' visit to Ashstead, 1667.*

Betchworth Castle, Fetcham Park, Bookham and Ashtead Parks, Woodcote, Durdans and Thorncroft. Pepys' little excursion can be worked out from John Lawrence's map of Ashtead dated 1638 (opposite).

John Evelyn

A contemporary of Pepys who also throws much light on his receptiveness to the spirit of place in his own local landscape is the diarist John Evelyn.[6] In 1694 he moved from Sayes Court in Deptford to spend the summers at Wotton in the Tillingbourne valley, his birthplace, which he inherited from his brother George in 1697. He was the younger son of Richard Evelyn, a landowner of considerable property at Wotton, who had himself inherited the family estate from George Evelyn, the diarist's grandfather who acquired his wealth from 1579 as a pioneer in establishing gunpowder mills in England. By investing in land he was one of the numerous Tudor entrepreneurs in the Tillingbourne valley district who sought social elevation by this conventional route. By John Evelyn's day, the family were as completely members of the gentry as any of the older families. His father had been sheriff of Surrey and Sussex and his brother George served in many Parliaments from 1641. Evelyn himself had been a founding member of the Royal Society and was by this time established as a polymath, connoisseur, arboriculturist, landscape gardener, philosopher, visionary, town planner, hydraulic engineer, antiquarian, historian and humanitarian rolled into one. He was not only so completely the perfect English gentleman (and with what perfection his district of Surrey subsequently produced countless more!) but one who was absorbed in the Restoration revolution in the natural sciences associated with persons such as Newton, John Ray the celebrated botanist, and John Aubrey the antiquarian, which involved the new approach of observing, collecting, collating, cataloguing of data with little sense of intellectual boundaries.[7]

Evelyn is not noted for a sense of humour but this emerges in his correspondence; when, for instance, Pepys requested his engraved head for his collection of virtuosi, Evelyn retorted that he only wanted to be remembered as a planter of cabbage (this was then his current obsession and his last book, *Acetaria*, was on the cultivation of salads). Guy de la Bédoyère sees him as the product of his own personality but it is difficult to resist the conclusion that his father, remembered in family tradition as a 'thriving, neat, silent and methodical genius', had a great influence on his son's interests, which in so far as his situation and times allowed, were apparently similar to those of his son's, and were worked out when woods and water were the basis of the family's prosperity. The diarist was attracted to industrial technology related to his family's activities. For example, he proved by experiment that gunpowder could be made with charcoal made from beech, instead of the usual dogwood and alder, and he promoted the Italian Ramelli's inventions in applied hydraulics, another family trait, and counselled people undertaking a Grand Tour to draw on their return 'models of useful engines for raising of water, carrying of burdens, suspending weights …'. He had not expected to inherit Wotton but his nephews had all predeceased their father, his brother. He took on the role of steward of the estate for the sake of his family's posterity and with something of the resignation, frustration and exaggerated helplessness of someone who has had to take an early retirement. The fact was that Wotton was isolated from London in his day (not really changing for the better until Westminster Bridge was built across the Thames in 1749). Evelyn enjoyed the bliss of summer at Wotton but at the heavy cost of losing touch with his friends, including Pepys, and all his intellectual contacts, which he made up for by residence at his town house in Dover Street during the winter.

He wrote to Pepys from Wotton in 1692: 'I have been philosophising and world-despising in the solitudes of this place whither I have retired to pause. And mourn the absence of my best and worthiest friend. Here is wood and water, meadows and mountains, the Dryads and the Hamadryads; but there is no Mr Pepys, no Dr Gale …'. In later correspondence with the elderly

58 *Portrait of John Evelyn, the diarist, holding a copy of his most famous book* Sylva.

and terminally ill Pepys, Evelyn tried to tempt him to sample 'the sweet breath of the Surrey Downs', but Pepys was not well enough to come and Evelyn, despairing of keeping his mind on stretch, had to explain that in the manner of the Patriarchs of old he passed the day 'in the fields, among the horses and oxen, sheep and cows, bulls and sows, the sewing [draining] of ponds and looking after his hinds in the manner which Cicero reckoned the best occupation for a senator in old age'. Earlier, at Sayes Court, Evelyn had shown enthusiasm for samples of plants from New England and Virginia which he wanted as seeds from Captain Nicholson, probably Francis Nicholson, who became Governor of Virginia.

Evelyn's writings show that in his day he was more than usually receptive to what became known as Romantic scenery. In his introductory account of the parish of Wotton, written for John Aubrey's *A History of Surrey* published in 1718-19,[9] he wrote, in language more typical of Thomson's two generations later, of the 'Sugar-Loaf mountains' south-west of Wotton, which with the boscage upon them, and little torrents in between, made such a solitude as he had never seen in any place more 'horridly agreeable and romantic'. This statement is of particular interest because it appears to be the first admiration of what later became known as 'a perfect piece of English countryside' around Friday Street. As previously noted, the prevailing taste in landscape in Evelyn's day was rather for the orderly and polished neatness of garden-like fields. The hillier, well-wooded parts of south-east England gave rise to different sensations, and did not conform to the conventionally accepted notion of the beautiful until the impulse of the Picturesque and Romantic movements at the end of the 18th century. It appears that Evelyn's love of the 'wildness' of the wooded glens of his birth-place had played to such an extent on his sensitive imagination that he was able to distil pleasure from such a landscape one hundred years or so before it became fashionable.

Evelyn was also ahead of his day in another matter of landscape aesthetics. In the 17th century curiosity in landscape was still so rare that far-spreading prospects ('landskips') of extensive and variegated views of countryside were little known or appreciated until the 'hill' or 'prospect' poem became established, such as Sir John Denham's 'Cooper's Hill'. In his letter to Aubrey, Evelyn mentions the now famous view from Leith Hill and describes it in more detail in his contribution to the section on Surrey in William Gibson's edition of Camden's *Britannia* (1695). It is worth quoting in full:

> Hereabouts is a thing remarkable, tho' but little taken notice of; I mean that goodly prospect from the top of Leith Hill … From hence one may see, in a clear day, the goodly Vale [of Horsham] and consequently the whole county of Sussex, as far as the South Downs, and even beyond them to the sea; the entire county of Surrey, part of Hampshire, Berkshire, Oxfordshire, Buckinghamshire and Hertfordshire; as also of Middlesex, Kent and Essex; and further yet (as is believed) into Wiltshire could one well distinguish them with the aid of a telescope. The like, I think, is not to be found in any part of England, or perhaps Europe besides; and the reason why it is not more observed is partly its lying quite off any road …*

Meanwhile major land-use changes had occurred in the Tillingbourne valley, with some of which the diarist was personally involved. Some of the earliest examples of the 17th-century landscape gardener's art, deliberately Italian in inspiration, are located in the Tillingbourne valley. This is marked by the surviving terraces at Chilworth Manor, lovingly restored by the late Lady Heald, and at the Deepdene, Dorking, where the Hon. Charles Howard re-modelled his grounds in a yet more Italian manner, aided by the naturally 'U'-shaped hill which could resemble a Roman amphitheatre and lent itself to terraced treatment. As David Watkin has remarked, the steep hills and rolling woods of central Surrey, which were regarded as so Picturesque in the precise sense in which the word was used in 1800, had evidently had their own effect on those wanting to make Italianate gardens more than a century earlier.

---

* We can forgive Evelyn for not knowing the similar stupendous view across the Midlands to the Welsh mountains associated with Piers Plowman but deeply regret that the present polluted atmosphere and the heedless growth of trees on former open heath now prevents one from seeing more than one quarter of the panoramas enjoyed by Stuarts and Georgians from the summit of Leith Hill. Is this not a case for a generous use of the axe to restore such vistas in Surrey? Since writing this plea a start has been made on this urgent matter.

59 *The terrace at Albury Park,*
designed by John Evelyn in 1679.

Wenceslaus Hollar's skilfully composed etchings of the Earl of Arundel's favourite country retreat at Albury in the 1630s (on the site of the present Albury House) depict terraced gardens opposite the Earl's 'poor cottage', sloping to shimmering light reflecting trees and a 'ruined' casino on a wide surface of still water.[10] This picture was one of the favourite recollections of the Earl during his final years in exile at Padua. Another of Hollar's etchings, intended to heighten the dream-like illusion of Albury in the Earl's mind, records a tree-lined walk along the edge of a naturally serpentined lake. These water features were a minimally modified landscape previously created by the diversion of streams and the building of dams for the purpose of milling and keeping fish. The almost photographic truth of Hollar's drawings of a chain of mill- and fish-ponds is authenticated by a contemporary survey of the Earl's estate in 1638.[11]

A decade later, inspired by his tour of Europe from 1641, John Evelyn was able to create with his brother's and cousin's aid in the midst of his cherished streams and woods at Wotton the aesthetic and philosophic use of water in landscape which was to make it one of the most magnificent of the Italianate canal-gardens in England. Evelyn brought water from the Tillingbourne stream against the loose sand which dissolved into the sand as sugar dissolves in wine. In this manner he made his steep terraces which were the normal accompaniment of the Italian villa such as at the Villa Lante and the Villa d'Este. Another significant technique was to draw off water from a leat 50 feet higher than the first parterre which supplied by gravity the fountain and circular *bason* at his Roman Doric garden-temple, then unique in England. It is characteristic of Evelyn that his practical skills in applied hydraulics employed in remodelling landscape were largely learned in Italy during his long residence there at the time of the Civil War.*

He was also directly concerned in garden design at Albury Park, noting in his diary in 1655 that he had visited Mr Howard there 'who had begun to build and alter the garden much'. This was Henry Howard, who earlier had bought

* The gardens at Wotton House have been restored and were re-opened to the public in 2004.

the property from his brother Thomas, and who later became Earl of Arundel and the 6th Duke of Norfolk. He had brought in his neighbour Evelyn to help with his landscaping. The diarist's design pivoted on two parallel terraces, each about 400 yards in length, well above the level of the River Tillingbourne, a central semi-circular *bason* with a fountain on the upper terrace and a grotto or 'crypta' driven into the sandstone hill for 160 yards, in imitation of the Grotto di Posilippo near Naples. Additionally, the river was widened to form two canals each 800 yards long and 80 feet wide. Beneath the principal terrace Evelyn made a cavern as a Bath House. Vines were planted on the south-facing slope above the river, protected on the upper side by a yew hedge. William Cobbett wrote with tremendous enthusiasm about these gardens, particularly the yew hedge, and pronounced them the prettiest he had seen.[12]

Evelyn, who was brilliant at the manipulation of water, chose to irrigate the vines and to supply the fountain by means of a high-level contour canal from the Sherbourne Pond (Silent Pool), which can still be traced as a dry channel, but he did not reckon on the opposition of the Risbridgers, yeomen of Cookes Place downstream, through whose land the watercourse passed and which threatened the loss of water for floating meadows, a technique introduced in the early 17th century. This practice was a triumph of agricultural art which required a skilfully managed sheet of running water, only about one inch deep, to trickle (not stagnate) periodically over water meadows for the sake of the luxuriant crop of grass or hay crop produced by its fertilising properties, just when it was most wanted. The warmer waters from springs on the south sides of hills were preferred because it was probably the warmth of water trickling over the surface which hastened grass growth and the calcareous particles in water from the chalk were the most fertilising. The meadows were re-shaped to take the water. Ingenuity lay in the accuracy with which the necessary amount of water

60 *Wenceslaus Hollar's sketch of the River Tillingbourne for the Earl of Arundel.*

was drawn from the catch-water system of drains which conducted flowing water along the upper edge of meadows by means of master feeders, dropping down on them by means of subsidiary feeders and gutters controlled by sluices. The Tillingbourne valley was ideal for floating on account of the numerous springs along the valley's sides and the conjunction of sandstones and clays.[12]

The most fiercely contested water resource in the whole valley was the water which flowed from the Sherbourne springs, except in the driest of seasons, as in 1741. As the water issued from the chalk it had fertilising powers to an astonishing degree and much ingenuity was employed in conducting water from it. At some indeterminate stage the Sherbourne Pond comprised additionally the Upper and Middle Ponds at different levels to facilitate the construction of a tier of master feeders. Subsequently a Lower Pond was artificially constructed by means of a trench from the Middle Pond. This appears to have been made subsequent to a survey of the Albury estate in 1638 and it apparently owes its origin to the bitter dispute over water supply between several generations of the Risbridgers and the occupiers of Albury House.

Mr Howard secured the permission from William Risbridger's widow for water from the pond but this lapsed when her son came of age. From 1673 onwards the new Risbridger owner interrupted the supply to the fountain from time to time. Howard sold Albury to Sir Heneage Finch who was an eminent national figure, solicitor-general to Charles II between 1678 and 1682. Lord Chancellor Finch fell foul of the Risbridgers who cut off the supply of water completely. Risbridger's widow was sued by Finch in 1696 and in 1700 judgment was given in his favour but with the injunction that this was not to be binding on the widow's infant son after the age of 21 years if he should show good cause within six months to the contrary. At the age of 21 years and five months the latest Risbridger petitioned the Lord Chancellor but the family was again unsuccessful, although a stipulation was made that Finch was to scour and amend the banks of the watercourse and allow enough water for the Risbridgers to 'float' their meadows. It is hardly surprising that the Chancery Court (which was the Lord Chancellor's own court) should have come down in favour of Finch when there was some doubt about the merits of the Risbridger case. Litigation flared up again after 1745 when Lord Aylesford was the owner of Albury House. He replaced a board which had been raised and lowered to regulate the supply of water to the Lower and Upper Sherbourne ponds with a locked penstock which cut off the water from the Lower Pond and to Risbridger lands. Legal proceedings dragged on until the then Risbridger, who had no heir, threw in the towel and sold his freehold properties to Lord Aylesford and surrendered copyhold land to him for £3,000, Risbridger retaining the properties for the term of his natural life. As R. Charles Walmsley has remarked, the heavy iron railings above the Risbridger vault by the north porch of the old church and the memorial tablet on the west wall are notable memorials of a yeoman family resident at Cookes Place 'thro many ages'. They are also lasting mementoes in a valley rich in the various historical associations of the developing art of directing water sources for the use and convenience of man.[13] Many relics of the mining industry still exist.[14] The similar importance of the Loose and Len valleys near Maidstone is discussed on pages 119-20.

Agricultural Change

Throwing some light on a rural community and its farming practices of the time is an Elizabethan survey of the manor of Gomshall in the Tillingbourne valley between Dorking and Guildford.[15] The lord's moated mansion had a hall, apparently a detached kitchen, two granges, a cow house, sheepcote, garden and water mill. There is mention of the 'common field of Gomshall' but this appears to have been separate from the lord's land which, described in furlongs, suggests that some of the lord's land had been enclosed earlier from that of the villagers. Thirty acres of the demesne in Southfield was in tillage, and valued at 6d. an acre. Fifty more acres were valued at 4d. and 28 at 2d. This poorer land was apparently only occasionally ploughed. Twelve acres of pasture was reckoned to be worth only 1d. as was 40 acres of woodland in Kingswood. The most valuable pasture was two acres of meadow valued at 1s. an acre which could sustain 300 wether sheep when not on the common or in the lord's other pasture. The overall impression is of modest husbandry which never failed to incur the wrath of later agricultural experts (see p.145).

A substantial community of small farmers also cultivated the land. A transition from medieval feudalism had already set in. Thirty-one landholders, mainly cottagers and small men, owed no customary services to the lord and were either freemen or had commuted their obligations for a money payment. Other copyholders, as a last-remaining symbol of their lowly status, were to provide five wagon loads of wood for the lord from the Churt Wood just before Christmas and others were still obliged to perform farming duties for the lord. Walter Parkhurst and others had to reap the lord's corn for two days with two men and when engaged on this task had the customary right to a meal a day which consisted of pottage, wheaten bread, cheese, or five herrings (and water, but no beer). In this way the smaller men could earn a decent meal. George Whitworth weeded the lord's corn and did carpentry work at the granges or commuted for 6d. When William Bromham went on the lord's business with sack and horse to the markets of Dorking or Guildford he was given 1s. 0½d. expenses if he could not return home within half a day. If he reaped the lord's corn, he had a rood of oats, one quarter-acre of wheat and one rood of barley for his trouble and he could have the lord's plough-team every other Saturday (or, if wet, on another day) for his own cultivation. William also kept 25 of his own sheep with the lord's two-year-old sheep and at his own expense folded them for 14 nights in the lord's sheepfold. For this he was entitled to one lamb, called a marking lamb, and the fleece of the wether sheep carrying the bell. Altogether the survey throws vivid light on a disintegrating medieval system of farming; some of the peasants might have actually welcomed the security and stability arising from a feudal paternalism. We also have a glimpse of farming at Wanborough in 1542. A little lightly-sown wheat was grown, but the main crop on the light soils was barley with some oats, sown at the rate of four bushels to the acre! Eight plough-oxen and a large sheep flock of over 800, including lambs, were kept.[15]

At this time the four great hollow lanes and several smaller ones crossing the sandstones between Pitch Hill and Winterfold Common and running more or less straight for several miles to the villages of Shere and Gomshall were in regular use, as they had been for centuries and as they were to continue, for moving across difficult country until comparatively recent times. The widest is the Windmill Hollow ('The Ride Way' which is now metalled and is the most direct route between Ewhurst and Peaslake, Gomshall, Shere and Albury. One of the narrowest is 'Horse Block Hollow', a former pack-horse road to Cranleigh. This mesh of trackways, foreshadowing the second-class roads and bridle ways of today, were the arteries along which men moved from the manorial headquarters of Shere and Gomshall for millennia, sometimes very slowly, driving swine into the depths of the Surrey Weald, collecting weary stragglers on their return in autumn around Oakwood and Wallis Wood; sometimes faster when mounted with sacks bound for the markets of Horsham, Dorking and Guildford. Generations of carters and wagoners, too, would have known the tedious ascents that might take them two hours to reach the Winterfold or Leith

61 *Sixteenth-century barn at Nursecombe, Surrey.*

Hill district, when they would be overtaken by free tenants and gentry making frequent court-going visits to manors on the banks of the Tillingbourne. There is also the network of grass lanes from the clean chalk of the Downs to the sandstones leading into the more important arteries, which would have been busy with local traffic.

A rental of 1559 throws much light on farming in Kent on the lean soils around Wrotham, Stansted, Hale, Wynfield, Nepacre, Borough Green and Roughway.[16] There were 103 tenants of the manor of Wrotham on these lands, of whom 18 were gentry. Two persons had holdings larger than 200 acres; eight held between 199 and 99 acres; and eight, between 98 and 49 acres. 24 tenants held between 48 and 97 acres and 11 were smallholders. Almost all tenants had gardens and held parcels of orchard and meadow. Many had small hemp plots (hemphaughs) which were suited to the sandy loam and old meadows. The hemp was presumably worked up locally into ropes, cables and huckaback towelling. Several fulling mills were operating on the bournes. A good deal of the land was described as parcels of *riddens* (a word derived from *ridde*, meaning land taken in from the waste and grubbed for agriculture) which implies that it was first taken into cultivation during the rise in population of the 13th and early 14th centuries. All holdings had a multiplicity of small fields. Christopher Alleyn, for example, who held 74 acres, dispersed them in 27 parcels, averaging only 2.75 acres each. This was probably Allen's Farm in Plaxtol. Thomas Cransden of Stansted occupied his 37-acre Romenlys Farm (now doubtless Rumney Farm) in nine parcels, and this was typical. Wrotham at this period was still a market.

The Estate Book of the Camer estate at Meopham gives agricultural information between 1726-54.[17] This belonged to the Smith Masters family who had settled in Meopham at Camer (Kemmer) from the 16th century at least and built Camer House in the 18th century. Katherine, the last of the Masters, married William Smith of Croydon, a brewer, in 1748. Numerous small purchases of land made in the first half of the 18th century were mostly in gavelkind. A typical entry reads: 'three-eighths part of the whole, being in the hands of the late John Rickman, Richard and Edward Meades, purchased of the three sons of Thomas, William and Henry Meades. The farmer was concerned to produce as much timber for farm purposes as possible. One shaw was grubbed up and several fields combined into one but basically the old field pattern continued and new shaws were planted up at the tail ends of fields. 'At about 1724 I planted about 1 acre 3 roods with ash.' He continued: '1740 planted with ash a corner of a field, will be hop poles in 13 years; 1743, 60 or 70 perches planted with ash; 1745 chestnut on 3 roods at end of a field; 1749 planted part of a field with ash and some chestnut and willow; 1751 planted ash at the bottom of Sheeplands; 1752 planted another corner of a field with ash; 1754 planted part of a field; 1755 planted willow, to be felled to make hurdles and gates, "it being a wappy sort"; crabs planted in hedgerows at the same time.' His old hedges were evidently grubbed up and became quicks. Meanwhile the farmer was paying close attention to his stock of bees and fruit. In 1742 he planted 'some very good sorts of cherry' and again in 1744, and followed it up for four successive years from 1747. He sowed trefoil in a three-year ley and purchased his Red Wheat seed from Hertfordshire. His fallows received four ploughings and heavy dunging.

Industry

The 16th and early 17th centuries was also the heyday of the local iron industry. The most striking effect in the landscape, apart from the hammer-ponds which supplied water to the forges and furnaces, is the surface of the commons 'furrowed as though a great plough had been drawn along'.[18] These gullies were adits varying from 10 to 40 feet deep and of various lengths, made in quest of thin bands of iron ore in the Folkestone Beds, the scars being now veiled by heather. (For further details see Brandon, *The Kent and Sussex Weald*.)

In the 16th century the woollen cloth trade shrank to the towns and villages of the south-west on the fast-flowing river Wey or its many tumbling tributaries. Guildford in the reign of Elizabeth I became 'one of the chiefest towns for making kerseys in England' and cloth made in south-west Surrey and Sussex was marketed as 'cloths of Guildford'. The aulnage returns for 1574 indicate that Godalming had then 39 clothiers, rather fewer than Guildford, Farnham 15 and Petworth 11, and their outlying villages such as Ash, Shere, Stoke, Wonersh and Lodsworth had some trade. The aulnage returns for the 1570s show that Guildford was the largest centre of cloth manufacture, closely followed by Godalming and that Farnham and Lodsworth and Petworth in Sussex were in the second rank.[19] Objections in the reign of Elizabeth I were made to the proposal to make Wonersh a clothing town on the grounds that it was 'an outlandish' place

62 *A former clothier's cottage, Shere, a former cloth-working village.*

of farmers and husbandmen with few houses suitable for clothiers and that it lay between Guildford and that town's supply of wood fuel which would be diminished if cloth was manufactured at Wonersh.[20]

By the early 17th century decay had set in.[21] In 1619 George Abbot, Archbishop of Canterbury and a native of Guildford, endowed the Hospital of the Blessed Trinity to alleviate the town's distress. This fine brick building, reminiscent of an early Tudor gatehouse, still survives with little alteration. It is likely that members of his extended family were in the cloth trade because three Guildford clothiers bore the surname Abbot. In 1629 a petition submitted to the Privy Council by destitute Surrey clothworkers led to instructions to magistrates to organise parish collections for relief. There was a second petition on the same lines in 1636 when it was reported that the imprisonment of Samuel Vassel, a London merchant, had disrupted the trade of cloth to Ragusa (Dubrovnik), then, apparently, the chief outlet for the Surrey manufacturers. Meanwhile

63 *Crossways Farm, near Abinger, early 17th century.*

attempts were made to increase the wages of clothworkers and a compromise was reached on legislation introduced in the reign of Philip and Mary regarding the length of fulled cloth.

At the end of Elizabeth's reign a series of poor harvests prompted concern that the expanding cultivation of woad for dyestuffs would prejudice tillage for corn.[22] The Returns collected in 1585 by justices for the government from the clothmaking area around Guildford made several objections to woad growing. It was alleged that as four persons to an acre were employed weeding the crop between the end of May and Michaelmas and in cutting and grinding the plant, farmers would have difficulty in finding harvesters for their corn. After three years' cropping it was said that the soil was exhausted and would take seven years to recover, when it was merely poor pasture.[23] Another critic remarked that every two acres under woad meant a loss of four acres of corn because farmers put their best land under the new crop.[24] Yet another was concerned that the men and women working together in the woad fields 'very lewdliedly used bushes and hedges'.[25] For a discussion on the implications of woad growing see Joan

64 *Hospital of the Blessed Trinity, Guildford, founded by Archbishop Abbot in the reign of James I to alleviate distress amongst clothworkers.*

Thirsk.[26] Worries in Surrey at the decay of tillage in the early 17th century were unfounded according to landowners and farmers threatened with penalties for not ploughing up their lands. They insisted that there was then no want of corn but of pasture and cattle 'for much woodland and barren grounds are become fruitful cornlands'.[27]

Aubrey reported that in 1684 Farnham, which had a hundred weavers a century earlier (clearly an exaggeration), had none then.[28] Heavy woollen manufacture was also dying at Guildford and Godalming. Taste in clothing was changing from long staples of wool, which needed combing by men, towards short wool for worsteds carded by women. A small worsted production began in Godalming and a flourishing stocking industry grew up later.[29] Farnham became a great corn market when legislation by the Stuarts and Commonwealth prevented new markets within 40 miles of London. Farnham was just outside this limit and trade later grew in hops. Where the cloth industry was important the houses are often distinguished by their comparatively large first-floor windows which lighted the loom, or wide overhanging upper rooms which provided additional space for weaving. Yet another device was a central balconied room set aside for weaving. Shere is a rewarding place for these features. Many a Surrey yeoman derived wealth and gentility from wool or cloth and his social enhancement was expressed in domestic architecture. The most celebrated example is Crossways Farm, Abinger, the brick-fronted home of a 17th-century wool merchant. The decline of the Kent cloth industry near Maidstone is discussed on p.119. Worsteds were made in Canterbury and Sandwich in the 17th century and lighter cloths were introduced under Elizabeth I. After the 1670s the silk industry, introduced by French refugees, flourished at Canterbury.

10

Industrial Evolution

Apart from mining and quarrying, two districts stand out as major industrial centres, both originating in the medieval cloth trade and then evolving into other forms of manufacture before finally closing down over a century ago. They were both sited at sources of convenient water power, namely on the rivers Loose and Len near Maidstone and on the river Tillingbourne in the Vale of Holmesdale in Surrey.

Maidstone

In the Maidstone district the decline of woollen manufacture was accompanied by religious persecution. Through long association with Protestant merchants abroad, particularly the Netherlands, weavers had acquired strong leanings towards nonconformity. At Maidstone the welcome granted to Protestant refugees had extended to giving them a church, St Faith's Chapel. The rapid spread of religious dissent led to a clash with Archbishop Laud who put severe restraints on nonconformists and eventually debarred Dutch settlers from worship in Maidstone. This caused their dispersal and the emigration of a number of Kentish clothworkers to Holland, some ultimately emigrating to America.

At the Restoration of the Stuart monarchy, the Act of Uniformity (1662) caused the ejection of the vicar of Maidstone and ten more ministers in the clothmaking district. The Conventicle Act (1664) forbade meetings of more than five persons for unauthorised religious worship. As a result, many local nonconformists were thrown into gaol, some left to die there, and others imprisoned for more than 20 years. The Quakers were harshly treated. Their founder, George Fox, visited Cranbrook in 1655, and after the Restoration a number of his followers were gaoled. Presbyterians and Baptists at Maidstone were also persecuted. One of the most influential Baptists was Simon Pine, a fuller of Tovil mill, who gave land in Tovil as a burial ground after the Declaration of Indulgence (1672) when they were able to gain a licence to worship there. The vicar of All Saints' Maidstone permitted work in the local fulling mills on Sundays until his ejection in 1643 when his Puritan successor forbade the practice.[1]

To walk downstream from Brishing near Maidstone is to encounter, one after another, the 13 watermills driven by the Loose stream and described by William Lambarde in 1570 as 12 fulling-mills and a corn mill, a density of mills only matched by that of the river Tillingbourne. This traverse takes one into Loose village, remarkable for the clear springs which flow rapidly down its streets to the wide water meadows that make the valley such a valuable open space today on the edge of expanding Maidstone. Another journey on foot down the river Len also reveals sites of fulling mills. It was to these mills that clothmakers of Cranbrook and surrounding villages in the Weald brought their cloth for finishing between the 14th and 17th centuries.

65 *Paper-making, 17th-century.*

The emergence of Maidstone as the main paper-making centre in 17th-century England and the rise of the two Whatmans, father and son, the greatest paper-makers in the country, has been recently demonstrated by Shorter.[2] He has shown that the first recorded paper-mill in Kent was in 1588 at Dartford and that by the 1680s the industry had spread to Eynsford and was spectacularly taking over former fulling-mills of the declining cloth trade near Maidstone. The distribution of Kentish paper-mills *c.*1740 is indicated on Fig. 66. Of the 25 mills, 14 were on streams near the county town, the river Len accounting for four, including the most famous of all, Turkey Mill, and the river Loose for five. On this evidence Balston concluded that Kent was close to being, if not actually, the most important white paper-making county in England.[3]

Early paper-makers needed a ready supply of rags as raw material and a market for their paper. They therefore sought places near large populations such as London. In 1711 paper at Turkey Mill was made from rags brought by 'straggling persons' chiefly from London: the best was made into white paper; the inferior, mixed with old ropes and sails, was used to make wrapping paper. They also needed pure spring water for producing high-quality paper and water-power such as was provided at fulling-mill sites. The conversion of a fulling-mill into a paper-mill was not difficult because the water-driven machinery for fulling consisted of great wooden hammers which beat the dirt out of cloth in a vertical movement, an operation similar to that of stampers in paper-mills producing pulp. Thus fulling mills were easier to convert into paper-mills than, say, a corn mill. In the manufacture of cheap brown paper the hammers could equally well be used to pulp rags for hand-made paper, the only process to be mechanised; and, even for a mill making high-grade paper which used more sophisticated pulp preparation, the acquisition of a fulling site was an immense capital asset. An embargo was placed on the import of French goods from 1678 and this, together with the wars that followed later, provided another stimulus to white paper-making in England.

James Whatman senior, a tanner's son from Boxley, married in 1740 the relict of Richard Harris, a paper-maker of Hollingbourne.[4] His son, James Whatman junior, inherited his father's mills on coming of age. At the age of 26 he was appointed High Sheriff of Kent. By 1785, when he had bought Turkey Mill on the river Len, he had established himself as England's foremost paper-maker. He had two daughters and no son. William Balston, aged 15 and a pupil at Christ's Hospital, became his protégée and, although on re-marriage Whatman had an heir, Balston succeeded him to found eventually his own paper-making dynasty. Whatman parted with his mills when in ill-health in 1794 and became a wealthy country gentleman residing at Vintners, a mansion near his works which became the basis of a considerable landed estate. He spent his last years adding to his

66 *Paper mills in the Maidstone District from the 17th/early 18th century.*

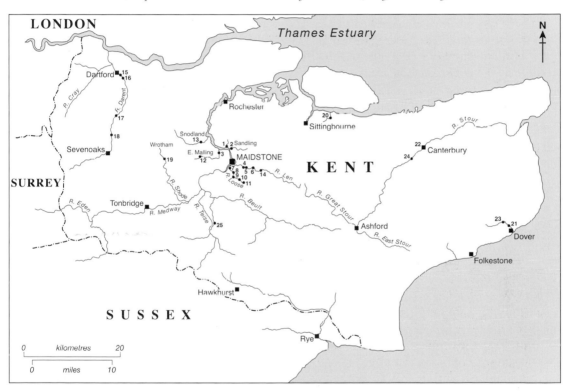

Maidstone area

1. Forstal Mill	Cossington Stream	White
2. Cobtree Mill	Sandling Stream	White?
3. Millhall Mill	East Malling Stream	White
4. Turkey Mill	River Len	White
5. Poll mill	River Len	White
6. Otham Mill	River Len	
7. Lower Tovil Mill	River Loose	
8. Lower Tovil Mill	River Loose	
9. Ivy Mill	River Loose	
10. Gurney's Mill	River Loose	White
11. Upper Mill	River Loose	
12. East Malling	East Malling Stream	
13. Snodland	Leybourne Stream	
14. Old Mill, Hollingbourne	River Len	White

West Kent

15. Dartford No.1 Mill	River Darent	White
16. Dartford No.2 Mill	River Darent	White
17. Eynesford Mill	River Darent	White
18. Shoreham Mill	River Darent	White
19. Basted Mill, Wrotham	River Shode	White

North Kent

20. Sittingbourne Mill		White

East Kent

21. Buckland Mill, Dover	River Dour	
22. Barton Mill, Canterbury	River Stour	White
23. River Mill, Dover	River Dour	
24. Chatham Mill	River Stour	White

South Kent

25. Goudhurst Mill	River Teise	
(may have been closed down by 1700)		

library and his notable collection of paintings and prints. In 1782 he paid £25 to Romney for his wife's portrait and subscribed to the octavo editions of Hasted's *Kent*. Like many employers after the French Revolution he was not immune from the many anxieties which afflicted well-to-do people and his fear of uprisings in England and even revolution induced him to hide a bag of guineas behind the door of a closet in his mansion. He evidently committed suicide in 1798, but whether it was from his ill-health, or the troubles of the age that preyed upon his mind, has never been determined. The tragedy that brought to an end such a distinguished career caused great grief amongst public figures in Kent.[5]

The Whatmans, together with a few others such as the Portals and William Lepard, brought the English paper industry to such excellence that it rivalled, or excelled, the French, Dutch and Italian. A correspondence Whatman junior would doubtless have treasured survives from A.C. de Poggi (undated) who noted Whatman's aim to raise the standard of English paper-making and to save great sums of money going out of the kingdom and congratulating him on a product 'far superior to French paper'.

67 *Site of Turkey Mill, Maidstone. This is now an industrial park. Paper-making continues at Springfield Mill nearby.*

The Whatman watermark conveyed such commercial prestige that it continued to be used long after James Whatman's sale of Turkey Mill in 1794. This came to light when Nabi Saheb wrote from India in 1946 regarding official documents held in an archive there bearing the watermark 'J Whatman, Turkey Mill, 1856'. Messrs Balston explained that two mills used Whatman watermarks after the sale of Turkey Mill, Hollingworths at Turkey Mill and Balston at Springfield Mill, until the latter secured sole rights in 1859 for £7,500.[6]

The world-famous watermark 'J Whatman' and its variants have themselves a most interesting history. James Wardrop of the Victoria and Albert Musem reported in 1935 that part of the autograph manuscript of Lamb's *Essays of Elia* was on blue laid paper watermarked 'Whatman'. He deduced that Lamb had written on the official stationery of the East India Company in whose employment Lamb was for the greater part of his life. Wardrop was also able to prove that falsification of the Whatman watermarks had evidently occurred in revolutionary France. He also observed that Whatman had produced the famous 'Antiquara' hand-made paper for the Society of Antiquaries of London in 1775 and that his letter regarding the mould was still held by the Society. Wardrop continued to hunt down Whatman watermarks and found that J. Hills's great botanical work *The Vegetation System*, published in parts 1760-1770, had been watermarked 'J Whatman' two years earlier than the formerly accepted date. Subsequently further important books and documents have been found to bear the watermark.[7]

Paper-making on the Loose and Len rivers is now almost as defunct as the old fulling industry, although the industry continues in a modern form at Springfield Mill, Balston's old mill. In 1839 numerous mills were still working but they closed down from competition from London and not one is now in work. The properties are mainly bought for the residential use of the mill-house, the derelict mill itself being demolished. The history of Upper Mill is not untypical. It was certainly a paper-mill in 1726. In 1774 James Whatman occupied it and Messrs Thomas Hollingworth followed. About 1850 it was converted to a water-powered corn mill until 1890 when a new mill was built alongside, equipped with a 12hp steam beam engine which closed in 1908. In 1689 Gurney's Mill, a former fulling-mill, was occupied by William Harris, papermaker. It was later in the possession of the Hollingworths until Henry Gurney bought it to make millboard. This also closed in 1908 so suddenly that 'everything was just as it was left, even down to the pennies on the office desks, the correspondence littered about, pens still in ink pots and quantities of account books on the shelves'. Great Ivey Mill was associated with a paper-maker from 1685 and became a prominent paper-mill until closed down just after the First World War. J. Barcham Green continued the tradition of producing beautiful hand-made paper at Hayle Mill into the 1960s, but the mill is now derelict. After Whatman, Turkey Mill made paper for the descendants of the Hollingworths until it was sold to Wiggins Teape who closed it down in 1976.[8] The site is now a Business Park, home to more than 45 companies employing *c*.500 people and was a National Landscape Award winner.

The Tillingbourne Valley

Paper-making was introduced into the valley when the Lower Works of the gunpowder mill at Chilworth were converted for this purpose and paper-making continued at two mills there until 1870. At the end of the 18th century, one of the Chilworth paper-makers, Charles Ball, took over the former corn mill at Albury Park and rebuilt it as a paper mill. When the original Albury settlement was moved to Weston Street downstream, Ball erected for his sons two new paper-mills at Postford (at a site used to power gunpowder mills) which continued operations until 1875. Earlier John Aubrey referred to two paper mills at Godalming in his *History*, written mainly in the 1670s. These appear to have been sections of Catteshall and Eashing mills which were converted to paper-making. Aubrey also writes that in the reign of James I coarse paper, commonly called whited brown paper, was first made in England, especially in Surrey and around Windsor. Around 1630 a paper-mill was erected at Stoke by Guildford.

The Tillingbourne mills eventually produced banknote paper. At the beginning of the French Revolution, the Count of Artois, afterwards Charles X, King of France, who is said to have lived at Shalford Rectory during his exile, attempted to undermine the Republic by forging assignats issued as worthless paper currency by means of bank notes with the same watermarks as the French currency from Charles Ball of Albury Park Mill, who did not discover his patron's role until after the event. Ball also printed Russian bank-note paper until he discovered the fact and was indemnified for the loss of his order by the Emperor of Russia. William Cobbett, who wanted to do away with paper-money (and gunpowder, too), which he linked to rising prices and a huge volume of National Debt, made his famous diatribe about 'the means of misery spreading over an entire nation' in 1822 when he passed through the Tillingbourne valley on the way to Evelyn's garden at Albury, the only redeeming factor in the situation to him being the rags which had been turned into his political journal *The Register*.

The sites of the paper- and other mills in the valley have been used in very different ways. Unwin Brothers occupied Chilworth Mill as a printing works until a fire in 1895 when they removed to Old Woking, where they still remain. The adjacent gunpowder works closed after the First World War. Some of the ruined buildings can be viewed from the footpath which follows the route of the former tramway along the wooded valley. The old waterwheel of Postford Lower Mill has been replaced for historical purposes by an overshot waterwheel

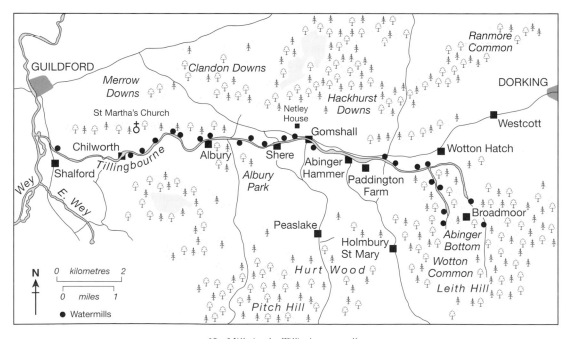

68 *Mills in the Tillingbourne valley.*

69 *George Mote's* Abinger Mill *(1883).*

from Clandon Park, the estate of Lord Onslow.[9] The former corn mill at Albury, vacated by the Botting family, is now a scientific laboratory. The attractive early 18th-century Shalford Mill, with its projecting upper storeys carried on wooden pillars, was worked as a corn mill until the First World War. Together with its equipment and internal waterwheel it was restored by a secret society known as Ferguson's Gang and presented to the National Trust in 1932. (Clough Williams-Ellis has been identified as 'Ferguson'.) Gomshall Mill has recently undergone restoration and is now a restaurant. Gomshall Tannery, which continues one of the traditional industries of the valley, now converts imported sheep skins into suedes. At the head of the valley, the mill-pond and cluster of cottages at Friday Street and Abinger Hammer are amongst the most picturesque spots in Surrey.

II

Sir John Evelyn of Wotton

Although the life, work and character of Sir John Evelyn (1681-1763) of Wotton have been totally eclipsed by his diarist grandfather, the central figure in Restoration gardening and planting, they serve to illuminate contemporary problems on southern English estates which were far from special to Wotton and also throw light on the new owner's changes in landscape design which brought the estate into the forefront of places devoted to early 18th-century naturalistic landscaping and brought Wotton renewed acclaim.

Evelyn's particular problem was that Wotton, at the foot of Leith Hill, had been largely stripped of its trees, 'its only best and proper husbandry the estate is capable of' in the diarist's own words, and was no longer the 'delicious seat' in charming grounds that had made it famous. The diarist's brother George, the previous owner of Wotton, had ranged the axe widely on trees planted by his father Richard to provide a marriage jointure for one of his daughters and to pay off some of his debts.[1] By the terms of his own inheritance, which was not until 1699, the diarist had been obliged to make generous provision for his brother George's grandchildren and for his only surviving child, his daughter Moll, who was understandably frustrated that as a female she could not inherit Wotton. The exceptional storm of 1703 had also taken its toll of trees. Thus the diarist only saved Wotton for his family at the expense of its trees. As he stated publicly, Wotton (i.e. Woodtown) was no more, being stripped and naked and ashamed of its own name. Privately, Evelyn grieved at this embarrassment and felt humiliated at the ironical circumstance of owning an estate which bore all the marks of over-felled woodland he publicly deplored in successive editions of *Sylva*, in which his tree-planting campaign had made him a national hero equivalent to another Virgil and which today marks him as the first of 'The Men of the Trees'.[2]

Evelyn's solution to the crisis was obsessively to train his young successor in his notion of estate manager.[3] The son of an ailing father who died young 'as a promising failure', as the diarist put it, was brought up from boyhood to bring renewed honour to Wotton and the family name. Even in his early teens the boy was urged to save presents of money 'towards the new building of Wotton' and he was furnished with excellent advice on the most appropriate form of estate management. The grandson never betrayed the trust placed upon him. By training, inclination and temperament he came to share in most of his grandfather's intellectual enthusiasm and he inherited much of his personality, notably a natural diffidence of manner and lack of ostentation. Everything he did at Wotton – his practical forestry, his building and landscaping, the keepership of the diarist's library and manuscripts, and his scientific and archaeological interests – reflects with the intensity of a mirror his deep attachment to Wotton and a life-long concern to do his best for it.

With frugality the grandson survived the lean years when he had little money to run the estate until his sales of timber began to alter the situation some 20 years later.[4] Although comprising 7,500 acres, the estate was mostly on poor soils. The low rents of the first two decades of the 18th century went against him and he found it difficult at first to maintain the gardens and grounds in good repair, still less to undertake much in the way of necessary improvements. The loss of his junior government post on the death of Queen Anne obliged him to reduce expenditure still further. At this time he wrote to his gardener expressing the hope that he would be 'very careful with his seeds and not want any more this great while; what I have now sent coming to a pretty deal of money'. A little later he ordered his bailiff 'to reduce the expense of the garden as much as is convenient with its being kept in pretty good order'. His financial stringency seems to have put paid to gardening on the lavish Brompton Park style of London and Wise. The latter sent him plants from Hampton Court and London came twice yearly as a consultant and had sent a skilled assistant to prune the fruit trees, who was conveyed by mail coach to Epsom, the remainder of the journey being by an estate vehicle. The bailiff was instructed to find out his diet and offer what the house affords, together with some strong beer now and then.[4] London's imminent arrival led to the order that he was to be treated in the best manner the bailiff was able. Evelyn had to curtail such expenditure later but nevertheless a weekly hamper, bursting with produce and also containing ready cash secreted amongst it to elude highwaymen, together with a letter giving details of estate work carried out in the previous week, made its regular arrival at the Evelyns' London house.[5]

Meanwhile Evelyn's primary concern was planting up the depleted estate and in this he proved to be a practical woodman of the first order, transforming the estate – rather like Earl Bathurst at Cirencester Park or Lord Bessborough at Stansted, Sussex – into a forest with rides and walks rather than of open grounds streaked with woods and coppices. His improving hand was everywhere: thinning neglected coppice; trimming boughs of standing trees; planting roadside trees for shade and beauty; and replenishing hedgerows with timber. His overall aim was to grow nurseries of trees so as to transplant seedlings on areas cleared previously and to extend timber onto worn out fields where none had previously existed.

Representative extracts from his bailiff's weekly letters and Evelyn's journal throw light on these developments:

1707   Thinning out in Deerleap Wood.
1709   Robert Lane (the gardener) transplanted 'above 500 trees of several sorts into the hedgerows and more intended'.
1710   Walks near the House re-laid with elm.

1712   Re-planted Pasture Wood (several hundred acres).

1714   Re-planted Heathy Lane Wood (250 acres).

1719   Paid Arge (a tenant) for saving trees in a hedgerow at Hoopwick Farm, he was not obliged to.

1722   Planted 300 young saplings on Garrot Hill (on high ground near Leith Hill) and 'about 3,000 more are needed'.

1724   Began planting at Noones (an arboretum at Friday Street mill-pond).

1729   Visited West End Farm below Leith Hill (tenant farm) and saw in a coppice not above two acres at least 1,000 tellers.

1730   The 'account of timber' above the hill (i.e. on the sandy flanks of Leith Hill) showed towards the end of his afforestation, oaks, 6,153; beech, 2,907; ash, 589; elm, 114; oak tellers, 3,000. Below the hill the figures were 4,972, 841, 849 and 320 respectively and tellers numbered more than 20,000.[6]

By 1736 fir plantations on Leith Hill extended over 19 acres. John Rocque's map of Surrey on a scale of six inches to one mile gives a good impression of the afforestation towards the end of Evelyn's planting career which brought trees into former fields on both sides of the River Tillingbourne downstream of the mill-hamlet of Friday Street and on the branch of the same stream at Broadmoor and across the intervening ridge, as well as up to Leith Hill. lt also provides evidence that in his plantings Evelyn was evidently strongly influenced by Stephen Switzer's 'rural extensive and forest gardening' into an extensive forest

70 *Sir John Evelyn's serpentining of the River Tillingbourne at Wotton.*

with rides, walks and glades cut out of it, advocated in his *Ichnographia Rustica* (1718, 1742). Switzer urged that 'The pleasures of a country life cannot possibly be contained within the narrow limits of the greatest garden; woods, fields and distant enclosures would have the care of the industrious and laborious planter'. It is also noteworthy that Evelyn followed Switzer's recommendation to raise a nursery of trees to stock and plant the 'exterior parts' of the estate. Unfortunately no visual evidence in the form of a sketch or painting has survived to show the care Evelyn took in varying the shapes and colouring of his trees and the skill by which he massed them. His interest in the chestnut, until the 1730s rarely planted in English hedgerows, is an indication of his concern for variety and repeatedly his collection was enhanced both economically and aesthetically with seeds of exotics obtained from America and the West Indies. His delight in the noble view of St Paul's some 24 miles away determined the steep, west-facing slopes above Friday Street as one of his major arboreta and a grove of beech nearby in which seats were erected had a special significance for his family because the diarist had successfully saved them from his brother's axe.

Evelyn's nurseries became so celebrated that he supplied many thousands of trees to neighbouring estates which were adopting his own landscaping example. Wotton should thus be seen as one of the mainsprings of a landscaping movement which eventually modified much of Surrey and the entire character of rural England. As early as 1715 Evelyn had supplied 3,400 beech from his own raising to John Parker of Neden. By 1723 he was growing both beech and fir from seed and had supplied large quantities to Sir Edward Nicholas of East

71 *Friday Street, a 'mill village' in the 16th and 17th centuries, which became one of the most popular 'honey-pots' last century. See pp.208-9.*

72 *Portrait of King George II engrossed on a deed relating to Fairlawne, Shipbourne.*

Horsley. King George I's estates were also in receipt of trees from Wotton as was Henry Pelham's Esher Place and Thomas Moore's Polesden Lacey where he was carrying out extensive alterations between 1735 and 1748. In some instances gifts of trees and plants were exchanged. For example, Revell of Fetcham sent Evelyn a gift of Spanish acorns which was reciprocated by a gift of Scotch fir. The longest lasting connection between Wotton and another 'improving' estate was with the Duke of Newcastle's Claremont at Esher. Between 1731, when an annual despatch of tree plants to the Duke was already an established custom, and 1746 there was scarcely a year when Claremont was not supplied with trees by Evelyn. In 1731, for instance, the Duke of Newcastle's gardener was supplied with 1,000 chestnuts and on other occasions with two hundred or more beech and oak. Evelyn had good cause to boast to Sir Edward Nicholas that 'for fir seed in my opinion you need go no farther than the trees of my own raising [these] being to the best of my observation as flourishing as any I have seen in this country'. These annual consignments of trees to Claremont resulted in a letter from the Duchess to Lady Evelyn which is a model of patrician brevity:

March 12 1739/40

Dear Madam

I am really quite ashamed of what I'm going to ask but the Duke of Newcastle has the courage enough to beg Sir John Evelyn would be so good to let him have ten or a dozen more pretty large Scotch firs from Wotton and if he comply's

with this request, the Duke of Newcastle begs he would send his orders to the gardener, because this is the time they are to be planted. I think when people are unreasonable, the less they say for themselves the better, therefore I wish only to ask your pardon and spare you, dear Madam, much.
From your faithful servant
    Newcastle

A keynote of Evelyn's forestry and gardening was his conscious attempt to harmonise design with local scenery. In this he was probably the first to take the Surrey hills as a leading motif. Leith Hill, which lay on his estate, had a profound influence on his plantings. Its commanding view of the South Downs and the intervening Weald was becoming better known with the new passion for prospects of 'extensive and variegated views'. The 'hill' or 'prospect' poem had become well established since Sir John Denham's 'Cooper's Hill' and Claude's paintings were the most popular prospects in painted scenery. By definition 'landskip' had become synonymous with prospect and John Dennis remarked of the view from Leith Hill in 1717 that it was superior to any he had seen in the Roman Campagna or elsewhere in Italy.

Sir John Evelyn's own delighted preoccupation with the open, splendidly arranged natural scenery of the Weald displayed from the great hill ranges of the region is evident in the repeated emphasis in his journal of the 'surprise' excited in him by the contemplation of the grandeur of immense sweeps of space afforded from his estate. In this pleasure the special fascination with his 'own' Leith Hill is also very evident. His visit to Syon House at Isleworth in 1722, for example, was made specially memorable by the view from the gallery 'which leads in a delicate prospect into Surrey as far as Leith Hill which I could plainly discern'. Of a visit to Secretary Cecil's old mansion and garden at Wimbledon in the same year his journal entry is confined to his admiration for the 'great view' from the terrace towards Leith Hill and Box Hill. An earlier instance of his love of scanning extensive panoramas was in 1720 when he observed of a tenant's farmhouse that it had 'one of the largest and finest prospects I ever saw, being situated on a hill which looks down upon the town of Dorking and as far as the South Downs and twenty miles off into Kent'. In 1728 Newlands Corner was visited for the sake of its views and in 1729 the fine prospect of Richmond Hill was appreciated from the Duke of Argyle's villa at Petersham. Evelyn also indulges in frequent descriptions of natural scenery, whether 'wild' or 'picturesque'. For example, of a view near Guildford in 1748 he writes '... I was pleased with the prospect St Catherine's Hill afforded me. If I have a right notion of a landscape it wants nothing but hanging rocks and that in some measure is remedied by two large chalk pits'. In such statements lies the genesis of the Picturesque amongst the Hanoverian gentry.[6]

This influence of prospect upon him is very apparent in his lay-out of outlying parts of his estate where the controlling features were the walks of Scots pine aimed on the distant but ever beckoning horizon of the South Downs. These were connected with the conjoined plantations of deciduous trees and the diarist's formal garden about Wotton House itself with alleys lined with elm and chestnut. The outcome was not so much geometrical as a pattern of 'naturalized' avenues on irregular courses related to the natural beauties of the site. They were a departure from the long accepted cosmopolitan style favouring exact geometry: in a departure from precedent, Evelyn's tree-lined walks and rides possess the landscape without dominating it. They are not aligned on the highest point of Leith Hill (which Evelyn later leased to Col Foliot of Leith Hill Place who built the famous tower) but to a focal point slightly north-west in order to converge on a horse road serving the estate's claylands 'below the hill', itself laid out for convenience and pleasure. Another notable feature was winding rides on the peripheries of his woods which formed a continuous circuit and brought one back to one's starting point, again designed for utility as well as recreation. Evelyn's walks on the outlying parts of the estate were lined by platoons (Fr. *peloton*), square clumps of 10 to 12 firs planted within small cattle-proof enclosures and sited at uniform intervals of 25 to 30 yards. Within each enclosure the firs were planted in rows analogous to the 'hollow square' disposed by a body of musketeers. When Arthur Young observed them on a visit to Wotton in 1793 he attributed them wrongly to Sir Frederick Evelyn, Sir John's immediate successor. He would seem to be remarking on the former's re-plantings of fir in the enclosures for in Sir John's journal and in the weekly letters from staff there is ample earlier evidence of the gradual construction of the original enclosures to Leith Hill. Thus in October 1727 Evelyn records: 'Cut out a circle on the common of 200 foot diameter, for my great walk of clumps of firs was to be continued'. This site can be identified with that on the southern edge of Abinger Common where Rocque shows inter-connecting vistas. These 'new walks on the common' were still being laid out four years later, and 'fir planting on the common' was still continuing as late as 1745, indicating that Evelyn was employing the minimum of labour on his improvements. Objects to embellish views from the walks were added sparingly. In 1738 gardeners were preparing timbers for an ornamental building to be set up opposite the Great Walk but there is no further reference to this eye-catcher. The summit of Leith Hill was planted with 'Nagansey' trees in 1730 and several species of fir were subsequently planted there. These were to be the prototype of landscape increasingly laid on the common lands in the valley of the Tillingbourne between Dorking and Guildford. Throughout this period, Evelyn was selecting keynote elements in his landscape: bluffs, ridges, summits, ponds, river banks and similar places of picturesque or romantic character and accentuating their beauty with trees and, occasionally, buildings.

When his layout of walks and rides was largely completed, Evelyn turned his attention to the final phase of his landscaping which was to introduce winding rivulets and cascades. His earliest work was between *c.*1736 and 1740 which makes it one of the earliest in the country – rather later than the 'digging of a river' at Castle Howard in 1732 and perhaps Kent's similar experiment at Lord Burlington's Chiswick Villa but rather earlier than his more mature work at Rousham. The decisive influence on Evelyn's water features appears to have been the works for the Earl of Carlisle at Castle Howard, for Evelyn made two visits there in 1732, when he observed the serpentine river under construction, and again in 1738, when his 'own river' was being serpentined. He was also doubtless familiar with similar work at Riskins, Middlesex, which he also occasionally visited. Basically, his 'New River' was a reconstructed course of the upper River Tillingbourne which was made to flow over an artificially constructed waterfall below Friday Street and a series of low falls between fish-ponds. At the same time the branch of the stream flowing from the Broadmoor valley was also serpentined. The work involved enlarging the bed of the river and cutting its course in a more winding and irregular manner through sheets of gravel, work which was under way by November 1736 when Evelyn wrote to his bailiff: 'I forgot in my letter to set down carrying on the serpentine river in the meadow ...'. Progress was slow. He again wrote from London in August 1737: 'Since there is no want of men, I hope you have employed as many as could work in the meadow these fine days.' In May 1738 stone quarried from Westgate Heath was being laid down for the waterfalls at which time Jacobsen's construction of an artificial cascade and falls on his neighbouring property was also influencing Evelyn's own fastidious stone- and brick-work.[7]

By 1740 Evelyn's most active period as landscapist was over, although he was left with nearly a quarter of a century to enjoy the fruits of his work. He had not failed to carry out the injunction of his grandfather to 'Restore the Name of Wotton, otherwise in danger to be lost and forgotten'.[8] His woods, some of his trees and his rivers remain but not his walks which today are traceable only on old maps and by the existence on the ground of the 'fir pounds', the purpose of which has been forgotten locally. Thus the Wotton landscape has come to bear two quite different states of the Evelyn imagination. The diarist's strong sensibility in the mid-17th century to Italian landscapes in the Inigo Jones tradition was to be complemented by his grandson's receptivity to Wealden nature itself in one of its most dramatically contrived examples of the 18th century.

12

The Farmer and the Landowner, 1750-1880

Introduction

This period witnessed a dramatic rise in the population of England and Wales. Gregory King reckoned it to be 5½ million in 1688; it had risen to nine million by the first census in 1801, to 16 million in 1851 and to nearly 23 million in 1871. This dramatic increase required spectacular innovations in agriculture, which attracted widespread European attention, to feed and clothe the people of London and the new industrial towns and cities. This averted the dearths of the 18th and early 19th centuries which had evoked the spectre of famine and the danger to security resulting from rising food imports.

This period was the heyday of English agriculture.[1] All classes, from the monarch and aristocracy downwards, responded as positively to the call for increased food as when the Kaiser's and Hitler's submarines sank merchant vessels during wartime in the next century. In our region the main thrust for improvement came from yeomen farmers who had for generations demonstrated their prowess in husbandry to a point beyond comparison with most parts of England. The contemporary agricultural writer Arthur Young praised these men of modest property for their efforts and ranked them above all others. He was especially critical of the aristocrat's attention to husbandry:

73 *Arthur Young, Secretary to the Board of Agriculture, editor of the Annals and a life-long publicist for the improvement of British agriculture.*

He resides in London with great splendour and expense for eight months of the year and when in the country has little interest apart from his morning's ride. Few bear a winter's residence in the country, can find amusement in viewing every part of their estate, in cherishing good tenants, in beautifying their neighbourhood by substantial farmhouses, convenient yards, comfortable cottages. Would to heaven

134

we had more such men who work their small properties. They are more valuable among the great, and all the mob of ministers, statesmen, orators and heroes at whose shrine the baser part of mankind are so ready to bend the knee.[2]

This savage indictment against the aristocracy is not fully merited because some of its members performed sterling service to English agriculture at this time, including 'Turnip' Townshend and the Duke of Bedford, but a fuller investigation of the contribution of the class in general may prove Young correct.

It is an irony of history that the men of the most modest holdings were to be inexorably squeezed out of existence by bigger farmers and landowners as the period progressed. In parishes all over the region the small men who typified the rural scene with farmhouses in village streets, and who still sometimes held land in common-fields and grazed the commons up to the early 19th century, had virtually disappeared by 1880. This trend was reinforced by government policy towards agriculture which committed support to larger farmers on the presumption that it was they who were most innovative in agriculture and uniformly grew more corn, beef and mutton per acre than those of small capital. John Boys of Betteshanger in Kent and the author of *A General View of the Agriculture of the County of Kent* considered that the smaller farmers in general worked themselves much harder and fared worse than labourers and journeymen mechanics, but he was inclined to believe that the exertions of the larger farmers, generally speaking, made the land more productive than smaller farmers did, tended to lower the price of provisions and increase population through their employment of large numbers of labourers. He conceded that a number of small farms on a given tract of land would have probably reared more poultry and produced more eggs, and perhaps more butter, than one farmer on the same quantity of land.[3] In this respect he was following the line of the Board of Agriculture. This policy explains the General Enclosure Act of 1801 which was designed to hasten the demise of small farmers. Farm labourers enjoyed a higher standard of living up to the end of war in 1815 but suffered distress during the period of the Swing Riots, when post-war farming declined with the peace until it revived from the 1840s.[4] Their wages, however, did not rise proportionately to the prosperity of farmers and landowners and the indifference to their poverty is a stain on Victorian society.

Not all parts of the North Downs and their adjacent hills, of course, responded equally to the general trend of agricultural improvement because some had more potential than others or had more enthusiastic farmers. The wealth of government reports, notably the County Reports of the Board of Agriculture and of the various Commissions into the state of English agriculture during the 19th century, together with the Tithe Survey of 1840-3 plus detailed estate and ordnance maps, has made differences between farming districts clearer. The greater awareness of these differences led to an appreciation of 'natural districts' which in the hands of William Marshall became a primary tool for explanations of the differing pattern of farming across the country. For William Cobbett this diversity of English farming was the very basis of his descriptions of the rural scene in his *Rural Rides*. If we travel, as it were, with Arthur Young we encounter him witnessing the extreme of agricultural development on the Isle of Thanet, one of the most productive districts in the country, and at Abinger in Surrey, singularly picturesque and romantic, but from a farming point of view a blank, for much of the land was in a state of total uncultivation in 1794. He thought that the deserts which foreigners were amazed to find so near the Colossus of London could be converted to arable with dunghills. Mercifully it has remained a gloriously unproductive countryside.[5]

Kent Farming

One of the jewels in the crown was the Kentish portion of the Vale of Holmesdale. We have already mentioned George Buckland's apt description of it (p.30) and its soil was as diversified as its farming.[6] Immediately at the foot of the chalk ridge was dry fertile land easily tilled though intermixed with flints' 'stone-hatters'. The Gault Clay which followed was surly, ill-tempered stuff, requiring six horses to plough it, but it produced good crops of wheat, beans, clover, tares and oats. Its hops, grown on sunny slopes, fetched high prices in the Borough Market. Waring's Imperial Green hop, raised by Mr Waring at Shoreham in the rich Darent valley nearly a century earlier, and 'Colgate' raised by Buckland's father at Chevening, from a single plant probably growing wild, were extensively cultivated.

The mid-Kent district around Maidstone was even more remarkable. Taking its range of agricultural productions together, there was no place in England to compare with it. Every inch of soil in this aptly named 'Garden of England' was turned to profitable account. The management of its hedgerows was unsurpassed (a fact known to William Robinson, the famed gardener of Gravetye in Sussex who engaged Kentish men to lay out his own hedges there). Every nook uncultivated was planted with trees. Great efforts to improve the fertility of the soil were made from the 1840s and this, aided by the southern warmth of climate, allowed intensive farming on the double-cropping system to operate: for example, on land which, after root crops sown as late as mid-summer and fed to folded sheep, could be subsequently sown with wheat before Christmas with benefit from the dung. Another sign of intensive production was the growing of hops, filberts and apples in the same ground, the hops affording shelter to young trees. Pears were trained on south-facing walls. R.I. Braddick of Boughton Mount was celebrated for his knowledge of fruit and grafted numerous sorts on the same trees. The southern slope of the ragstone hills overlooking the Weald was the most favoured strip of land. The soil was provincially known as 'coomb', the debris of the sandstone hills mixed with Gault Clay. The land was so inherently rich and well maintained by enormous expenditure on various manures, including guano, that there was no regular rotation of the high-yielding crops. Double-harvests and the nearly two-thirds of home-grown fruit supplied to Covent Garden market meant that farmers lived in comparative comfort and happiness. Cottages were comfortable and roomy and labourers were better paid than in most other districts.

An example of improvement by a landowner determined to spare no expense in improving his whole farm was that of Lord Middleton at Teston who sent a widely publicised report to the Board of Agriculture. When he commenced to improve the farm the rent was 14s. an acre. This he was able to more than double. It was ill-managed and out of heart when he acquired it in 1770 but by dint of lavish manuring, draining and excellent arable husbandry over more than 25 years it produced prodigious yields of crops, great numbers of fat beasts, and became self-sufficient in hop poles.[7]

Another celebrated farming district was the Isle of Thanet. Its gentle chalk down swell was covered in a deep mantle of self-draining calcareous loam, so that no drains or ditches were needed. The Church institutions who held the land in the Middle Ages had spared no pains or cost to keep the land in good heart and this example had been followed ever since. The wide, open country was virtually treeless and exposed to the fury of the wind.

74 *Badlesmere Court Farm, near Faversham, an example of a Kentish yeoman's improved farmhouse of the 18th century.*

A large portion of the chalkland east of Canterbury – around Ash, Worth, Wingham and Preston – was mostly covered with a rich deep loam (derived from loess) of a variable nature, including the round, water-worn pebbles at Wingham called by local farmers 'sea drift', which was capable of producing under ordinary management the largest crops of the finest quality. Ash was singled out by Arthur Young as the most prosperous parish in Kent. This was the home of the famed 'Kentish Round-Course' system of husbandry based on a rotation of wheat, beans and barley, the land never fallowed[8] or the 'Norfolk Four-Course system of turnips, barley, clover and wheat, which was preferred by livestock farmers who folded sheep upon the fodder. The sheep were either Romney Marsh or the 'New Kents' which Richard Goord had originated on Colshall Farm near Milton from 1795. The use of a drill plough enabled hand-hoeing of crops to keep them absolutely free of weeds and so obviated the need for a fallow. After a heavy sea, farmers would be seen carting seaweed to manure their lands.

John Boys of Betteshanger published an important treatise on paring and burning, then the accepted method of improving downland for arable cultivation.[9] This practice was called Denshiring (from its reputed origin in Devonshire) and involved the cutting of the turf which was burnt to ashes and applied to the land. He demonstrated that this process of ploughing-up the sheep downs resulted not in a reduction of sheep and wool, as opponents of the practice believed, but actually supported more sheep on the extra fodder, in addition to the profits from arable cultivation. One of the Boys family, Henry Boys of Mailmans Farm near Betteshanger, was prosecuted by his landlord, the Revd Viscount Guildford, for an alleged under-payment of rent after improving Barville Down by paring and burning in 1835. He was acquitted of the charge by a jury. He had earlier encountered trouble from the noble clergyman who had prosecuted him for shooting game on his tenanted farm, but the fine was quashed on appeal. The outraged Henry, who recovered most of his costs from Lord Guildford, published an account of his misadventures, adding '... I do yet indulge in the hope (however vain that hope may be) that his Lordship's high station and Christian calling will prompt him to let me live in peace during the few years I am compelled to remain his tenant'. This appears to have had the desired result.[10]

The thinner chalk soils on the high downs and ragstone hills of Kent were not so productive. The expanses plastered with a stiff soil and literally covered with flints and stones ('cledge') were difficult and expensive to manage and in dry summers its cultivation was impracticable. Fallowing was necessary to rid the land of weeds. In places, as at Detling and Boxley, there were tracts of woodland of such very great extent as the Wealds of Surrey and Kent could not equal.

The crop book of the Camer estate at Meopham in 1823 gives full details of the operations during the farming year:

January Prepare clover seed and manure hop fields with sprats.

February Time for laying Cliffe marshes in readiness to taking Bullocks in May

March Sow barley, oats, peas, beans. Hoe out the soil for drills of Long Pod beans. Sow rye grass and Gupsham.

April Roll sainfoin. Roll wheat and harrow. Stir fallows, if dry, 9½ Vents to a rod (16½ feet) Clean yard. Roll tares, Dip sheep. Thatch buildings with reed. Pole hops. Cant wheat. Best time for making hurdles and gates. Dig couch out of beans, Finish rolling peas and beans, Hoe beans, weed wheat, hoe Potatoes, Nidget hops.

May Sow trefoil and sainfoin Send steer cattle and heifers into the marshes. Begin work on fallows, carry out dung, brush orchards.

June Hoe round hops and earth up. Break clods in hop grounds. Clear out barns.

July Carry out dung for turnips. Keep hedges brushed. Nidget Hops.

August Harvest turnips, cut oats, cut wheat and beans. Make and Mend hop bins. Brush off weeds on roads. Hoe beans before Harvest. Maintain buildings, paint wagons.

September Manure and plough tares gratten [stubble] for rye. 300 Loads of manure per acre. Sow rye. Dig up potatoes. Land up for wheat.

October Dig plantations. Carry out manure for wheat. Thresh and Sell beans and peas. Set hops. Sow wheat. Plant ash in Woods. Plant quicks and mend them.

November Begin to fell woods. Plough for beans. Fallow as soon as Wheat is in. Send for heifers and steers from marshes. Begin to feed off sheep on turnips Harrow in oat stubble. Catch rats in barns.

December Manure 15 loads an acre for spring wheat where the fold Was; 32 in other places. Get ware out of woods.

Explanation: 'landing up', ploughing heavy land in ridges to facilitate drainage. 'Gratten', stubble; 'laying marshes', removing weeds and improving drainage. Rye was customarily eaten off green as a crop by sheep in spring.

Further information was provided. A hop plantation of four to five acres required an oast 16 feet square. Winter tares were sown on wheat stubble ploughed once. Oats were sown on barley gratten at the end of August (a spring crop was also sown in February-April, a practice much impressing Arthur Young). Peas were invariably grown on wheat stubble. The sheep fold was placed over ground needed for wheat and turnips. In the park an old cedar still existed in 1900 which was thought to have been planted c.1700, one of the first in the country, and c.1850 a fir was sown from seed from India. Successors kept up tree planting; The Prince of Wales's wedding in 1863 was celebrated with Wellingtonia gigantea and the Jubilee of Queen Victoria in 1887 with Douglas and Scotch fir. These trees, with other plantings, are now accessible to the public in the Meopham Country Park.[11]

The survey of crops in 1840 in preparation for the Tithe Award reveals that there were 41 occupiers of land in Meopham. Nearly all grew small acreages of hops and out of a total acreage of 4,694 arable occupied 3,026, grass 508 and woodland 877 acres. Wheat was the most important arable crop followed by sainfoin for three-year leys. Peas, beans, tares, barley, clover, oats, turnips, rye and potatoes were also grown. Fallowing had been reduced, but it still comprised 7.5 per cent of the arable acreage. This required ploughing with eight horses as the land was heavy.

Surrey Agriculture and 'Pleasure Farming'

James Malcolm's three volumes on the agriculture of the County of Surrey (1805) are an invaluable insight into the conditions of farming at that time. He was particularly concerned at the deficiencies of roads, both highways and minor roads, and exposed their deleterious effects on farming, which in any case never matched the productivity and prosperity of Kent's.[12]

75 *Unimproved road, early 19th-century.*

Although profound social and economic changes were being wrought by some turnpikes from the 1750s (an example being that running through the Vale of Mickleham which was not readily accessible to London until it became a thoroughfare on the Epsom to Horsham turnpike in 1755) the *general* effects should not be over-rated before the 1820s, when smooth roads and fast public coaching services to Brighton and other coastal towns made England the envy of the Continent. Writing of Surrey roads in 1805, Malcolm makes clear that they did not reach the standards they were to attain a generation later, despite the county being already 'the most admired, the most fashionable, the most healthy and as much frequented as any in the kingdom'. The incompetent management of many of the Trusts invoked his censure as did their reluctance to spend enough on maintenance. The frequent tolls also made the carriage of bulky goods expensive. The turnpike from Godstone to Westerham (part of the present A25) was sound, and hedges were cut low to admit sun and air, but a branch from a turnpike to Smitham and Titsey was deplorable, as was the turnpike from Leatherhead to Epsom which abounded in standing water, ruts and holes. The Clandon and Kingston roads to Guildford were poor and, as for roads beyond Guildford to Godalming, Milford and Haslemere, it was difficult for any carriage to go along without overturning. The road to Farnham over the Hog's Back which should have been a showpiece was in bad condition through lack of maintenance, although flints for this purpose were everywhere in profusion.

As for the minor roads in almost all Surrey parishes, Malcolm felt a sense of shame and the purely local ones he considered scandalous; the further from the metropolis, the deeper the mire. He noted shrewdly that, if none of these roads happened to lead to a gentleman's house, in the worse order and the more impassable they were, and the lower was the rent of farms bordering them. His list of 37 parishes with roads 'as bad as some of the most inaccessible and uninhabited parts of Ireland' is mainly Wealden but includes Chaldon, Chelsham, Chipstead, Ewell, Frensham, Godalming, Hambledon, Hascombe, Limpsfield, Merstham, Oxted, Tandridge, Thursley, Warlingham and Witley, all places where road materials were more easily obtainable than in the Weald. His explanation for this sorry state was that the management of local roads had got into the hands of shopkeepers and small farmers whose object was to give themselves the least trouble. Malcolm also alludes to the almost total lack of road signs on turnpikes and local roads alike. He was repeatedly cursing his inability to find his way, bewildered by intersecting roads on commons, heaths and downs, and went miles out of his way, to the hazard of his life. It was worse still in the Weald where he had to take guides in the winter months.

The economic malaise which was a consequence of the deplorable roads at the beginning of the 19th century was vividly exposed by Malcolm. Anticipating the doctrine of Von Thünen's of concentric rings, he observed that, in Surrey generally, agricultural rents fell with increasing distance from London, those of farms within the innermost ring of up to half an hour's drive from the 'Stone's End' of Southwark being almost double the rentals in the next zone, up to one hour's distance, and six times as much as those in remoter parts. On the Downs he put rents at about 20s. an acre, on the sands, 16s., compared with £6-12 in the innermost ring. It is plain that Malcolm considered that the lack of accessibility to London was a leading factor behind low rentals outside London and his remarks on the improvement of farm rentals are corroborated by a detailed valuation of Francis Scawen Blunt's estate around Horsham and Worth in Sussex in 1811, which proposed increases in farm rentals which were related in part to recent turnpikings.[13]

When these rapid changes were taking place, William Cobbett in 1825 drew a distinction between the unselfconscious face of the traditional farming landscape of Surrey and the 'artificial' landscapes of the new country gentry spreading out of London in the wake of the turnpikes. Sarcastically he cast his exact, quick glance over the 'improvements' which frustrated his express aim of seeing the country's agriculture and its working farmers and labourers. The experience of a day's journey across Surrey led him to conclude that the traditional sights and habits of rural England survived only along rutted hollow-ways, unusable to carriages. Beside the high roads from London the new gentry, which were his aversion, were expelling yeomanry and re-arranging landscape for their sensuous delight, activities associated in Cobbett's mind with the topsy-turveydom created by the repulsive eruption of the Great Wen: 'Those who travel on turnpike roads know nothing of England – from Hascombe to Thursley almost the whole way is across fields or commons or along narrow lanes. Here we see the people without any disguise or affectation. Against a *great road* things are made for *show*'.[14] Cobbett's distinction between two contending forces in the landscape of south-east England, the one sustaining a working farmscape of mean farm buildings rented to round-frocked farmers, and the other creating a new design worked on for pleasure like a piece of stage scenery, is amply borne out by other writers, not all of whom would have agreed with Cobbett as to which was the baser and which the better.

Another of Malcolm's grievances was the continued existence of common-fields and commons, which hardly existed in Kent. In 1794 their extent on the Downs between Croydon and the Clandons was still appreciable and the author felt he could not rest until there was not a single acre of either left. He lists 1,200 acres of common-fields at Beddington, Wallington and Carshalton; 200 at Sutton and Cheam; 800 at Epsom; 200 at Leatherhead; 700 at Ashtead; 130 at Fetcham, for example. Within the two years before his publication Great and Little Bookham, Effingham, East and West Horsley, Clandon, Merrow, Send and Ewell had been enclosed and now Malcolm was wanting to be rid of the rest. He also lists large amounts of common-land in the area, including Mitcham, 530 acres, Addington and Shirley, 300, Warlingham, Walton, Kingswood and Banstead, 1,500, Sutton 250, Cheam 320 and Epsom and Leatherhead 1,200 acres.

In defence of the enclosure of common-fields and commons he cited the official government policy that England could not grow corn or stock enough for the consumption of the present population without their eradication and added: 'I am the last man who be desirous of erasing the dwelling of the cottager from the map of society, because I know well that society, as it is now formed, could not do without them; notwithstanding, they are too often the abodes of wretchedness and plunder, and like the picture so ably described by Mr Gilpin [a single example of a dissolute heathman in the New Forest!].' In reality the common-fields in Surrey in Malcolm's time were not so inefficiently run as one might have thought from his strictures. The large numbers of smaller farmers were rapidly diminishing and the strips of land were already being enclosed piecemeal. Their final demise involved the greater change of the enclosure of commons. Fortunately, many were saved by conservationists for posterity (pp.204-5). It is relevant to note that, although heathmen were distinctive as rougher in speech, dress and habits than people elsewhere and were regarded (as were many other commoners) as just about the lowest in human society, they found a champion in the Revd Charles Kingsley, the novelist and naturalist of Eversley in Hampshire, who admired their rosy, dark-eyed children and all the simple, healthy comforts of the heath-cropper's home:

> The clod of these parts is the descendant of many generations of broom squires and deer stealers … But he is nevertheless a thoroughly good fellow. Civil, contented, industrious, often very handsome. A far shrewder fellow too – owing to the dash of wild forest blood from gipsy, highwayman, and what not – than his bullet-headed and flaxen-polled cousin, the pure South Saxon of the

76 *George Scharf's impression of Farnham, 1823. The Bishop of Winchester's castle is in the background.*

chalk downs. Dark-haired he is, ruddy and tall of bone; swaggering in his youth but when he grows old a thorough gentleman reserved, stately, and courteous as a prince ... True he seldom goes to church, save to be christened, married or buried, but he equally seldom gets drunk.[15]

Another sturdy defender of the heathmen was George Sturt ('George Bourne') of Farnham, author of *Memoirs of a Surrey Labourer* (1907), *Change in the Village* (1912) and *The Wheelwright's Shop* (1923), who brilliantly conveys the aspect of Surrey Heaths before they were broken up by London 'improvers'. As late as 1870 heath stretched continuously from Heath End west of Aldershot as far east as Woking. Sturt bitterly expresses his disapproval of widespread building of spacious houses on every ridge and slope:

Their desolation has gone, their silence, their savagery, their impressive beauty ... Gone too are the traditional small-holders, the 'broom-squires', who eked out a frugal living on the heaths by using the commons. The feed of the commons kept his pigs and his cow and pony and just enabled him to make a little money by them. The rough scrub of the commons gave him his fuel, the gorse and bracken litter for his livestock which became manure for his patch of land. Also gone are the many farmer-potters of the heaths, men who dug their own clay and fired it with turf, sprays and gorse.[16]

Sturt noted that the name Whitmore Bottom had been changed to Whitmore Vale and that on Hindhead villas seen from a distance seem to have broken out upon the once majestic hill like a red skin eruption. There had been a time when he could not see Hindhead without gladness; now there were times when he would rather look away than endure to think what had gone from it for ever.

It would be most interesting to know more about the responses of people dispossessed from the common-fields, or bought out by larger proprietors and those who lost the right to depasture livestock and to roam over them at leisure. There was opposition to the enclosure of the Leatherhead Common in 1865 but this appears to have been muted. The objections to the proposed Banstead Common and Walton Heath from 1864 are noted on p.204. Silence appears to reign as to reactions of occupiers of common-fields. There must have been some 'John Clares' who deplored the new public roads, footways and drains staked out, the new allotments with their fences, gates and 'No Trespassing' signs, trees cut down and streams stopped in their course, so that ditches could be made straight. To some people, doubtless, enclosure was perceived as the destruction of the traditional rural community: 'You could talk to the man working the next strip, you could see the shared ditches, you could tell the time of the day by the movement of the common flock and herd from the village pound out to the heath and back.' Once a year everyone would gather to 'beat the bounds'. But as we have noted, the Surrey common-fields were not like those of the east Midlands and by the 1800s they had comparatively few occupiers and many fewer small men suffered from enclosure.

With Malcolm we can traverse the Surrey Downs above Croydon, noting that most of them were then under the plough, although the soil was generally heavy and flinty. Crops, which had to be 'landed up' in ridges to allow rainwater to disperse more freely, were moderate in favourable seasons. The most successful farmers folded sheep on turnips on a large scale and with the aid of their dung might produce as many as 12 saleable crops in 15 years. Farmers like William Ashby of Woodmansterne, with abilities above the ordinary, had exemplary arable equal to any in the Kent Downs. The irrigation of meadows, introduced in the 17th century, was in decline (as in Kent) because the then generation of farmers thought that, although irrigation improved the quantity of grass, its quality was lower and did not support as much stock for the London market. Malcolm was most scathing about husbandry at Merstham, Nutfield and Gatton where ditches were unscoured, briars, brambles and mole-hills were everywhere and there was so much trumpery that 'one might actually fancy oneself transported to the wild of America'. This might be explained by the quarrying of Fuller's Earth in the vicinity.

Malcolm vividly explains the technique of paring and burning old pasture on the surface of the enclosed commons.[17] Effingham Common was being improved by General De Lancey. This had been tolerably thickly covered with brushwood – furze, hawthorn, blackthorn, juniper, etc. – and the stiff soil abounded in stones. Breaking in the land was an arduous undertaking. The man who used a breast-plough for the task attached a stiff piece of board to his legs with leather straps, and pushed with such exertion with his thighs into the skin of the turf as frequently to force the blood from his nose. Having cut the turf by repeatedly using the grind-stone on his plough-share, he turned it upside down. After drying for two or three months, it was laid in heaps and burnt, every acre producing between 40-50 bushels of good ash which was ploughed in for turnips, followed by wheat in the next season. The chemical value of the ash more than compensated for the cost of cutting the turf and clearing any brushwood. Paring and burning was also universally adopted by heathmen on worn-out pasture or on encroachments on the waste. Women and children turned the sods frequently to dry them, as they did for turf fuel, setting them up on their edges to allow the wind to dry them better. If the fire burned too fiercely it was necessary to dampen it by putting on sods, for the goodness of the ashes depended on their being consumed rather than burnt. As we have previously noted, the Kentish turn-wrest plough was in general use, though a small wheel plough was used on light lands around Dorking and Guildford.

Some parts of the Downs rose above the general level of Surrey husbandry, notably the Mole valley between Leatherhead and Cobham and the Vale of Farnham. William Marshall and later writers admired the hop culture of the latter place which had spread to Alton on former common-fields, trees being planted as sheltering screens marking out former strips. The fertility of the land was largely due to the chalkiness of the loam soils. Cultivation of hops at Farnham was quite different from that of Kent. Labour was manual, not horse-drawn as in Kent, because the hops were grown on fewer hop-poles and harvested at an earlier stage of ripeness. This difference helps to explain why Farnham hops tended to fetch a higher price than Kentish. Wagons taking hops to Weyhill Fair returned with cheeses and other dairy produce. Hop-pickers celebrated the end of the season by dancing in the streets of Farnham to the music of fiddlers and, bedecked in ribbons and coloured handkerchiefs, returned to their homes in wagons carrying thirty or more persons, 'altogether in a sort of glee and merriment rarely met with', observed William Marshall (presumably spending most of their harvest money in pubs).[18]

A district which fell below the average in farming competence was parts of the Tillingbourne valley which had clearly lapsed since the great days in the 17th century of the Evelyns. James Caird in his *English Agriculture* (1851) illustrated the backwardness of its agriculture on a tour from Gomshall railway station by remarking on 'undrained marshes, ill-kept roads, untrimmed hedges, rickety farm-buildings, shabby-looking cows of various breeds and dirty cottages' – the very character visitors from London found so appealing a generation or so later. He attributed much of the neglect to the pernicious custom of letting farms on yearly leases, a practice much favoured by tenants who fraudulently 'worked-out' a farm and received from the incoming tenant payment for 'imaginary improvements and alleged operations', a bad system which was the staple of Surrey land agents and valuers whose shiny brass plates were a feature of every little town in the county.[19]

There was another reason for the decline in practical agriculture in parts of Surrey. The 'pleasure farmer' was invading the more picturesque parts by the 1860s. This process had its origins in the late 18th century when a simpler

77 *Bury Hill, near Dorking, the home of Charles Barclay who assisted emigrants to Upper Canada.*

and more obviously useful type of ornamental farm than the *ferme ornée* made its appearance. An early site of natural gardening was the Rookery at Dorking. Daniel Malthus, the owner, was a friend of Jean Jacques Rousseau who stayed there briefly in 1766. In this delightful rural retreat of glens, pools of water and serpentine paths Malthus laid out a garden on the natural principles enunciated by Rousseau in Julie's garden in *Julie ou la Nouvelle Héloïse* (Thomas Malthus, the famous writer of the *Essays on the Principle of Population* was brought up by his father on the educational principles advocated by Rousseau in *Emile*.) One of the most influential advocates of the pleasure farm was Thomas Ruggles, a Suffolk and Surrey farmer, who devoted much attention to the topic in the 1780s.[20] He advocated a turreted farmhouse surrounded by woodland opened up by wide rides to give prospects of farm cottages and well-bred livestock. He noted that farmers ploughed to the very brow of their ditches in Surrey and broke their shares against roots growing in the banks of their hedges, as if their land would bear nothing if it did not bear corn. He advocated grassy margins to give the farmer pleasure to walk round his fields and see the growing produce of his industry (an idea which is now being adopted for conservation reasons). He advised the repair of old hedges with whitethorn, crab, holly, sweet briar and honeysuckle and the planting up of 'short-lands' in the fields with Scots pine, silver fir and Weymouth pine. He also recommended trees natural to watersides – aspen, white poplar, black poplar, Carolina pine and Lombardy poplar to improve meadows and brooks. Ponds were a main feature, shaded by willows. It is interesting to note that he was not an advocate of trees in hedges, especially on arable land, but he made an exception in favour of the apple, delightful to the eye in blossom as in Normandy, a characteristic of a kind of landscape he called *riant*. He observed that this kind of farming would provide a legacy of beauty that children and their children's children would enjoy. His vision of a new Surrey landscape was enthusiastically taken up by later proprietors who imparted a widespread park-like appearance of farmland which has been ever since one of Surrey's glories. An example of Ruggles' model of a pleasure farm was Thorncroft at the head of the Vale of Mickleham. The mansion was built in 1760 for an ornamented estate of 121 acres which was laid out in regular 14-16 acre fields well planted up with trees and luxurious hedgerows. Its ambience is well preserved in the exquisite and ingenious map of F.T. Young (1822), itself a minor form of art. This depicts in perspective view the variegated autumn foliage, spiked with poplar and conifers, and tree-shrouded buildings reflected in the waters of the River Mole. His fundamental question was how to bring arable lands into the most convenient shape for the plough, and yet preserve in great measure the beauty of the landscape. None of this 'picturesque farming' was held to compromise 'the absolute attention to good cultivation'. This may have been so in the 18th century but the Victorian successors were more concerned with beauty than commerce. A response to the 'pleasure' or 'model' farmer by a practical small-holder at the end of the 19th century is discussed on p.148.

A later type of newcomer who put farmland to ornamental use was one of the first migrants to the Haslemere district, James Henry Mangles, who bought Valewood House below Blackdown in 1860.[21] He was enchanted by the scenery but a more important consideration was that the soil and climate were ideally suited to the cultivation of rhododendron. This would have been immediately obvious as the lower parts of the valley sides had already been invaded by self-sown R ponticum, introduced in the previous century as game coverts. Mangles had already become passionately fond of the rhododendron genus which was to dominate the rest of his life. He was particularly excited by the many species of Himalayan rhododendron introduced by Joseph Hooker as a result of his exploration of Sikkim. Mangles' life work was to hybridise species not reliably hardy in this country with some of the hardier species, and hybrids already established in Britain. His adviser was Sir William Hooker, the father of Joseph, and Director of Kew, where the Sikkim seedlings were under cultivation. 'Nearly twenty years ago', wrote Mangles in 1879, 'I walked with Sir Wiliam Hooker through the gardens at Kew, and in the Temperate House he gave me some pollen of the finest Rhododendron arboretum there, with which I made my first essay in hybridising'. From then until his death in 1884 he never ceased to create improved varieties of rhododendron. His impressive contribution to gardening was acknowledged by his election as a Fellow of the Linnaean Society in 1874. Some time earlier he had begun visits to other growers of Sikkim rhododenrons in Britain and on the Continent, which he reported in articles in the gardening press. Most of these articles were reprinted with an introduction by Gerald Loder of Wakehurst, himself an ardent devotee of rhododendrons. J.G. Millais, the historian of the genus, described Mangles as the 'high priest of the rhododendron cult'. He died at the age of 52 and is buried in his parish church of Lurgashall. (The subsequent widespread rhododendron invasion on heathland in west Surrey is discussed on page 243.)

Although no champion came forward to aid the common-field farmer, the cottager and small-holder did not lack support. The Surrey heaths and woodlands were traditionally their preserve and wherever a strip of land could be cultivated there were old cottages dotted here and there in what was 'three acres and a cow' country. Here the 'litter' (bracken, gorse, heather and grass) was cut to spread in the cattle barns and the turf cut for fuel was returned as potash to the fields. Here lingered a stubborn spirit of independence that forbade oppression and resented interference. It was in this partially tamed district of ragged ponies, straggly cows and heath-cropper's donkeys, that the idea was first conceived of giving agricultural labourers the chance of owning a small-holding as a cure for their poverty. Eli Hamshire (1834-92) of Ewhurst claimed to have originated the idea.[21] He was the son of a small-holder of about three acres on Ewhurst Green who supplemented his living with a carrier's business. Eli himself started life with his father as his carrier's boy and as early as aged 14 had rented a field of his own. He became a chicken dealer and a small-holder. As a young man he sang radical songs of his own composition in the beer-house and tap-room to the accompaniment of the first concertina heard in Ewhurst. Later he became a well-known 'character'. Attired in his slate-coloured smock he feared no man and tirelessly crusaded for the rights of the oppressed. He criticised the powers of the gentry, the clergy and the lawyer, the system of poor relief, the treatment of women and children and bemoaned the poverty of the agricultural labourer. Basically, he backed politicians who publicly supported the labouring classes, such as Joseph Chamberlain and Joseph Arch, who had founded in 1872 the National Agricultural Labourers' Union. The agricultural historian Thorold Rogers encouraged his activities, noting that the legislature was ill-informed about farmworkers.

Hamshire wrote under the pseudonym of 'The Carrier's Boy' two books which he dictated to his children as his ability to write was limited. His *Source of England's Greatness* (Pamphlet, 1885; second edition 1894) was followed by *The Three Great Locusts* (1889). Of dissenting stock, he based his demands for social reform firmly on the teachings of the Bible. As a 'practical farmer' he deplored the 'model farmers' who had invaded the district and who were monopolising the Ewhurst and Cranleigh area. They had each bought up a number of little farms which had supported traditional rural life. He knew of 20 of them formerly producing butter and milk which were then dormant. The same newcomers were enclosing waste and roadside verges where the poor man kept his cow and pig. Farmhouses were standing empty and cottages were being demolished. Fields were being converted to parks and in their grounds were planted laurels and 'other evergreen rubbish of no earthly use for the sustenance of man'. Pheasants, newly introduced for the battue in the autumn, damaged newly-sown fields. Rectors who administered the sacrament on Sunday engaged in stag-hunting on Monday, a sport which Hamshire considered cruel, and destructive of the poor man's property. Although he did not succeed in his principal aim of securing support for his three acres and a cow policy, W. McEager has rightly said, 'He voiced the countryman's grievance and made demands on behalf of the agricultural labourer which then seemed Utopian, but would now be universally recognised as just and reasonable'. Later advocates of the revival of British agriculture on the basis of 'peasant' farms and small-holdings were Charles F.G. Masterman, Hilaire Belloc and G.K. Chesterton.

13

Nineteenth-Century Labourers

Westerham

We now turn to the situation of the poor and Westerham is an excellent place to start. The population of the parish in 1801 was 1,344, in 1851, 2,113. Visiting the large parish church (mainly 15th-century but in such a bad state of repair that the church was re-opened in 1883 by the Archbishop of Canterbury), and surveying the memorials we are struck by an Edenic civilisation, the air of well-being in general, the ambience of ease and leisure, in fact, an impression of universal prosperity which seems to have been attained as readily as the air people breathed. There are 12 hatchments on memorial slabs on the floor. General Wolfe (who lived in the village) is commemorated as are seven to eight families who bore arms, including merchants and lawyers from the 16th century, who had London connections, and landed estate owners. The Wardes of Squerryes handsomely supported the church with a new organ, oak case, windows, etc. A very elaborate reredos, including opus sessile and painted glass by Powell and Sons of Whitefriars, Lambeth, and a sanctuary lamp donated by Sir Winston and Lady Churchill are amongst the more modern features.

But now, examine the parish registers and other parish papers and another side of Westerham appears which is not represented in the church itself nor even in the tombs in the churchyard. A close examination of these reveals that 168 persons out of a population of about 1,437 persons (8.4 per cent) lived in 1817 at the expense of public charity. This number rose to 202 in 1830. Of the 1817 total, 116 were labourers, 18 tradesmen and mechanics, 40 were old and infirm. Forty-five were single men or married without children, 43 had families not exceeding three children and 42 had more. The diet of the poor house was adequate but monotonous:

Breakfast Lunch Supper
Monday Bread and cheese
Tuesday Hot beef pudding.
Wednesday Broth and Gruel, Cold meat, bread. Bread and cheese,
Thursday daily Hot beef pudding daily
Friday Cold meat, bread.
Saturday Bread and cheese
Sunday Hot pudding.

Bread at dinner was withdrawn and rice substituted. This was cheaper than bread and was claimed to be 'most nutritious and heartening, particularly for children'. After 1824 soup was substituted on Tuesdays and Saturdays. It was reckoned that a man earning 15 shillings could support a wife and three children. Further evidence of poverty at Westerham is provided by the assistance given in the terrible year 1816, which rose from 14 families assisted with flour in June and steadily rose to a maximum of 37 in February 1817.[1]

Poverty and Emigration

The problem at Westerham was not exceptional. Throughout Surrey and Kent, as elsewhere in England, the situation was much the same. Charles Wayth of Bearsted House near Maidstone was so appalled at the severity threatening the labouring population in 1834 that he addressed a printed letter to landed proprietors and parochial authorities pointing out the insufficiency of out-door relief in the 1834 Poor Law Act and the need for allotments at rentals the poor could afford. Stepping out of line on Poor Law matters could be harmful to tenants. A Mr Barrett had to give up the tenancy of a farm at Brasted because he apparently worked the farm not in accordance with Earl Stanhope's wishes and for taking an active part in the new Poor Law as a Guardian.[2] As late as 1847 the *Examiner* newspaper of Kent was drawing attention to the suffering among poorer classes, 'with bread too dear by half', and arguing that the working man should be relieved of taxes on timber, windows, paper and bricks which if repealed would increase employment and diminish poor rates and crime.

One solution to relieving the poor was by assisted emigration. The Overseers of the parish of West Malling received a letter in 1833 from a firm willing to contract for the conveyance of families, labourers and poor persons to the British Colonies in North America, Australia and the United States and 'to victual them if required'. Trading ships departed from London twice monthly and special services from more local ports were organised if a sufficient number of emigrants were offered.[3] Wateringbury Vestry sent six families to Canada in 1832 by these means and four more went to Australia in 1838.[4] In 1845 seven children died of scarlet fever. So many poor families from the parish of Mereworth were emigrating to New South Wales in 1838 by the same shipping line that a special collection was organised for them to assist in clothing and other necessities. In all, 45 persons (including children) were assisted to Australia.[5]

Many other expedients were also practised. Yalding employed out-of-work persons to assist in diverting the course of the river there to ease flooding in 1830. Wages of 1s. a day were still being paid for this purpose ten years later. In 1841, 71 families were issued with potato tickets of two bushels each and others bought at reduced prices. Coal tickets were also issued. Meanwhile seven males and nine females went to South Australia and 16 male and 19 females left for Sydney.[6] Coal was also given to 35-41 Sellinge parishioners in 1845-6.[7] At Stowting soup was issued up to 11 times to 20 families in 1836/7.[8] Boxley overseers held for years that it was not expedient to encourage emigration by defraying the expenses of good labourers but finally resolved to send a family to New Zealand in 1841[9] as had Westwell in 1834.[10] At the latter place one organiser stated that, 'If I had been a rich man I can only say I would outfit dozens of families'.[11] His advice was taken, apparently, for 52 persons were assisted in travelling to London or Liverpool.[12]

Charles Barclay of Bury Hill introduced a plan for assisting persons from Dorking to emigrate to Canada. He founded the Dorking Emigration Society which raised the passage money for 75 individuals by subscription in 1832, almost all of whom had received parish relief, their outfits being paid for from the rates. In letters he edited, received by relatives and friends at home, Cornelius Cousins wrote after a nine weeks' passage that he liked the country very much: 'It's a far better place than old England [thinking of Dorking, Coldharbour and Broadmoor].' The wife of William Wilar, the mother of seven boys, wrote to her sister that she was happily settled on 12 acres of cleared land with 'beautiful spring water like your orchard water in Milton [Street,

78 *Spade used for cutting turf for fuel on heathland.*

Dorking]' and that whereas the family could hardly get a taste of meat in Surrey they could now afford to roast a large joint. John Worsfold thought his new town of Hamilton was as good as Dorking and in a few years would be better. Numerous letters were in the same vein.[13]

Aylesford was so overwhelmed with poor that the parish decided that medical expenses 'for strangers employed at harvest time and hopping time' would have to be paid by employers in future.[14] Six adults and 16 children were considered for emigration at Linton in 1842.[15] Loose in 1848 acquired part of Coxheath for the purpose of 'grubbing stone' to benefit out-of-work labourers.[16] Other parish business throws interesting light on various social matters. In 1819, a rate was imposed for the purpose of enlarging the church payment made to a man for keeping order in the church and churchyard during Divine Service, and a warning had to be issued to shopkeepers that their shops should be closed on the Sabbath under pain of incurring penalties enacted by law. In 1835 the parish payment for sparrows at one farthing a head was discontinued. (This was a widespread custom throughout England intended to reduce the damage done to crops by wild birds.)[17] Boughton Monchelsea clothed over 100 persons in the 1830s, including Richard Wood, given a suit of clothes 'for his better appearance in church'.[18] Earlier at Wrotham there are details of the diet at the local workhouse in 1813. Each pauper was provided with food costing up to 5s. 6d. weekly. On Sundays, Tuesdays and Thursdays breakfasts for men were one quart of bread and gruel. The women had bread, two ounces of cheese and one ounce of butter. At dinner men and women were fed with ten ounces of beef, vegetables and a suet pudding. For supper there was more bread and cheese. On Wednesdays and Fridays dinner was confined to bread and broth and on Mondays and Saturdays an even more frugal dish was offered. Men were supplied with one pint of beer at dinner (Wednesdays and Fridays excepted) and half a pint at supper every day. Children's helpings were proportional.[19]

It was not only agricultural workers who experienced poverty after the Napoleonic Wars. The boatmen of Deal and Dover suffered a great decline in their service when naval forces stationed there were disbanded and convoys broken up. Further decline was brought by the substitution of hemp for chain and the introduction of steam vessels. The Deal boatmen explained that for centuries their forefathers had made a living, day and night, cruising to westwards in readiness to assist homeward-bound vessels by putting pilots ashore from outward-bound vessels, conveying letters and despatches and the supply of fresh provisions. They also frequently came to the assistance of ships in distress, even in the direst circumstances. As Edward Darby put it:

> In gales of wind ships are unable to assist themselves in the Downs; they break adrift and then they want the assistance of the Deal men, who, the harder it blows, the more they are afloat; and but for their assistance would be lost by going on shore on the flats at Sandwich, or in attempting to get to Ramsgate pier, and be lost at the back of the Heads …

Deal men also rescued ships stranded on the Goodwin Sands. In Deal some 440 boatmen were employed in 1833, at Dover somewhat less than half that number. By that time they had been reduced to penury; they were debilitated, unable to face the hardships at sea, their houses were dilapidated, and there was scarcely a family that did not receive food from the Poor Rate. As a result of an investigation into their conditions their earnings were improved.[20]

The 'Swing Riots'

These were rural disturbances which began in east Kent in August 1830 and reached their peak in November, when they had spread into Sussex, Surrey and most of south-east England. They were so called because of threatening letters to farmers purporting to come from a 'Captain Swing' but in fact there was no overall leadership. The violence included the destruction of threshing machines, burning of ricks and barns, attacks on Overseers of the Poor and intimidation of farmers and landowners to force up wages. For a brief period the whole countryside fell into the hands of labourers and was convulsed by the destruction of property; every peaceable family was alarmed. William Cobbett had often predicted in his *Weekly Political Register* that the burning and destroying would happen and that it would begin in Kent or Sussex, not on account of discontent being greater there than elsewhere, but because the radically-minded agricultural labourers would be the first to rise in protest.

Hobsbawm's and Rudé's account of the riots in *Captain Swing* (1969) has been re-addressed by Carl Griffin.[21] He has found evidence that the insurgence was not simply spontaneous, and quite at random, as Hobsbawm and Rudé thought, but that gangs were in communication with one another and his detailed study of the riots in east Kent greatly extends both their spatial extent and their intensity. The first action against a threshing machine was in May 1829 at Lyminge when the barn and lodge of a local farmer were set on fire to destroy a threshing machine within them. Fifteen months later violence got under way at Wigmore Court on the border between Elham and Barham and spread rapidly through east Kent. The Lower Hardres incident, which Hobsbawm and Rudé thought the earliest, was in fact four days later. Griffin finds evidence that the 'Elham confederacy' destroyed 16 threshing machines in nine parishes. Sir Edward Knatchbull, the chairman of the East Kent Quarter Sessions, leniently sentenced the Elham gang to three-day imprisonments and this apparently incited a renewed outbreak of destruction which did not abate until 1831.

79 *Memorial at the Gatton Rotten Borough, near Reigate.*

In connection with the Wigmore Court incident Ingram Swaine confessed that he was in the taproom of the *King's Arms* public house in Elham when a man asked him whether he was not going with their company 'a machining' that night? He was charged on his own confession that he had destroyed two threshing machines of William Dodd at Upper Hardres. Two other labourers were convicted for the same incident.

William Dodd, a yeoman farmer of Upper Hardres, explained that he was in the market room at Canterbury when he learned that men were coming to break his machine that night. He galloped home. He ordered his servant, John Cramp, to keep a look-out after supper. After some considerable time he heard 'a great hallowing and singing' from nearly 60 men who came into the yard and broke down the barn door. From their dress he thought that most of them were not of the labouring class, but above it. They attacked the wood and iron of two threshing machines for about half an hour with sledge hammers and a saw and broke them into pieces. George Youens, a labourer, was charged upon his own confession with having destroyed four threshing machines on the night of

20 September in the parish of Barham. In November 1830, 25 labourers and a cordwainer were sentenced at Canterbury for destroying threshing machines in Ash, near Sandwich, Stourmouth, Wingham, Bekesbourne, and Patrixbourne. The aggressive mood of labourers is indicated by one who stated that the first machine that comes into Paddlesworth will be broken.

The scale of relief under the Poor Law Amendment Act, 1834 provoked riots in 1835 in east Kent at Doddington, Lynsted, Throwley and Rodmersham, districts within the Faversham Union. In each case up to 250 labourers, some armed with sticks and bludgeons, besieged workhouses and forced paupers to return the tickets for bread they had received from Relieving Officers. Daniel Gooshen came out of the Doddington Workhouse with 6d. in money and a ticket for bread valued at 2s. He was ordered by the mob to return his relief. He tried to escape through the rear of the premises but was apprehended by some of the mob. He then left his ticket with the Parish Guardian and began working, whereupon he was seized by some rioters who said 'it is no use your being queer' and was so fearful of them that he went along with them. A Relieving Officer was threatened and a magistrate, the Revd Dr John Poore, assaulted. The mention of 'strangers' amongst the mobs suggests that activists were drawn from a number of parishes in east Kent and that the riots, staged on different dates, were on the basis of a preconceived plan.[22]

At Farnham land was let by individuals in small plots of half an acre to two acres and some farmers permitted labourers to grow potatoes on their land. At Albury 'the active benevolence and zealous mind' of Mr Drummond, the principal and almost sole proprietor, let his cottages, of a superior kind, with large gardens at low rents. This liberality was not exercised in the neighbouring parish of Shere, nor in the whole district from Dorking to Guildford. At Shere lawless outrages were committed in the Swing Riots of 1830-1 'and the respectable inhabitants, owing to the demoralised and disaffected state of the labouring classes, are now living in a continual dread of fires, or other destruction of property'. Repeated attacks were made on Captain Hay, who was acting as a special constable, and his property. The worst offenders were the 'Shere Gang' who were the terror of the whole neighbourhood. 'The members of it have always money, without any ostensible means of earning or obtaining it, as they neither work nor apply to the parish for relief.' One of the most notorious was hanged for burning Albury Mill in the winter of 1830-1 and seven or eight had been transported at various times. The new beer shops were regarded as extending 'every kind of vice and immorality among the lower orders'. They were frequently kept by persons of notoriously bad character and were often situated in remote places where persons of 'idle and loose character of both sexes could congregate without being observed'.[23] At Oxted, by comparison a peaceful parish, the common lands were regarded as helping to provide a decent standard of living for labourers, and employers sought to provide work in the winter.

14

A Nobleman's Estate: Linton Place

Few places could have been more fit for a nobleman than the great estate of the Mann and Cornwallis families centred on Linton Place which was bought in 1724 and built up in the 18th and 19th centuries to embrace several thousand acres, mainly in Linton, Egerton, Cranbrook, Sissinghurst and the neighbourhood. Lord Cornwallis' children in 1827 playfully called it a 'terrestrial paradise' in their 'newspaper', as in fact it presumably actually was.[1]

Detailed accounts for work done in the mansion, gardens, pleasure grounds, park and home farm at Linton Park for the years 1864-73 throw considerable light on the Cornwallis family, members of one of the most powerful landed élites in Kent. They illustrate to some extent their changing style of landscape gardening, its costs, the plants acquired, and what it was like to work for them, amongst other social and economic matters.[2]

The accounts themselves are worthy of mention. They are meticulously and minutely compiled on the same format throughout, presumably by the steward or his deputy. The cost of labour for every worker for every single day of the year

80 *Linton Place, residence of the Mann and Cornwallis families.*

on various parts of the estate – mansions, gardens, park and home farm – and a day-by-day weather report was supplied, doubtless to explain the work done on a particular day by each member of the over forty-strong workforce (excluding servants). It was thus possible to discover what a particular employee was doing on every day, whether working in the hot houses, sowing in the kitchen garden, maintaining the park pale, preparing for the return of the family or helping with the annual ball and the shoots when a 'great amount of company' could be expected. This makes the accounts fascinating today. We can keep track of some of the long-serving employees, even in retirement, because those suffering from disablement and ill-health were provided with generous weekly pensions. Current staff were not given annual holidays but had 'treats' instead: in 1868 fifty men and their families were given a free day's excursion by train from Maidstone to Hampton Court. The annual running costs of each department on the estate were abstracted at the close of the year, exactly as if they were being prepared by a commercial firm for a present-day auditor. Everything bought, sold, or produced, was accounted for: not a quart of milk or pound of butter from the dairy, a truss of hay at the stables or a man's harvest supper went unnoted.[3]

The family looked for some economic returns from their estate – sheep skins and fruit to London markets, and some beasts to the local butcher, but the receipts were trifling and purely incidental compared with the huge costs incurred in the refurbishment of the mansion and maintenance of the garden and estate generally. Prodigious supplies were needed to run the establishment, including in 1865, for example, 34,802 quarts of milk, 1,582 lbs of butter, 103 sheep and lambs, and over 200 tons of coal and coke for domestic heating, the laundry and hothouses. Presumably, this ostentatious life-style explains the need for accurate financial returns to avoid temptation into financial irresponsibility, which arose at Chatsworth and other places.[4]

The period of the extant accounts covers the time when the gardens were extensively altered, a new conservatory and fernery built, and much new space for trees and plants was required, especially for the various specimen pines 'being brought to England from foreign parts'. They exemplify the immense importance attached by mid-Victorian aristocracy and gentry to their mansions and grounds as a way of demonstrating their wealth, prestige and power. There were never fewer than nine or ten full-time and as many as 19 part-time gardeners at work. The total running costs of the garden compared with the maintenance of the mansion and the total expenses of the estate, rounded off to the nearest pound sterling, is shown in the following table:[5]

Year	Garden	Mansion	Total estate costs (£)
1864	743	515	2430
1865	832	612	3067
1868	978	664	2505
1869	980	633	3002
1871	604	271	1488
1873	681	345	1750

The fame of the Linton gardens pre-dates the 1860s and 1870s. As far back as 1805 the kitchen garden was described as 'capital' and the pleasure grounds and trees exceptionally beautiful. For the 1840s extant invoices and catalogues show that plant purchases were then mainly from London nurseries – King's Road and Hans Square, Chelsea, the Edgware Road, Clapham and at Kingston and Epsom – and that they would sometimes be conveyed by 'luggage train'. This was at the fashion for bedding-out and Catleugh, the family's supplier off Sloane Square, could supply in 1843-4 135 varieties of geranium, 155 of dahlia, 181 of calceolaria, 49 of verbena, 82 of fuchsia and 271 of roses. At the same time huge amounts of coal were being used in the hot-houses and greenhouses; T. Jackson of Kingston-upon-Thames was willing to supply 34 varieties of fern for the stove-houses and 16 more for the greenhouse, together with 406 further species of tender exotics which need heat.[6]

During the period of detailed accounts, 1865-72, the family occasionally bought special plants at auction. From Combermere Abbey in Devon came orange trees bought for the new conservatory, including those acquired by

---

SUPPLEMENT FOR 1842,

TO THE CATALOGUE OF PLANTS CULTIVATED FOR SALE BY
T. JACKSON,
NURSERYMAN, SEEDSMAN, AND FLORIST,
Kingston, Surrey.

CONTAINING THOSE NOT IN HIS GENERAL CATALOGUE, AND ALL THOSE OF WHICH AN ALTERATION IS MADE IN THE CURRENT PRICE.

T. J. begs to assure all those who favour him with their commands, that their orders will be executed with care and dispatch.

N.B. It is requested that correspondents will send with their first orders a remittance or satisfactory reference.

STOVE.

	s. d.		s. d.		s. d.		s. d.
Achimenes longiflora (strong)	15 0	Cattleya labiata	- 31 6	Oncidium divaricatum	- 15 0	Aspidium filix mas	- 1 6
Alamanda cathartica	- 2 6	Mossiæ	- 21 0	flexuosum - 3s. 6d. to	21 0	* molle	- 2 0
Amaryllis striatifolia	- 10 6	Skinneri	-105 0	Harrisonianum - 5s to	10 6	* nitens	- 3 6
Angelonia grandiflora	- 3 6	Cirrhæa viridi-purpurea	- 15 0	inophyllum	- 15 0	* patens	- 2 6
Begonia species Mexico	- 3 6	Warreana 15s. to	31 6	juncifolium	- 15 0	pectinatum	- 2 0
Bignonia speciosa	- 5 0	Cœlia Baueri	- 5 0	Lanceanum - 10s. 6d. to	21 0	† pennigerum	- 2 6
Tweediana	- 5 0	Cœlogyne fimbriata	- 5 0	leucochilum 42s. to	63 0	spinulosum	- 2 0
Browallia speciosa	- 3 6	nitida	- 15 0	luridum guttatum		Asplenium ebeneum	- 2 6
Ceropegia stapelieformis	- 5 0	Coryanthus speciosus	- 31 6	10s 6d. to	21 0	† flabellifolium	- 2 0
Columnea Schiediana	- 2 6	Cycnoches chlorochilon	- 50 0	ornithorhynchon	- 21 0	marinum	- 2 0
Croton variegata - 2s. 6d. to	15 0	Loddigesii	- 42 0	papilio - 5s. to	15 0	* præmorsum	- 2 6
Echiveria secunda	- 7 6	Cyrtochilum maculatum	- 31 6	pictum	- 10 6	* pubescens	- 2 6
Epiphyllum Russellianum		Dendrobium aureum	- 42 0	pumilum	- 10 6	* striatum	- 2 6
2s. 6d. to	15 0	Calceolaria	- 21 0	sanguineum	- 42 0	*Cheilanthus Dicksonioides	3 6
truncatus elegans	- 5 0	chrysanthum	- 31 6	stramineum	- 15 0	* profusa	- 1 6
Gesneria faucialis	- 2 6	cuculatum	- 7 6	Suttonii	- 21 0	*Cistopteris atomaria	- 2 0
Gloxinia rubra - 2s. 6d. to	10 6	fimbriatum 10s. 6d. to	21 0	Ornithidium coccineum	- 7 6	*Daria cicutaria	- 10 6
Glycine Harrissonii - 5s to	15 0	Gibsonii	-105 0	Paxtonia rosea	- 21 0	†Davallia canariensis	- 1 6
Goldfussia glomerata	- 2 6	Jenkinsonii	- 42 0	Peristeria Barkeri	- 21 0	*Diplasium decussatum	- 10 6
Hibiscus lilacinus	- 2 6	macrostachya	- 15 0	cerina - 7s. 6d. to	21 0	†Doodia aspera	- 2 0
Inga Harrissii - 3s. 6d. to	42 0	moschatum 15s. to	31 6	elata - 10s. 6d. to	31 6	† caudata	- 1 6
Ipomea batatoides	- 3 6	multicaule	- 7 6	pendula	- 10 6	† Kunthii	- 3 6
learii - 1s. 6d. to	10 6	nobile	- 21 0	Phaius maculatus	- 10 6	Lycopodium denticulatum	- 1 0
sellowii - 2s. to	15 0	pulchellum - 5s. to	15 0	Pholidota pallida - 3s. 6d. to	15 0	* stoloniferum	- 1 6
Manettia splendens	- 3 6	Epidendrum asperum 5s. to	15 0	Pleurathallis prolifera	- 5 0	*Lygodium scandens	- 3 6
species nova	- 7 6	cochleatum	- 3 6	Renanthera coccinea - 5s. to	15 0	*Niphobolus sinensis	- 2 0
Mandevilla suaveolens	- 3 6	cuspidatum	- 10 6	Rodriguezia secunda	- 10 6	*Polypodium angustifolium	2 0
Milla biflora	- 1 6	lancifolium - 10s. 6d. to	21 0	Saccolabium papilcosum	- 21 0	* aureum	- 2 0
Morinda odorata - 3s. 6d. to	10 6	machrochilum	- 10 6	Sarcanthus macranthus	- 21 0	Billardierii	- 2 0
Osbeckia canescens	- 2 6	pastoris	- 10 6	rostratus - 7s. 6d. to	15 0	calcarium	- 2 0
sinensis	- 2 6	patens	- 15 0	Schomburgkia marginata	- 31 6	decumana	- 2 0
Passiflora nigellæflora	- 2 6	tibicinis	- 42 0	tibicina (Epidendrum)	42 0	dryopteris	- 2 0
Roscoea purpurea - 5s. to	10 6	variegatum	- 7 6	Stanhopea aurea -		falcatum	- 2 6
Ruellia Sabiniana - 2s. to	5 0	Eria pubescens	- 5 0	Devoneana - 31s. 6d. to	84 0	fraxinifolium	- 2 6
Stephanotus floribundus	- 5 0	Gongora alba	- 10 6	eburnea	- 5 0	iridifolium	- 2 0
Thrvallis brachystachys	- 3 6	maculata - 5s. to	15 0	gracilis	- 15 0		
		mexicana	- 15 0	grandiflora - 7s. 6d. to 21 0			

81 *Extract from a nurseryman's sale catalogue, 1848.*

Lord Combermere from Paris in 1816 when they had belonged to the Empress Josephine, and they successfully bid for 140 rare Japanese plants just introduced into England. Spring bulbs were often bought at Stevens' auction rooms at Covent Garden. For a new fernery a truck load of peat was sent by railway from Wimbledon Common. Roses were supplied from Uckfield and Piltdown in Sussex, and 1,000 laurel plants came from Derbyshire. The hothouses still reigned supreme. Yet tastes in planting had changed. There was much less bedding-out and more interest in exotic trees. A 'wild' aspect was given to the park with the planting of 3,000 furze plants from Devon, for example, and rhododendrons and azaleas came to the fore. The former, in particular, were the family's new pre-occupation. Hybrids and 'new kinds' were annually added to their collection of over 6,000 from nurseries at Sunningdale in Berkshire and Matlock in Derbyshire. Wellingtonia, which had also become fashionable, was bought as seed.

The Countess Cornwallis' acquisitions c.1869 included (apart from 4,000 spring bulbs): 135 rhododendron ponticum, 160 rhododendron (other varieties), five variegated willow, 12 red-berried hollies, 170 azalea (seven varieties), 50 red and white cedars, 24 evergreen oak, 30 cypresses, 12 beech, 25 Chinese arborvitae, six weeping willow, 25 American arborvitae, 25 Weymouth pine, 22 hemlock fir, 25 white spruce, 54 magnolia (six species), 20 black spruce, 20 large cedar of Lebanon, 25 juniper, one acacia ('North American').

We also learn something about the domestic arrangements at Linton during the period c.1830-50. At this time 23 servants are listed with their wages. The highest paid was the steward at £105 per annum. A butler and under-butler headed the list of others. The housekeeper, paid £48, was next in seniority to the butler. The cook's salary was only fractionally less, at £47 10s. Two coachmen and a stable boy were needed and Lord and Lady Cornwallis had a footman each. Then followed the maids for kitchen, scullery, dairy, two for laundry, three further housemaids for Linton and two engaged at the London house, together with a maid for the stew room there. The head gardener, paid £40, and a schoolmaster completed the list. The movement of the family between London and Linton meant that servants frequently changed locations with their employers. At one time in 1838, for example, seven men and eight women servants were in one place and only two men and three women remained at Linton.[7]

The servants' weekly luncheon menus were prescribed in detail. On Sunday roast beef and plum pudding or cold meat and potatoes were available. Monday's meal comprised a meat pie and rice pudding; Tuesday's a leg of mutton (from the Home Farm) and apple pudding; on Wednesday it was boiled beef and dumplings and cabbage; on Thursday they made do with a pea soup, bubble and squeak or a bullock's heart; Friday was the day for a bouillon soup and Irish stew with a fruit pudding and on Saturday they were back to leg of mutton. The men servants' breakfast comprised cold loin of mutton, with an occasional fish dish. Suppers for all servants 'consisted of what was left from my lord's table'. Tea, coffee and sugar 'were not found', the wages making an allowance for this.

Servants were also given specific instructions signed by Lady Laura Cornwallis. The cook was required to order fish and poultry daily and to serve meals 'with

82 *Monument in Linton church, designed by Richard Bentley for Horace Walpole's friend, Galfridus Mann.*

due regard to economy', the prime joints being for his lordship's table and inferior pieces for the household. The laundry maids were expected to rise on Mondays at 3 a.m. and to complete washing before their normal day's work. The lord's dressing room fire was to be lit before 7 a.m. The dairy maid made butter, cheese, cream and the household bread and in addition plucked poultry and game, collected the eggs, froze ice, and was never to go out without leave of the housekeeper. She had to be in the dairy by 6 a.m., but thankfully did not have to milk the cows. The scullery maid was to perform her regular duties by 9 a.m. leaving the rest of the day for kitchen duties. The stillroom maid was responsible for confectionery, fancy bread, preserves, barley water and lemonade and cleaned the housekeeper's room and laid the table for meals in the kitchen, where she was joined by the dairy, scullery and stillroom maids. The kitchen maid rose before 6 a.m. and did not leave her post before 10.30 p.m. She also prepared the men servants' meals and made broth for the poor.

Meanwhile, the ladies Louisa and Elizabeth Cornwallis were engaged on the family's restoration of Linton church with many memorials of the Mann and the Cornwallis families, including a monument commissioned from Richard Bentley for Galfridus Mann, a brother of Sir Horace Mann, by Horace Walpole. Richard Hussey, who was later to design Frittenden church nearby, was selected as architect. He submitted plans for the church to the sisters over the period 1860-2, but the proposed restoration had evidently been in the minds of the family for some time, a plan of the church having been made by J. Reeves in 1857. That they had actively influenced the design is apparent from Hussey's

83 *Monument in Linton church to a young member of the Cornwallis family.*

plan of April 1860 which increased the amount of accommodation in the church from 373, proposed on a plan a month earlier, to 409 persons. On the south elevation Hussey restored an old window west of the doorway which had been crudely blocked up. His sketches for coloured glazing in the monumental chapel and for the stone altar piece in June 1862 evidently put the finishing touches to the new church.[8]

15

After Eden

In 1901 the novelist and agricultural writer H. Rider Haggard travelled across the greater part of rural England in the manner of Arthur Young and William Marshall a century or more earlier, to write up in the columns of the *Daily Express* his conclusions as to the state of agriculture.[1] His account of Kent affords a great contrast with the earlier reports of Buckland and Caird, for agriculture was suffering from competition from overseas imports, resulting from the far-reaching doctrine of Free Trade. Around the charming village of Wingham hops had taken over more of the well-farmed land, and poplars had replaced the old quickset hedges as shelter belts. The cultivation was on a new system, the 'east Kent', whereby a network of galvanised wires was suspended on uprights of chestnut or larch soaked in creosote to preserve them for a generation. This was a more efficient method than growing hops on single poles which lasted only a few years. The orchards were more intensively used than ever before; shorter trees were being planted to obviate the need for ladders; strawberries were grown at the foot of cherries, salad crops and vegetables were also intermixed amongst young trees, and the grass orchards were fed heavily with sheep whose manure nurtured the fruit trees (a practice recently questioned on hygiene by the EEC but which will apparently be allowed).

Apart from hops and fruit in east Kent, which offered a hard-working man a good living, Haggard had no very cheerful tale to tell. Many farmers had recently gone bankrupt after losing money month by month, and many more had compounded with their creditors and vanished. On the poorest lands, said a Canterbury auctioneer, farmers wrung a bare living from the soil and some 'were almost starving and owed money'. Poor corn-growing land meant poor tenants. Even prime hop and fruit land had fallen in value by up to 60 per cent from 1870. Cereal land was fetching only one-third of its value 30 years earlier. The resident 'yeoman' type of farmer was particularly hard hit and the small men most of all. For centuries the Kentish yeomen and small squires of moderate means had been the backbone of Kentish agriculture and society, but now they were engulfed, and territorial magnates were speculating in land. Labourers were leaving the poorer lands on the high chalk downs which were going down to grass, and migrating to the richer lands, only to stay awhile on their road to the towns. 'We live on hope in this district', added the auctioneer, little knowing that conditions would not improve until the First World War when more home-grown food was needed.

On the way between Wye and Romney Marsh, Haggard passed over a great stretch of undulating country of average quality which grew gradually poorer and more sodden-looking towards the crest of the ridge. Even in the richer lands of the 'Garden of England', farmers were now hard-pressed, hanging on in the hope of a change for the better. The country banks were chary of lending money even for hops, and although the pick of the land, e.g. around East Sutton, Leeds and Langley, still commanded high rents, the value of hill land had tumbled greatly. In conclusion, Haggard was considerably disappointed and discouraged by his visit to Kent. The condition of the poor lands and those who worked them was bad, if not desperate. Fruit and hop farming was now uncertain. Throwing a shadow over all was the question of labour. He could only trust that he was unduly pessimistic and that time would bear him out.

Haggard's visit prompted a discussion about the conditions of hop pickers initiated by the philanthrophist Miss Mary Russell. She complained that their habitations were tin huts, fitted with doors and iron ventilators, but without flooring or windows. A covered-in brick oven was provided for communal use and two or tree sanitary huts, but no coppers for washing clothes. Water was supplied to some pickers in a tank brought by a cart; in others the 'hoppers' had to fetch it, with the straw they slept on which was only rarely changed. Adult pickers were illiterate but younger children could sometimes read a little. The majority of adults had no thought of anything but drink, the children were infested with lice, and those who suffered from ophthalmia caused by dirt were covered in sores. The question arose, 'Who was to better this?' Hop farmers insisted that they made no more than a living, and to improve the sanitary and moral surroundings of the hop pickers they would send them to the workhouse; local authorities declared that rates were already too high; the government already staggered under its obligations and no more could its broad back carry. Rider Haggard's own suggestion was to let things go on as they were and to trust to philanthrophists to better them; after all, in the festering slums of London, conditions were no different, and on their holiday pickers had the sweet fresh air and blue skies of the ravishing Kent summer. Despite the conditions Miss Russell described, the balance of good was about right when one considered the yearly exodus from slums to the evil-smelling shanties of the Kent gardens 'with its accompaniment of healthful labour in a pure atmosphere sweetened by the sights and sounds of Nature undefiled'.

Haggard's impressions are corroborated and extended by the unique survival of more than 1,200 letters addressed to Lord Sondes of the Lees Court estate by his agents, Frederick Neave and his son Ivo from their office at Faversham.[2] From this remarkable archive on the day-to-day running of the estate of some 10,000 acres a broad picture can be ascertained of the fortunes of tenants and of the estate over a period of more than thirty years.

Broadly speaking, farming was at a very low ebb between 1900-4, gradually improved to a more satisfactory situation in 1910-14, became more buoyant in the First World War and then rapidly fell back to a pre-war condition which worsened in the later 1920s and 1930s. The introduction of dairying and fruit-

84 *Lees Court, the former home of the Sondes family and once the centre of a great landed estate.*

growing in the first decade of the 19th century, together with hop production, meant that farmers were fully engaged on a variety of other tasks. Despite these difficult farming conditions the estate provided better amenities at farmhouses, such as bathrooms and better kitchens.

During the exceptional circumstances of the First World War arable farming regained profitability and the farms on the brickearth were well cultivated and fully cropped. The hill farms on the Downs proper and corn farming were not sufficiently productive from 1900 and hops were also unpredictable owing to over-production. Fruit farming and dairying tended to emerge as alternatives. The latter activity needed considerable expenditure on the conversion of barns to cow stalls, the provision of water supply and equipment, costs which were shared between the estate and tenants. In July 1909, 22 farmers were owing arrears of rent and the more marginal hill farms on the Downs at Molash and Throwley were working at a loss. Reductions in rent were general and the poorest land was put down to grass. Some tenants left farms in a foul condition. Although traditionally an arable area, a proposed sugar beet plant in 1911 failed to win local support. The farms around Molash and Throwley were turned round again in the First World War. From 1917 the War Agricultural Committee compulsorily purchased land; beech were planted at the considerable extra cost of fencing against rabbits which had become a pest. The agent himself saw to the re-planting of underwood on cleared grounds. The interest in trees had much to do with the shooting rights over 900 acres of the coverts which were highly profitable.

The harvests of 1922 and 1927 were particularly disastrous. Grassland on poor land was again laid back. The Wheat Act of 1931, which fixed a minimum price for the crop, was a salvation. Before that farmers lost money from corn farming. V. Higgs of Owen's Court Farm detailed his losses:

1927	£277 5s. ½d.
1928	£624 17s. 4½d.
1929	£1397 12s. 10½d.
1930	£526 18s. 2d.
1931	£409 1s. 5½d.

Two sources throw light on rural society at and near Kemsing over the past one hundred years or so. The Archdeacon's Visitation Report on Kemsing, 1880 tells of a population mainly composed of labouring poor of whom only 20 were regular communicants and ten occasional. This low figure he put down to dissenters and that seats in the church, although not let for money, were appropriated for the various classes by the churchwardens at their discretion. Publicans came in for criticism for not regulating the amount of beer drunk and one of the churchwardens was reprimanded for not being regular in his duties. The moral condition of the people was low; they tended to be rough, headstrong, coarse and not self-controlled. The archdeacon even suggested that 'notably immoral people' should not receive burial service at the hands of clergy. Were we to have more such accounts we would know much more about rural societies at this time.[3]

The memories of Jack Hollands, who was born in 1920, of the simple life on East Hill on the high downs between Kemsing and Eynsford illuminate this remote and somewhat mysterious place. He tells of the people whose work up there was 'farming and wooding', who supplemented their diet by catching wild rabbits as everyone did up there. Big families lived in the cottages, a number of people sharing each of the few bedrooms. Some cottages, later condemned, had no stove or kitchen range, so everything was cooked in a pot over an open fire. Other cottages lacking a kitchen range had pothooks hanging down from the chimney. 'Hill children', as they were called, walked to school in Kemsing and left early in winter so that they could reach home before dark. The inns still brewed their own beer before the First World War and baked bread – with their yeast for sale – in an oven heated with faggots and cord wood. One pub also sold general goods. Woodcutters were the main customers; after they had been paid they would be on the doorstep at six o'clock in the morning. A butcher came up on horseback from Otford, carrying his meat in one basket, so that he could travel by the shortest route along bridleways. Horses were in general use until tractors began to be employed from the early 1940s. Farm workers were still housed in some farmhouses; casual workers often slept in barns or out-houses. A dish of bread and milk was supplied to them at breakfast. Before piped water became general from the 1950s wells were dug on farms up to five hundred feet deep. Cottages used to have underground storage tanks to store rainwater off the roof. Drinking water was so precious that farmworkers would bring a bucket of water home from a farm which had a piped supply.

85 *Lime Avenue, Fairlawne, mid-18th century.*

The farmers' main crop was hay from permanent pasture which was run over with a seed barrow to add some clover and other seeds. Their hay and wheat or oats was sold for horse feed. Sheep from Romney Marsh were collected, driven by local drovers in four days to Wrotham, and wintered there until the late 1920s. Many farmers supplemented their income with other activities. There was more money, however, made from the coppice woods than from farming. Coppicers often set up a rough shelter by banging four hazel stakes in the ground and covering them with a tarpaulin. The markets were mainly Dartford and south London. From the early 1930s the inns had a different clientèle. Droves of ramblers caught trains out of London at week-ends to Eynsford, Shoreham or Otford and walked over the hills to the inns. 'On a summer Sunday, or a bank holiday, there were hundreds of people up here.' Fields were let out for camping, a holiday camp was set up, and plots of land were sold for retirement bungalows.[4]

16

London's Playground

'Give me the clear blue sky over my head, and the green turf beneath my feet, a winding road before me, and a three hours' march to dinner – and then to thinking!'
William Hazlitt, 'On Going a Journey', 1822

As London spread itself over farmland and woods with ever-growing streets and suburbs, people were driven each year further and further afield to find natural scenery unpolluted by smoke, and free of noise and bustle. Eighteenth-century Henry Thrale, who owned a brewery in Southwark and befriended Samuel Johnson, lived the life of a country gentleman at Streatham. When Leigh Hunt in the 1850s wanted some veritable home-brewed country ale and a change of air, he had to go no further than Putney Heath or Wimbledon Common, and at the same time the novelist George Eliot, always searching for a rural scene, could find it as near as at East Sheen. The subsequent expansion of the capital into the largest city in the world distantly separated people from their places of work and leisure and put an unhealthy smoke canopy over them. The London that had been praised by Charles Lamb and which inspired Dr Johnson's famous aphorism, 'He who is tired of London is tired of life …', was virtually a new city. A representative of Victorian London was Sir Leslie Stephen, editor of the *Cornhill*, the most famous literary journal, founder of the *Dictionary of National Biography* and father of Bloomsburyites Vanessa Bell and Virginia Woolf. For him, daily experience of London was an endurance test involving long journeys through crowded streets and requiring compensating annual holidays and weekend breaks away from London as a restorative from the dirt and grind of the city.

Amongst the first to go on long-distance walking excursions on periodical escapes from London, that was growing so vastly, was William Hazlitt, who after a day's walk from Farnham to Alton combined his pleasure in a comfortable inn with reading Congreve and sipping elegantly-served coffee with excellent cream, bread and butter.[1] Other pioneers were the Mills – James and his son, John Stuart, the future famous political economist – who were rambling in Surrey before 1830, when they took a cottage at Mickleham below Box Hill for use on their leave from the East India Company. They were invited to 'Conversation' Sharp's famous breakfasts (from 10 a.m. to 3 p.m.) and had Carlyle down as a guest when they were not sightseeing, geologising or botanising. The Mills had taken advantage of the growing network of turnpike roads out of London and the increasing stagecoach services down the present A24 road to Worthing.

The younger Mill was a particularly ardent walker and naturalist and the extant journals of his tours record him leaving Leatherhead by the Chichester coach for a walking tour in Sussex with two close companions in 1827. Mill apparently took notes of his sightseeing from carriage windows and, absorbed by the beauty of the Vale of Albury and the diversified appearance of the country around Hindhead and Blackdown, thought it the most agreeable he had ever experienced. In the following summer vacation with three companions his walking tour took in Guildford and St Martha's chapel which, in the arrangement of fold after fold of hills, one after another, and the richness of the appearance of the country, entirely eclipsed that of the Chiltern Hills he had just left behind him. In July 1832 Mill's walking companion was (Sir) Henry Cole, a future organiser of the 1851 Exhibition and the first director of the Victoria and Albert Museum. They went by the Southampton coach to Alton and set off on foot, evidently equipped with topographical and geological maps with which they tried to make sense of the kaleidoscope of little local landscapes they encountered. A highlight was the long-desired pilgrimage to Selborne, the home of Gilbert White, author of *The Natural History and Antiquities of Selborne* (1789). Henry Cole made numerous sketches, including that of White's house, and his own diary of the tour survives.[2]

It was the paddle steamer and steam train which really created popular tourism.[3] The former supplanted the sailing hoy and brought thousands from the city on excursions from Thames piers to Margate which, unlike most seaside resorts, owed nothing to royal patronage, but everything to the cockney pleasure-seeker in the 1820s.[3] Soon afterwards various railway companies were furiously competing with one another and excursion fares came within the limits of even the poorer classes. The countryside was also quickly exploited commercially by railway companies. As early as 1844 John Thorne's guide for walkers, the earliest literary production of the London, Brighton and South Coast Railway, led city-wearied pedestrians across countryside hitherto inaccessible.[4] With the aid of railways, the acquisition of country cottages by the comfortably off, mainly for use in summer, steadily increased. The rapid transport made frequent commuting to town practical for the first time. Cole

86 *Margate steamer from Gravesend or Tower Hill which replaced the sailing hoys.*

was one of the first to take advantage of this by taking his family for country air in the summer, travelling between Kensington and Elm Cottage, Shere, whenever he could, using Gomshall railway station which had opened ten years earlier. His weekend visitors included W.M. Thackeray and the photographer Capt. Francis Fowke, who took surviving pictures of the house. Whilst residing at Shere, restless enabler as he was, he demonstrated how influential townie newcomers were to come amongst 'backward' local communities. He founded with others' help the Tillingbourne Association which offered prizes to cottagers exhibiting fruit and vegetables at an annual horticultural show, which continued until the Second World War. He also introduced Arthur Sullivan as conductor when he was roped in by the Bray family to help organise a concert for 'the gentry' to raise money for coals for elderly women in the village. Cole was so pleased with his efforts that he wrote a long letter to *The Times*, explaining how other villages could do the same. He later moved to Witley, where an artistic colony began to flourish, also within commuting distance from London by train.[5]

No Londoner's published comments over such a long period evoke the longing for the country more than those of the writer George Eliot, regarded at the end of her life as the leading English novelist.[6] She suffered great ill-health and when in London was rendered helpless by nausea and headache, so she was forever going into London's countryside. A dun-coloured fog left her ailing, oppressed and chilled. In the first hour of stillness amidst fields, lanes and commons she had a delicious sense of repose and refreshment. The countryside she craved for was 'true country air, free of London haze', with wide horizons giving her a sense of 'standing on a round world', and not impracticably far off from frequent trains. Thus much of her life was spent searching for fresh air 'and the thoughts that come with it'.

In 1862 she warned against Ramsgate, 'which is a strip of London come out for an airing', but was so charmed with Broadstairs, which Dickens had made popular, that she thought that she might retire from the world, and live there for the rest of her days.

In 1868, however, she was in the quietest and most beautiful part of Surrey, four-and-a-half miles from the nearest railway station, where the deep calm of fields and woods of the Leith Hill district had a beneficial effect on her. The following year found her at Limpsfield Chart, 'far away from the sound of railways', and at Shottermill, Brookbank, Haslemere, the home of the author, Mrs Anne Gilchrist. This district was to provide her with the 'round world' countryside and the sense of distance from London hurry that she most loved.

This had its disadvantages.

> The butcher does not bring the meat, everybody grudges selling new milk, eggs are scarce, and a expedition we made yesterday in search of fowls showed us nothing more helpful than some chickens six week old which the good woman observed were sometimes 'eaten by the gentry with asparagus'. One cannot get a screw for a door handle nearer than Guildford and one has to scour the country and offer up petitions in order to get butter, fowls, and vegetables ...

She eventually settled at Witley, near Haslemere, a stone's throw from the railway platform, whence she obtained provisions from London. Her idea of countryside was clearly that of her generation – a place near a cab rank and a railway station.

By the 1860s the London suburban train service network had developed sufficiently to allow rambling groups to leave the capital from one railway station and to return to another after a circular walk, a practice regularly adopted by George Meredith for his London friends. His sheer joy of life, his intense pleasure in walking and his love of the countryside are expressed in his correspondence:[7]

> Yesterday being fair, I marched me to the vale of Mickleham. An English Tempe! Was there such delicious greenery? The nightingale saluted me on entering and departing. The walk has made of me a new man. I bathed anew in the Pierian fount. I cannot prose. I took Keats with me to read the last lines of Endymion at the spot of composition. [To W.C. Bonparte Wise, 27 April 1861]

> O Corsican! The naval man and the poet of Copsham [near Esher] have combined to arrange an expedition over Mickleham, and along the hills of laughing Surrey, into the heart of pastoral Hampshire … We lunch lightly at Copsham … then like arrows from Tartar's bow, out we sally; and away we go knapsack on back, singing – Hey, nonny nonny. [To Wise, 7 May 1861]

The walking habit was spreading when a new note was struck by Sir Leslie Stephen's Sunday Tramps, a walking club of London intellectuals founded in 1878, as important a milestone in the secularisation of the Sabbath as in the history of leisure. The free-thinking Tramps included retired mountaineers

87 *An idea of the new village created by the motor car in* Punch *magazine.*

II.—THE VILLAGE. NEW STYLE.

like Stephen himself who with advancing years had come to regard the long uninterrupted stretches of the southern slopes and crest of the North Downs and the heaths of the Leith Hill range as a geriatric substitute for the Alps. Meredith gives an account of one of the Tramps' excursions to Leith Hill in 1880 where they consumed a sack of cold sausages, Pollinharis and Hock before scrambling down 'the piny clefts' of Friday Street into the sloping meadows of the Tillingbourne and leaping through Evelyn's Wotton and along under Ranmore to his cottage for dinner.

The invention of the safety cycle in 1894 had quite momentous consequences for recreation and made the playground of the North Downs and Surrey Hills even more accessible. (The headquarters of the Cyclists' Touring Club was appropriately at Godalming.) Cycling became not a mere whim, as many expected, but a permanent passion. It was rapidly seized upon as one of the most stimulating and exhilarating forms of exercise of which the human body was capable. Seemingly, the whole world was awheel by 1900, exploring what was then a strange and half-forgotten rural landscape. Denton Welch has told of his exhilaration of riding down Wrotham Hill into the sunshine.[8] Clerks and shopmen, who thronged trams and gas-lit third-class waiting rooms on railway stations on weekdays, rode joyfully in bicycling clubs down the Portsmouth Road to Ripley on a Sunday from west London over Putney and Kingston bridges, or aimed to take a shandy gaff after their invigorating descent to the inn at the bottom of Liphook Hill, or after a scorch to the Mole Valley at the foot of Box Hill. Of the latter route it was noted: 'To the cyclist this is the last lap before the second shandy-gaff. To the Box Hill picnicker it is a way to heaven; to the Meredithean, the road to Mecca ...'. The cycle did much more than give exercise. As *The Spectator* wrote in 1894, 'For those who love "to sing the song of the open road" and whose idea of delight is to go somewhere where they have never been before ... the cycle has no fellow'. This was the theme taken up by H.G. Wells' new genre of cycling literature ushered in by Mr Hoopdriver, the Putney draper's assistant in *Wheels of Chance* (1896), whose world was unexpectedly opened up for him through cycling out of his suburb in his new brown cycling suit.

THE PEAK OF THE HIKING SEASON.

88 *Mr Punch's impression of the consequences of week-end rambling in the country in the 1930s.*

Moreover, the cycle was an emancipator; it levelled rich and poor and made it possible for both sexes to meet informally. Unchaperoned cycling couples led to the introduction of beer gardens and tea shops since no nice young girl entered the bars of pubs. Furthermore, as Malcolm Muggeridge has noted, a love of nature, partly promoted by cycling, and inspired by Brighton-born Edward Carpenter and American Walt Whitman, was proclaimed by his Edwardian generation as an enlightened alternative to religious worship. At weekends and on Bank Holidays Muggeridge's parents marshalled the family for country walks and bicycle rides. He never forgot the occasion of a 'tremendous feeling of exultation' near the church at Chipstead when the light of the setting sun slashed the trunks of trees, so that they were half gilded and half in shadow.[9] Richard Church has recalled his father's bicycle and trailer used by the family on holidays between Battersea and Alton. His father broke into song recklessly with not a care in the world:

> Oh merry goes the day
> When the heart is young

And as the roads were not tarred but paved in colours of the different stones by local councils in this variegated geological district, '… the fine choking powder gradually settled along the creases of our skin, our garments, and on every plane surface. By the time we reached Guildford we were three millers and the trailer gave the appearance of a load of limestone …'.[10]

With the more general use of the cheap motor car, the motorcycle and the charabanc, beauty spots within 30 miles of St Paul's, which could be reached with greater convenience than ever before, became crowded with trippers. By 1900 in spring and summer so many hundreds of people passed through railways stations to Shoreham in Kent that the village had six inns and extra carriages were put on trains to take them home to London. Many more came down in horse-drawn brakes, pony-traps, dog-carts and cycles to traverse the narrow country lanes and view the flower be-decked cottages, the bluebells, foxgloves, wild violets and bee orchids and the swift river Darent (then strongly flowing brimful before modern water abstraction drastically reduced the volume of this once perfect chalk stream).[11] Present-day weekend ramblers at Romney Street above Kemsing in west Kent see clearly the Post Office Tower near Oxford Street, the gigantic offices at Canary Wharf and the Thames Barrier a dozen miles away below them and yet can still exult in the pure air, wide views, silences and serenity of the uplands.

By the late 19th century, too, railways from Waterloo and Cannon Street provided easy access to Box Hill, which for the Londoner, even more than Burnham Beeches or Richmond Hill, has been the supreme place to enjoy the pleasures of scenery, whence views of the sandhills towards the Hog's Back stretch forward like many natural bastions into the oak-covered Weald below. Delighted recreationists and field naturalists, the latter equipped with haversacks, geological hammers, botanical vasculums, maps, compasses, gauze nets, clinometers and aneroids, unveiled the varied and wonderful world which lay around them, so unsuspected and yet so near! Never were happier people than those who brought back home at the close of a summer afternoon their specimens of plants, shells and rocks.[12] The Cockney was out in force on Sundays and Bank Holidays. Walkers explored it along the line of the old Pilgrims' Way and cyclists turned it into a mecca by the 1930s, flying along the cycling tracks, surely amongst the finest in England, alongside the A24 road to Worthing. Then the motorist arrived to sport up the mountain road with its hairpin bends or to park in ranks outside the *Burford Bridge Hotel*. On bank holidays and weekends in summer fleets of London buses carried passengers to and fro to climb this glamorous stretch of open downland and admire the panorama of the south country from the summit. Yet thanks to donations to the National Trust, which guards it so effectively and imaginatively, and the great efforts of the Surrey County Council and other organisations, the Hill remains virtually free of bungalows and other indiscriminate development. The man or woman who follows George Meredith's footsteps up the 'Happy Valley' on the northern flanks of the Hill is the heir to exceptional foresight and vision in the conservation of the English countryside.

Car-borne sight-seers also congregated at places like Newlands Corner, and the Silent Pool (so successfully 'boomed' by Martin Tupper whose historical romance *Stephen Langton* [1858] was intended to give the district a special 'literary lift' that it became one of the most photographed landscapes). Friday Street, below Leith Hill, also gave yearly pleasure to thousands, as did Ranmore Common, Headley Heath, the wooded and heather-clad hills of mid-Surrey and Kent, or wherever there was an extensive view. Of Newlands Corner before the motor-age, Amabel, the daughter of St Loe Strachey, editor of *The Spectator*, who subsequently married Clough Williams-Ellis, wrote of her father's week-ending there for more than forty years:

> No one who knows the two roads over the hill today can have the slightest idea of what a desolate spot Newlands Corner was in the year 1890. There was no post, there was no water; there was no noise of any sort. Occasionally a cart rumbled past the high hedge which bordered the farmhouse garden and no one at all seemed to drive up Clandon Hill.[13]

89 *Relics of Ten Acres Holiday Camp, Ewhurst, created in the 1920s. The proprietor reluctantly accommodated cyclists whom he thought too rowdy.*

Week-Ending

By the mid-1920s the habit of owning or renting a country cottage or wooded cabin for weekend use by physically exhausted Londoners during the summer for recreation, exercise, or simply for a change of air, became a middle-class cult. Harold Monro, the poet who kept the famous bookshop in Southampton Row, conveys the ecstasy and anticipation with which second-homers greeted Saturday:

> The train! The twelve o'clock for paradise.
> Hurry, or it will try to creep away.
> Out in the country everyone is wise
> We can be only wise on Saturday.
> There you are waiting, little friendly house:
> Those are your chimney stacks with you between,
> Surrounded by old trees and strolling cows,
> Staring through all your windows at the green.
> Your homely floor is creaking for our tread;
> The smiling teapot with contented spout
> Thinks of the boiling water and the bread
> Longs for the butter. All their hands are out
> To greet us, and the gentle blankets seem
> Purring and crooning; 'lie on us, and dream'.[14]

Meanwhile country walking in the 1930s (and even more the popular hiking movement founded by *The Daily Herald* in 1931 called the National League of Hikers) became even more urban in impetus and outlook, coinciding with the mass portent of urban civilisation in Germany of the *wandervogel* and similarly providing opportunities for hard physical exercise, a simple existence and contact with Nature lacking in everyday life. Adventurous hardy youngsters of both sexes, connected with workers' organisations and various Church and political bodies, became enthusiasts for such shared aspects of outdoor life as community singing, organised games, youth hostelling and camp life. A continuous stream of ramblers through places like Clandon followed the arrival of each London train during the summer and a ramblers' rally at St Martha's in 1934 attracted over 2,000 persons to whom messages were addressed by the

90 *Gustave Doré's London epitomised late Victorian congestion, dirt and noise.*

Archbishop of Canterbury. Appropriately, ramblers from all parts of London and the Home Counties gathered at Leith Hill in 1929 for the dedication of a memorial to Edward Sefang-Taylor, better known as 'Walker Miles', who more than any other writer has popularised the extraordinary loveliness of the countryside of his favourite county. Holiday camps sprang up all over the Downs and Hills such as Ten Acres Holiday Camp at Ewhurst, Surrey where the cabins survive.[15]

The impact of these various leisure pursuits on a rural community can be illustrated by Shere, Surrey, which even at the end of the 19th century rather smugly established its claim to be the most beautiful village in England. When its wild and sequestered loveliness was first discovered the smock-frock was still worn and the noise of the flail sounded in barns. By the 1880s the village had become a favourite haunt of landscape artists whose white umbrellas sprouted like mushrooms along the banks of the river Tillingbourne and by the old mill. These newcomers combined successfully to prevent the demolition of the old bridge over the stream on the grounds that it would deprive the village of much of its picturesqueness and so both impair their calling and the tourist business. In the 1890s cyclists discovered it. This reinforced the need to conserve the village; 'So much of the prosperity of Shere depends on its visitors that nothing must be allowed which would tend to throw any doubt as to its sanitary condition', said the current lord of the manor in 1898.[16] Today few villages in Surrey can surpass it for the combination of those qualities which make up the ideal village.

During the inter-war years Reginald Bray (pp.182-4) struggled to reconcile the conflicts between agriculture, forestry, conservation and recreation at a time when government, whether national or local, hardly had any power or influence – indeed hardly any interest – to become involved. Ideologically committed to the provision of outdoor recreation in the health-giving climate of his district, his most important step was to bring the Hurtwood and adjacent commonland of more than 2,000 acres under the provisions of the Law of Property Act, 1925, consequently giving the public freedom of access, subject to regulation in the common interest. He also scheduled another open space, the Churt, extending to 350 acres. A board of trustees, the Hurtwood Control Committee (which still exists), was set up to supervise the open spaces with the help of a countryside warden. Such developments have since become commonplace, but in Bray's day they were revolutionary.[17]

Bray also generously afforded facilities for outdoor recreation for people of limited means. He leased land for a holiday camp for the Bermondsey Settlement and helped to set up the National League of Hikers. He strongly identified himself with the Youth Hostel movement and provided sites for hostels at Holmbury St Mary and Ewhurst in 1935, amongst the first in the country. His connections with the Boy Scout and Girl Guide movements, and similar organisations, made his estate one of the most popular for camping.[18]

Bray enjoyed the intellectual company of weekenders (as had his predecessors) and their patronage of summer drama and music festivals helped to invigorate village life. The plays performed by the Otherwise Club in Shere Barn became

91 *George Vicat Cole,* Harvest Time *(1880).*

locally famous. Concurrent was the Leith Hill Music Festival founded in 1921 by Vaughan Williams. He enjoyed finding, adapting and building suitable property for townsmen who ran down from London on Saturdays. From weekend cottages on his estate in the inter-war years musical scores, books and journalism were delivered to their publishers and poetry, sketches and watercolours were created for his friends who included (Sir) Adrian Boult, Miss Helen Waddell, (Sir) G.M. Trevelyan, Wilson Harris (editor of *The Spectator*), the radio commentator Raymond Gram Swing, artist Mary Freeman and architect-planner Clough Williams-Ellis. But the main function of Shere weekend houses was to provide short periods of relaxation from London. J.W. Mackail, the biographer of William Morris and a leading literary critic, wrote in 1934 from Quaker's Orchard in Peaslake (a house previously rented by Sir Adrian Boult), 'It is a beautiful bit of country just on the edge of Hurt Wood, with any amount of woodland walks …'. There is some irony in the fact that the spirited attack against the spreading infection of the bungalow virus in southern England was mounted by Clough Williams-Ellis whose family were the occupants of a weekend cabin deeply buried in a wooded glade overlooking a perfect paradise of Surrey landscape! (The building still exists on the Downs above Shere.)[19]

Although some of the weekend fraternity entered fully into village life and found some of their closest friends there, other 'comers and goers' found it less easy to come to terms with the country and its life. Moreover, weekenders not only wanted new and different facilities, they developed a different awareness of the environment from that of the villager who resented these 'fly-by-night' rich suburban-minded and totally non-country stock.[20] For example, the 'blossoming

92 *John Clayton Adams,* Surrey Heathland.

gorse' valued by newcomers as a landscape resource was traditionally cut and burnt by local brick-makers. Furthermore, when Bray in 1924 sought to find a site for a village hall in Holmbury St Mary, a ludicrous situation developed. Bray saw Holmbury as 'a small place up in the hills which stands sadly in need of some centre where meetings and entertainments could be held'. Opposition to his proposal came mainly from weekenders with smart London addresses who feared for their weekend peace. The finally chosen site lies on the remotest edge of the settlement, buried in woodland. More perniciously, weekend visitors in the mid-1920s were offering high prices for workmen's cottages, getting out the tenants by some means, and converting the cottages to weekend villas. The working people became very bitter when local men who wanted to marry had to wait a considerable time before obtaining a cottage.[21] It was not only the weekender who was causing the problem. The building of large country houses had created a famine for chauffeurs, gardeners, and the like. In the late 19th century the really big householders had built their own suites of cottages in Holmbury or at farms; now it was more customary for newcomers to take over village cottages for their servants' use. By the late 1930s the situation had changed for the better because the shortage of domestic servants in the area meant that fewer wealthy people could contemplate a move from London.[22]

Bray recognised that the welfare of the country people on his estate was being prejudiced by the habit of weekending. 'The weekenders are the curse of this district', he wrote to the Minister of Agriculture in 1925.[23] By a strict control on the number of weekend cottages he built or let, he avoided the twin problems of the wooded hutments or caravans which were rapidly disfiguring parts of Surrey, and the potential social disintegration of the various village communities around him. To minimise damage to the locality Bray's hutments were confined to the Devil's Oven district of Ewhurst and Farley Green, and none of his own cottages was let to other than local workers.[24]

Limpsfield is famous for Beatrice Harrison, the leading British cellist of her time. She became known to millions in 1924 when, in BBC outside broadcasts, she played her cello in duet with a nightingale in Foyle Riding in Limpsfield 'at one of the most heavenly corners of Surrey'. The broadcasting experiment was repeated in 1925 and HMV made recordings which sold phenomenally. Visitors in hundreds came to Foyle Riding annually and children from the East End were bussed down to hear the nightingale sing to the cello.[25]

93 *Limpsfield churchyard, famed for its memorials to musical composers including Delius and Sir Thomas Beecham.*

'The country has me by the heart' brigade inevitably produced a satirical reaction. The most amusing is George Bernard Shaw's account of his walk from Farnham to Tilford to visit his friend, Henry Salt, who was then living there the Simple Life. Shaw recalled his route as one of dusty hedges, a ditch with dead dogs, rank weeds and poisonous flies, groups of children torturing something, a savage tramp, and the 'dull, toil-broken, prematurely old agricultural labourer'. He perceived the walk back as 'a leap from the brutalising torpor of Nature's tyranny over Man into the order and alertness of Man's organised dominion over Nature'. The only thing he liked in the weekend was the blackcurrant jam and boiling water that Mrs Salt administered to him when he arrived drenched through to the skin and cold to the wrist. There are also some other hints that in fact the parodist actually rather enjoyed himself.[26]

17

The Estate Management of the Brays of Shere

The Brays were the direct descendants of a nephew of Sir Reginald Bray (he dying without issue in 1503), whose acquisition of the manor of Shere and Gomshall on the attainder and execution of Lord Audley in 1497 began the family's association with these delightful places which still continues unbroken for more than five hundred years. The succeeding Brays were men of modest wealth and pretensions. In the manner of the 16th- and 17th-century landed gentry they became improvers and ironmasters. As landowners they ranked below the Evelyns of Wotton, whose estate, built up by the diarist's father and grandfather, exceeded 7,000 acres and supported a baronetcy from 1713, or the Onslows of Clandon, whose luxurious mansion and park bespoke of political distinction. Instead, the Brays found advance through the law, either as a country solicitor, or at the Bar, or in the Church, and it was the Revd George Bray and his brother William (1736-1832), who re-laid the fortunes of the family by purchasing farms which had previously been sold off. William, a solicitor by profession, was an amateur painter and student of the Picturesque as was the habit of his day. He was also an informed antiquary and took over and completed *The History of Surrey* from the Revd Owen Manning. He lionised John Evelyn and was the first editor of his Diary. He was also the first to appreciate the national and regional importance of the Loseley manuscripts. By his son's marriage to Mary Catherine Malthus, a daughter of Daniel Malthus of the Rookery, Dorking, and father of Thomas Malthus, the author of the economic classic on population, an additional strain of strong radical thinking was imparted to the Bray family connections. Reginald Bray, William's second son, married Frances, a daughter of T.N. Longman of the publishing house. His son, Reginald More Bray (1842-1923), was an eminent lawyer, appointed a judge of the High Court in 1904. His wife, Emily, a daughter of Arthur Barclay of Bury Hill, Dorking, was a writer of children's stories.[1] An account of Reginald Arthur Bray, the judge's eldest son (1889-1950), will conclude this chapter.

An Eighteenth-Century Surrey Squire in his Landscape

It is evident from the voluminous extant Bray family and estate muniments that successive generations were zealous lords of the manor of Shere and Gomshall, who invariably imparted their skills in estate management to their heirs. One whose Day Book was kept up for over forty years until his death, that of the Revd George Bray, is particularly illuminating on his life style and activities

94 Shere, Surrey, *a painting by Helen Allingham, c.1890. The oak has been replaced but little else has altered in this picturesque village.*

as lord of the manor between 1760 and 1803.[2] As a sportsman he frequently bought flints and guns from Mr Attree, a general dealer in the village of Shere, and his casting nets from a netmaker in Guildford. He was a heavy smoker and something of a gourmet with a liking for Bohea tea, Cheshire cheese and pickled salmon, items also supplied by Attree. Some of his wines came from London in a quarter cask which he bottled on his premises, but mostly he bought three dozen hampers of wine at a time. His port wine, bought by the dozen bottles, was delivered from Dorking, the empties being returned with payment. He bought malt and yeast to make his own beer. He paid quarterly for his laundry and the mending of his stockings. He bought ready-made breeches locally but for best wear his clothes were made up by a tailor from worsted and serge. When he wanted writing paper he went to Chilworth Mill to obtain it. He occasionally bathed at Littlehampton.

As lord of the manor, he received all the manorial dues, although his younger brother and successor, the solicitor William Bray, held the courts, usually at the clergyman's house, and received the standard legal fees for doing so. Beer was supplied by the court beadle to all who attended. Bray insisted on all the ancient manorial dues such as heriots and deodands. Two payments of the latter resulted from fatal accidents on the manor. A fine of 10s. became due when his employee, James Whitebread, was killed by a wheel when he fell from his wagon loaded with turf for fuel. Another deodand was received in respect of Abraham Heather, another employee, who died when a wagon overturned and fell on him. Bray also kept up the custom of beating the bounds. Each year a different part of the manor boundary would be traversed and participants were refreshed with beer. The bounds of manorial sheepwalks on the Downs had evidently become less well known than in the past and Bray went to great lengths to get them re-established.

When Bray had some building work to do at his house, Tower Hill, he burnt his own grey chalk for lime in a kiln fed by his own furzes from his 'waste' at Cranleigh, selling any surplus to requirements, quite a normal practice amongst landowners and farmers at the time, because furze was used as a fuel for baking and brick-making and small farmers bought it for their own lime-making. Building stone was dug on Holmbury Hill. For fuel he burnt turf (another general custom of the district), as well as faggots, but never coals which the manor did not supply. He allowed copyholders to sell oaks and ash who paid him one-third of their value, deducting the expenses of viewing. On occasion such payments were made long after felling to get a higher price for seasoned timber. In one instance, Bray's share of the money for oaks cut in May, but not sold until a year later, was not paid until Christmas. Another source of regular income came from the sale of oak bark sent to the tannery in Gomshall. Wayleaves through his property were granted by the token payment of a pullet. His damaged tools and kitchen equipment were regularly mended and not thrown away.

George Bray's Wages Book records work done by 11 labourers on a weekly basis in 1802.[3] They received bread and cheese for lunch; carters had beer. January was the month in which he planted beech and spread chalk on the meadows. February was the season for wheeling earth from the mixen on to meadows, chalking any not previously done, and repairing hedges with quickset. March was the time for planting acorns and picking stones from the fields. In April ashes were applied to meadows and bushes cut down in pastures. May was for planting larch. June and July were hay-making months, two quarts of beer being supplied to each harvester. In August earth was shovelled up from roads for fertiliser before reaping began. September was for nut and apple harvesting. In October and November three gallons of whitethorn seed and two of briars were sown in hedges and ditching began. The close of the year saw trees being planted in the Hurtwood.

Bray's memoranda also show the extent to which he was re-purchasing copyholds sold off by forebears. He purchased cottages, barns and land on 11 occasions from copyholders on his own manor. This suggests that the traditional rural society of small farmers was in its death throes. Several of these small fry had scraps of land in the last surviving common field which were converted

95 *The Bray Estate, Shere.*

to gardens or incorporated into Bray's own fields. The purchase of Edward Lambert's butcher's shop, 'at a great price', was for the sake of the amenity of Tower Hill. 'I foolishly missed the opportunity some years ago, when I could have had it much cheaper', he wailed.

Bray's accounts reveal him as a tree planter of the Ruggles sort. Having bought the manor Shere Eboracum in 1772 he at once obtained over 1,500 of Sir Frederick Evelyn's beech seedlings to plant round the old chalk pit at Combe Bottom. 1774 was the year when he planted 13,600 more beech on the estate, mainly on the old downland sheepwalk which was no longer being heavily grazed (a trend throughout the Surrey Downs at this time). In 1775, 8,000 Scots fir and 100 Weymouth pine were put in. In 1776 he planted firs on the Churt common and a poor field went under ash. In 1777 he was planting small oaks in the 'hedge rews' and clumps of fir on the sheepwalk on the Downs. In 1778 and 1779 he was engaged in planting the 'land's ends' of fields with beech and ash, and another poor field was converted to woodland. Some Scots pine went into hedges and box trees were planted on the Downs. Bray was also refurbishing the orchards and kitchen garden walls with fruit trees right up to his death. Thus Bray emerges as a landscapist who had a major effect on the appearance of his locality, which became an example which others followed. His younger brother thus secured a goodly inheritance to add to his legal fees and set him up for editing John Evelyn's Diaries.

A Twentieth-Century Squire in his Landscape

It is a fallacy to assume that the scope for estate management by the surviving 20th-century squires had fast dwindled into insignificance before the Second World War when government interference, both national and local, was greatly increasing in such matters as housing, employment and health. Reginald Arthur Bray, in fact, found that estate work gradually took up more and more of his time and energy until it became virtually a full-time occupation, although his father and predecessors had carried on estate business as a labour of love in their spare time. This was partly because of the growing bureaucratic complexities and the increased burden of taxation and death duties on land initiated by the Finance Act, 1910, together with the more business-like attitudes to property this necessitated.[4]

Reginald Arthur Bray (1869-1950) became the squire of Shere when he inherited the estate of some two thousand acres of farmland and woodland and two thousand acres of commonland. He retained to his death the privileges, power and position of the squirearchy at this period but he was untrue to this type and few men with his antecedents had a more unaffected attitude to life or prescribed more to social progress. He never hunted, he seldom even rode, did not race horses or indulge in country house luxury. His work and pleasure was engaging conscientiously in estate management from 1896 and to meet the needs of the community. He saw his role as vital in the transitional period between traditional paternalism on the one hand, and the still delayed advent of the Welfare State. His ideas and actions have an added significance because he was not only a manager of neighbouring rural estates but also spent much time between 1900 and 1919 as a social reformer in working-class Camberwell, as a councillor on the London County Council. From this unaccustomed and illuminating dual position he left a lasting mark on the education policy of the metropolis, and his later achievements proved eventful in the history of town and country planning.[5]

Bray developed his interest in social reform with Charles F.G. Masterman,[6] who became junior minister in Liberal administrations, through their joint work for the Cambridge University Settlement in Camberwell from 1904. Between then and 1910 Bray was a member of an *avant-garde* group of historians-to-be, G.M. Trevelyan and R.C.K. Ensor, and the future politicians Charles Trevelyan, Noel Buxton and F.W. Pethick-Lawrence-Bray and his friends regarded the disproportionate growth of London as one of the greatest social evils of the day. For them, the most characteristic feature of the metropolis was the chaotic, coagulating inner suburban ring of labouring poor who had been sucked in from the surrounding rural districts. Masterman's picture of their monotonous daily lives, their long journeys to work, their wolf-up meals, 'the engine-like activity and moroseness even of pleasure', in short the bleakness and futility of human life in places such as Lambeth, Camberwell, Deptford and parts of Wandsworth is sketched in vivid but unexaggerated phrases. The contrast between the beauty and serenity at Shere and the world of man as drably created in inner South London stirred Bray's conscience and remained a consistent source of inspiration to him, and from his dual perspective he was uniquely equipped to become absorbed in the attempt to reduce the tensions arising between town and country around London and to draw them more closely together. As a Fabian, between 1905 and 1948 he chose to work towards improving the London environment through the medium of education which he saw as the means of helping working-class people both to play a more effective role in society and to enrich their own lives.

Estate Management

Bray's involvement with the Shere estate lasted 54 years. He began to assist his father in running it in 1896; in 1904 (the year of his father's appointment as a High Court judge) he took over full responsibility; and in 1923 it became his inheritance. Bray's father became a country squire at weekends free of judicial duties in London, as had his own father, who had combined a flourishing solicitor's practice in London with periodic visits to Shere where he also enjoyed being at the centre of real village life. Reginald Bray saw estate management more as a social responsibility and a hobby than a source of private income, until it became virtually a full-time occupation. This he did on a shoe-string. 'I can afford neither clerk nor agent and have to do all the clerical work myself', he wrote of his affairs in the mid-1920s.

Bray's first major task was to re-evaluate and adapt the estate management in the light of the provisions of the Finance Act, 1910, and the heavy burden of death duties and income which this portended.[7] These bore

96 *Reginald Bray's forestry at Pitch Hill near Shere.*

hardly on Shere and other estates verging on the Downs because their market value was substantially based on amenities such as scenic beauty and historical connections, which were taken into account, for the first time, by the new legislation. Broadly speaking, Bray's plan was similar in many respects to other landowners in the same circumstances. He was obliged to reduce the costs of building and repairs, to cut the estate work-force and re-organise the tenant farms for dairying. His decision to invest in forestry because he perceived that it had long-term prospects over agriculture (misguided as it turned out) gives his work added interest.

His policy with regard to estate cottages was characteristic. Over-crowding was still a problem despite the flow of labourers to London and other cities, and Bray still whole-heartedly regarded the provision of cottages as a function of the landowner. In all 86 cottages were owned, of which 32 were erected between 1896 and 1914 and five more between the two World Wars. His aim was to modernise cottages without sacrificing their external appearance. The tenanted farms numbered 16 and proved a specially heavy burden. Improvements were periodically necessary – barns and granaries before 1914, piped water and conversions for dairies in the 1920s and '30s. The bad farming years of 1921 and 1925 led to a deterioration in the land and in the quality of farmers. By the end of the 1920s Bray found it difficult to get good farmers for some of the poorer farms and was obliged to offer reduced rents to their successors. Steadily the position worsened. Field after field was given up to thistle and ragwort. (During the Second World War the War Agricultural Committee compulsorily requisitioned two farms and part of another and ploughed up 150 acres of old pasture.) Very profitable in comparison were shooting rents from people who rushed down from London in their cars on Saturdays and rushed back when time was up.

On his comparatively poor land on the heavy, water-retentive soils of Surrey, the sandy, limeless soils of the sandstones and on the 'clay-with-flints' on the North Downs, Bray turned his thoughts to afforestation (as had his 18th-century predecessor) and in this respect was a notable creator of new landscapes. It must be borne in mind that in prosperous times for agriculture in England, Caird in 1850-1 found Bray's district an 'island' of comparative neglect. In the 1890s several farms on the Bray estate were in a dilapidated state, the roughest parts being used for shooting and poultry rearing, and poor farming practices prevailed throughout the Tillingbourne valley and its environs up to 1939.[8]

The art and practice of forestry afforded Bray his happiest experiences and was the source of his most controversial decisions. He appears to have been strongly influenced by a Fabian tract on forestry and the popularity of afforestation with the new Labour Party as a means of relieving rural unemployment. Before the First World War he raised plantations of larch and spruce in the Churt adjoining the Hurtwood and from 1923 replanted under various government schemes for the unemployed and later under subsidised Forestry Commission schemes. The fine high forest of Spanish chestnut on the North Downs in West Horsley, the beech stands around Hollister and Medlands farms in Shere, and plantations of now flourishing Corsican pine, Douglas fir and larch in the Churt are of this period. Some 10-20 acres of woodland were planted annually, the maximum the estate could afford in terms of costs, though Bray appreciated it should have been larger. This was rectified after the Second World War when in 1949 he entered into a dedication scheme with the Forestry Commission for a 10-year planting programme on the Hurtwood Common, the Churt and other parts of the estate. This decision gave a completely new look to the district. Neither the trustees of the commons, nor Sir Jocelyn Bray, his successor as lord of the manor, approved of such a drastic change on what had been largely open heath, and Bray was much criticised by the Council for the Preservation of Rural England, ramblers' associations and other amenity bodies. Bray took the view that national considerations of timber supply should take precedence over any others.[9] This afforestation of former heathland means that the former carefree heather walking can only be recaptured in Victorian landscape paintings, such as by John Clayton Adams, who expresses with great élan the charming appearance of the Victorian landscape.

18

The Victorian Church, Rural Arts and Crafts, and Attempts at Religious and Social Reform

The Victorian Church

Surrey has more Victorian churches than Kent because it was changed by railways from a sparsely populated county into one of the most densely inhabited parts of England and, as more and more commuters took up residence, church-rebuilding and restoration gathered momentum. Late 18th- and early 19th-century watercolours may reveal the nature of churches before the Victorian changes. Henry Petrie's painting of Headley church in 1798 and a Cracklow print of 1827 show a simple three-cell structure comprising chancel, nave and western tower with buttresses at the angles, and a small west porch.[1] This was replaced by what Ian Nairn calls 'a harsh conjunction: nave and chancel by Salvin and appalling tower, 1859 by Street, and not bad, if hard ...'. J. Hassell's watercolours of Tandridge church painted between 1820 and 1830 show the original Norman building, the original Norman chancel arch and the lack of side aisles, box pews, a gallery and three-decker pulpit, all of which were to be greatly changed by 'restorations'. Similarly, a picture emerges of a small and simple church at Ashtead which was evidently too poor to afford the normal addition of aisles. This had fallen into such a ruinous state by the early 19th century that Paget wrote:

> When Ashtead church was first known in 1817 it was remembered much in the condition in which most rural churches were seen half a century earlier. It was damp and cheerless; for by the accumulation of soil through frequent interments anyone standing on the outside of the south-eastern window of the nave could have had his feet nearly on the level with the desk of the pulpit within ...[2]

The writer's recollections seem to carry him back to a strunk-shaped plaster ceiling and an edifice chocked up with high pews, dark and cellar-like. A musicians' gallery stretched across the west end of the nave, painted bright blue. The first and gentlest wave of ecclesiastical revival came to Ashtead in the 1820s. A complete restoration followed in 1862; 'a preposterous job', remarked Nairn. A different fate awaited Haslemere: Sir Robert Hunter protested, successfully, against the enlargement of the church on the grounds that it would destroy its character and the harmony with its setting.[3]

The influence of Sir George Gilbert Scott (1811-78) on the restoration of churches was immense. To him, more than any other individual, is owed the architectural movement known as the Gothic Revival. He was inspired by Augustus Pugin and the Cambridge Society and came to realise that France was the real cradle of Gothic church building when he visited Amiens, Beauvais and Chartres. An incomplete list in *The Builder* records 732 buildings with which Scott was connected as architect or restorer. These included 29 cathedrals, 476 churches, 26 public buildings and 43 mansions. He told his son at the end of his life, 'I have been one of the leading actors in the great architectural movement which has occurred since the classic Renaissance. I only seek to be placed before the public fairly and honourably, as I trust I deserve'. His remark was inspired by an attack on him by William Morris, who severely took him to task for over-zealous restoration, specifically at Tewkesbury Abbey, and co-founded the Society for the Protection of Ancient Buildings on the strength of that. Scott himself claimed that he was strictly conservative in his work, but for which many of our finest churches would simply have fallen down, so bad was their state of repair. Nevertheless, there is a belief that he was guilty of energetic renovation instead of restoration in some cases.

Blatch considers St Mary's Shackleford (1865), built of Bargate stone in the early English style, one of his best.[4] Scott added the south aisle to St Peter's, Tandridge in 1874 and most of the windows are restorations by him. He also replaced the original Norman chancel arch by the existing pointed arch. Holy Trinity, Westcott was an entirely new church built by him in 1851-2 for a new parish of about 1,000 persons which had hitherto been

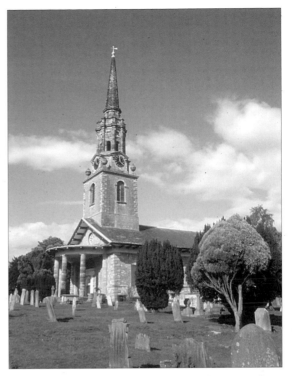

97 *Mereworth church, completely rebuilt in the early 18th century.*

98 *Betchworth church before restoration, from a photograph taken in 1915 of a pencil drawing c.1861.*

99 *Ranmore church, 'the Church of the Downs', one of the finest works of Sir George Gilbert Scott.*

100 *Interior of Ranmore church.*

part of the large parish of Dorking. The cost of the building was raised by subscription and Charles Barclay of Bury Hill, the initiator of assisted emigration (p.151), was the principal benefactor. In dressed flint with a shingled spire, it imparts an appropriate village atmosphere. A south aisle was added in 1855 and an unusual mosaic reredos was erected in 1882. The beautiful east window depicting the Ascension was the work of James Powell and Son of Whitefriars, and was given by a member of the Barclay family in 1889. The tall slender spire of St Barnabas' at Ranmore Common standing on the downs 700 feet above sea level, and one of the greatest landmarks in Surrey, is visible across the Vale of Holmesdale from the porch of Westcott church. It was built at the sole expense of George Cubitt, M.P., the son of Thomas Cubitt, the London builder who retired to his mansion at Denbies. The church was intended to serve the 300 or more estate workers and their families. The octagonal tower, lavish marble shafts and rich naturalist vaulting of the cross and the elaborate fittings, especially the font, pulpit and rich reredos, make this a veritable *tour de force*.

It is a striking foil to Henry Woodyer's St Martin's at Dorking. Woodyer's practice was based in Surrey and, with Scott, he is the leading figure in the county. Buckland, Burpham, Grafham, Hascombe and Wye are his. In his own parish of Grafham he built and paid for the apsed chapel of 1861-4 and Buckland, built of Bargate stone in 1860, received from Nairn the accolade of 'village church building at its best'. Most of Bramley is Woodyer's. Hascombe (1864) was the inspiration of Canon Vernon Musgrave who was shocked at the state of the parish church with its high box pews and commissioned Woodyer to create a church of his own in Bargate stone. Musgrave paid for the chancel himself and persuaded four local landowners to finance the rest. Musgrave also decorated the church piecemeal as money became available. The entire nave is devoted to the theme of the Miraculous Draught of Fishes and the chancel glows with colour. 'Every inch of wall and ceiling is decorated, even the window splays. The rafters, cusped and gilded, spread out from the apse like a giant fin, as if trying frantically to cool the heat below … The walls are covered with murals or mosaic. Angels trumpet from the embroidered altar frontal …'. Together with its vivid stained glass, it is one of the most exciting Victorian churches in the country. Musgrave, who attended to every detail in the building over 44 years, is commemorated in medieval style by a brass in the chancel floor.[5] Notable amongst Woodyer's restoration was St Martha's (1848-50) on the Pilgrims' Way. This was in ruins and was almost re-built by Woodyer, using old materials as far as possible. The drawing of pilgrims climbing the hill was given to the church by E.H. Shepard, the illustrator of *Winnie-the-Pooh*. Other restored churches along the line of the Pilgrims' Way include Peper Harrow, Albury (see p.191) and Gatton. The latter is so laden with the furnishing acquired during Lord Monson's travels in Europe that Dr Charles Cox denounced it as 'absolutely unsuitable for God's worship in an English village'. (But there is no village, Gatton being a notoriously Rotten Borough with a toy Town Hall.) The north transept is an undespoiled family pew, the perfect example of the English nobleman's desire to worship in comfort. It has a fireplace, panelled overmantel, padded benches and comfortable chairs.

101 *Congregation of Woodlands Church near Kemsing.*

A strong personality who dominated the Victorian church at Albury was Henry Drummond (1786-1860), a wealthy banker, country gentleman and Tory M.P. for Surrey. He shared with J.B. Cardale (the pillar of the Apostles who died at Albury in 1877) the founding of the Catholic Apostolic Church. Drummond had been stirred by Edward Irving's apocalyptic eloquence in London and he built in 1840 the large church in Albury intended as the spiritual centre and administrative base for the newly-formed body of Christians whose fervent conviction was that the Second Coming of Christ was imminent, a thought brought about by the conclusion of traditionalists that the French Revolution, the rise of industrialism and seemingly irreversible changes in urban and rural society had created a state of crisis. Twelve members of the Church, several of great distinction, were known as the Apostles and an octagonal chapter house was built off the north transept for their deliberations. By the middle years of the 19th century the Church was flourishing at home and abroad. The Gordon Square church (now the central church of the University of London), largely funded by Drummond, was used for the monthly gatherings of members of seven other churches in the capital. Yet when the Apostles finally died out in 1901 ordinations and full rituals could no longer take place so that when all the ministers, priests and deacons who had been ordained by the Apostles were also deceased (in 1929, 1971 and 1972 respectively) the churches, including Albury, closed.[6]

Drummond was also responsible for building a new parish church for the village of Albury in 1842 at Weston Street (notable for the wonderful flourish of fluted chimney stacks) and for closing the ancient parish church which stands

102 *Albury old church, replaced by a new church at Weston Street.*

near the Albury Park mansion. He took over the south transept of the old church to serve as a mortuary chapel for his family, designed by Augustus Pugin, then only 27 years of age. Long before Drummond's time, traces of the old village of Albury, which had originally stood around the old church in Albury Park, had disappeared. The villagers had moved to the hamlets of Weston Street and Little London in the present parish of Albury. In 1839 the Bishop of Winchester authorised Drummond to build a new parish church in the new village as a replacement for the old church which was in a bad state of repair. The old church is notable for the incumbent William Oughtred, vicar for 50 years, tutor to Wren and a gifted mathematician. It is also remarkable for the wall painting depicting St Christopher full length, probably executed *c.*1480. This was plastered over, probably by Oughtred during the Commonwealth period to preserve it, and it was only re-discovered in 1844. The Duke of Northumberland, a great-grandson of Henry Drummond, preserved the remains of the fresco and it was treated with preservative again in 1919 when the eminent restoration architect and antiquary, Philip Mainwaring Johnston, made a survey of the church.

Drummond's closure of the old parish church went much against the feelings and wishes of some of the congregation. Martin Tupper (d.1899), an occupant of Albury House and famed in the early Victorian era for his moralising *Proverbial Philosophy* (1838-67), was angered at the loss of burial rights in the old churchyard where he had buried two children. Louisa Charlotte Bray, daughter of Edward and Mary Ann Malthus and grandchild of William Bray, also observed in her diary her grief when the last service was performed in the old church in 1841. She thought that the saying that he who moves a church will lose his heir, was literally fulfilled in Mr Drummond's case, who lost his three sons, one after another.

On account of the appalling neglect of church fabric during the 17th and 18th centuries it is often unjust to blame Victorians for their drastic methods of restoration. An example is Stockbury in Kent which was burned down in 1836 and Richard Hussey's re-building is considered 'harsh' by John Newman.[7] Victorians saw things differently. The archdeacon's visitation reports on the church for 1871 and 1876 are distinctly favourable. He was impressed by the zeal and taste of the incumbent, the Revd David Twopenny, who held the benefice for more than forty years and was a much loved and respected vicar. He was one of many wealthy 19th-century clergy who devoted their lives and fortunes to the revival of their church. It was noted that his affectionate care for the structure and furnishings of his church had had a positive effect on neighbouring parishes. Hussey had designed a church with 286 seats in all. Seats in the north transept were reserved for poor families, and single men and women were segregated. At Loose, where the vestry agreed a special rate for the enlargement of the church in 1819, a beadle was then appointed at the rate of one shilling a week to keep order in the church and the churchyard during Divine Service and shopkeepers were reminded that their shops should be closed on the Sabbath.[8] The two people who contributed towards expenses were granted single pews in the body of the church.[9]

Another example is Luddesdown, hidden in a fold in the hills. The writer Denton Welch met in 1946 the daughter of the vicar who rebuilt the church in 1856. The previous incumbent spent his week in the British Museum and he did his visits, took the service every week and was off again to his books. The church had been utterly neglected by the absentee and was allowed to get into such a ruinous state that it all had to be taken down. Although he was told that everything was saved that could be saved, Welch thought they had been very sparing with their preservation. The pitiful remnants of the old church were 'gripped and held in a glistening mass of new flint' and imagined 'greedy architects and contractors fatly thinking how well the tottering church would pull down …'. The re-building vicar had built two schools as well. 'There used to be fifty children in each. There weren't twelve when they were closed', because the young people had left the village and only the old ones stayed.[10] Welch had earlier visited Burham Old Church, lying derelict and utterly bare. It was then still roofed and with fragments of glass in the windows and had evidently been larger, with side aisles, several centuries earlier. Troops had been billeted there during the last War.[11] St Giles' Shipbourne was re-built in 1722 by Lord Barnard of Fairlawne, incorporating parts of earlier buildings. When Edward Cazalet, a wealthy merchant in the Russian trade, bought the Fairlawne estate in 1871, he eventually persuaded the villagers to allow him to replace it and the new church was opened for worship in 1881. Contemporary accounts in newspapers described it as 'one of the most charming country churches to be found anywhere', but opinion is more divided today. As Simon Jenkins has observed, 'The modern eye has yet to appreciate restored art other than as a defacing of art'.[12]

Happily surviving in a once simple village church restored out of existence by Carpenter and Slater are two medieval stained glass windows at Stowting. Of perhaps the first half of the 14th century, is a vivid red, gold and green rendering of the Virgin and Child. The other, perhaps of the middle 15th century, depicts three saints under canopies, and below each a group of kneeling donors. An inscription relating to the latter mentions Richard Stotyne and his wife Juliana, who may have been the wealthy benefactors.

Attempts at Religious and Social Reform in the Countryside

By the 1880s many men's minds were oppressed by a profound sense of disillusionment with mechanical mass-production and increasing urbanisation. In a mood of nostalgia and regret was dreamt the lure of the simple life and a purer, pre-industrial world. For the vast majority of Londoners it remained a dream. Some, indeed, like the earlier generation of Samuel Johnson, William Hogarth, William Blake, J.M.W. Turner and Charles Lamb the essayist, were quintessential Londoners who would not be torn from their 'loadstone' of the capital and remained wedded to the crowds, the smoke, the dirt, noise and violence. Some were lucky enough to live in 'greener' parts of London such as Mayfair and artistically-induced Edwardian home-buyers could reside in what John Betjeman called 'the best and earliest of garden suburbs', Bedford Park at Turnham

Green, marketed at the end of the 19th century as 'the healthiest place in the world'. Here the Bedford Parkers could combine elements of rural charm with urban practicality without 'needing the rest of London'. A very few (but who had far-reaching effects on the re-shaping of landscapes and societies, domestic architecture and interior design) were inspired by Ruskin's and Morris's outrage at what they perceived as the damage to human life and culture, took the matter to its logical conclusion and abandoned the city for the country.

Such people took cottage life, rural handicrafts and the ordered regularity of the country workshop as their ideals, with all the charms of the countryside that went with them. C.R. Ashbee's Guild of Handicrafts in the Cotswolds was a magnet but so also were villages in Sussex and in the North Downs and Surrey Hills. With them came the *nouveaux riches* and aesthetes restoring old manor houses and buying Arts and Crafts houses with Gertrude Jekyll gardens, slightly earnest pots and beautiful textiles. With their nostalgic hang-ups about industrialisation they developed their own set of political and moral principles.

PEASANT ARTS GUILD

17 Duke Street, Manchester Square, W. 1

(near Selfridge's; 'Phone Mayfair 4347)

This Guild is a Society of those who believe in the spiritual and economic necessity for the restoration of simple country life and crafts. Its craft-workers produce and its Depôt exhibits varied and inexpensive examples of the work of its own and associated craftsmen. Woollen Jerkins, Scarves, etc., vegetable-dyed, hand-spun and hand-woven ; Linens ; Cottons ; Books ; Toys ; Pottery ; Metal Works ; Welfare Talismans and Prints.

Welcome extended to all, whether coming as purchasers or interested visitors.

Catalogues on application

HASLEMERE
WEAVING INDUSTRY
KING'S ROAD, HASLEMERE, SURREY

In the famous Hindhead district, forty miles from London : Rail from Waterloo ; Road through Kingston and Guildford.

Established thirty years ago, this hand-weaving craft produces fabrics for dress or furniture in linen, cotton and wool.

London Agency and Showrooms :
PEASANT ARTS GUILD
17 DUKE STREET
W. 1

10

103 *Advertisements for Arts and Crafts, c.1925.*

Haslemere was one of the outstanding centres of rural arts and crafts created by a loathing of urban life and industrialisation which sprang from the influence of John Ruskin and William Morris, the inspired advocate of the revival of handicrafts. Its origin was a remarkable partnership of four persons: the barrister Joseph King and his artistic wife, Maude, who started hand-weaving in Haslemere in 1894 and Godfrey Blount and his wife Ethel (sister of Maude King), who moved to Haslemere in 1896 and set up the Peasant Arts Society the following year in the belief that the spiritual and economic restoration of simple country life and crafts was a necessity to national well-being. The sisters were daughters of Henry G. Hine, noted for his water colours of the South Downs.[13]

Blount was the pivotal figure. He was a distinguished artist and craftsman who had been for a time a student of Professor Sir Hubert von Herkomer at Bushey and had attended the Slade School. He provided the designs for carpet and rug

104 *Jonathan Hutchinson's sanatorium, Haslemere, now converted into a private residence.*

weaving and other textile industries at Haslemere; made wood carvings which gave a distinctive beauty to furniture; worked on lino and acquired a hand-printing press so as to produce widely varied pamphlets for his causes. The Peasant Arts Society, with which he and his wife were associated for over 35 years, encouraged handicrafts, enlightened the public to their value, and found selling organisations in London and elsewhere. What made Blount exceptional, however, were his deep moral and religious convictions and his almost messianic belief that he could lead people's return to the land, revive country life and crafts, and so eventually accomplish his ultimate object, the reformation of English society. His New Crusade, with religious, moral and social overtones, launched in 1903, was a re-thinking on Christian principles to counter the materialistic tendencies hindering what he regarded as the indispensable revival of old country customs, such as the May Day Festival and the restoration of folk music, singing and country dancing. In essence it was an appeal for simpler ways of living than in London and other cities and a rejection of machinery and mechanisation. He saw the setting up of a museum of traditional Arts and Crafts, craft workshops, and a new church, 'The Country Church', an indispensable way forward to his goal. This was based on the principles of simplicity, self-sacrifice for the community and the sacredness of all living things.

Blount inspired his colleagues to provide strong support. Joseph King was a Liberal M.P. and an active educational reformer and congregationalist who offered the site for the proposed Museum of Peasant Arts, had the Weaving House built in 1898 and together with Greville MacDonald started the Vineyard Press to publish the Peasant Arts Society's reports and magazine devoted to tales of peasant life. MacDonald, who married another of the Hine sisters, was a surgeon who bought the collection of Peasant Art objects from the Revd. Gerald Davies and donated it to the Peasant Arts Society. King's wife, Maude, was inspired by Godfrey Blount to be an educational reformer and ran the Haslemere Weaving Industry with Catherine Hird-Jones. She was also a writer of short stories and novels on 'progressive' country themes. Her sister Ethel was co-founder with her husband of the Peasant Tapestry Industry and ran a craft school of spinning and weaving.

105 *G.E. Street's Holmbury St Mary church.*

Under the aegis of these remarkable people, Haslemere sprouted handicrafts on a substantial scale but few businesses survived more than a short while, though they strove to find a London outlet such as Liberty's or Heal's. Blount's wider appeal to the country at large appears to have been unsuccessful. As Europe still had a peasantry which carried on traditional crafts which had long ceased to flourish in Britain, inspiration was sought there, and in particular, Scandinavia, which provided the design of hand-looms and many of the objects acquired for the unique Museum of Peasant Arts (now the Haslemere Educational Museum). Textile industries were the most important of the Haslemere crafts. The starting point of the settlement was the Haslemere Weaving Industry which became established in the Weaving House in King's Road. Then came the Blounts' St Cross Industries (based on their house) which produced tapestries, appliqué work and hand-woven pile carpets. Luther Hooper wove silk, worsted and linen damasks, brocades and velvets whilst Edmund Hunter brought silk weavers from Spitalfields who wove magnificent church vestments, hangings, curtains and dress fabrics. Besides the textiles Radley Young had established a hand-made pottery at Hammer near Haslemere, and Romney Green made hand-made dining tables, armchairs and other furniture in English oak and walnut. Other handicraftsmen bound books, smote iron and cleaved and carved wood. James Guthrie (who later moved to South Harting in Sussex) operated a hand-printing press. The central purpose of all these craftsmen was to make useful things as beautifully as may be for the sake of the community.

The most successful business after the First World War was that of the Inval Weavers. This was established in 1922 by two pioneering women, Ursula Hutchinson and Hilda Woods in the grounds at Inval, just outside Haslemere, of the physician Sir Jonathan Hutchinson, Ursula's father.[14] The old Quaker Meeting House at Inval became their showroom; a derelict coach-house and stables were used as a dye-house. Eventually more looms were added to an upper floor above the stables. On the grass outside a range of clothes lines was put up on which skeins of dyed wool were hung to dry. (The premises are identifiable, although they are now in residential occupation.) The sisters learned the craft of hand-loom weaving at Ethel Mairet's famed workshop at Ditchling, Sussex. Only natural dyes were used, initially from hedgerows. Fleeces increasingly came from agricultural shows at which the weavers were exhibitors. As the business expanded, however, so the number of spinners and braid-makers working from home increased, and full-time help was needed in the weaving and dye-sheds. A full-time dressmaker made up woven material into clothing until the business ended in 1936.

Haslemere attracted numerous others of an unorthodox spirit and forward-looking minds. One was Sir Jonathan Hutchinson, a Quaker and an internationally-known medical practitioner and President of the Royal College of Surgeons, who in 1872 bought Inval as his holiday home. Although keeping up his medical contacts in London, he farmed, brought up his children in country air and enjoyed shooting parties. His dream was to make the pure air of the healthy and beautiful country of Haslemere easily accessible to people of moderate incomes. In this he was in large measure successful. He made extensive purchases of land on which his younger son designed and built more than 70 houses. Provided local materials were used he had little regard for design. He preferred timber construction, dry and inexpensive, to brick, which was liable to damp at a time when damp-courses were exceptional. Some of his houses were very cheaply built but by using local tiles and thatch and covering the exterior with rough larch 'slabs' they fitted into their rural surroundings. These simple dwellings were mainly used for weekending and holiday parties from London before the days of youth hostels and camping sites. The elder Hutchinson's friends and others who were early visitors included Edward Nettleship, the eminent oculist, and his brother Jack Nettleship and Tristram Ellis, both artists. In 1898 he built a country home for sick London children which still exists, though now converted into a residence. Hutchinson was a warm friend of Sir Robert Hunter and an ardent supporter of the National Trust. He was such a convinced supporter that *c.*1914 he voted in a minority of three for the provision of a new road along the ridge to Blackdown. All Haslemere had turned up in opposition. Hutchinson justified his position by describing the view from Blackdown as a national asset and that everything should be done to enable the greatest possible number to enjoy it. The majority wanted Blackdown to remain an unspoilt place and not become like Hindhead with a motor car behind every bush.

106 *Albury House, home of Henry Drummond, the banker, and subsequently of the Duke of Northumberland.*

107 *Durbins near Guildford, designed by C.A.F. Voysey.*

In later life, under the impact of Darwinism, Hutchinson became passionately fond of natural history, and teaching, through the medium of educational museums, became the object of his life. His own collection of objects formed the basis of the first museum at Haslemere in two large barns at Inval. In 1894 the museum was moved to specially-built premises in East Street before finally reaching its present site. He himself lectured at the museum which had the skilled E.W. Swanton as the first curator. Hutchinson was initially criticised by religious groups for his natural history teaching, for his convictions seemed to clash with preconceived opinions and doctrines but the atmosphere changed with the coming of Canon Barnett as rector in 1897.[14] When Hutchinson died in 1912 similar educational museums were being set up all over the country. He could never have envisaged how his pioneer work would have developed, for example, into the work of the Field Studies Council at Juniper Hall in the Vale of Mickleham after the Second World War.

Arnold Dolmetsch re-established English instrumental music *c.*1500-1700 as a modern movement and created a revolution in music as great as Morris in furniture and Philip Webb in domestic architecture. He established the Haslemere Festival from 1925, an annual event which brought music lovers from all over the world to hear the tranquil smooth-flowing sounds, which were a refreshment to a noise-ridden society, and to visit his famous workshops where hand-made harpsichords, clavichords, recorders, viols and other instruments on which the old music was performed were manufactured.[15]

Although George Sturt (Bourne) of Farnham also advocated resistance to change in the countryside, he was more realistic than the Haslemere reformers. He saw some disadvantages in the traditional rural life – the waste of time brewing one's own beer, or baking one's own bread and that peopled aged prematurely, children lost charm, and the loveliness of girls was gone before they grew up. He realised that there was no going back to traditional peasant life on the old terms but he was concerned at the 'spiritual' state of rural Surrey in the first decade of the 20th century. With the end of peasant life he thought that most of the meaning of the landscape, and half its charm, had been lost. He hoped that a greater sense of social

108 *Sir Edwin Lutyens' Goddards, Abinger.*

and economic justice would one day supersede the present order. The feature of old Surrey society which was all-important to Sturt was the instinctive regard for the needs of others. Individualism with its aggressive ambition to assert one's own interests now prevailed. Noting the well-kept villas, trim lawns, hedges, pergolas and the retired colonels and parsons who manifested 'country' values then, he argued that there was no room for these new residents where there was true country life, for those people who outwardly manifested rural values and yet made 'a sort of toy or harlot of the beautiful country – keeping it to themselves, or setting it, without true understanding'. He wanted to recover 'the folk attitude to life' and to re-assert its knowledge and care of the environment. His message is of immense importance to the modern world and the world of the future. A memorial tablet on the wall of Farnham parish church by Eric Gill commemorates Sturt's literary gifts. His wheelwright shop at 84 East Street has gone, but Vine Cottage remains much the same as when the Sturts came to live there in 1891.[16]

Arts and Crafts Domestic Architecture and Gardening

Ralph Nevill's *Old Cottage and Domestic Architecture in South-West Surrey* (1889) is significant because he was the first architect to study and interpret the Surrey vernacular in connection with his alterations and additions to old houses.[17] His drawings had considerable influence on a great number of architects. John Betjeman has argued that it was G. Edmund Street who was the real founder of the Arts and Crafts Movement, associated with the names of Norman Shaw, William Morris, Sedding and Philip Webb, all of whom worked in Street's office.[18] He certainly left a deep mark on Surrey with, for example, his church and home, Holmdale, at Holmbury St Mary. By the end of the 19th century Norman Shaw (1831-1912) and two of his pupils, Mervyn McCartney and Ernest Newton, were re-creating styles and building techniques of indigenous southern English architecture. Shaw's flair for creating comfortable and sensibly planned country houses for the *nouveaux riches* is illustrated by 'Pierrepoint' near Frensham (1870), 'Merrist Wood' near Guildford (1877), 'Burrow's Cross' near Gomshall (1885) and 'The Hallams', Shamley Green (1894-5). 'Merrist Wood' was one of

109 *Clough Williams-Ellis's cottages at Merrow.*

110 *(below) Philip Webb's Coneyhurst.*

111 *(right) Wycliffe Building, Guildford.*

the first moderately-sized houses to combine half-timbering, tile-hanging and locally quarried Bargate stone in his 'Old English' style and this and his other works in many ways anticipate the later vernacular work of Edwin Lutyens.

This vernacular inspiration was powerfully influenced by the Arts and Crafts Movement led by William Morris. Major figures in this were Philip Webb, C.F.A. Voysey and many less well known but equally successful architects. One was Thackeray Turner, the first professional secretary of the Society for the Protection of Ancient Buildings (who designed his own home, Westbrook, near Godalming in Arts and Crafts style, using rough-hewn Surrey stone). Although articled to Sir George Gilbert Scott, he learned much to be avoided by the restoration architect and acquired an almost instinctive revulsion from the Gothic Revival in all its forms. C. Harrison Townsend, Baillie Scott, Harold Falkner, who transfigured Farnham in harmony with one of the handsomest Georgian towns in England, and Curtis Green, a fine architect and draughtsman who wrote *Old Cottages and Farmhouses in Surrey* (1908), should also be mentioned. Oliver Hill, a protégé of Lutyens and Jekyll, designed country houses between the wars 'which combined modern standards of convenience with a traditional attitude to life'. Voysey has four major houses, including 'Greyfriars' on the Hog's Back. He articulated an approach to life and work based on simple principles and was 'fortunate in finding enough vegetarians and Fabian socialists to keep him in business'.

Philip Webb made alterations and additions to Great Tangley Manor over 20 years from the late 1880s, in an attempt to reproduce the spirit, not the letter, of traditional skills. Coneyhurst, which he also designed near Ewhurst, was a collaboration between landowner, house owner, architect and builder, each of whom had an instinct for the handling of local materials and a deep appreciation of what the landscape could assimilate. The initial request of Miss Ewart, a niece of Gladstone, for land for the building of a house was turned down by R.M. Bray for he had preserved the highest parts of Coneyhurst Hill for amenity. An alternative site was found for her at the foot of the hill with a southern aspect overlooking the Weald. Webb designed the 'small dwelling' (large enough to be converted into four quite substantial modern homes). He agonised about how he should 'least mar the site with the coming house' and resolved the matter on the spot with the prospective owner, the landowner, and the builder, King of Abinger Hammer (who later developed his experience by working for the architect Goodhart-Rendel in local Surrey tradition in East Clandon). For 25 years Miss Ewart lived at the new house dispensing philanthropy at Ewhurst with the liberality of the spinsters, Augusta and Rosa Spottiswoode, in the adjacent hamlet of Peaslake who paid for its church. As for Coneyhurst, it was the progenitor of other country houses, so unobtrusively fitted into the wooded landscape that they are only clearly visible from a helicopter.[19] Baillie Scott came to work as sensitively as Webb; he thought that the greatest compliment paid to him was that he had built more houses doing less damage to the landscape than any man in England.

All Gertrude Jekyll's young years were spent in Bramley and on her return to that place she was inspired by Ruskin and Morris to study the vernacular traditions of west Surrey with renewed interest and published her childhood memories of cottage life in *Old West Surrey* in 1904. She rescued from destruction all kinds of household objects from local cottages and farmsteads, chiefly lighting and cooking utensils which were becoming obsolete, and now these form 'the Jekyll collection' in Guildford Museum. She was also deeply concerned about the preservation of the cottages themselves now that there was an increasing demand for houses by railway commuters travelling to London. Her interest in vernacular architecture was further stimulated by her friendship with the young architect Edwin Lutyens, whose first major commission was 'Munstead Wood', near Godalming, built for Gertrude Jekyll in 1896. As her eyesight began to fail, she took up her own type of gardening: woodland cottage gardening blending with the local heaths and woodlands made familiar to her by the cottage paintings of her friend, Helen Allingham, at nearby Witley and as seen by her own artist's eye. This produced a new impressionistic pictorialism in gardening where gardens melted imperceptibly into the wooded landscape and which through her partnership with Lutyens and her many contributions to *The Garden* (edited by William Robinson of Gravetye, whose 'wild' gardening she admired) swept across the face of England from the west Surrey scene, the source of her inspiration for the new art and familiar to her from childhood.

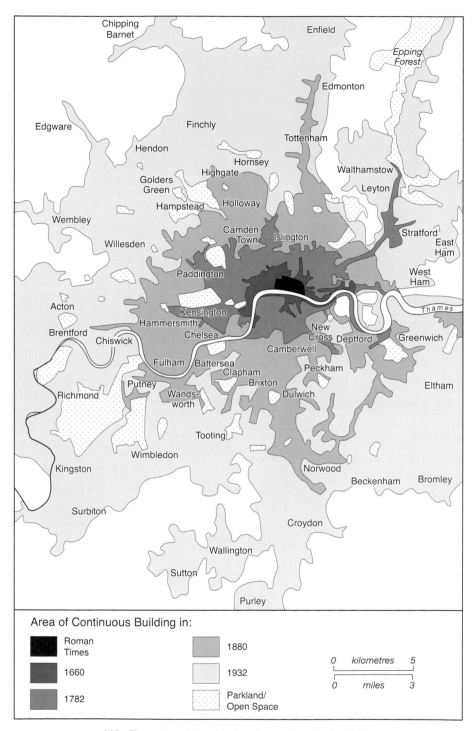

Area of Continuous Building in:

	Roman Times		1880
	1660		1932
	1782		Parkland/ Open Space

0 kilometres 5

0 miles 3

112 *Expansion of London from Roman times to the 1930s.*

19

The London Octopus and Rural Landscape Protection

'There is nothing for it but a letter to *The Times* and to hand round the hat.'

> John Maynard Keynes in *Britain and the Beast*,
> ed. Clough Williams-Ellis (1937), p.2.

Hanoverian London, as we have noted, had been relatively compact and coherent, enveloped in its fields and market gardens. By contrast, thereafter, it became virtually a new city that was 'more excavated, more cut-about, more rebuilt, and more extended' than at any time in its previous history. In terms of physical growth, London expanded from the 8.5 square miles on John Rocque's 1746 map, to about 23 square miles on John Cary's in 1822, to some 50 square miles in 1851, and then continuously to more than 120 square miles in 1901 and to over 200 square miles in 1939. (In the 1980s the extent of London was 610 square miles.)

One of the earliest issues, which was to reverberate over and over again, was that of railway proposals. A notable conflict arose in the 1830s over Robert Stephenson's proposed London to Brighton railway that would have passed through the Vale of Mickleham and down the Adur valley to Shoreham to avoid the heavy costs of tunnelling under the successive ridges of the Weald which the direct route to Brighton (ultimately laid out by George and John Rennie) would incur.[1] This met with organised opposition from local landowners with extensive parks and pleasure grounds who were joined by John Stuart Mill, a leading protagonist of public rights, who had week-ended there in his youth (p.167). He was greatly concerned at the possible havoc railways might have caused in beautiful districts when little thought was given to the matter. He considered that the beauty of the Vale of Mickleham 'was unrivalled in the world for the exquisiteness, combined with accessibility, of natural scenery' and thought it disgraceful that, although Members of Parliament would 'hold forth by the hour about encouraging the fine arts', hardly one cared for natural beauty. 'The truth is,' remarked Mill, 'that in this country the sense of beauty as a national characteristic, scarcely exists.'[2] The opposition to the Vale route was so effective that the engineer abandoned the route altogether on the grounds that the consents of the owners of Leatherhead and Norbury Parks, and from Hope of Deepdene, amongst others, would be impossible to obtain, or too expensive to indemnify. When a railway was eventually built through the valley it went under Norbury Park in a tunnel and special landscaping measures were insisted upon to mitigate intrusion.

The spread of London's ever-growing streets and suburbs over commons, field and woods also created a backlash amongst conservationists. The first controversies centred on the commonlands in south London which became the earliest vulnerable to development. The bitterest and longest struggle involved the Banstead Downs and Walton Heath, within easy reach of London and in the bracing air of its summit. As soon as the value of the common land for building in this area became recognised, the lord of the manor made an attempt in 1864 at enclosure and his trustees tried again shortly afterwards, both cases being thwarted by commoners. Sir John Hartopp acquired the manor and sought to enclose by buying up commoners' rights one by one, 'spending money like water', with the object of covering the commons with 'eligible villas'. Meanwhile Sir John was paring turf and carting topsoil off the commons, a wholesale destruction greatly injurious to sheep grazing. He was restrained by a Court Action and went bankrupt but his disappointed mortgagees waged an even more furious battle for enclosure. Finally in 1889, after 13 years of litigation, the commons were rescued. A great role was played by new residents to the area who did not relish giving up their 'breathing grounds'. The London branch of the Commons Preservation Society had played a notable part in this, advised by one of the greatest conservationists of the time, (Sir) Robert Hunter, a partner in the firm of Fawcett, Horne and Hunter, and Honorary Solicitor to the Commons Preservation Society.[3]

Hunter's description of the commons and of the justification for their rescue is memorable:

> They lie on the summit of the North Downs in a neighbourhood perhaps the most bracing to be found within a short distance of the city. From either extremity

113 *George Cubitt's Denbies, since demolished; part of the former estate is now a vineyard.*

they command striking views, in one direction of the valley of the Thames, and in the other of the weald of Surrey and Sussex. Timber they cannot boast, but in every other mark of wild, open land – smooth springy turf, stretches of brake and gorse, tracts of moorland heather – is to be found in one spot or another. To roam and gallop over such commons is the breath of life to those who have emerged from the smoke and noise of London, while to those who never set eyes on a blade of grass from one year's end to another they still serve as a reservoir of pure air, to make town life more healthful.[4]

After the triumph of Banstead other branches of the Commons Preservation Society battled, in most cases successfully, for the survival of their commons, notably at Coulsdon, Sanderstead, Godalming and Limpsfield. At the latter place the lord of the manor, Granville Leveson-Gower, diverted two footpaths and stopped up a third which included a route which the Commons Preservation Society considered would be invaluable now that the area was becoming suburban in character. An irregularity in voting at the Vestry allowed the Society to win the case on Appeal.[5]

The Tentacles of the Octopus

The inter-war years coincided with the spread of indiscriminate and unaesthetic building in the countryside, following the electric train, the motor car and the motor bus revolutions. London suburbs south of the Thames multiplied like mushrooms at this period and spread outwards nearer the North Downs and the Surrey Hills, for example, at Raynes Park and along the railway at Wallington, Carshalton, Sutton and Cheam, Coulsdon and Purley. Old mills on the Wandle at Merton and Morden were now swamped with housing. Esher and Oxshott filled with villas and Claygate was engulfed. Ewell, Ashtead and Epsom, Stoneleigh, Worcester Park and Motspur Park (the two latter with 'Ye Olde' names to suit their pseudo-Tudor semi-detacheds) are other examples with large housing estates encroaching on green fields. Populations almost doubled at New Malden and Mitcham. Petts Wood, developing fast from 1928, and Bexley Heath, a dormitory for Thames-side workers, and Bexley village's middle-class suburb, together with places such as Bromley and Orpington, were also expanding on the Kent side of London within a 12-mile radius of Charing Cross. Meanwhile, apart from this private speculative building, the LCC, 'a colonizing power, like Ancient Rome', was out-housing slum residents in new cottage estates on the outskirts of London, including the St Helier's estate of 40,000 people astride the 1926 Sutton by-pass, and at Downham, Whitefoot Lane and Mottingham a combined total of more than 30,000 houses was built.[6]

Until the rush to the suburbs began Malden was the small township of Old Malden. It became a target for developers at the beginning of the 20th century but it was the opening of the Kingston by-pass in 1927, which became lined with factories, which sent housing hectic. By the mid-1930s the conversion of market gardens to rows of semi-detached houses was in full swing and then came pubs, petrol stations, 'parades' of shops with service roads and New

114 *A Sale at Deepdene, symbolising the decline of the country house and estate after the First World War.*

Malden was in being as a dormitory. Paul Vaughan has written evocatively of a certain excitement and even prestige about his family's proximity to the tumultuous new highway of the by-pass. Smart new road houses were the haunts of 'dashing young men with tooth-brush moustaches and "sports" jackets with pleated pockets, driving the SS Swallows or Javelins we could see cruising past the lounge windows of "Wayside" at a shocking sixty mph …'.[7]

It was not only the inner suburbs which were fast encroaching on London's green fields. All round the outer suburban ring in Surrey and Kent well-to-do Londoners were migrating from the suburbs. It brought a sheen of prosperity and general well-being but it came at the price of creating a landscape which was neither rural, suburban nor urban, for which in 1931 the term 'rurban' was coined. As H.E. Bates remarked in 1936, the English were sometimes masters of the art of destroying what they most professed to love. The 'working landscape' had been steadily re-shaped with pleasure farms, private parks, wild gardens and arboreta, pheasant shoots – in fact, a contrived artificial landscape tributary to country houses. Around railway stations 'squadrons of villas' were being pegged out and land was selling at what were fabulous prices. This urban growth was resulting from the unregulated spread of pockets of housing in the deeper countryside, creating places such as the Horsleys and the Clandons. John Connell has described their development and pointed out that whereas Haslemere was largely a creation of the railway companies, the 'New Guildford Line' was situated near the northern end of the four parishes and, although its presence was almost unnoticed for thirty years, it quietly heralded a new era in the history of the locality. In fact, even in the early 1920s, the district was still recognisably rural and their inhabitants largely engaged in agricultural pursuits. East Clandon was an estate village controlled by the squire, the architect H.S. Goodhart-Rendel of Hatchlands. Until shortly before the First World War almost all of East Horsley was part of the Lovelace estate, which also covered parts of adjoining parishes, including

Ockham, Effingham and Abinger. The catalysts were the breaking up of the Lovelace estate following its sale in 1920 and the electrification of the 'New Guildford Line' in 1925, which was described as 'a bold venture, for the areas served were still largely rural, but the traffic came'. The land was sold in small lots and catalogued as 'excellent sites for the erection of good-class houses'. Frank Chown, a local architect and surveyor, acquired the majority of the lots and it was he who imposed conditions on the layout and style of houses but there was no conception of overall planning. For example, no shops were built. In the inter-war period West Clandon near the railway station developed in the same way as at East Horsley. Connell's study of the four villages showed how in the inter-war years agriculture declined in importance and a wave of migrants entered who were of the new type of countrymen with links in both village and city.[8] In Pahl's felicitous phrase, these villages had become metropolitan villages, *urbs in rure*. When Basil Cracknell described the villagers in 1970 he perceived them as a 'dreadful middle-class uniformity differentiated only by the particular train they caught each morning, and by the make, but not the size, of their motor car'.[9] He went on to say that 'No part of Surrey has changed more in a single lifetime than the northern edge of the chalk from Croydon to the Clandons'. This was the time when one would find nearly all the stockbrokers in the country in the vicinity of Guildford. More modest passengers left Waterloo for Dorking in the rush hour in 1936 with up to 21 in a compartment. People who had to adapt to the change included gipsies. Near Shere they turned to the Hurtwood as their last refuge. These indigenous peoples were rough and tough, living in tight self-supporting and self-protecting communities. They spoke in dialect, now practically lost.

The whirlwind of social change raging over London's countryside from the 1920s produced the cocktail, 'G-and-T' and stockbroker belt, and the two-class metropolitan village, a split society polarised spatially and also socially into middle- and working- class sectors. The former, the immigrant professional and managerial people with 'lots of cars and posh hats', and the latter, the old-

115 *Westbrook, near Godalming, the former home of conservationist-architect Thackeray Turner.*

established villagers, could not have been more apart. The middle-class people came in search of a community and by their presence destroyed whatever community was there; so many people moved in and out every week that any sense of belonging was lost. The myth of bowler-hatted men waiting for the 8.05 at a rural station leaving behind neurotic women in their rural retreats became part of the folklore of the pop sociologist and had a grain of truth in it before one car or more in a household made life feel less isolated.

Another habitat especially vulnerable was that of cliffed coastlines. Bates thought it a crazy paradox that, despite the nation proudly singing and declaiming its coastline, only a fraction of it was held by the National Trust and preserved for the nation, and yet it was at the mercy of speculating jerry building. Dr Vaughan Cornish had done a great service by publishing a pamphlet entitled *The Cliff Scenery of England and the Preservation of its Amenities*. It helped to arouse disquiet at the development on cliffs at Hythe, Folkestone, and St Margaret's Bay on the Isle of Thanet.

By the mid-1930s the danger threatening some of the most beautiful places within thirty miles of London had become fully recognised. It was symptomatic of the current crisis that the narrator at the Pageant of Surrey held at Pyrford Court, Woking, should have been the Surrey woodman and his son who told, in the manner of a chorus in Greek drama, events since the clearing of the wood. The programme illustration shows him narrating in medieval dress against a background of trees. The only advertisement for a motor-car was for a Rolls-Royce depicted in a woodland glade and the crow scene, alluding to Surrey's rapidly disappearing countryside, comprised hikers, campers, cyclists, picnickers, typists, builders, motorists, house-viewers and tub-thumpers, etc.

At about the same time, at an Abinger pageant associated with the novelist E.M. Forster, the narrator declaims:

> Houses, houses, houses! You came from them and you must go back to them. Houses and bungalows, hotels, restaurants and flats, arterial roads, by-passes, petrol pumps and pylons. Are these going to be England? Or is there another England, green and eternal, which will outlast them? I cannot tell you, I am only the Woodman, but this land is yours and you can make it what you will. If you want to ruin our Surrey fields and woodlands it is easy to do, very easy, and if you want to save them, they can be saved. Look into your hearts and look into the past, and remember that all this beauty is a gift which you can never replace, which no money can buy, which no cleverness can refashion. You can make a town, you can make a desert, you can even make a garden, but you can never, never, make a country, because it was made by Time.[10]

In the absence of any governmental assistance, public appeals for money to buy land threatened with development were launched in newspapers and periodicals, outstanding in this respect being St Loe Strachey's *The Spectator*. One of the first beautiful spots to be rescued would have become 'a choice freehold building estate, absolutely unrestricted at Friday Street'. With 10 days to run before a sale, £3,000 was still needed but at the last minute donors subscribed enough to a well publicised Preservation Fund to save this lovely corner which

XVII Autumn Path, *watercolour by A.M. Parkin of Kemsing.*

XVIII Bluebells on the North Downs, *a watercolour by A.M. Parkin.*

XIX *Samuel Palmer,* Evening at Shoreham.

XX The Song of Samuel: *Graham Clarke's representation of Samuel Palmer at Shoreham. A hand-made etching using the same techniques as Palmer.*

XXI *Theodore Jacobsen, architect of the Foundling Hospital, London and designer of grounds including a waterfall at Lonesome Lodge. Wotton church appears in the background.*

XXII *A Kentish landscape by Rowland Hilder.*

XXIII Flowers of the Hills, *a 1920s poster of the Surrey Uplands.*

XXIV *The six-spot burnet moth on Green Hill, Kemsing in a habitat being restored to encourage the abundant flora and wildlife of chalk grassland of a century ago.*

XXV Wild Flowers of the Surrey Heathland, *a painting by Ethel Wyn Shiel.*

still remains undefiled. In a similar way Colley Hill near Reigate was saved in 1912. Grayswood Common was a wild, wooded place just north of Haslemere which had become a tangled undergrowth of birch, holly and ash. Publicity in *The Times* and in *Country Life* in 1906 resulted in judicious thinning and steps were taken to prevent its enclosure. The origin of efforts to preserve Leith Hill is in the public appeal reported in *The Times* in 1929 – £9,000 was raised, the summit bought and handed over to the National Trust for preservation. In 1930 and 1931 the possibility of housing there again became pressing. A speculator was planning to build 94 houses but by the efforts of Captain Bray and others the proposal was stopped. In 1936 the plan to construct overhead power lines in beautiful parts of Surrey was modified in respect of properties from Westcott to Abinger Hammer.

The future of Box Hill at this time was a matter of great anxiety. *The Spectator* in 1913 outlined the case for its preservation, writing that, 'It is one of the most glorious stretches of open downland within reach of London' and that it was more than a hill with its plantations of box trees and literary and historical associations of its own. Meredith, Keats and Nelson were mentioned and 'Juniper Hall and Fredley Farm under its flank have gathered half the names of a century – Fanny Burney, Madame de Staël, Talleyrand and the guests of Conversation Sharp from Wordsworth to Coleridge to Huskisson and Lord John Russell'. Box Hill was indeed the clasp and jewel of the whole of London's countryside and building on it would have led to its complete and irreparable ruin. Hunter lived long enough to learn that Leopold Salomons of Norbury Park had made a generous donation to the National Trust which saved the Hill. Other donations followed. For those who love Box Hill the good news in 1951 was that the National Trust had secured an additional 88 acres of land on the escarpment, so keeping safe the breezy views from the summit. This allowed people to walk the slopes, where the whitebeam gleams against sombre yew, and enjoy the sunsets. The Hill and its surrounds is one of the largest National Trust properties.

As John Julius Norwich has stated, 'Hunter was an outstanding lawyer and a man of charm, modesty and resolve. He not only conceived the idea behind the National Trust but also supplied its name and a legal framework which has survived almost unaltered, although greatly enlarged, for a century'. It should also be remarked that Hunter drew attention in 1894 to the fact that, although public opinion was then favouring restraints on individual owners of land in the matter of the protection of historical buildings and beautiful landscapes in the national interest, in Britain there was inadequate provision for this compared with most European countries (*Places of Historic Interest and National Beauty*, 1898). Hunter was knighted for 31 years' service to the Post Office in 1894 but had devoted his spare time to the provision of open spaces and the protection of access to the countryside.[11]

Towards the end of his life this was directed to the commons of south-west Surrey around Haslemere, where he had retired. He was an active member of the Haslemere Commons committee, formed for the protection of surrounding open spaces in 1884, including Blackdown and Hindhead, on which the attractiveness

116 *National Trust volunteers at Leith Hill, c.1910. The natural setting has been changed completely with the encroachment of trees.*

of the district depended. The main provocation was the enclosures on Hindhead which been proceeding on a large scale for some years. The motives of the committee were not entirely altruistic. Were the heather-clad hills enclosed, or the picturesque bits of commons and bounding roadside waste absorbed into adjacent fields, the charm and value of enclosed property would eventually have been much diminished. As Haslemere and Hindhead were becoming better known, there was a great risk that large inroads would be made into common-lands, particularly where, as at Hindhead, controversy existed over their bounds. Amongst landowners incurring anxiety in this respect was Lord Egmont, then owner of the Cowdray estate, who declined to join the committee. At a meeting soon afterwards, William Allingham, the poet, and husband of landscape artist Helen, attended together with Edward Whymper the mountaineer. The formation of the committee was announced in a letter to *The Times*, 6 February 1885. Haslemere was claimed to be a natural home of the movement, 'lying as it does in the very lap of the huge mass of Hindhead and Blackdown' (then largely a mass of heather) whence were seen panoramic views of the whole range of the South Downs. It deplored the enclosure of 'huge tracts' on Hindhead arising from the sudden popularity of the place as a residential centre and resort (p.223). The Committee undoubtedly arrested the encroachments and alerted public opinion to their vulnerability. It led to numerous donations to the National Trust of attractive open spaces which would have been built upon.

A Case Study

To Reginald Bray of Shere this crisis was seen not as an occasion for narrowly restrictive attitudes, but as an opportunity for experiments in rural re-construction which would yet preserve the balanced pattern of life with its basis in a well integrated town and country. The countryside was to him a living organism which had evolved over generations through its landlords, yeomen and peasants to meet changing practical needs: it could not be exempt from change. He therefore saw the problem of his generation with regard to the countryside as not to arrest change but to direct it into courses producing new prosperity and beauty. He fully appreciated that country space was no longer the prerogative of country people. His broad objective was a design which preserved the essential character of the Surrey countryside but which allowed adequate room for development. Few people, indeed, were more impatient with the standard negative and protectionist attitudes in preserving countryside amenities than Bray. In this outlook can be recognised that of a planner.[12]

His most tangible planning achievements were the voluntary agreements he secured with landowners for protection from speculative builders of the wooded and heathy range of hills dominated by Leith Hill and the crest and southern slopes of the North Downs between Merrow and Ranmore, in all 20 square miles of the loveliest Surrey scenery. He was not the first to appreciate the need to protect this area. Seven years earlier a consultant's report to the Surrey Joint Town Planning Committee had remarked of the Leith Hill district that there was 'no more important duty that it had to perform than to take adequate steps to preserve intact this gem of rural England'. Of the North Downs it spoke of the preservation of the crest and slopes 'as much of national importance as the preservation of the South Downs' (then the subject of intense national concern on account of the rash of bungalows and shacks spreading like treacle). But the lack of adequate planning powers at the time meant that both these tasks were beyond the capabilities of the Planning Committee and they awaited someone with the commitment, energy, patience and tact to get landowners to agree to preservation. Bray was ideally suited to this role and his success will prove to be the most enduring of his life's work.

The planning schemes fathered by Bray were big by the standards of the 1930s – and larger than Surrey County Council had dealt with up to this time – and their importance was out of all proportion to the area of the land involved because of the high landscape value of the districts concerned and the example they set to others. For their ultimate success the schemes were dependent upon a 'combined operations' exercise involving the cordial support of landowners, that of the Chairman of the Surrey County Council, James Chuter Ede (later Education minister and Home Secretary in the post-war Labour government), and Capt. E.H. Tuckwell, the chairman of the county's Town and Country Planning Committee, and officials of the Ministry of Health, then responsible for planning. There was also active help and encouragement from various voluntary amenity bodies and propagandists, such as the Council for the Preservation of Rural England and Clough Williams-Ellis whose influential book *Britain and the Beast*

(1937) alerted people to the threat of despoliation.[13] But Bray's own contribution stands out. He and his brother Jocelyn were the originators of the schemes; through his tireless efforts they were launched, and through his great skills as a conciliator they finally triumphed. It was his sure instinct of a Surrey landowner that persuaded him to make the proposals and it was his ability to expound their first principles, as never before in English planning, which finally won the day.

Bray's fundamental principle, outlined in a memorandum which was widely discussed nationally and put across to Surrey landowners by correspondence or at meetings during 1934, was that in the county it was strongly to the advantage of landowners to preserve amenities, because they added market value to adjoining landed property which potentially outweighed the loss of revenue from building land elsewhere. Such an argument, if not acceptable in the new mood after the Second World War, was a valid one at a time when compensation was statutorily payable for the loss of building 'rights'. Bray's 'market law' was a way round the impossible compensation requirement and offered a means towards the protection of relatively large areas, not simply of 'beauty-spots'.[14]

Bray's initiative was much praised, but had inherent weaknesses. It was most applicable to the grander scenery which there was a general desire to save. The idea that it would pay a landowner to preserve 'ordinary' scenery was not widely understood at the time. His schemes were potentially much cheaper than the buying of lands as public open space which was the essence of the London Green Belt proposal, but unfortunately they did not work in favour of the small landowner, who often felt unfairly treated.

The effects of such objections to Bray's schemes can be traced in the history of the Leith Hill district from 1934.[15] The object was to make special provision for the delightfully wooded district of some 5,500 acres by restricting building to a minimum and carefully controlling every aspect of land use to ensure that it remained in its existing condition. The intention was to create what was in effect a public park on privately-owned land. It began as a scheme of big landowners, including the largest, the Wotton estate, and then proceeded to an outline local agreement with the support of 38 smaller occupiers. In 1935 the Surrey County Council took over the responsibility for the scheme with a view to the payments of necessary compensation. It was such a special scheme that it drew a lot of attention from the officials of the Planning Division of the Ministry of Health. Yet such were the long delays in negotiating compensation with smaller landowners that even in May 1938 the scheme was considered at the Ministry as being still 'in the embryonic stage'. At the outbreak of the Second World War it had still not reached the stage when it could be the subject of a Planning Inquiry. Bray's North Downs protective scheme, modelled on the Leith Hill proposal, was then at a still more rudimentary stage, although an outline scheme with the larger landowners had been reached five years earlier. Nevertheless, the spade work had been done for the post-war generation.[16]

Bray encountered no fewer than 487 written objections to a proposal for a new road replacing the A25 between Chilworth and Abinger Hammer and the zoning of several hundreds of acres of exceptionally beautiful woodland for house building, which he advocated when chairman of the county's Planning Committee.[17] Much of the opposition came from a vocal group of new residents.[18] Bray's aim for the building development was based on the belief that the still overcrowded London of his day required healthy rural spaces in which people could enjoy a happier existence. The rift which developed between Bray and the opposition was symptomatic of the fast-waning powers of a squire in the growing democratic climate of the late 1930s. After the war the scheme was trimmed down in the light of the Green Belt policy then prevailing. The proposed new road has not been built and in the 1960s a short by-pass alleviated traffic congestion in Shere; the woodlands and farmland remain unviolated.[19]

In effect, Bray's drastic schemes for landscape protection in mid-Surrey fell short of perfection and were too ambitious in scale for the rudimentary planning machinery of the day. Ultimately they were superseded by the tougher measures of post-war planning legislation. Yet they were considered examples which might well be followed elsewhere and were, in fact, the parent of a number of voluntary schemes in south-east England. At a time when so many airy futilities were being talked and so few useful things done, Bray's work stands out as exemplifying pioneering practical idealism and so deserves a niche in planning history. He also achieved his immediate object, for, although a formal scheme did not materialise, landowners honoured their 'gentleman's agreement' of 1934 which proved invaluable with the rising public use of the finest parts of the Surrey countryside until local authorities possessed rougher planning powers.[20]

From 1944 the need to control and disperse London for reasons of growth and space led to the concept of the Green Belt. This was a zone with physical planning restrictions to curb the outward growth of the capital. It was being advocated by Lord Meath before 1901 as a 'green girdle' around London on the example set by American cities who were seriously putting such proposals into effect.[21] Unhappily the Belt now includes a medley of land uses, many existing before its designation, producing a strange hermaphrodite sort of landscape, which has become of extremely doubtful value to Londoners or to anyone else (Hall, 1974, 52-8). Yet an extension of Green Belts is still needed to protect more of London's countryside from development.

It is appropriate to end this chapter with a mention of Octavia Hill (1838-1912), who was one of the most influential reformers of the 19th century. Her lifelong vocation was to preserve open spaces and provide access to the countryside for urban dwellers, especially the working classes, to which end she put the whole strength of her personality, clear sightedness, singleness of purpose and unbounded enthusiasm. Her mentors included the Revd R.D. Maurice, the founder of the Christian Socialists, and John Ruskin, artist, art critic and social reformer. Her early work, not always successful, was a premonition of the National Trust of which she was a co-founder and its inspiration. She was herself a donor of land to the Trust at Mariner's Hill at Crockham Chart where she lived in retirement. Her tomb is in the church.

20

The Literary Inspiration of Downs and Hills

For centuries the exquisite landscape and characteristic features of the North Downs and Surrey Hills have urged the poet and writer to contemplative delight and deep satisfaction which has given them an enduring expression in creative art. Immediately brought to mind is William Cobbett; Jane Austen's *Emma* set in the Box Hill district and of the local Kent society around Godmersham Park and Chilham which finds its place in *Pride and Prejudice* and *Sense and Sensibility*; of Dickens' north Kent and of Kipling's poem on Merrow Down.

This love of the Downs and Hills and the urge to express it in literature stretches back well into the Middle Ages:

> The nihtegale bigon tho speke
> In one hurne of one breche
> And set upone veyre bowe
> That were aboute blostme ynoo
> In ore vaste thickke hedge
> I medy myd spire and grene segge

So wrote a poet in the Surrey dialect of the late 12th or 13th century to celebrate a nightingle singing in a wooded nook (*hurne*), in a woodland clearing (*breche*), using 'v' for 'f' as in 'veyre' (fair). *Hurne* and *breche* were common place-name elements

117 *The Earl of Surrey.*

and people took their surnames from them. There was a John ate Hurne living at Albury in 1380 and John ate Breche in Gomshall in 1332.[1]

Another pre-Chaucerian rhymester was William de Shoreham of Kent, the able and devoted parish priest of Chart Sutton, who about the mid-14th century rendered didactic Latin into catchy little rhymes in Kentish dialect to edify his flock. Appealing to the ear of his listeners, his verses answered their questions on such matters as baptism, divorce (sprousebreche) and the Immaculate Conception, for which he used the familiar image of sunlight passing through glass:

214

Ase the sonne taketh hyre pas
Wkyth-out breche throrgh-out that glas
They maydenhad on-wemmed hytewas
For here of thene chylder.[2]

Chaucer's *Canterbury Tales* immortalised the pilgrimage from the *Tabard Inn* in Southwark along the great road to Canterbury along the edge of the North Downs:

… Ane specially, from every shires ende
Of Engelond, to Caunterbury they wende
The holy blissful martir for to seke
That hem hath holpen when that they were seke …

And although he built little topographical detail into his poem he wrote affectionately of one place:

… Wite ye nat wher ther stant a litel toun
Which that y-cleped is Bob-up-and-doun,
Under the Blee, in Caunterbury weye?

John Skelton, a leading literary figure of the reign of Henry VIII, usually addressed lyrics to high-born ladies at Court, but his poem *Elinour Rumming* is about a low-born landlady of *The Running Horse* in Leatherhead and her sordid customers. The building may be that bearing the inn's name today although John Blair is doubtful. It is a hilarious tale in a vigorous metre, close to the bone and none too clean. The tipsters, apparently mostly foul sluts, creep out to the ale-house when their husbands have left for theirs. To pay for their drink they barter goods, some rancid, in lieu of money and in return Dame Elinor supplied stale ale from vats which were not free from drowned rats:

Cisly and Sere
With their legs bare
And also their feet
Fully unsweet
Their kirtles all to-jagged
Their smocks all to-ragged
With titters and tatters
Bring dishes and platters
With all their might running
To Elinor Rumming
To have of her tunning.

118 *Elinour Rummin from a 17th-century print.*

The poem gets wilder and lewder as it proceeds and then Skelton remembers he is a clergyman and a Poet Laureate and that he should be a moralist. He is not very convincing when he denounces drunken, dirty and loquacious women and the belchings of Elinour Rumming. His rumbustious verses offer a unique insight into the coarse and rough but otherwise unknown life of 16th-century villagers and to read him is to come into contact with a contentious person who was not quite like anyone else in his oddnesses.[3]

Sir Thomas Wyatt of Allington Castle struck a new note in the realm of English poetry with his 'Renaissance' sonnets inspired by Petrarch, discovered on his stay in Italy. He was writing in the 1530s and 1540s as a precursor of Spenser and Sidney. His achievement was to raise literary standards and establish new models in English verse, some based on the most recent developments in Italy and France, but some inherited from the late medieval love lyric. He describes life in the seclusion of Allington:

> This maketh me at home to hunt and hawk
> And in foul weather at my book to sit;
> In frost and snow then with by bow to stalk;
> No man doth mark where so I ride or go.
> In lusty leas at liberty I walk;
> And of these news I feel nor weal nor woe ...

It is unsurprising that its landscape, so 'full of observables' to attract the Elizabethan, should have inspired William Lambarde to write in 1570 *A Perambulation of Kent*, the first of county histories and amongst the earliest antiquarian studies in England. He was not born in Kent but he is as much an ambassador for the county as its ancient families and is buried in the church of St Nicholas, Sevenoaks. He divided Kent into agricultural regions: 'The Isle of Thanet and those eastern parts are the grange, the Weald, the wood, Romney Marsh is the meadow plot, the North Downs be the coneygarth, or warren, and Teynham with thirty other parishes lying on each side be the cherry garden and apple orchard of Kent.' Like a true son of Kent he tells us that neither sun nor 'fat soil' was lacking to make the fruit unequalled in the realm since Master Harris, Henry VIII's fruiterer, had planted pippins and cherries at Teynham. The Chart country he knew well and noted that although the soils were poor it was a healthy place in which to live. By this time the Weald of the Kentish franklin and yeoman had become proverbial and its society was more mobile and individualist and so free of feudal restraints that Lambarde writes memorably, 'In a manner every man is a freeholder and hath some part of his own to live on'.

Edward Bolton, one of the most learned men of his time and a leading poet in the first anthology of pastoral poetry, *England's Helicon* (1600), is drunk with the beauty of the 'chalky downs' and, as Edmund Gosse has remarked, 'he feels the sunlight in his eyes and the perfume of spring in his nostrils. His invocation of 'wood-gods in every grove' suggests that it was the North Downs of which he writes.

It is in Michael Drayton's *Polyolbion* completed in 1622 that Kent is described in the most extravagant phrases:

O famous Kent
What country hath this Ile that can compare with thee,
Which hast within they self as much as thou canst wish?
They Conyes, Venson, Fruit; they sorts of Fowle and Fish:
As what with strength comports thy Hay, thy Corne, they Wood:
Nor any thing doth want, that any where is good ...

One of the later writers inspired by Lambarde and Drayton was Christopher Smart whose *Hop Garden* (1752) was not only a Georgic in praise of Kent's most famous agricultural production, 'the English vine' which fills the air in autumn with its fragrance and which long typified the landscape of Kent, but a paean of praise for all that was great in Kent tradition:

... Hail, Cantium, hail!
Illustrious parent of the finest fruits,
Illustrious parent of the best of men!

Smart flatteringly praises Fairlawne at Shipbourne (pronounced Shibbun), the seat of Lord Vane, 'where nature and art hold dalliance', admiration which paid off when the owner and his family bought 18 copies of his work! Sir Harry Vane, executed by Charles II in 1662, is buried in the church. The Vane family's lime avenues survive and the foliage of the woods and copses is as attractive as when Smart wrote. There can be few places in England as exquisite as Shipbourne, Plaxtol and Ivychurch with their views to the wooded slopes of the Greensand hills and to the charming square orchards and plantations of cobnuts with their shelter belts of lime and beech on the sunny hillsides. The hops which were Smart's theme have, however, gone.

One of the earliest specific references to the North Downs in verse was from the humble 'peasant poet' Robert Bloomfield (1766-1823), whose local attachments and interest in wild flowers influenced John Clare's cottage tales. Bloomfield yearned for Shooter's Hill, the health-giving green-topped Surrey Hills, and specifically where the River Mole, 'all silence glides dwells Peace – and Peace is wealth to me!':

And far away where last as now I freedom stole,
And spent one dear delicious day
On thy wild banks, romantic Mole.

No poet or writer has been more inspired by the North Downs than the poet-novelist George Meredith (1828-1909) who resided at Flint Cottage, below Box Hill, for more than forty years. He clearly felt reverence and an almost mystical attachment to his chalk headland. The grassy slope of the majestic hill swept 'from his doors up into the clouds' and his chalet in which he wrote and sometimes slept afforded him, he thought, a view unsurpassed outside the Alps, the dark line of the hill running 'up to the stars' and the valley below a 'soundless gulf'. (The site is now noisy with road traffic routed in a by-pass through the Vale of Mickleham instead of to the west of it.) It was at Flint Cottage that he wrote of the Downs in 1882, 'Nowhere in England is richer foliage, or wilder downs and fresher woodlands'. He was an environmentalist and conservationist before these terms were invented and an amateur naturalist of distinction. He expressed awe in nature, deplored the over-sophistication of modern man that endangered his feeling for Earth and taught people how to enjoy the Surrey landscape who would 'cast off the yoke of toil and smoke' in the city.

> You live in rows of snug abodes,
> With gold, maybe, for counting;
> And mine's the beck of the rainy roads
> Against the sun a-mounting.

He was also inspired by the exceptional diversity in his landscape encountered even on a short walk, as expressed in *The Orchard and the Heath* (1865) when he was moved to contrast farmers' children in the mellow orchard country of the Vale of Holmesdale with the gipsy ragamuffins playing on the heath above. As Edward Thomas remarked, Meredith was the Londoner's poet and his country was London's countryside.

119 *George Meredith's Flint Cottage below Box Hill.*

Meredith was a rapid and strong walker who attacked his countryside with tremendous strides in all weathers. We can readily conjure up an image of him walking for fun in the wind and rain. It sent the blood coursing to his brain and going through woods, over heaths and along footpaths, which he could not have done if he had ridden, his tramps could take on a hectic, almost violent character. He gathered a multitude of images and sights which he transmitted to his poetry. Like Hilaire Belloc, he exulted in rain, and wrestled with storm and the south-west wind. He scorned discomfort of wet clothes and squealing boots: 'Let him be drenched, his heart will sing' and courted 'the clouds of the south-west with a lover's blood'. It was the music of the storm he most wished to hear, the snapping of branches, the bending of the tree-tops, the animation of the leaves and the great noise on the land in a downpour of 'eager gobbling, much like that the swine's trough freshly filled'.

> Pour, let the wines of Heaven pour!
> The golden harp is struck once more
> And all its music is for me.

Pour, let the wine of Heaven pour!
And, ho, for a sight of pagan glee!
Hear the crushing of the leaves;
Hear the cracking of the bough
And the whistling of the bramble,
The piping of the wind!

Meredith was particularly sensitive to trees. Their changing colours attracted his eye and his ear was fascinated by the sound of their varying music. He imagined each tree to be a harp with foliaged strings played by the wind. He learned that the aspen was the first to tremble at an impending storm, that the storm-cock (missel thrush) then begins to trill an alarm from a bough, the grass now rustles slightly, the hazels, briars and brakes that line the dells 'like straggling beetling brows' come in and sing their individual shrill music – and then the storm breaks, 'heaven's laughter':

... and now the whole
With savage inspiration – pine,
And larch and beech and fir, and thorn,
And ash, and oak, and oakling rare
And shriek, and shout, and whirl and toss,
And stretch their arms, and split and crock
And bend their stems, and bow their heads,
And grind, and groan and lion-like
Roar to the echo-peopled hills and
Ravenous wilds ... with melody sublime.

Trees, indeed, were the very substance of his poetry, as in the youthful *South-West Wind* (1851), *Ode to the Spirit of Earth in Autumn* (1862), *Woodland Peace* (1870), *Dirge in the Woods* (1870) and *The Woods of Westermain* (1882).

His poetry is today unjustly neglected. An exceptionally perceptive critic was the historian G.M. Trevelyan who edited Meredith's poetical works (1912), wrote a literary criticism and found a wife for himself, a daughter of novelist Mrs Humphry Ward, through their collaboration on these projects. The historian would recite Meredith's poem *Love in the Valley* (1878) as he strode over his Northumberland hills and placed it above anything in Milton and Wordsworth.[4] Meredith's novels contain some of his loveliest landscape pictures, such as of the country around the Hampshire-Sussex border in *Evan Harrington* and of the Vale of Holmesdale near Dorking in *Diana of the Crossways*.

Richard Jefferies' essays were well calculated to appeal to those who subscribed to the new enthusiasm for the open-air and long country walks. Even suburbanites were encouraged by Jefferies' *Nature near London* (1883) to appreciate natural beauties to be found within strolling distances of their own doorsteps. '... The path brings you in sight of a railway station. And the railway station ... presently compels you to go upon the platform, and after a little puffing and revolution of wheels you emerge at Charing Cross, or London Bridge, or Waterloo or Ludgate Hill and with the freshness of the meadows clinging to your coats, mingle with the crows.' Essays like 'Hours of Spring' or

'The Pageant of Summer' were the forerunners of a host of imitative nature notes in magazines and newspapers. Jefferies' Surbiton residence enabled him to range to Claygate and beyond to Ewell where the land begins to rise up towards the Downs. Here he had never seen such numbers of small birds flying up from the stubbles, a sign that farming was not intensive.

Alfred, Lord Tennyson's view from his study at Aldworth on Blackdown had a view which took in some fifty miles of countryside. Three of his poems deal specifically with his house and neighbourhood. The verses forming the prologue to 'The Charge of the Light Brigade at Balaclava' include the well-known lines describing the scene from the terrace at Aldworth:

> You came and look'd and loved the view
> Long known and loved by me
> Green Sussex fading into blue
> With one gray glimpse of sea.

Another is 'The Roses on the Terrace' and a third was 'June Braken and Heather' in a poem dedicated to his wife in which the poet speaks of the 'wild heather round me and over me' on the top of the down near his home at Aldworth.

The Spread of Literary Colonies

By this time authors were beginning to emulate artists in their summer habits and, taking advantage of railways, to write books in the countryside free from the distractions of London life. An example is George Eliot, whose novels were partially written in the Surrey countryside (pp.168-9). Some close-knit groups of intellectuals congregated in colonies in summer. One was that of Fabians and Russian émigrés at Crockham Hill on Limpsfield Chart, founded after the opening of the railway from London to Uckfield in 1898. Edward Garnett and his wife Constance, Richard Heath, Henry Salt, Ford Madox Ford, E.R. Pease, Stephen Crane, E.V. Lucas and others built houses or dachas overlooking the Wealden panoramas where they were visited by Edward Thomas, D.H. Lawrence, Prince Kropotkin, Stepniak, Montague Fordham and H.E. Bates.

From this incongruous setting on the fringes of London came publications aimed at nothing less than the retrieval of a fast-dissolving rural culture. They included Edward Garnett's *The Imagined World* (1898); Richard Heath's *The English Peasant* (1893), a kind of modern Piers Plowman committed to a non-industrial, unorganised society, rooted in the soil; Henry Salt's edition of Thoreau; and Montague Fordham's *Mother Earth* (1908), which, despite its title, outlined a realistic blueprint for the revival of agriculture, only partially fulfilled long afterwards by the Wheat Act of 1931 and government planning during and after the Second World War. Constance Garnett translated the Russian novelists. The Limpsfield colony lives on in literature in Ford Madox Ford's satirical *Simple Life Limited*.

Another remarkable colony of Victorian and Edwardian intellectuals was that of 'hilltop' writers who moved away from the smoke and grime of London to the

120 *George Eliot's home at Witley.*

121 *Cearn at Crockham Chart, the weekend home of Edward and Constance Garnett. This was the nucleus of a literary colony.*

wildly beautiful Surrey hills around Hindhead. Some members consciously turned their backs on the metropolis. They had a deep sense of estrangement from natural life and, with London as foil and background, perceived the countryside as something of the supernatural. Foreigners failed to appreciate what a tremendous difference London made to the perceived freshness of the air, the beauty of the views and the feeling of repose. They also did not recognise how alienated some 'hilltop' writers were to what they considered the baneful influence of city life. The elevated landscapes of the Surrey Hills were particularly favoured by those who wanted to make a vigorous protest against the modern artificiality of life. They tended to become contemplative reclusivists, deliberately distancing themselves from the city, expressing unrest or disillusionment, introspection and anxiety. They could not fit with late 19th-century civilisation for they hated the expansion of London and what it stood for and the progress of the huge economic movement which was taking Britain, and the whole world, from agriculture towards industrialism by means of the machine. They fled from it and wrote from some studio preferably commanding enormous views of broad open woodland and purple heath. Grant Allen, a devotee of Thoreau and whose influence on H.G. Wells was considerable, resided successively on the 'free hills' of Leith Hill and on Hindhead, a venue which became so popular with 'progressive' writers that it was dubbed an 'Observatory of State'. He considered London to be full of injustices, joylessness and smugness but, like Blake, he went too far in his denunciations:

> I am writing in my study on a heather-clad hilltop. When I raise my eyes from my sheet of foolscap, it falls upon miles of broad open moorland. My window looks out over unsullied nature. Everything around is fresh and clean and wholesome … But away down in the valley, as night draws on, a lurid glare reddens the north-eastern horizon. It marks the spot where the great wen of

London heaves and festers. Up here on the free hills, the sharp air blows in upon us, limpid and clear from a thousand leagues of open ocean; down there in the crowded town, it stagnates and ferments, polluted with the diseases and vices of centuries[5]

and he tells us what Hindhead meant to him as he listened in the evening to the night-jar, the bird of the heather and bracken, murmuring George Meredith's lines:

Lovely are the curves of the white owl sweeping
Wavy in the dusk lit by one large star,
Lone on the fir-branch, his rattle-note unvaried,
Brooding o'er the gloom, spins the brown eve-jar

and perceiving it as 'a genuine relic of the older, the wilder, and the freer England ... before the whirr of wheels and the snort of steam drove the wild things far from us' (Grant Allen, *Moorland Idylls*, 1896). His flight, of course, failed, but it is easy to appreciate how in a time of upheaval he was tempted to disgust at the loss of his world of the spirit and of tradition. His conviction that something irreplaceable had been destroyed drove him to seek inner compensation in the fog-free countryside.

Stopford Brooke, the religious thinker and distinguished amateur water-colourist, chose the summit of Pitch Hill, Ewhurst, for his eyrie. George Meredith wrote from his chalet on the slopes of Box Hill. Even nonsense verse enters this

122 *Hindhead, a drawing which captures a malevolent character of the Punch Bowl.*

special arena. Edward Lear's great Gombolian Plain that stretches towards the skyline of the hills of the Chankly Bore owes much to his childhood fantasies dominated by Chanctonbury (in dialect, Chanklebury) Ring.

Anne Gilchrist was one of the first writers to settle in the Surrey Hills. She chose a cottage at Shottermill near Haslemere in 1862, completing there her husband's *Life of William Blake* (1863). Tennyson visited her at Shottermill in 1866 and she was largely responsible for introducing him to Blackdown. It was Mrs Gilchrist who also invited George Eliot down to her cottage which led to her renting it and writing a large part of *Middlemarch* there. She eventually retired to nearby Witley. Tennyson's audacious move to Aldworth on Blackdown led to his friend William Allingham the poet, and his artist-wife, Helen, residing in the district.

A remarkable development occurred from 1883 when the scientists John Tyndall and Rollo Russell first arrived on Hindhead.[6] Tyndall was an experienced mountaineer and, as a direct result of his influence, Hindhead became known as 'the English Switzerland' and famed for the freshness of its air. Frederick Pollock, the lawyer and confirmed mountaineer and walker, followed, together with Frederic Harrison the historian, Manley Hopkins and Frank Smythe the mountaineer. Nearby Grayswood attracted Mary (Mrs Humphry) Ward and dramatist Henry Pinero, who were both there in 1890. The Pearsall Smith family acquired Friday's Hill House in Fernhurst in 1889 which was to become another centre of literary activity. Bertrand Russell, who married one of Pearsall Smith's daughters, wrote his first book in the neighbourhood. A branch of the Strachey family also moved into Fernhurst. Meanwhile Margaret Oliphant had moved to Hindhead; Grant Allen came in 1893; the Beveridges, father and son, settled at Pitfold House on Woolmer Hill; the Revd S. Baring-Gould wrote his gruesome novel *The Broom Squire* against the beautiful local setting and described it in 1896 as 'one of the loveliest parts of fair England', though the Devil's Punch Bowl, delineated in vivid detail, was the focus of repeated tragedy. In 1896 Conan Doyle built 'Undershaw' in Hindhead and there wrote some of his historical novels and some of his Sherlock Holmes stories. George Bernard Shaw arrived in 1898 and Flora Thompson, postmistress at Grayswood between 1897-1900, eventually wrote about the locality and its people in *Heatherley* (1979), published posthumously. Other distinguished intellectuals included Henry Mangles, the rhododendron specialist; the family of Jonathan Hutchinson who built Inval as his country house and became a focal point in the community through the educational museum he founded, and Joseph and Maude King and Godfrey Blount of Haslemere (pp.193-4). By the early 1900s the spread of country houses in and around Hindhead had destroyed much of its earlier charm. Pollock left in 1904 for this reason; Conan Doyle left for Crowborough in 1907.[7]

Mrs Humphry Ward, in *Robert Elsemere*, struck a new note about the Surrey heaths which did not conform to the conventional notion of the beautiful until the mid-19th century:

> A nature wild and solitary indeed, but still rich, luxuriant and friendly to the
> sense of the traveller, even in the loneliest places. The heaths and woods of

123 *Undershaw, Hindhead, built for Sir Arthur Conan Doyle.*

some districts of Surrey are scarcely more thickly populated than the fells of Westmoreland [*sic*]; the walker may wander for miles, and still enjoy untamed primitive earth, guiltless of boundary or furrow, the undisturbed home of all that grows and flies, where the rabbits, the lizards, and the birds live their life as they please, either ignorant of intruding man or strangely little incommoded by his neighbourhood. And yet there is nothing forbidding or austere in these wild solitudes … These Surrey commons [are] not a wilderness, but a paradise …[8]

and so did Charles Kingsley who wrote of his heath at Eversley in terms of natural history and who claimed to have learned more, studying over and over again for 15 years his sand and gravel heaps, than he would have by roaming all Europe in search of new geologic wonders.[9]

Aldous Huxley wrote more than fifty books which earned him a world-wide readership. His *Brave New World* (1932) became one of the best-sellers of the century. Much of the lurch to the New World took place in west Surrey, Huxley's native home. Beyond London's satellite suburbs, helicopters ceaselessly hummed and roared, carrying Gammas and Beta-Minuses on the 'down-line' to Guildford via Witley to Portsmouth, the 'up service' being via Tongham, Elstead, Grayshott and Puttenham. Elstead had a 14-storey tower block; Puttenham a vitamin-D factory but Huxley took good care that the Brave New World does not savage the Surrey heaths. This had been done by H.G. Wells who was familiar with Woking and Broadstairs. He has Martians fresh from their annihilation of London calmly and methodically wreaking total destruction around Broadstairs and Deal and 'over the blue hills that rise southward of the river (the Thames).

H.E. Bates of Great Chart was a great nature writer excelling in descriptions of the Kent scene. He also wrote *The Darling Buds of May* (1958), instantly a phenomenal success in many languages. With wanton Chaucerian robustness and fun, his novel was told with joy and relish, and flouting all conventions, was a 'blower away of the blues'. 'From all quarters came reports of laughter … of the Larkins working miracles in hospital wards.' Bates explained that he was driving through a Kent village in 'apple orchard country' when he encountered, outside a shop, a ramshackle lorry painted in a violent electric blue containing the high spirited family, which was the source of inspiration for his tales: 'Wild laughter ranged through the village street and the whole scene might have come out of Merrie England.' Its flavour is the Kent world at its ripest. The Larkins can be read on two planes; purely for the sheer joy of their enviable way of life, but also as a reflection on the revolution that had overtaken the post-war countryside. As Bates himself remarked:

> In the early thirties not a single farm worker in my village had a car, many not even a bicycle; today many have two cars, many a cottage is inhabited by a family displaying four, five or even six cars; few village shops sold anything but mousetrap cheese, fat bacon, candles, paraffin, tart oranges and boiled sweets; today everyone has its deep freeze dispensing scampi, smoked salmon, Spaghetti Bolognese and exotics of every kind.

Vita Sackville-West, who wrote *The Land* and *The Garden* at Sissinghurst in the Weald, wrote an amusing piece when on the Downs:

> She was wearing the coral taffeta trousers
> Some one had brought her from Ispahan,
> And the little gold coat with pomegranate blossoms,
> And the coral-hafted fan;
> But she ran down a Kentish lane in the moonlight,
> And skipped in the pool of the moon as she ran.
> She cared not a rap for all the big planets,
> For Betelgeuse or Aldebarna,
> And all the big planets cared nothing for her,
> That small, impertinent charlatan;
> But she climbed on a Kentish stile in the moonlight,
> And laughed at the sky through the sticks of her fan.[10]

The Landscape Artist's Inspiration from the North Downs and Surrey Hills

It was the landscape painter who increasingly supplied impressions that could not adequately be expressed in poetry or prose. In 1792 J.M.W. Turner was introduced to William Frederick Wells of Knockholt in Kent where he made a small series in oils of the beech trees in Chevening Park in 1799, out of doors which he had never done before. He was also apparently indebted to Wells for his encouragement of his exquisite *Liber Studiorium*.[1] Turner endlessly captured in hundreds of pencil sketches his excited visual pleasure at glimpses of the varied and richly wooded landscape (as in the Wey Gap at Guildford where he sought paintable tree groups and landscapes framed by trees) and some were elaborated in the medium of watercolour, such as the fair on St Catherine's Hill and Dover Castle.[2]

An artist much inspired by Turner and also by William Blake and his mentor, John Linnell who suggested Albrecht Dürer to him, was Samuel Palmer (1805-1881), whose ecstatic visions at Shoreham in Kent have been re-discovered since the 1960s and are now regarded as the work of one of the few English artists of the 1820s of international stature. Shoreham in the Darent valley was only 20 miles from London but in the 1820s hardly influenced by it; as Palmer's friend Edward Calvert remarked, 'It looked as if the Devil had not yet found it out'. In this rich landscape of immemorial antiquity he found a *Genius Loci* beyond price. His inspiration came from its breast-like hills, little cottages, cornfields, blossom and fruit in enamelled orchards, hop fields, flocks of sheep, brilliant stars, gnarled ancient oak, beech and chestnut trees, shady lanes and innumerable little dells and nooks and 'wild places'. This not only inspired his art but virtually shaped it, and haunted him all his life. As Carlo Peacock has written: 'Had he been actually born into it [the Shoreham valley] instead of discovering it in his most impressionable years, it might have affected him less profoundly; but coming as it did, with Blake's influence like a ferment in his mind, this little corner of Kent took on for him the character of an earthly paradise.'[3] These were perceived with a religious and poetic intensity unequalled except by Blake, and called up a dreamy reverie of a prodigal garden, of 'heaped-up richness' he called it, as in *The Magic Apple Tree*, *The Shoreham Garden*, *The Pear Tree* and *Pastoral with Horse-Chestnut*, the shadowy world of twilight and moon-lit nightfall being recurring themes.

After Shoreham, Palmer and his new wife went to Rome, where the impact of Italian art weakened his vision. As time went on the dominating personality of John Linnell, his tyrannical father-in-law, proved to be a source of friction and the death of a son caused him much grief. This had an inhibiting effect on Palmer. He was haunted by a sense of deprivation in Kensington and moved finally to Furze Hill House near Reigate which had distant views of the Weald. His etchings from here were a re-flowering of his inner vision at Shoreham.

124 *Portrait of Samuel Palmer.*

Jaded urban dwellers in hugely expanding London who felt increasingly separated from their natural environment developed a new outlook on nature which had a powerful effect on landscape artists. To the generation of *c.*1830 London still provided in its many *rus-in-urbe* enclaves an inexhaustibly rich source of inspiration to the landscape-water-colourist, and the artist's receptive appreciation of beauty in the urban scene was inherited from the intellectual tradition that the city was the formative centre of civilisation. Moreover, difficulties of travel before the coming of railways obliged artists to seek beauty and diversity within London itself. The following artists' generation had to come to terms with the spectacular expansion of the metropolis, the first world capital to grow so huge so rapidly, that was in the 1860s 'more excavated, more cut about, more rebuilt and extended than at any time in its previous history'. Landscape artists then preferred to ignore all Victorian components in London and escape from the many urgent challenges that the noisy, crowded, smoky precincts were throwing up and, with the new opportunities provided by railways, paint the green girdle around London.

The master-evil oppressing the city, amongst a crowd of other dispiriting phenomena, was its smoke canopy. *The Times* of 1856 declared:

> London is a colourless metropolis. It is like a landscape in sepia, without the finish of a line engraving or the gloss of a pencil drawing. Everything matches; the houses are black or whitey-brown; the streets are dirty; the sky semi-opaque and the clothing of the passengers dark and dusty ...

Broadly in proportion to its growing size, London became blacker and more acridly smoky. 'The Smoke' became cockney slang for the capital and repeatedly newspapers returned to the subject of urban malediction. In December 1890 *The Times* again let out a cry of despair and lamented:

> ... Can we dispel that overhanging canopy of gloom which makes London in winter a city of dreadful and almost everlasting night? ... What would London

give, what indeed would it not give, if some man of science would tell it how to get rid of that intolerable winter gloom which destroys now so unnecessarily, lowers its vitality, impedes its labour and destroys its happiness?

Another powerful weapon for bringing the idea of the Victorian city into disrespect amongst artists was John Ruskin's concept of a barren-blighted landscape that he eloquently campaigned against in his *Modern Painters* (1834-60). In response to these circumstances painters from the decade of the 1840s developed to a fanatical degree a passion for 'the country'. In this process a few rural districts near London were brought into general artistic consciousness for the first time. An example is the middle Thames valley between Cookham and Pangbourne where Frederick Walker and George Price Boyce went to paint in the 1860s; but the gravitational centre to which most of the would-be landscapists drifted was predominantly the North Downs and the sandstone hills of Surrey. John Sell Cotman exhibited at the Royal Academy in 1800 when he was only 18 years of age two sketches made at Ashtead when on vacation, and an elegant etching survives by Henry Eldridge RA depicting Thomas Hearne (d. 1817) sitting on a tombstone in Ashtead churchyard making a sketch of the manor house. Later the Pre-Raphaelites were associated with the district near Ewell. Holman Hunt painted the landscape for his 'Hireling Shepherd' in Ewell meadows north of Ewell Court Farm (his maternal uncle's) and his 'Light of the World' captured the light of the moon from Worcester Park Farm. Millais used the river flowing through the Lemprières' family property for the background to his Ophelia (the subject herself was painted in a bath tub).[4]

Migrating Artists

The most attractive place for migrating artists to learn their painting skills was the Vale of Mickleham and the adjoining Dorking district, which became known as the most interesting natural habitat within 30 miles of London. Before railways widened artists' options the district became recognised as a suitable trainee-artist's workshop on account of the richly varied and supremely wooded course of the River Mole under the slopes of Norbury Park and Box Hill, combined with its accessibility to the capital. Notable here were the pupils of Dr Thomas Monro, who inherited a senior position at Bethlehem Hospital in London and was a consultant to King George III. He was an enthusiastic patron of the arts and taught young artists, among them Turner, Girtin, John Linnell, John Sell Cotman, and John Varley, at his house in Adelphi Terrace and at his country house in Bell Lane, Fetcham.[5]

With the coming of railways the North Downs and Surrey Hills became a rallying point for migrating artists and subsequently a centre from which new naturalistic movements radiated. No other environment in lowland England possessed anything like its visual significance for mid- and late 19th-century artists.

The spark of grumbling revolt at the constraints of London as a subject for landscape painting among Ruskin's generation[6] was lit by the academician Richard Redgrave, the first breakaway London artist who gave up a successful career as a genre artist in London in 1849 and was to spend no fewer than 37 successive summers painting directly in the open air at Abinger. John Linnell independently abandoned portrait painting in Bayswater in the same year and returned to his first love of landscape by removing to Redstone, on the crest of the sandstone hills near Redhill. J.C. Hook, then a figure painter at Brompton, joined Redgrave at Abinger for the 1853 season in the company of William Rose. Hook settled permanently in Surrey from 1856, first at Witley and subsequently at Churt. Later arrivals at Abinger were George Vicat Cole (the first landscape artist to be admitted to the Royal Academy for 30 years), Edmund Warren and G.P. Boyce. Cole's friend, Benjamin W.

125 *Richard Redgrave.*

Leader, also became familiar with the same locality at this time, although he did not take up residence near Gomshall until 20 years later.

To the pioneer artist Abinger had an unmatched potency. As the English 'Barbizon' it not only boasted of exceptionally varied scenery within walking distance, but also afforded distant prospects over extensive woods and heaths which, although near to London, were remote and 'wild' enough to feed the imagination of artists who were addicted to uncultivated places as a foil to London. Meanwhile, another artists' colony was developing at Witley. At Hook's suggestion, Birket Foster, long frustrated as an illustrative draughtsman in London, joined him there in 1861. Frederick Walker came too, and the Witley circle soon included (Sir) Henry Cole, Redgrave's superior at the South Kensington Museum (Victoria and Albert), himself a water-colourist of distinction. These were followed by Helen Allingham and by writers and poets including Tennyson and George Eliot. Most of these artists followed the practice of working in the country air during most of the year, but returning to the capital for the winter season for exhibitions, business contact and the enjoyment of social life. This double-life placed artists among the first to turn the region into commuter country and among the first to reverse the townward drift of population.

The predominant image depicted by artists of the Redgravian generation was not a tamed landscape, but a half-wild one. Theirs was a vision animated by quasi-scientific curiosity in the morphology of rocks and plants which in the region of the Weald was then engaging widespread interest and controversy. It was in effect the compound of chaos and order which earlier engaged the rapturous attention of Turner and was currently observed with preternatural vivacity by Ruskin whose injunctions and advice were followed:

They must be careful that it *is* nature to whom they go, nature in her liberty, not as a servant of all work in the hands of the agriculturist, nor stiffened into court-dress by the landscape gardener ... As far as the painter is concerned, man never touches nature but to spoil; he operates on her as a barber would on Apollo. The only advice I can safely give the young painter is to keep clear of clover fields and parks and to hold to the unpenetrated forest and unfurrowed hill.[7]

Another consistent advocate of the intrinsic worth of the natural environment then in abject retreat was John Stuart Mill's eloquent plea in defence of nature which had as powerful an influence as it should today:

A world from which all solitude is extirpated is a very poor ideal ... Nor is there much satisfaction in contemplating the world with nothing left to the spontaneous activity of nature; with every rood of land brought into cultivation, which is capable of growing food for human beings; every flowery waste or natural pasture ploughed up, all quadrupeds or birds which are not domesticated for man's use exterminated as his rivals for food, every hedgerow or superfluous tree rooted out, and scarcely a place where wild shrub or flower could grow without being eradicated as a weed in the name of improved agriculture ...[8]

Although the region had been developed for agriculture for millennia, there was an uncommon profusion and diversity of nature, matching to perfection the spirit of the age which rejoiced in exuberance, intricacy, opulence and smallness of detail. Samuel Palmer at Shoreham had made this superabundance of detail even more excessive by a dazzling compendium of minutely rendered vegetation 'heaped up like the produce on a market stall' in the belief that exuberance

126 *Helen Allingham's* Surrey Cottage.

is beauty. It was a country with paradoxically opposed qualities of landscape melting into one another, deeply humanised and utterly wild by turns. Its garden-like richness alternated with austere heaths and downs and dense woodland, a 'disordered order' and 'fertile wildness' as Patrick Heron described its lushness, not only inspiring in the 'deep secret recesses' loved by Palmer but also the general settings in spaciously open landscapes of grandeur and dignity which inspired Linnell and later followers such as John Clayton Adams.[9] This was all the more miraculous for being so close to London, one of the world's most artificial environments.

Richard Redgrave (1804-88) is chiefly remembered for his early genre paintings which were powerful evocations of human dilemmas such as *The Emigrant's Last Sight of Home* (1858) and other paintings, in richly-wooded Abinger, his beloved country place, there where he found the necessary relaxation and renewal from his busy administrative duties in the metropolis. He became fixated with the most charming characteristic features of the Surrey Greensands – its little streams, woodland glades, reflecting pool, rocky outcrops and sunken lanes – and painted with the realism of minute detail urged by Ruskin and appealing in the age of the Pre-Raphaelite Brotherhood. These 'natural truths' were captured in his sheer bliss at being in Abinger with his family, sampling the simple pleasures and beauty of country life: 'Sweet sunny hours we had? How can life offer anything happier?', he wrote.

His successors, such as George Vicat Cole and Clayton Adams, also sought to capture the beauty, activity and complexity of undisturbed woodland but also explored undiscovered qualities in the landscape, notably the panoramic effect, for which they chose to reside on summits commanding the most glorious outlooks across the vales of Surrey, Sussex and Kent. This delineation of extended space involved technical difficulties which could only be overcome with extreme patience and concentration. As the contemporary artist Herkomer wrote: 'To paint vast nature in all its changing expression of cloud and light the painter's mind must be stored with a mass of fact which has accumulated for years of sketching, note-taking and observation.' For lengthy study of aerial effects, artists constructed special outdoor studios (sky parlours) and to lengthen the season of *plein-air* painting the painter resisted rough weather by guying his easel to a heavy suspended stone. The power of this kind of landscape art to refresh minds wearied by the dual shocks of industrialism and urbanisation was conceived by artists as a social responsibility and they struck a genuine vein of popular taste. In the words of G.F. Watts, a contemporary artist resident in London and at Compton, near Guildford, it was the urban patron's ideal of landscape to see nothing beautiful around him 'excepting always sky and trees and sea; these as he is mainly a dweller in cities he cannot live enough with'.

The master of Wealden panorama was John Linnell (1792-1882). In his youth he was taught by John Varley and William Mulready to paint directly from nature when there was seemingly inexhaustible richness in the 'old London scene'. Yet by middle age, and after more than fifty years' residence in the city, Linnell had developed such a strong antipathy to 'the new London' that he

127 *Rowland Hilder country.*

sought an idea of, and approach to, landscape painting that was diametrically opposed to anything London stood for. That he should have thereby become England's most popular and prolific landscape painter when over sixty years of age, and established the sylvan distances of the Weald in the minds of the newly enriched industrial and business leaders of the Midlands and the North, is one of the most remarkable events in 19th-century social history. Linnell was the subject of much undiscriminating over-praise and there was a sharp fall in his reputation after his death. This had something to do with the hackneyed and repetitious pictures produced at his Redhill 'art factory' which revealed the declining powers of his old age. Moreover, the recent rise in stature of his friend William Blake and of his son-in-law Samuel Palmer had cast a deep shadow over Linnell personally so that his own accomplishments were in danger of almost total eclipse. Fortunately, Katharine Crouan took advantage of the centenary in 1982 of his death in 1882 by choosing and cataloguing a selection of his work for exhibition at the Fitzwilliam Museum, Cambridge, which demonstrated that Linnell made a significant contribution to English landscape painting.[10]

Linnell stands apart from such artists as Redgrave and Birket Foster in being a generation older, and like others of his time, caught between two worlds, which made him a thinker on the utterly new human organisation that England had become. Whereas, for example, Foster was really a public relations man, exploiting the media of watercolour in favour of rural scenery, Linnell had a moral message to convey, though he was not averse to pandering to his patrons' nostalgia as well. The nightmare which stalked his middle and old age was similar to Ruskin's and Arnold's fear of civilisation under threat. He shared the Victorian fear of a godless society and his visions of social decay in such works as *On the Eve of the Deluge* (1848) and *The Last Load* (1852) show that he was responding to what he considered to be the loss of human values through the spread of cities and the tremendous altercation with nature that their growth entailed. As Crouan remarked, 'Linnell's impulse towards landscape was bred in the heart of the city'.

The favourite pictorial devices of later landscape artists tend to be places of withdrawal, such as the old-fashioned cottage and garden, the water-mill, the gorse and heather on the common, woodland glades, deliberately chosen archaic features evoking the domestic English scene and prized as a countervailing heaven on earth by an urban society desperately wanting another Eden. The garden has always been archetypically symbolic of pleasure and retreat and was now a painter's concept to ward off the modern terror of urbanisation and its accompanying rushed living and high-pressure work. The theme of the old-fashioned garden, with its image of peace, variety, continuity and tradition, contrasted with the uniformity and ugliness of urban building and was the clearest signal of a town weary society. The cottage and the cottager, which still existed in considerable numbers in the Downs and Hills were seen as the epitome of an essentially English type of landscape, as much as oak-studded hedgerows and village greens. Birket Foster, *the* watercolourist of his day, was popularising this image at Witley in the 1860s and it was developed as the main motif by Helen Allingham. C.S. Elgood, P.L. Clifford, Alfred Parsons and others followed with studies of gardens. Their pictures brought out the contrast between the serene loveliness of the region's ancient landscape and the crowded precincts of encroaching London. Bought avidly by Londoners and inhabitants of provincial towns and cities, they introduced west Surrey as an ideal place for retirement and ever since it has remained the garden of gardens amongst the fictional regions of the mind.

By the 1890s landscape artists were descending on west Surrey in clouds (to the resentment of some farmers and millers) and multiplying artists' colonies were turning the south-east into a vast open-air studio from which emerged artists, who for convenience might be called the Wealden School, which became the paramount school of English painting between the decline of the Norwich school and the rise of the Newlyn impressionists. Shere was a magnet for artists as early as the 1860s. In the 1920s and '30s up to a dozen would be resident at any one time. Mary Freeman so fell in love with the place that, with an art woman friend, she slept in the fields. Then someone allowed them to sleep in a corner of a barn and then a shepherd's hut. Reginald Bray then towed it up to a woodland site at the top of the hill and himself marked out land to make a garden. Freeman was later joined by Margaret Johnson, a book illustrator, and together they lived for years without any amenities. William Hyde, the illustrator of Housman's *Shropshire Lad*, had his studio called Sayers overlooking the Tillingbourne stream and Edward Wilkins Waite (1854-1954) resided at Abinger. Amongst numerous other artists, George Marks lived at Shere between 1887 and 1926 and Benjamin Leader was at nearby Gomshall; Ethelbert White lived in a caravan at Shere in the 1930s.[11]

Rowland Hilder (1905-93) put the Darent valley at the heart of much of his work. It was only after he and his artist friends began sketching and painting at Shoreham that they realised that this was 'Samuel Palmer country'. The illustrator for the Highways and Byways series of books, F.L. Griggs, passed on this information to Graham Sutherland and Paul Drury. Hilder unknowingly recorded the barn at Sepham Farm which appears in several of Palmer's drawings. (This has now gone.) Hilder looked at the stunningly beautiful landscape of the Shoreham valley with new eyes once Palmer's visionary genius had been revealed. After the First World War his studio was at St Julians, just south of Sevenoaks, commanding a glorious view across Knowle Park. The English winter, his speciality, had not been tackled before. His 'Hilderscapes', such as *The Weald of Kent* and *Oasts under Snow*, have a strong linear quality and his Kentish landscapes in winter garb are perceptive delineations of the scene.[12]

Thomas Hennell, the countryman, artist and writer, was born at Ridley, high on the Downs above Wrotham, of which he wrote that 'lanes turn and twist' and 'not easy was the wayward road to find'. He spent most of the time between late 1935 and mid-1943 in the same district and in watercolour and ink made some fine renderings of barns and farming implements.[13]

128 *Ethelbert White's representation of the Shere district.*

22

Nature, Man and Beast

Downland

From as early as 1548 when the 'father of botany' William Turner recorded the sea cabbage, samphire and yellow sea poppy on the cliffs around Dover, the plants of the chalk of the North Downs which find the dry, warm, calcareous soil amenable to their growth have been eagerly studied by generations of naturalists.[1]

It is now accepted that turf is not natural to chalkland, but has resulted from human and animal clearance of deciduous woodland that with the gradual climate warming from *c.*10,000 BC replaced the juniper, pine, hazel and birch of the colder phase. As woodland clearance proceeded, sun-loving plants so common in chalk were able to expand in numbers and territory. It is difficult to ascertain where these plants came from. Dr Francis Rose suggests that chalk-loving plants may have survived as relict species in 'refugia' during the advance of the woodland after the last Ice Age, e.g. on the edges of sea- or river-cliffs. There is also the possibility that suitable habitats existed in grassy patches within the woodland. The Dutch ecologist Vera has recently stressed the role of large herbivores in the 'wildwood' such as the auroch (a species of large cattle), the wild horse, boar and deer which may have created open, grassy clearings in woodland before Man began to reclaim it.[2]

A remarkable characteristic of old chalk grassland is its springiness, which, where it survives post-war intensive agriculture, makes walking almost effortless. The reason for this cushion-like effect is that for several inches below the well-drained light soils of the chalk, a dense mass of roots of intertwined plants give it elasticity. Uniquely, the turf harbours more species than any other habitat in Britain. According to English Nature there may be up to forty species in one square yard, including numerous herbs and other plants as well as even more abundant grasses such as sheep's fescue. Some are exceedingly small like the aromatic thyme and marjoram, rock rose and horseshoe vetch, the food source of the Chalkhill Blue butterfly and the even rarer and more beautiful Adonis Blue. This fragrant chalk turf is now largely confined to the south-facing escarpment of the Downs and other hillsides too steep to plough. Such fragments now constitute one of the rarest habitats in western Europe and the fact that they are a haven for species of insects, fauna and flora declining elsewhere makes them even more important.

It is still not fully understood how many species can survive in such close proximity but it is thought that the need for tolerance or adaptation to extended

129 Autumn Trees on the North Downs, *A.M. Parkin of Kemsing.*

periods of water nutrients shortage, coupled with the unpredictable and random effects of grazing, creates such a variety of advantages and setbacks for each species from year to year that no one species or group of species can come to dominate the rest. Another apparent factor is that chalk is not a particularly good soil-forming rock. The result is very shallow soil which is highly alkaline in reaction with a high pH. The high level of bases tends to reduce the availability of important plant nutrients such as nitrates, phosphates and certain metallic trace elements, imposing severe limitations on growth. Such soils have a large number of leguminous plants such as the pea family, which manufacture nitrate from atmospheric nitrogen with the aid of root nodules containing nitrogen-fixing bacteria. The scaling-down of plants gives the impression of a greensward as smooth as a billiard table or garden lawn. Ordinarily, the plants would have grown taller, but wind, shallow infertile soil, very dry conditions and close and selective grazing by sheep and rabbits, in contrast to the lighter and more uniform grazing by cattle, has meant that they hug the ground tenaciously.

The Kemsing Down Nature Reserve is an excellent example of such chalk grassland. It is managed by the parish council with the help and advice of the Kent Trust for Nature Conservation and lies on the escarpment of the Downs

130 Wild Marjoram on the North Downs *by A.M. Parkin of Kemsing.*

above the village with many indented slopes of varying aspects. Left entirely to nature such downland habitats would be invaded by dogwood and thorn scrub and in the very long term would develop into mature woodlands, principally of ash, beech and oak. Since the Reserve was formally established in the late 1970s there has been some sensitive clearance of scrub, brambles and dogwood to restore the sward. Twenty-seven species of butterfly have been recorded on the Reserve and even more moths. Forty-five species of birds are supported. The flora is very rich and includes eight varieties of orchid. Wild spindle is also abundant. This is the loveliest of downland plants when the seed pods split open.[3]

Three other areas of the Kent Downs escarpment are important areas of chalk grassland. The extremely rare silver-spotted skipper butterfly was re-introduced to Barham Down in 1998 and has begun to breed in the reserve. Amongst colourful day-flying moths is the Six-spot Burnet moth. Darland Banks, lying south of Gillingham, was an area of invasive hawthorn scrub which is being cut back in winter by volunteers. Cattle browse the seedlings and this is allowing the grassland flora to return. One of the most spectacular areas of chalk grassland is Queendown Warren, midway between Hartlip and Bredhurst, which is renowned for its variety of orchids. Other examples of chalk grassland are met with in parts of Box Hill and in the undercliff of the Wye National Nature Reserve.

English Nature advise that, as such chalk grassland is a pasture habitat developed over centuries of grazing management, cutting and mowing can only provide interim slowing down of damage owing to the lack of grazing. Grazing by stock is essential in the long-term, and no management other than grazing can maintain it indefinitely. Grazing should cover the spring and summer when vegetation is most nutritious and thorny shrubs are not harmed by having their flowering shoots eaten. Stocking in wet winter weather is to be avoided. Mixed grazing creates a particularly good sward. Rank swards are often unpalatable but animals able to cope are Galloway, Highland, Sussex or Welsh Mountain cattle, some mountain breeds of sheep, native ponies and goats.

Clearance of developing scrub is an important aspect of chalk grassland management. This task is an immensely difficult one and many a farmer has given up the struggle. The steep slopes of downland do not lend themselves easily to mechanised scrub clearance and heavy machinery is liable to damage the thin soil structure and cause erosion. The only effective method of clearance is regular and arduous hand clearance which is undertaken by voluntary members of a local Nature Conservancy. Work is carried out from late autumn to early spring to avoid damage to wildflowers and disturbance to nesting birds and animals with young. It is becoming essential that as much of the chalk grassland as possible is conserved while it still exists because its creation can take hundreds of years. In other areas grassland is being subjected to the plough as sheep husbandry becomes uneconomic or the grassland is being 'improved' by the application of artificial fertilisers and re-seeding, which encourages the dominance of the more nutritious rye grasses, but which discourages most of the unique flora.

On typical short downland turf the first pale scentless flowers of the hairy violet appear in early spring. Cowslips flower by early April and dense mats of honey-scented crosswort and salad burnet appear. In May the downland slopes are bright with flowers of the tiny common milkwort and various leguminous plants are abundant including red and white clovers, black medick, bird's-foot trefoil, hop trefoil and various vetches. Orchids then appear – bee, man, common spotted, pyramidal, and fragrant orchids. In July the bright yellow flowers of the common rock-rose are widespread and during the summer season the delightful aroma of the thyme/mint family pervades the downland including wild thyme, marjoram and wild basil. In August the harebell comes into flower. Among other interesting flowers are common eyebright, fairy flax and squinancy-wort.[4]

Collectively, the miniature herbs and flowers growing in the short dense turf have always been responsible for much of the beauty and fascination of the Downs, so it is easy to understand why their natural riches have received such notice. A number of plants are entirely confined to chalk on account of their specialised requirements. Such plants often send deep roots down into the ground, and some develop a hairy or waxy skin to avoid dessication, like the autumn gentian and many of the orchids. Some other species, such as the man and bee orchids, die down after flowering to avoid the hottest months. The high density of flowering plants and herbs makes the greensward very coloured and scented, its colour varying from season to season. Chalk grassland also supports many species of invertebrates, apart from the Chalkhill Blue and Adonis Blue butterfly and moths already mentioned, such as grasshoppers and crickets.[5]

Some animal species are either mainly or completely confined to chalk. There is an abundance of snail, some diminutive, due to the availability of calcium for shell-making. An exclusive species is the round-mouthed snail; another, though with a wider horizon, is the Roman snail, generally concentrated in rougher downland sward; other species favour woodland and others rabbit-grazed turf. Owing to the scarcity of surface water amphibians are rare.

The wild rabbit is the most important of all wild mammals on downland because it has the closest connection with man and in the feral state they have been, and remain, important agents in modifying chalk grassland. Unlike the hare, it is not indigenous to the British Isles. Hitherto it has been considered an introduction of the Normans, though the recent discovery of a skeleton of a rabbit at Thetford in Norfolk at a Romanised site may indicate that it was known much earlier.[6] Rabbiting began in specially created warrens known as coney-garths (coney being the original name for an adult rabbit) and gorse, juniper, bramble and other prickly shrubs were planted or managed for their food. Although chalkland provided ideal well-drained soils for burrowing, breeding was encouraged by the erection of massive mounds of earth known as 'pillow mounds' which can be as long as 100 feet, 15 feet wide at the base and four to five feet high. To the chagrin of farmers and golf course greenkeepers, rabbits are now re-occupying parts of the Downs after the ravages of myxomatosis in the 1950s. The survivors have developed a degree of immunity to the disease which is passed from one generation to the next and have become particularly tenacious pests in many places. The chalk shows white where rabbits have excavated burrows and, unless kept down, they do tremendous damage to growing crops and to tree and plant species. This is very evident from the contrast between vegetation inside and outside rabbit-proof enclosures.

Of great potential interest to field naturalists are liverworts, mosses and lichens (bryophytes). Francis Rose has shown that the chalk range of the North Downs provides in Box Hill what is the richest locality for bryophytes on the English chalk. This is because it combines a wide selection of slopes of different aspect and degrees of steepness with a rich variety of vegetation types. The steep escarpment of Box Hill overlooking the Weald to the south is very warm, dry and exposed. On the northern sides there is a series of steep-sided

131 *Juniper Hall students at fieldwork.*

valleys where conditions are more sheltered, with round-topped ridges between them. The summit plateau capped with clay-with-flints provides acid conditions because no calcium carbonate is present to neutralise the acid humus formed by vegetation. The open chalk areas were formerly sheepwalk, dominated largely by a short close turf of sheep's fescue (*fescue ovina*) but owing to the cessation of grazing (even by rabbits) large areas are dominated by taller upright brome grass, locally by coarse aggressive tor grass. The plateau has developed birch scrub which in places has culminated in typical oakwood climax. Each of these communities has its own bryophyte flora. On the dry south face of the escarpment, typical 'calcicole' or chalk mosses are found. Some of these, such as *pleurachaete squarrosa* which has tiny yellow-green stars in winter, are confined to warm spots in southern England. The chalk turf of the north and north-east facing slopes is in general deeper and damper. Here the sun's rays fall at a steeper angle at midday and so less heat energy reaches any given surface area than on the south facing slopes. These slopes, being in valleys, are also sheltered and thus the humidity of the air just above the soil level is high. This is shown by the way in which both dew in mild weather and hoar frost in wintry weather lie far longer on these slopes than on the southern ones. As a result a much more luxuriant bryophyte community is found. Also in the short turf of the northern slopes there are remarkable calcicole bryophytes whose main home in Britain is the limestone hills of the wetter west and northern parts of the country. Four of these in particular deserve notice as they are confined on the North Downs to the north slopes of Box Hill, though widespread on the escarpment of the western South Downs which faces north and has a higher rainfall.[7]

Characteristic birds of downland fields include the red-legged and grey partridge and the lapwing, which nest in corn before it has grown too high. From March the first of the summer migrants arrive; wheatears and chiffchaffs are often the earliest, followed by willow warblers, blackcaps, nightingales and swallows. Others from Scandinavia such as bramblings, redwings and fieldfares are winter visitors. The skylark, which everyone associates with downland, has lost most of its preferred nesting sites in rough grassland with the intensification of agriculture. Insects and other invertebrates provide food for amphibians, lizards, many species of birds and the numerous creatures including the common toad, common and pigmy shrew, mole and hedgehog. Brown hares are at home in cultivated fields as much as in grassland.[8]

The sea cliffs have species of their own. The fulmar petrel now nests in small numbers around Folkestone and Ramsgate. The kittiwake is also a recent colonist of the cliffs. Herring gulls also nest on cliff-edges as do the sparrow hawk and hobby. Feral pigeons and jackdaws breed in crevices. Plants special to sea cliffs include wild sea cabbage, which has lovely pale yellow flowers from May to August on the White Cliffs of Dover, sea beet, rock samphire, long prized for its fleshy leaves which can be used for food, yellow horned poppy, seaside thistle and dwarf centaury.

Many of the shrubs, wildflowers and other plants of the chalk have had such a long association with downsmen as to have written themselves into folklore

XXVI *Paul Nash:* The Battle of Britain.

XXVII *Industrial crops on the Lees Court Estate.*

XXVIII *Exmoor ponies grazing on the Dover cliffs.*

XXIX *Denbies Vineyard, Dorking.*

XXX *A Eurostar train speeding through Kent, providing the most comfortable and convenient travel to and from the continent from Ashford.*

and the imagination. This is because they played a large part in the practice of magic and entered into daily lives as food, cosmetics, colourings and medicine, as well as ceremonies. This is discussed in the present author's *The South Downs*[9] and it is unnecessary to repeat it here, but it should be mentioned that on the Downs at Kingston near Canterbury wild plants are again being gathered for restaurants.

The Vegetation of the Sandstones

The abrupt and strong contrasts of marsh, wood, common, bog and heath sum up the vegetation of the sandstone ridges and differentiate them fascinatingly from the chalk. In boggy patches, sedges are the commonest plants, but it is the spread of sphagnum moss which is particularly significant because its habit of absorbing wetness up to 16 times its weight, and squeezing it out like a sponge wherever it spreads, leads to the formation of boggy land. The largest expanse of this light green plant with its tufted cushions was the bottom of the Devil's Punch Bowl in the Hindhead upland at the upper end of the great valley nearest to the Gibbet Hill ridge, but only small patches now survive; trees have overgrown the site. This is simply one instance of vegetation change in the district since E.C. Matthews wrote *The Highlands of South-West Surrey* in 1911. In other wet places is found the bog pimpernel, the lesser-jointed bog-rush and the bog asphodel, a little iris-like plant bearing exquisite gold flowers and orange-coloured fruits, earlier used as a dye. Cotton grass, with its silky-white tufts, is the commonest plant of boggy swamps. The whortleberry, hoary cinquefoil, long-leaved sundew and hare's foot trefoil are amongst the wild plants thriving on the sands. All three kinds of heather are found on the heaths – the ling,

132 *Gilbert White's house, Selborne.*

most widely spread, the fine-leaved heath, with its large, deep, crimson bells and the paler, pink-tipped cross-leaved heath. Gorse grows tall and luxuriantly, but a shorter variety occurs on the sterile sands, the pretty whin or dwarf gorse. The Scots pine has adapted to the sands with ease. Hothfield Common is one of Kent's few remaining fragments of open heath and has the last four valley bogs left in the county. The aim of the Kent Wildlife Trust here is to redress years of neglect by controlling bracken and birch invasion, restoring the valley bogs and maintaining a mosaic of grassland heath.

Of particular relevance to the sandstone hills is what Chris Howkins calls 'the heathland harvest', the uses of heathland plants through the ages.[10] There was so little foliage on heaths that cattle and sheep browsed on sprouting birch stools in spring. When the stools had grown the 'heathmen' earned a steady trade by making besoms. Birch Wine and Birch Water were so highly prized for kidney disorders and gallstones that Evelyn gives detailed directions in his *Sylva* for drawing sap by penetrating into the bark, but not so far as the heartwood. Oil from the bark was also used in tannin and other medicines. Almost every cottager on heaths was a beekeeper producing honey, 'the nectar of the gods', and beeswax for articles like candles and polish. The traditional skeps on their stools imitating natural nests was a familiar sight in cottage gardens. Heather was used as an antiseptic; it was also used to make ale and for thatching. Heather (and furze) was also important before coal became cheap enough for general use in the early 19th century. Turves of matted roots and litter from the heather were cut in early summer with a special spade which had a cross-bar to the handle upon which the cutter put his weight. Broom, a member of the legume family, was long cultivated as a medicine and young buds were harvested as a salad, as Evelyn noted in his *Acetaria* (1699). The cottager found endless use for sweet gale, including making beer, flavouring food, making dyes and repelling moths.

Of critical importance amongst commoners was a source of fertiliser known as 'litter' or 'brakes'. This comprised anything on common-land that made good bedding for beasts in barns (straw being scarce on their little holdings) which could afterwards be ploughed into their lean, hungry soil as dung. An annual supply of brakes (bracken) or 'litter' (mainly young heather) was thus indispensable for the maintenance of a little farm and even larger properties made use of it. It involved back-breaking work and the small farmer's family would descend on a common, the men scything, the women and girls raking, and boys swinging their own little hooks. Potash from bracken was used in the manufacture of glass and soap. The latter was made by women for the cloth industry by running water through bracken ashes to make an alkaline solution known as 'lye'. The 'Old Soap House' at West Horsley is considered one place where soap was made; in its garden was soapwort, a beautifully scented plant that obtained its name from this use. Furze (gorse or whin) is highly inflammable and burns fiercely and hotly. The twiggy tops were used for fuel in baking and the thick stems as fuel for making bricks and tiles. It was also an important fodder, especially for horses. In autumn whortleberries ('whorts' or 'hurts') were harvested for wine, liqueur, jam or fresh fruit.

The Commonlands

Broadly speaking, commons have evolved with a similar history. Up until the late 19th century for generations they were an integral part of the farming system and jealously guarded by commoners against encroachment and enclosure. The decline of small farmers, however, greatly reduced their importance and, with the emphasis on livestock improvement, fewer animals were depastured on commons. By 1914 most commons had lost much of their grazing value and during the inter-war years most commons were even more lightly used. Since the Second World War commoning has virtually died out. This allowed the growth of scrub, bramble, rhododendron and trees on the heather and grass sward, so completely altering their character. The management of most commons is now vested in committees, many of which have now delegated or handed over the responsibility to local authorities and other larger bodies. Since the last war different methods of birch, bracken and gorse control have been attempted to allow heather to grow freely. Chemical scrub killers are not long-lasting in effect and birch still regrows after a physical clearance by volunteers. On Headley Heath (a place-name meaning a clearing overgrown with heather), a lost vista of Ranmore church spire was re-created in three days by 250 Scouts and Guides in the 1960s but the advantage was lost after a few years and although the name Ranmore Vista is retained for the path then made, the tall spire can no longer be seen. On burnt areas, the practice on Headley Heath was to remove charred growth, uproot stumps by machine and swipe the surface. Heather, grass and bracken come up from seed or roots. The gorse and bracken was swiped two or three times a year above the level of the heather, which is not then shaded out, and so is gradually coming back again. In recent years management techniques have moved away from the use of mechanical equipment towards more sustainable methods. Sheep and goats are being used to graze heathland and the use of cattle, such as Highland cattle on Headley Heath, which are not unduly disturbed by people and dogs, is proving a successful alternative. The maintenance and extension of heathland remains a key priority for the future and, with new techniques as yet unpractised, this may be a realisable objective.

On Albury Heath, part of the Albury estate of the Duke of Northumberland, heathland restoration has been undertaken on 57 acres since 1990 where an old resident can recall open views across heather, grazed twice-weekly by a large flock of sheep. When work started, the open areas were dominated by wavy-hair grass and bracken. This was experimentally stripped piecemeal on a 10-year programme of heathland restoration under the Countryside Stewardship Scheme, and another similar programme has been embarked upon. Moist growing conditions have best favoured heather growth which has an abundant natural seed bank, but some of the turf-stripped areas became heavily invaded by birch which has been controlled by herbicide in summer in a manner which causes little damage to heather and grasses beneath. Goats brought in to attack another generation of birch were popular with locals but ate the heathers and wavy-hair grass and ignored the birch![11] Further establishment of heather will take place mainly on areas currently under bracken or secondary woodland.

On Blackheath, partly privately owned and managed by Waverley Borough Council and partly by the Albury estate, Scots pine seeded freely on land disturbed by military training in the last war, and secondary woodland and bracken have also flourished. The Council have been clear felling since the late 1980s, at first slowly against local scepticism, but subsequently on a larger scale when public support became stronger. By 1990 bracken had moved almost completely across wavy-hair grass in cleared areas on one patch near Lipscombe Cottage. As the land was uneven, rotoration by tractor was practised (without prior spraying) but bracken has regained its abundance since, and although heather regeneration is disappointing there, a good woodlark habitat has been created, a reminder that heathers are, of course, only part of the heathland picture. Similar work is now proceeding on the estate land under the encouragement of English Nature's Wildlife Enhancement Scheme.[12]

23

The North Downs at War

The Vale of Holmesdale
Never wonne, ne never shall.

The Dunkirk evacuation in May and June 1940 was directed by Vice-Admiral Ramsay from Dover Castle. He assembled 15 passenger ferries at Dover which began to rescue British troops from the French beaches. These were augmented by naval ships, coasters, cargo vessels, fishing smacks, trawlers, pleasure steamers and barges. 338,226 British and Allied troops were taken off in seven days in an extraordinary military manoeuvre, unprecedented in history. All told, 22 naval vessels and 800 civilian craft joined the operation. Ships were crowded to bursting. Mentally it was too much for some exhausted soldiers who ran into the water screaming after waiting days for rescue. Six destroyers and 243 ships were sunk; the killed, missing or wounded numbered 68,000. Dover was the busiest port of disembarkation but trains also carried troops from Ramsgate, Margate and Folkestone. Many of the wounded were taken to Pembury hospital.

Immediately after Dunkirk, preparations were made against the invasion which Hitler ordered on 16 July. Seafronts and beaches were closed; gun emplacements and pill boxes sprang up. Concrete blocks were built on beaches and barbed wire was coiled everywhere. Open spaces were strewn with obstacles. German paratroopers were poised to drop on high land around Lympne and Lyminge and secure the Canterbury to Folkestone road. Infantry and panzers were to land between Folkestone and Dungeness and at other points along the English Channel. On 12 August German shelling of Dover and Folkestone began from the Pas de Calais. On 24 August 250 high explosive and incendiary bombs were dropped on Ramsgate, leaving 31 killed and 1,200 homes destroyed. Some people who had lost their homes spent the rest of the war in catacombs under the town.

Maidstone was bombed on five occasions during September 1940 and a casualty list was posted outside the town hall, the worst occasion being 27 September when 22 people were killed. On 31 October 14 more people died in a bomb attack on the town. Despite this Eastenders fled to the hopfields during the London Blitz. At underground chambers in Godmersham Park were the secret headquarters of the civilian guerrillas who were trained to harass invading Germans. Patrols were based at Badlesmere, Challock, Wickhambreaux, Hastingleigh, Ash, Manston, Dover and Folkestone. Meanwhile Maidstone was ringed with barbed wire and tank traps by the chief constable whose aim was

NOTICE

To the Members of the Congregation.

An appeal in the Nation's hour of need. — Eat less Bread. —

THE sinking of foodships by German Submarines and the partial failure of the World's wheat crop have brought about a scarcity of wheat and flour which makes it imperative that every household should at once reduce its consumption of BREAD.

The Food Controller asks that the weekly consumption of Bread throughout the Country should be reduced to an average of 4 lbs. per head.

In order to get down to this average everyone must eat less bread than before, and must reduce his or her consumption by at least one lb. per week. Every possible step must be taken to AVOID WASTE.

COMPULSORY RATIONING
will be costly, difficult and extremely irksome
Let us all try our utmost to avoid it by
VOLUNTARY RATIONING.

Will you start Rationing in your Home at Once?

This announcement is posted at the request of the National War Savings Committee, Salisbury Square, London, E.C.

F. C. No. 15.

133 *Notice regarding consumption of bread in the Second World War.*

to turn the town into a fortress. It was anticipated that people would flee the town in the event of an invasion so police were instructed to use force to prevent panic. By the end of 1940 more than 4,000 air raids had occurred in Kent alone. Victor Cazalet of Fairlawne personally recruited personnel for his Light Anti-Aircraft batteries.

At Chislehurst in 1941 some 15,000 people slept in the underground caves under the town. At Dover, which was shelled continuously, thousands of people sought refuge at night in secure tunnels beneath the castle. It was also a naval headquarters which controlled the gun batteries from the North Foreland to Hastings. At the height of the town's sufferings in July 1941 the American Nat Burton wrote the stirring words of the song destined to become a wartime favourite, 'The White Cliffs of Dover', which symbolised the hope that peace would soon return. For Dover the sacrifice was a terrible one: 199 persons were killed and 2,998 buildings severely damaged, mainly from shell-fire across the Channel. Folkestone also suffered severely. In 1942 Canterbury was seriously damaged by a Luftwaffe raid after the British devastation of Cologne. St George's Street was totally flattened and incendiary bombs wrought havoc elsewhere. Ashford in February 1943 had even more fatalities when new Fokke-Wulf bombers attacked from a low altitude. Few towns suffered as badly as Margate. The population dropped from 40,000 in 1939 to 9,000 as residents moved inland, shops closed and boarding houses pulled down their blinds and locked their doors. By the end of the war Margate had received 83 enemy attacks, 9,170 of its premises were damaged and 268 destroyed.

The Battle of Britain

Nothing illustrates more clearly the relationship between the North Downs and London than the role of the RAF stations during the Second World War. Biggin Hill and Kenley in Surrey together with Kent airfields such as Detling, Hawkinge, Lympne and Manston were sited on the North Downs in the front line of 'Hell-fire Corner' for the defence of the capital. The Downs lay across the central-line of the intended invasion by German armies which was planned to take place from the coast between Folkestone and Bognor. In August and September 1940 they were heavily engaged in the Battle of Britain ordered by Goering on 13 August 1940, which was centred on Surrey and Kent. When Goering switched the air attack from airfields to London, the city was bombarded every night between 7 September and 3 November. The Germans made their supreme attack on London and south-east England on 15 September. Two days

134 *Victims of the Blitz in a Kent town.*

later Hitler postponed the invasion 'indefinitely': the Battle of Britain had been won.

Harold Nicolson and Vita Sackville-West were spectators from their own garden at Sissinghurst of a great part of the Battle of Britain. On 18 August the air-raid siren sounded as they sat outside. They remained where they were and witnessed thin streamers from the exhausts of two waves of German 'planes and the air battle overhead. On 26 August Nicolson wrote as enemy aircraft droned overhead:

> It seems incredible as I sit here at my window, looking out on the fuchsias and the zinneas with yellow butterflies playing round each other, that in a few seconds above the trees I may see other butterflies circling in the air intent on murdering each other. One lives in the present. The past is too sad a recollection and the future too sad a despair.

When he went to bed there was still the drone of aeroplanes and from time to time a dull thump in the distance, to all of which he listened with fatalism. On 2 September he recorded a 'tremendous raid' with the whole upper air buzzing and zooming with the noise of aeroplanes and many fights 'over our sunlit fields'. He soon learned to keep indoors during a raid for machine-gun bullets were found in the lake-field and one came through the roof of their garden shed. On 12 September was the first main daylight attack on London. This coincided with the massing of invasion barges in the French Channel ports and the invasion was expected at any moment. As Nicolson typed in his diary late at night, the guns were still booming. From 15 September an average of 200 German bombers raided London every night for 57 days in succession and Londoners took almost more than they could stand. Nigel Nicolson noted, 'It was only in the next year that an adequate defence against nightbombing was found in radar-controlled anti-aircraft guns and night-fighters'.[1]

The RAF stations on the North Downs were again at fever pitch during the Normandy landings from 6 June 1944, and on 15 June 1944 Wing Commander 'Johnnie' Johnson reported to his intelligence officer that he had been overtaken in flight by 'a strange aircraft which seemed to be on fire'. He had in fact witnessed a V1 pilotless bomber heading for London, the first of which were unleashed on 12 June. Hundreds of guns and great reserves of ammunition were positioned on the North Downs although later the batteries were re-sited on the coast between St Margaret's Bay and Cuckmere Haven. The balloon barrage remained. In all 8,000 V1s ('Doodlebugs') were launched, many falling on open countryside in Kent until the Allied Armies overran the bases in late August. A notable casualty was the parish church of Little Chart. A new church was consecrated in 1958 on a new site but the gutted remains of the Norman church still stand. A much more serious incident was at Swanscombe where 13 people were killed, 22 seriously injured, eight houses were demolished and damage done to almost one hundred other properties. In the first week of the bombardment some 10,000 casualties occurred in London but by July only one 'doodlebug' in seven was penetrating the fighter, anti-aircraft and balloon barrage screens.[2]

135 *Battle of Britain fighter pilots at Biggin Hill.*

On 12 September 1944 fell the first V2s, the German long-range rocket, which carried a ton of explosives and reached a height of 50 miles before dropping without warning on London 200 miles away. As Nicolson observed, 'It caused less anxiety and fewer casualties than the V1, but the British never found an answer to it other than by bombing the launching pads. About 1,300 were fired on London between September and March.' Many of these landed on or near the North Downs. Two rockets, for example, fell on Sevenoaks and the countryside around was peppered by them. The rural districts in the Darent valley were the most severely damaged by V1s and V2s. Shoreham in the valley became known as 'bomb alley' and to this day it is estimated that many hundreds of unexploded bombs lie buried beneath the farmland.[3]

Chuter Ede's Diary

Another diary which records much information on the effects of the Second World War is that of James Chuter Ede who was Chairman of the Surrey County Council before the War and was a junior Minister of Education before becoming Home Secretary in the Attlee administration from 1945.[4] His lifestyle at Epsom was utterly different from the Nicolsons'. Although a government minister, he travelled everywhere by bus like almost everyone else, patiently queuing like other

136 *Battle of Britain Hurricanes over Kent.*

citizens for meagre rations and the irregular 'special treats' at his local butcher and grocer. His entry for 23 December 1944 reads as follows:

> Shopping [in Epsom] was a rather tedious process this morning. Only very thin flank bacon was on the counter when I reached Nuthalls at 10.30. So I returned one hour later when I was given some rashers from the back and collar. Had to wait a long time outside the United Dairies for some sausages but my being on the spot when they arrived, I succeeded in getting a pound.

He kept a record of the London blitz in 1940 and again in 1944 when Epsom lay above 'flying bomb alley' and became a target for V2s. From his diary we can glean information about the disposition of the Armed Forces in south-eastern England in the Second World War. In November 1941 he was allowed by a sentry to go across the Stepping Stones over the River Mole at Box Hill but huge coils of barbed wire blocked the way and the military had occupied the *Burford Bridge Hotel*. On 21 June 1944 he encountered a stream of camouflaged vehicles hidden under the trees on the south-bound carriage of the Mickleham by-pass. On 8 July he again watched heavy military vehicles at Mickleham and in November was able for the first time to see how great the damage had been to Netley Heath which had been used for tank training.

He was greatly sustained by Norbury Park in the Vale of Mickleham which he had been instrumental in saving just before the War when Chairman of the Surrey County Council. The beauty of the beeches, the placid kingfisher reaches of the River Mole and the tranquillity of the surroundings lured him again and again by bus in the closing stages of the War.[4] He vowed to continue to protect this inexpressibly beautiful place after the end of the hostilities and his efforts were crowned when half the Labour Cabinet, including Prime Minister Attlee, crossed the River Mole by the Stepping Stones on the occasion of the newly opened long distance footpath at the foot of the Downs in 1951.[5]

Meanwhile appeals were made to agricultural workers to intensify their efforts in working the land. Lord Cornwallis, Lord Lieutenant of Kent, had this message for them in March 1942 at a time when women and boys of the Land Army were chopping, burning, tearing down bushes and clearing everything for growing wheat.

> ... A great deal has happened during the last year. The War has spread to the East. The difficulties of getting food to this nation have tremendously increased. Our Armed Forces have 'Backs to the Wall'. What about us? It is not only a cry of 'Back to the Land' but our bounden duty to put our Back into getting every ounce of food that is possible out of the land. Your employers are being ordered to increase their production and must give way to better men if they do not respond. Farm workers have at last got better wages. Now is your chance to show the country and the world that you are worthy of these better conditions. The blunt fact is that we are fighting for our lives ... We are all in the Battle. Let this be our Battle Cry. 'By my determination and work by every extra effort I can make, I am going to save a ship and save the lives of sailors and make sure that Britain shall not starve'.[6]

Surrey Defences and the Downs in the Final Stage of the War

Immediately after the evacuation of the British Expeditionary Force from Dunkirk preparations began by General Sir Edmund Ironside to defend London by building concrete pillboxes and anti-tank traps on a GHQ line which extended from the River Medway into Somerset. This followed, where possible, natural features which could easily be defended to create a continuous defence. In Surrey it ran from Farnham and then followed the River Wey to Shalford, the Tilingbourne to Wotton, the Pippbrook to Dorking, the River Mole to Horley and along the headwaters of the River Eden to Lingfield, whence it continued into Kent. Some pillboxes were camouflaged to make them unrecognisable. One on the A25 at the Silent Pool was made to look like a petrol station. Another at Elstead Mill was disguised as a summer house.[7]

Preparatory to 'D-day' in Normandy, huge amounts of equipment and stores were concentrated between Westerham and Wye. On Albury Heath is a monument recording that General Bernard Montgomery addressed troops there in February 1944 on the eve of their departure to the Normandy Beaches. He would doubtless have talked in his familiar sharp-lipped sentences in a curiously high beaky voice. His travelling road show, given three hearty cheers, went on to Mote Park in Maidstone. Enormous lengths were taken to delude the enemy into thinking that the allied invasion of the continent would take place across the Straits of Dover. Inflatable tanks and dummy military vehicles and other fakes were built and every effort was made to give the impression of massed armies poised to attack.

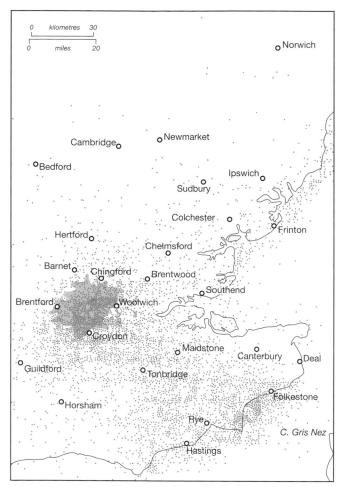

137 *Distribution of flying bombs in the Second World War.*

24

The Present and Uncertain Future

'The Garden of England?' More like a corridor to and from Europe, say the lorry drivers travelling on the two motorways in Kent near Ashford, the great transport node, as do passengers on the high-speed railway line between London, Brussels and Paris.[1] At night time it is no longer possible to see the stars so well as before, for lighting on the motorways at Polhill, Wrotham and more distantly around Kemsing emit reflections into the sky 'so that young children who have never seen the Milky Way confuse that miracle of wonder with a popular sweet bar'. Tranquillity is also a disappearing commodity in an overcrowded, noisy, traffic-filled, work-skewed Britain. According to the Campaign to Protect Rural England there are only three true tranquil 'reservoirs' left in Britain and the south-east has none of them. Yet there still remain, as we have noted, significant areas of high tranquillity in the North Downs and Hills and places with a complete absence of traffic noise in the background. Hence the noises are natural noises – water running, wind blowing and birds singing in an unspoilt landscape we can look out across. In such places the only lights are in a distant house and the stars are fantastic.[2]

New Crops, New Livelihoods

Moreover, although now without most of its hops, cherries, apples and strawberries, there is some especially good farming despite the enormous pressure agriculture is experiencing. This is largely through Kent's shift into alternative agriculture. This has been driven by a dramatic decline in the demand for hops used in beer-making. Breweries use fewer hops with more efficient methods and there is a trend towards beers which are less 'bitter' which need fewer hops. Growers have also had to face severe competition from overseas. Some new plantations are producing new breeds of hops with significantly increased disease resistance which are grown on low wirework systems. So far these have not checked the decline of hop gardens set with oast houses, which used to typify the landscape of Kent, partly on account of inertia amongst growers who need to make a significant investment in plants, machinery and equipment.

Meanwhile, a booming market for essential oils and herbs has occurred. These are becoming growth industries for the brave farmers who cultivate them, encouraged by the change in climate and culinary tastes introduced by the Asian community. Three farms in the Darent valley in a flinty soil on a chalk base now grow lavender and herbs, so bringing to Kent one of the famous

138 *Walkers on the North Downs Way.*

scents and sights of Provence. There is a distillery to extract valuable oil as soon as flowers are harvested. These British-grown herbs are helping to keep alive the horticultural tradition of the county.

A forward-looking enterprise is the Lees Court Estate of 4,500 acres near Faversham within the Kent Downs Area of Outstanding Natural Beauty, on which a major farm diversification project is the growing of industrial crops.[3] In 2001 chemical-free wheat-germ oil was raised from milled wheat and exported to the USA. Other non-food varieties include bio-diesel rape and echium. Trial plots of calendula ('pot marigold'), which has various industrial uses as a dilutent of varnishes and paints, and sweet quinoa are being assessed. The move to these unusual crops has been through Springdale Crop Synergies Ltd of the East Riding of Yorkshire, which has expertise in the food, industrial, pharmaceutical and energy market areas. The estate owner, Lady Sondes, has become one of the foremost advocates of non-food crops since taking over the estate on the death of her husband, the 5th Earl Sondes, in 1996. She estimates that non-food crops could take up to one-third of the country's arable within a decade. The benefits of growing calendula and echium are that they need little nitrogen, are hugely attractive to birds, insects and other wildlife and in a crop rotation the new crops prepare ground well for traditional farming.

A major new development in this part of Kent, which has throughout history been in the vanguard of England's agriculture, is the collaboration being worked out between the Lees Court Estate and the United Nations organisation which is being designed to introduce non-food crops to the developing world. In this is the chance of a revolution in agriculture worldwide.[4]

Meanwhile, the estate is engaged in research with the Game Conservancy on the impact of farming on the game management of partridges and pheasants. The aim is to demonstrate on an economically-viable southern England estate the ability to integrate wild and reared gamebird management which enhances the sporting quality of the shoot. In addition there is a rolling programme of woodland management on the estate. Hedges have been planted or gapped, grass margins have been planted around field edges and insect strips (beetle banks) have been placed strategically to help maximise wild bird life. Already research indicates that a big increase in song birds has occurred. Despite these conservation measures yields and gross margins have not suffered. The estate in hand, mainly on primarily Grade One agricultural land, is producing yields of wheat and rape higher than the average for the area. The estate has also entered the Countryside Stewardship Scheme which has provided wider access to the public.

Rural enterprise now often means finding other ways of supporting and managing the rural economy than farming. This means usually converting farm buildings into office and workshop space, but the owners of Cold Blow Farm on the top of the Kent Downs at Thurnham near Maidstone have turned premises into a camping barn. Another unusual enterprise is the initiative of two entrepreneurs who gather wild plants in Kingston Woods near Canterbury to provide succulent salads in London restaurants. At Shere a small brewery has opened in a former milking parlour.

Turning the Tide

Very encouraging is the government's new farming strategy as part of the reform of the Common Agriculture Policy announced in March 2005. This offers an opportunity to alter for the better the way the North Downs and hills look and function. For the first time farmers will be paid for caring for the environment instead of for the amounts of food they produce. Wildlife habitats will be safeguarded, less fertilizer will be put on grassland, fewer pesticides will be applied, grass margins will be kept round fields, hedges cut less frequently and stubble will be left in fields until mid-February for birds to feed on in winter. Higher payments are available for conserving archaeological sites and flood plains, conservation headlands and water meadows. Hay meadow restoration and the conservation of chalk grassland are to be encouraged. Organic farmers will receive special payments. In this era of farming there will be more birdsong, more wildflowers and more colourful butterflies.[5] Only a few years ago Graham Harvey was vividly describing in *The Killing of the Countryside* (1997) the vast featureless fields of agribusiness drained, sprayed, artificially fertilised, tidied, a land devoid of insects, birds, mammals and people – in short, an industrialised desert. Marion Shoard's earlier book *The Theft of the Countryside* (1980) did much to hammer home the same message. The government's strategy of balancing production and conservation is an alternative to this nightmarish situation.

Setbacks in Rural Life and Future Urbanisation

On a sadder note, Mereworth and Mersham lost their village stores in 1998 and this is the story all over the region. Thirty years ago local people still did a big shop at the village stores. Now they shop at superstores and petrol stations and some villagers never come near the village shop. This is a great blow to the rural community, especially if the village store was also the post office. The latter was a kind of mini-community centre at which people exchanged information, and its loss, particularly amongst older people without a car, is a serious setback to rural life.

A serious threat to the North Downs and its adjacent hills would arise from a recent suggestion of the Royal Town Planning Institute that the Green Belt should be considered for limited development in order to free up space for housing. The Institute refers to the spiralling cost of housing which is pricing out first-time buyers and to the continuing shortage of council and social housing. Lord Falconer, the Minister for Housing and Planning, has rejected this view on the grounds that the government's strategy of favouring brownfield development is more environmentally sound. The *Independent* newspaper has argued that we should not retain 'an irrational belief that the green belt is, like some tribal burial ground, always and everywhere sacrosanct'. It is to be hoped that this view will not be sustained and that tougher planning controls, not weaker ones, will prevail.

This is all the more important because of the vulnerability of the Downs and Hills to more housing. Only eight miles from the English Channel in Kent and 61 miles from London is Ham Street, a tiny hamlet on the Ashford and Canterbury Road, which town planners have been considering for several decades as the site of a new town. Professor Peter Hall anticipated its creation in his *London 2000* (1963) when it was to receive its first family in 1973 and by 1980 to have grown to a population of 120,000. This included the young Dumills who had moved from London soon after their marriage. Hall envisaged a tight, enclosed, compact town with a central shopping district near enough to be reached on foot. The road system was planned 'in a series of gigantic one-way loops', passing over and under pedestrian walkways to the New Kent motorway to London and the Channel. Mr Dumill was to catch daily the 8.28 semi-fast from Paris which has entered the Channel Tunnel with commuters. Is Hall's vision to become reality?[6]

An important problem for the next generation will be managing tourism to cope with the pressure of visitor numbers in a sustainable leisure programme. Everyone will have more leisure in the 21st century and the North Downs will become more valuable with each year that passes, because they provide an enormous reservoir when more and more people are looking for something worthwhile to do. Furthermore, the disposable income available to the general population has become greater and, as urban life becomes more artificial and technically driven, so the value of the Downs as a source of physical challenge and spiritual refreshment will increase. This will be particularly important for a region that is easy for large numbers of Londoners to reach. The implications are profound. For it to retain its integrity, its needs and special qualities must come before visitor considerations. The Kent Downs is the least popular section of the North Downs for rambling, apart from the honey-pot around Wye. They do not have the 'brand image' of the Surrey Hills or the South Downs. Attempts are now being made by various organisations, such as Tourism South-East, the Kent Downs AONB and Rights of Way officers, to promote them as the 'Explore Kent' Local Heritage Initiative, which is lottery funded. The quest for new stabling facilities is evidence of the area's growing popularity for riding and mountain biking. On byways increased use of four-wheel-drive vehicles is causing damage, conflict with other users and loss of tranquillity. The new access land created by the CROW Act has been extremely limited, principally due to the strict interpretation of what constitutes 'downland' or 'heathland'.[7]

Epilogue

Nature made the North Downs and the Surrey and Kent Hills one of the loveliest and most diversified of all English regions. Despite their shrinkage and shabbying, they still give as much of the wildness of nature and

139 *Motorcyclists at their favourite rendezvous on the flanks of Box Hill.*

traditional fields and hedgerows as one living in a crowded island can reasonably hope to possess. The sharp slopes of the chalk hills and their congruence with the clays, sands and sandstones harbour for future enjoyment an inexhaustible richness of wildlife. The beauty of the country does not cease to astonish, for happily there is still much of the world's finest scenery still unspoiled within reach of a day's excursion from London. People choose to retire to it and are satisfied to remain in it for the rest of their days. We have observed the extraordinary affection and love the enchanting region has inspired over generations, and it continues to haunt the imagination of artists, some exploring ways in which landscape can interact with modernity. Clearly the hill ranges rank as one of the most significant components of our national possessions, by whatever criteria they are judged, or in whatever period of history they are viewed. We need to consider not only how to continue to conserve them but how we can enlarge their appeal to benefit the generations to come.

In the past one hundred years they have suffered insidious obliteration from house builders and road construction and they remain under threat. Managing this enchanting heritage sustainably will be one of the greatest challenges for the next generation. A new period of change hopefully lies ahead of it, oriented towards the health, beauty and permanence of the landscape and a better deal for harassed farmers and all others working or living there. Looking forward into the future is the visitor centre, perched above the Dover ferry terminals, opened by the National Trust, where Exmoor ponies have been introduced to revive traditional grazing and encourage plant-rich chalk grassland. This is intended not only as a gateway to Britain but as a means of demonstrating the new millennium of sustainability and of understanding the heritage. The similar innovative initiatives spreading elsewhere also give hope that they will become widespread. Meanwhile, as we have noted, attempts are being made to re-create the noble wild scenes of heath and scattered pines and whortleberries that were beloved by Victorian painters but are now covered with masses of rhododendron and tangled trees. A modest start has also been made to recover

140 *Dover Harbour, for centuries the leading port for continental traffic.*

the vistas, enjoyed by Georgians, to famous landmarks now hopelessly lost in impenetrable jungles.We should not, however, simply look back into the past. Bryn Green has reminded us that we should take the opportunity to 'conceive, design and create new landscapes fit for the social and economic needs of the 21st century'.[8] In fact, changes deeper and more far-reaching doubtless lie ahead but this does not preclude the creation of new forms of beauty.

It is no miracle nor sheer good fortune that the North Downs and Surrey and Kent Hills survive, nor is it the result of accident. Their continued unspoiled existence, in an age when fields have lost much of the charm of their original setting and fewer have been left each coming year, has been due to the constant vigilance and energetic action of landowners, farmers, planners, public spirited individuals and voluntary bodies. The one thing we can be sure about the future is that these precious hills will need a similar army of fearless defenders to prevent them from becoming a vanishing landscape bereft of what we inherited and are dutybound to leave to the generations to come.

Only in this way will future Londoners and others continue to find their 'holy ground' in our overworked civilisation and experience spiritual refreshment in a sense of peace that is sought in vain elsewhere. The interpretation of the past will be one of the best guides to sensitivities in the present and aspirations for the future.

Notes

Manuscript sources are given in full. Articles and books are given by author and date, by which they can be located in the Bibliography.

Abbreviations

Ag. Hist. Rev.	*Agricultural History Review*
A.C.	*Archaeologia Cantiana*
Annals	Arthur Young (ed.), *Annals of Agriculture*
BL	British Library
BPP	British Parliamentary Papers
Econ. Hist. Rev.	*Economic History Review*
FSC	*Journal and Reports of the Field Studies Council*
CKS	Centre for Kent Studies, Maidstone
Inst. Brit. Geogr.	*Transactions of the Institute of British Geographers*
LDLHS	Leatherhead and District Local History Society
PRO	Public Record Office
SHC	Surrey History Centre, Woking
Shere	The Archive of the Shere, Gomshall and Peaslake Local History Society, Shere Museum, Surrey
South. Hist.	*Southern History*
Surr. Arch. Coll.	*Surrey Archaeological Collections*
Surr. Hist.	*Surrey History*
V&A	Victoria and Albert Museum

Preface

1. In Wooldridge S.W. and Goldring, F., *The Weald* (1953), viii.

Chapter 1. Introduction

1. Brandon, 1998, 1-19; Burton and Davis, *passim.*
2. Salt, 1922, 17.
3. For more information on *bocage* see Brandon, 2003, 4-9.
4. Scruton, 2004, 11.
5. Young (ed.), *Annals* 1 (1790), 93; 10 (1798), 433-4.
6. Marshall, 1798, i, 59-63.
7. Malcolm, 1805, vol. 2, 205.
8. For a fuller reference to hedges see Brandon, 2003, 65-8.
9. Frank Smythe, 4.
10. Lister (ed.), 647.
11. Cuming, 1924; 1927.
12. Cobbett, 1930, 132.
13. Walpole, vol. 1, 72.
14. *Don Juan*, Canto 10, 76.
15. Perey, L. (ed.), 494-5.
16. Arthur Young thought he would remember his ride to Dover to the last hour of his life and considered Dover as 'perhaps the most interesting spot in England', arguing that it gave more force to the imagination by impressing awe on the mind than any other situation. *Annals*, 23, 1795, 379-80.

Chapter 2. Natural and Man-Made Setting

1. Gibbard, 1995, 15-26.
2. Forster, 1924, 146.
3. Harrison, 1928.
4. Gibbons, 1981, 41.
5. Gallois, 1965.

6. Jones, 1981, 58.
7. Everitt, 1986, 322.
8. Allinson, 1997.
9. Pye-Smith, 1995.
10. Nairn, 1962, 17.
11. Blunt, 1932, 143-4.
12. Forster, 1951, 366-71.
13. Denton Welch, 1950, 99.
14. Baker, R., 1982.
15. Cobbett, 1930, 306.
16. Cobbett, 1930, 140.
17. Everitt, 1986, 50-52.
18. Fagg and Hutchings, 1930.
19. Hutchings, 1960.
20. CKS, Lubbock Mss.U 6 97.

Chapter 3. Mining and Quarrying
1. Paul W. Sowan, Pers. Comm.
2. Highley, 1975.
3. SHC Loseley Mss. M 16.
4. Worssam and Tatton-Brown, 1993.
5. CKS L23/14.
6. CKS U14/27.
7. For the immense quantities of lime applied in the Weald see Cobbett in Cobbett, 1930, 198.
8. CKS U 1015/T6.
9. Burgess, 1977.
10. Abercrombie, 1927, 431-8; Abercrombie and Archibald, 1928.
11. Booth, 2001, 51-2.
12. Dover District Council, 2002.
13. Briefing Papers, South East England Development Agency (SEEDA) 2002-4.

Chapter 4. Early Man
1. Glass, 1999, 189-20.
2. Quested, 2001, 2-4.
3. Owen and Frost, 2002.
4. Harrison, 1928.
5. Prestwich, 1869, 127-297; 1895, 617-28.
6. Pitts and Roberts, 1997.
7. Wymer in Bird, J. and D.G., 1987, 17-30.
8. Rankine, 1956.
9. Keene, 2001.
10. Burton and Dunn, 1992.
11. Rose, 1997.
12. Vera, 2000, 1-60.
13. Parfitt, 1998.
14. Bird, 1987, 49.
15. Bird, 2004.
16. Philp, 1984(a).
17. Reynolds, 1976.
18. Bird, 1987, 88.

19. Philp, 1984(b).
20. Andrews, 2001, 25-42.
21. Philp, 2003.

Chapter 5. Anglo-Saxons
1. Campbell, James (ed.), 1982.
2. Gillingham, 1983, 183, 19.
3. Everitt, 1986, 69-92.
4. Bennett, 1988, 14.
5. Everitt, 1986, 49-50.
6. Bird, 2004, 169-75.
7. Philp, 2002, 215-20.
8. Philp, 2003.
9. Maitland, 1897, 13-14.
10. Darby and Campbell, 1962, 364-562.
11. Urry, 105.

Chapter 6. Living on the Land in the early Middle Ages
1. Du Boulay, 1966, 50.
2. Smith, 1943.
3. Rigold, 1966, 1-66.
4. Smith, in Roake and Whyman, 1973, 50.
5. Gray, 1915, 302.
6. Campbell, B.M.S., 1988, 26-46.
7. *Hosbonderie*, 1890 edn.
8. Thirsk, in Witney, 2000, xv-xvi and Smith in Roake and Whyman, 1973, 37-50.
9. Du Boulay, 1966, 149.
10. Bishop, 1938, 38-44.
11. Bannister and Watt, 1997.
12. Baker, 1964, 1-23.
13. PRO C 130/9/5.
14. Behrens, 1926, 42.
15. Cal Pat. Rolls, 1232-47, 270.
16. May, 1967, 1-31.
17. PRO/134/188/14.

Chapter 7. The Later Middle Ages
1. Baker, 1966, 1-5.
2. Saaler, 1992, 19-40.
3. Mate, 1984, 331-43.
4. Du Boulay, 1959, 116-24.
5. Clarke and Stoyel, 1975, 92, 96.
6. CKS U55/ M/63.
7. Du Boulay, 1966, 228-6.
8. Brown, 1977, 145-56.
9. Du Boulay, 1966, 188.
10. Clarke and Stoyel, 1975, 77, 81.
11. Turner, in Bird, J. and D.G., 1987, 223-61.
12. Philp, 1973.
13. Spain, 1973, 159-81.
14. Pearson, 2001, 315-49.
15. Glasscock, 1965, 61-8.

Chapter 8. Early Churches and Religious Houses

1. Tatton-Brown, 1996.
2. Wormald, 2003.
3. Taylor, 1997; Tatton-Brown, 1994.
4. Everitt, 1996, 181-9.
5. Blair, 1991, 91-103, 133.
6. Evelyn, Dobson (ed), iii, 10.
7. Street, G.E., 1850, 49-58.
8. Walkden G., pers. comm.
9. Everitt, 1986, 250-4.
10. Berg, 2002, 113-42.
11. Urry, 1967, 191.
12. Zarnecki, 1953, 17-26.
13. Brandon, 1998, 45-6.

Chapter 9. The Late Sixteenth to the Mid-Eighteenth Centuries

1. Defoe, 1724, 83-4; Repr. 1971, 63-41.
2. Aubrey, 1717-18, 27.
3. Macky, 1732, 141.
4. Defoe; Repr. 1971, 153-4.
5. Latham, diary entry 14 July 1667.
6. Hiscock, 1955; Bowle, J., 1981.
7. Piggott, 1976.
8. Bédoyère, 243, 271.
9. Gibson, *Camden's Britannia*, 1695; repr. 1971.
10. Griffiths and Kesnerova, 1983.
11. Parry, 1980.
12. Cobbett, 1930, 141.
13. Brandon, 1984(a), 75-107.
14. Brandon, 1984.
15. Shere, 149(a).
16. CKS U 5561/112.
17. CKS U 1127/P5.
18. Baring-Gould, 1896, 303.
19. SHC LM 1985/1969.
20. SHC LM 1543/1-42.
21. Crowe, 1973, 38.
22. SHC LM 1985-1986.
23. SHC LM 955/1.
24. SHC LM 1985-1986.
25. SHC LM 1965 -1966, 2-5.
26. Thirsk 1977, 15, 17, 24, 28 and *passim*.
27. SHC LM 1843.
28. Aubrey, 1717-18.
29. Crocker, 1989-94.

Chapter 10. Industrial Evolution

1. Balston, 1955, 67.
2. Shorter, 1975, 46, 51 and *passim*.
3. Balston, 1957, 171.
4. CKS Whatman Mss. Envelope, A6; Box A.
5. CKS U 289/ T31, 2.3; C21;F 16; U 289/A9-
16.
6. CKS, Whatman Box, 3/18, A5; 11/18; 5/18; 10/18.
7. CKS Balston on the Whatmans and wove paper.
8. Spain, 1973, 159-81.
9. Crocker, 1989, 1992, 1994; 1988.

Chapter 11. Sir John Evelyn of Wotton

1. W.G. Hiscock, 1955, 201-3; 236-7.
2. John Evelyn, *Sylva* (1706 edn), 581.
3. John Evelyn, *Memoirs*, 1926, 17.
4. Sir John Evelyn Mss. BL 8514, A-F.
5. BL 78482-4.
6. BL 78485-90.
7. BL 78513,4.
8. *Memoires*, 17

Chapter 12. The Farmer and Landowner, 1750-1880

1. W. Smart, 311, states that Louis Simond reported after his Tour of 1815 that England 'is probably the only country in the world where people make fortunes from agriculture' and that every gentleman's conversation was taken up with turnips, clover, enclosures and [field] drains …'.
2. Young, *Annals* 8, 1787, 163-4; Young did not under-estimate the contribution to agriculture made by numerous great landowners and the gentlemen farmers in general, *Annals*, 21, 1993, 229-30. For Young's praise for the yeoman farmer see *Annals*, 2, 1783, 135.
3. Boys, 1813, 360, 374.
4. Mingay, 1995, 54, 85, 93.
5. *Annals*, 22 (1794), 195-9; see also Simmond, 146.
6. Buckland, 1846, 269.
7. CKS U 194/E4; U 194/Z19.
8. Boys, 1813, 84.
9. Boys, 1813, 243-92.
10. Behrens, 1926, 243-292.
11. CKS U 1127/E11.
12. Malcolm, 1805, vol. 3, 286-336.
13. WSRO Lytton Ms.11.
14. Cobbett, 1930, 288. Malcolm, 1805, vol.i, 99; vol ii, 243; vol. iii, 42, 45.
15. Kingsley, 1859, 134-62.
16. Bourne, 1967, 242.
17. Malcolm, 1805, vol ii, 205-8.
18. Marshall, 1798, ii, 73-4.
19. Caird, 1852.
20. Ruggles, 1786, 1787, 1778.
21. Trotter, 1996, 148, 150, 213-14.

22. Stemp, 1995.

Chapter 13. Nineteenth-Century Labourers
1. CKS 389/8/1.
2. CKS 1590/C173/1/177.
3. CKS P243/18/1-64.
4. CKS P 385/8/2.
5. CKS P 247/12/20-21.
6. CKS P 408.
7. CKS P329/8/2.
8. CKS P 12/6/1.
9. CKS P 40/8-10.
10. CKS 20/8/4.
11. P 390/18/100.
12. CKS P 406/18/17.
13. Barclay, 1833.
14. KCS SP 12, 8/1.
15. KCS P229, 12, 2.
16. KCS P 233/1.
17. KCS P 233/8/6.
18. KCS39/8/4.
19. KCS P 406/18/17.
20. Macfie, 131-6.
21. Griffin, 2000.
22. Wells, 1991, 32-81.
23. BPP 8 (1834), 866-67; 869-70.

Chapter 14. A Nobleman's Estate
1. This is the mansion which Horace Walpole declared 'had all Kent as its garden', Walpole, 7, 421. The inscription on the plaque in Linton church commemorating Lord Cornwallis (d.1935) refers to him as 'affectionately called the squire of Kent'.
2. CKS U 24, T4.
3. CKS, U 24 F21; F25.
4. CKS, U 24, F7, 22.
5. CKS U 24/A7.
6. CKS U 24/A8.
7. CKS U 24/E.
8. CKS U 24/A9, A1O, A11, A12.

Chapter 15. After Eden
1. Haggard, 1906, vol.1, 137-74.
2. CKS U1175 E39/2;E39/3;E39/5;U1175/ E388.
3. Bowden, 1994, 108-9.
4. Parkin, 1998.

Chapter 16. London's Playground
1. Hazlitt, *Table Talk*, 1821-2.
2. Mill, 1827-32, vol. 27, 556-63 and *passim*.
3. Whyman, 1981, 111-38.
4. Thorne, *The Environs of London*, 1844, 1-4.

5. Bonython and Burton, 2003, 169-70.
6. Eliot, 1954-6.
7. Meredith, *Letters* (ed. Cline), 27 April 1861; 7 May 1861; 16 June 1880.
8. Welch, 1950, 99.
9. Muggeridge, 1971, 50-1, 57-8.
10. Church, 1956, 81-2. See also 'This Great Club of Ours', The Cyclists' Touring Club, Godalming, 1953.
11. KCS P335/2128/1.
12. *Leisure Hour*, 1898, 402.
13. Williams-Ellis, A., 1928, 16.
14. Monro, 1923.
15. Brandon, 1982, 1.
16. *Art Journal*, 1882, 129-31.
17. Brandon, 1982, 192.
18. SHC 85/38/5a.
19. SHC 85/38/5a; pers. comm. Dr J. Scott Lidgett.
20. SHC 85/38/9a.
21. SHC 5341, 5342/6/1-5.
22. SHC 5341, 5342/6/1-5.
23. SHC 85/38/14a; 85/38/5-8; Brandon, 1982, fnt. 65, 9.218.
24. SHC 85/29/12.
25. Cleveland-Peck, 126-35, 146.
26. *Pall Mall Gazette*, 1897.

Chapter 17. The Estate Management of the Brays of Shere
1. Brandon, 1982, 192.
2. Shere, 12(b).
3. Shere, 13(c).
4. Brandon, 1982, 200.
5. Brandon, 1982, 192.
6. See Masterman 1903, 1904, 1911.
7. SHC 85/38/10a; 85/38/5a, *et seq.*
8. SHC 85/38/43.
9. SHC 85/38/43.

Chapter 18. The Victorian Church, Rural Arts and Crafts and Social Reform
1. Cracklow, 1979, plate 69.
2. Paget, 1873, 179.
3. Rawnsley, 1915, 239.
4. Blatch, 1997, 44.
5. Jenkins, 1999, 676-7.
6. Walmsley and Standring, 1980.
7. Newman, 1969b, 950-1.
8. CKS P 3248/8.
9. CKS P 233/8/6.
10. Brooke, 1952, 213-7.
11. Brooke, 206-7.
12. *The Spectator*, 25 November 1995, 44.

13. Blount, 1898, 1898, 1911.
14. Hutchinson, 1946, 172-83.
15. Dolmetsch, M., 1958.
16. Sturt, *Journal*, 20 April 1900.
17. See, for example, Brandon, 1982, 210-11; Lethaby, W.R., 1935.
18. Betjeman PP 3275, London Library.
19. Brandon, 1982, 210-11.

Chapter 19. The London Octopus and Rural Landscape Protection

1. House of Lords Archive, HC/CH/PB/ 23117, vols 17, 18.
2. Mill, 1965 edn, 938.
3. SHC 1621, Box 2/8, Box 3/14, 15/2.
4. Hunter, 1893; Rawnsley, 1914.
5. SHC 1621, Box 2/8.
6. Brandon and Short, 1990, 285.
7. Vaughan, 1994, 55-60.
8. Connell, 1978, 73-76.
9. Cracknell, 1974, 112.
10. Forster, 1936, 351.
11. Hunter, 1898.
12. Brandon, 1982, 209.
13. Williams-Ellis, 1928 (repr. 1975); 1937.
14. PRO HLG 4/3642, 3352.
15. Brandon, 1982, fnt.85, p.219.
16. PRO HLG 4/58, Parts 1 and 2; *The Listener*, 15 August 1934, 22.
17. *The Spectator*, 27 July 1934, 9d.
18. *The Spectator*, 25 June 1937, 1117.
19. PRO HLG 4/58; HLG G4/2780.
20. *The Spectator*, 25 June 1937; *The Surrey Advertiser*, 2 February 1935, 9; 27 July 1935, 6; SHC 85/38/10; 85/38/13a.
21. *The Spectator*, 22 June 1901, 916.

Chapter 20. The Literary Inspiration of the Downs and Hills

1. Yates, 1964, 12-13.
2. Wheeler, 153-61.
3. Forster, 1951, 158-9.
4. Rowse, 2003, 301-4.
5. Allen, 1896, 2-3.
6. Partridge, F., 1980.
7. Trotter, 1996, 224.
8. Ward, 1888.
9. Kingsley, 1860, 134-63.
10. Gosse, 1923, 235.

Chapter 21. The Landscape Artist

1. Wilton, 1987, 72.
2. Gage, 1987, 115-16.

3. Peacock, 1968, 18.
4. Kaufman, 1984, 124; Vardey, 1992, 138-40.
5. Vardey, 1992, 138-40.
6. Brandon, 1984(b), 55-74.
7. Ruskin, 1834-60 (1873 edn), 1, 419-20.
8. Mill, 1965 ed., Book IV, 756.
9. Heron, 1955, 1-5.
10. Crouan, K, 1982, ix-xxiv.
11. Pers. comm. Ron Weller.
12. Thomas, 1987.
13. Macleod, 1988.

Chapter 22. Nature, Man and Beast

1. Lousley. 1950, 49-50.
2. Vera, 2000, 1-60.
3. English Nature, Wye; Kemsing Parish Council.
4. Hutchings, 1953, 35.
5. Burton and Davis, 1992, 94-101.
6. *The Daily Telegraph*, 20 April, 2005, 12.
7. Rose, 1982, 180-94.
8. Hutchings and Sankey, 1968, 18-27.
9. Brandon, 1998, 143-5.
10. Howkins, 1997.
11. Dr R. McGibbon. Pers. comm.
12. The heaths and commons are well described in Owen, J.A. (ed.), *Man of the Marshes*, 1891, 48-51;1893, 111-72; 1896 173-5.

Chapter 23. The North Downs at War

1. Nicolson, 1967, 109-14.
2. Ogley, 1990, 1992, 1994.
3. Brooks, 1998.
4. BL Additional Collections, 59690-59700.
5. *The Times*, 1951, 5 September, 5d.
6. KCS SU 24/210.
7. Shepheard and Crocker in Cotton, *op. cit.*, 2004, 245-53.

Chapter 24. The Present and Uncertain Future

1. *The Daily Telegraph Week-End*, 12 March 2005, 14.
2. Bowden, 1996, 4.
3. Lees Court, Faversham, Newsletter 2004.
4. UN *Chronicle*, vol. XII, No. 4, 2004-5, 34-5.
5. *The Independent*, 9 May, 2002, 16.
6. Hall, P., 1969.
7. Information from the North Downs AONB; The Ramblers' Association; Mrs D. Pilkington and Surrey Rights of Way Officer.
8. Green, 210.

Bibliography

Abercrombie, Sir Patrick, 'The Development of East Kent', *Royal Institute of British Architects Journal*, vol. xxxiv, no. 13, 1927

Abercrombie, Sir Patrick and Archibald, John, East Kent Regional Planning, Final Report, 1928

Allen, Grant, *Moorland Idylls*, 1896

Allingham, H. and Radford, D. (eds), *A Diary of William Allingham*, 1907

Allinson, H., *Bredgar: The History of a Kentish Parish*, 1997

Andrews, Colin, 'Romanisation: a Kentish Persepective', *A.C.* 121, 2001, 25-42

Anon, *The Life and History of Swing: The Kent Rickburner*, 1830, reprinted CKS

Arnold, Matthew, *New Poems*, 1867

Arnold, Matthew, *Letters, 1848-1888*, ed. G.W.E. Russell, 1895

Aslett, C., *The Last Country Houses*, 1982

Aubrey, J., *The Natural History and Antiquities of Surrey*, 1718-19, reprinted 1975

Baker, A.R.H., 'The Field Systems of Kent', PhD thesis, University of London, 1963

Baker, A.R.H., 'Open Fields and Partible Inheritance on a Kent Manor', *Econ. Hist. Rev.* 17, no. 1, 1964, 1-23

Baker, A.R.H., 'Some Evidence of a Reduction in the acreage of … cultivated Land in Sussex during the thirteenth Century', *Suss. Arch. Coll.* 104, 1966, 1-5

Baker, Rowland, 'Holy Wells and Magical Waters of Surrey', *Surr. Hist.* vol. 2, no. 4, 1982

Balston, Thomas, *William Balston*, 1955

Balston, Thomas, *The Whatmans: Father and Son*, 1957

Bannister, N. and Watt, Trudy, *Wye: A Thousand years of a Kentish community in the Landscape*, 1997

Barclay, Charles, 'Letters from Dorking Emigrants to Upper Canada 1833', photocopy, Dorking Museum

Baring-Gould, S., *The Broom Squire*, 1896

Bates H.E., *The Darling Buds of May*, 1958

Bédoyère, Guy de la, *Particular Friends: the Correspondence between Samuel Pepys and John Evelyn*, 1997

Behrens, I.B., *Boys Memorial Volume: Under Thirty Seven*, Kings, 1926

Bennett, Paul, 'Archaeology and the Channel Tunnel', *A.C.*, 106, 1988

Berg, Mary, 'Patrixbourne church: Medieval Patronage, Fabric and History', *A.C.* 122, 2002, 103-34

Bird, D.G., *Roman Surrey*, 2004

Bird, Joanna and D.G., *The Archaeology of Surrey to 1540*, Surr. Arch. Soc., 1987

Bird, M., *Holmbury St.Mary: One Hundred Years*, 1979

Bishop, T.A.M., 'The Rotation of Crops at Westerham, 1297-1356', *Econ. Hist. Rev.* 9, 1938, 38-44

Blair, John, 'Medieval Deeds of the Leatherhead District', *LDLHS* vol. 4, no.2 (1978); no. 3 (1979); no. 4 (1982); no. 6 (1983); no. 7 (1984); no. 8 (1985)

Blair, John, *Early Medieval Surrey*, 1991

Blatch, M., *The Churches of Surrey*, 1997

Blount, G., 'The Gospel of Simplicity', BL U 1220 3e 7/8, 1893; 'For Our Country's Sake', BL U 8275, m 38, 1894

Blunt, W.S., *My Diaries*, 1932

Bonython, Elizabeth and Burton, Anthony, *The Great Exhibitor: The Life and Work of Henry Cole*, 2003

Booth, Alan, 'The Economy of Kent: an Overview' in Yates, N. (ed.), *Kent in the Twentieth Century*, 2001

Bourne (Sturt), G., *The Bettesworth Book*, 1902

Bourne (Sturt), G., *Change in the Village*, 1956

Bourne (Sturt), G., *Journals* ed. by M.D. Mackerness, 1967

Bowden, V.E., *The Story of Kemsing in Kent*, 1994

Bowle, John, *John Evelyn and his World*, 1981

Boys, J., *A General View of the Agriculture of the County of Kent*, 1795

BPP, Select Commission on Agriculture, 1833; on the Poor Law, 1934

Brandon, P.F., *A History of Surrey*, 2nd edn 1998

Brandon, P.F., 'New Settlement and Farming Techniques in South-East England' in Joan Thirsk (ed.), *The Agrarian History of England and Wales*, vol. ii (1042-1350), 1988

Brandon, P.F., 'Designed Landscapes in South-East England', *Inst. Brit. Geog. Special Number*, No. 10, 1979

Brandon, P.F., 'A Twentieth Century Squire in his Landscape, Reginald Bray of Shere, Surrey', *South. Hist.* 4, 1982, 191-220

Brandon P.F., 'Land, Technology and Water Management in the Tillingbourne Valley, Surrey', *South. Hist.* 6, 1984(a), 75-107

Brandon, P.F., 'Wealden Nature and the Role of London in Nineteenth Century Imagination', *Journ. Hist. Geog.* 10, 1984(b), 55-74

Brandon P.F., *The Tillingbourne River Story*, 1984

Brandon, P.F., *The South Downs*, 1998

Brandon, P.F., *The Kent and Sussex Weald*, 2003

Brandon P.F. and Short, Brian, *The South-East from A.D. 1000*, 1990

Brooke, J. (ed.), *The Denton Welch Journals*, 1952

Brooks, Robin, *Kent Airfields in the Second World War*, 1998

Brown, A., 'London and North-West Kent in the later Middle Ages: the development of the land Market', *A.C.* 92, 1977, 145-56

Brown, Jane, *The Gardens of a Golden Afternoon*, 1982

Brown, Jane, *Lutyens and the Edwardians*, 1996

Buckland, George, 'On the Farming of Kent', *Journ. Royal Agric. Soc.* 6, 1846

Bullen, A.H., *England's Helicon*, 1886

Burgess, Peter, 'Dene Holes in Surrey', *Surrey Local History Records*, vol. 4, 1977

Burton, F. and Davis, John, *Downland Wildlife: A Naturalist's Year in The North and South Downs*, 1992

Byron, Lord George, *Don Juan*, 1819-24

Caird, J., *English Agriculture in 1851-2*, 1968

Cameron, W. and Maude, Mary McDougall, *Assisting Emigration to Upper Canada: The Petworth Project*, 2000

Campbell, B.M.S., 'Agricultural Progress in Medieval England', *Econ. Hist. Rev.* 36, 1983, 26-46

Campbell, J. (ed.), *The Anglo-Saxons*, 1982

Chalklin, C., *Seventeenth Century Kent: A Social and Economic History*, 1965

Church, Richard, *Over the Bridge: an essay in autobiography*, 1956

Clark, F.L., 'The History of Epsom Spa', *Surr. Arch. Coll.* 57, 1960, 1-41

Clarke, P. and Stoyel, A., *Otford in Kent: A History*, 1975

Cleveland-Peck, *The Cello and the Nightingales*, 1985

Clifton-Taylor, Alec, *Six More English Towns*, 1981

Cobbett, W., *Rural Rides*, ed. G.D.H. and M. Cole, 1930

Connell, J., *The End of Tradition: Country Life in Central Surrey*, 1978

Cotton, J., Crocker, G. and Graham, A., *Aspects of Archaeology and History in Surrey*, 2004

Cracklow, C.T., *Views of Surrey Churches*, ed. K.W.E. Gravett, 1979

Cracknell, B.E., *Portrait of Surrey*, 1974

Cresswell, A., *The Swing Riots*, CKS 2000

Crocker, Alan, *The Paper Mills of the Tillingbourne*, 1988

Crocker, Alan, 'Paper Mills of Surrey', *Surr. Hist.*, vol. 3, no. 2, 1989; vol. 4, no. 4, 1992; vol.6, no.5, 1994

Crocker, Glenys, 'A Guide to the Chilworth Gunpowder Mills', Surrey Indust. Hist. Group, 1985

Crocker, Glenys, 'The Godalming Framework Knitting Industry', *Surr. Hist.*, vol. 4, no. 1, 1989-90

Crocker, Glenys, 'Seventeenth Century Wireworks in Surrey: the case of Thomas Steere', *Surr. Hist.*, vol. 5, no. 3, 1999

Crocker, Glenys and Crocker, Alan, 'Gunpowder Mills of Surrey', *Surr. Hist.*, vol. 4, no. 3, 1999

Crouan, Catharine, *John Linnell: A Centennial Exhibition*, 1982

Crowe, A.L., 'The West Surrey Wool Industry', *Surr. Hist.*, vol. 2, 1973

Cuming, E.D. and Shaw Sparrow, W., *Robert Smith Surtees*, 1924

Cuming, E.D. (ed.), *The Hunting Tours of Surtees*, 1927

Cyclists' Touring Club, *This Great Club of Ours*, Godalming, 1953

Darby, H.C. and Campbell, E.M.J., *The Domesday Geography of South-East England*, 1962

Davey, John (ed.), *Nature and Tradition: Arts and Crafts Architecture*, 1993

Defoe, Daniel, *A Tour through the island of Great Britain*, reprint 1971

Dolmetsch, Mabel, *Personal Recollections of Arnold Dolmetsch*, 1958

Dover District Council, *Aylesham Expansion Programme*, 2002

Drayton, Michael, *Polyolbion*, 1622

Drewett, P., Rudling, D. and Gardiner, M., *The South-East to AD 1000*, 1988

Du Boulay, F.R.H., 'Late-Continued Demesne Farming at Otford', *A.C.* 73, 1959, 116-124

Du Boulay, F.R.H., *The Lordship of Canterbury: an essay in Medieval Society*, 1966

Ede, Chuter, Diaries, unpub. BL

Eliot, George, *Letters*, ed. Gordon C. Haight, 1954-6

English Nature, *Landscape Profile: the North Downs*, 1998

English Nature, *Landscape Profile: the Greensands*, 1999

Evelyn, J., *Sylva, or a Discourse of Forest Trees*, 1664 and later edns

Evelyn, J., *Preface to John Aubrey*, 1718-19

Evelyn, J., *Diary* (ed. Dobson), 1906

Evelyn, J., *Memoires for my Grandson*, ed. G. Keynes, 1926

Everitt, A.M., 'The Making of the Agrarian Landscape Of Kent', *A.C.* 92, 1976, 1-31

Everitt, A.M., *Continuity and Colonization: the Evolution of Kentish Settlement*, 1986

Fagg, C.C. and Hutchings, G.E., *An Introduction to Regional Surveying*, 1930

Ford, Ford Madox, *Simple Life Limited*, 1909

Fordham, Montague, *Mother Earth*, 1908

Forster, E.M., *The Longest Journey* (1924 edn)

Forster, E.M., *Abinger Harvest*, 1936

Forster, E.M., *Two Cheers for Democracy*, 1951

Gage, John, *J.M.W. Turner: a Wonderful Range of Mind*, 1987

Gallois, R.W., *British Regional Geology: the Wealden District*, 1965

Garnett, Edward, *The Imagined World*, 1898

Gibbard, P.L., 'The Formation of the open Strait of Dover' in Preece, R.C. (ed.), *Island Britain: A Quaternary Perspective*, Geol. Soc. Spec. Pub. No. 96, 1995, 1-15

Gillingham, John, *London Review of Books*, November 1983, 19

Glass, Helen, 'Archaeology of the Channel Tunnel Rail Link', *A.C.* 119, 1999, 189-220

Glasscock, R.E., 'The Distribution of Lay Wealth in Kent, Surrey and Sussex', *A.C.* 80, 1965, 61-8

Gosse, E., *More Books on the Table*, 1923

Gray, H.L., *English Field Systems*, 1915

Green, Bryn, 'The Farmed Landscape' in Jenkins, J. (ed.), *Remaking the Landscape*, 2002

Griffiths, A. and Kesnerova, G., *Wenceslaus Hollar: Prints and Drawings*, 1983

Griffin, Carl, 'There was no law to punish that offence: Re-assessing Rebellion in east Kent', *South. Hist.* 22, 2000, 131-65

Haggard, H.R., *Rural England*, 1901-2, 1908

Hall, P., *London 2000*, 1969

Harrison, E.R., *Benjamin Harrison of Ightham*, 1928

Harvey, G., *The Killing of the Countryside*, 1997

Hasted, E., *The History and Topographical Survey of the County of Kent*, 1797-1801, repr. 1972

Heath, Richard, *The English Peasant*, 1898

Heron, Patrick, *Ivon Hitchens*, 1955

Highley, E.E., 'The Economic Geology of the Weald', *Proc. Geol. Assoc.* 86, 1975, 559-69

Hiscock, W.G., *John Evelyn and his Family Circle*, 1955

Howkins, Chris, *Heathland Harvest*, 1997

Huish, M.B., *Birket Foster*, 1890

Huish, M.B., *Happy England as painted by Helen Allingham*, 1892

Hunter, John, *Another Chapter in the Rescue of the London Commons*, 1893

Hunter, John, 'Places of Historic Interest and Natural Beauty', *Nineteenth Century*, XX, 1898

Hutchings, G.E., *The Book of Box Hill*, 1953

Hutchings, G.E., *Landscape Drawing*, 1960

Hutchings, G.E., 'The Hill Farm, Stockbury', Unpub. 1937, Juniper Hall, Dorking

Hutchings, G.E. and Sankey, J.H.P., 'Animal Life of the Chalk Country', *FCS* 4, 1968, 18-27

Huxley, Aldous, *Brave New World*, 1932

Jackson, Alan A., *Semi-detached London*, 2nd edn 1991

Jefferies, Richard, *Nature near London*, 1883

Jekyll, G., *Old West Surrey*, 1904, new edn 1999

Jekyll, G., *Wood and Garden*, 1898

Jenkins, Sir Simon, *England's Thousand Best Churches*, 1999

Jessup, F.W., *A History of Kent*, 1974

Jolliffe, J.E.A., *Pre-Feudal England: the Jutes*, 1933

Kaufman, C.M., *John Varley*, 1984

Keen, M., *Kent Arch. Review* 145, 1986

Kingsley, Charles, 'My Winter Garden' in *Miscellanies*, 1860

Lambarde, W.A., *Perambulation of Kent*, 1576

Lamond, E. (ed.), *Hosbonderie*, 1890

Latham, R.C. and Matthews, W. (eds), *The Diary of Samuel Pepys*, vol. 8, 1974

Lethaby, W.R., *Philip Webb and his Work*, 1979 edn

Lever, R.A., 'John Lawrence's Survey Map of Ashtead, 1638', *LDLHS*, vol. 4, 10, 1986, 275-9

Lister, R. (ed.), *Samuel Palmer and his Etchings*, 1969

Lousley, J.E., *Wildflowers of the Chalk and Limestone*, 1950

Macky, J.A., *Tour through England*, vol. 1, 1732 edn

MacLeod, Michael, *Thomas Hennell*, 1988

Maitland, F.W., *Domesday and Beyond*, 1897

Malcolm, J.A., *Compendium of Modern Husbandry*, 1805

Marchington, T., 'Wartime Defences between Box Hill and Shalford', *LDLHS*, vol. 6, no. 3, 1999, 70-6

Markham, G., *The Inrichment of the Weald of Kent*, 1638 edn

Marshall, W., *The Rural Economy of the Southern Counties*, 1798

Masterman, Charles, *The Heart of the Empire*, 1911

Masterman, Charles, 'From the Abyss' in Lucian Oldershaw (ed.), *England: a Nation*, 1904

Mate, M., 'Agrarian Economy after the Black Death; the Manors of Canterbury Cathedral Priory, 1348-1391', *Econ. Hist. Rev.* 37, 1984, 331-43

Mate, M., 'Pasture Farming in S.E. England', *Agric. Hist. Rev.* 20, 1998

Mate, M., 'Farming Practices and Tecniques in Kent and Sussex' in Thirsk, Joan (ed.), *Agrarian History of England and Wales*, 1990

May, Teresa, 'The Cobham Family in the Administration of England, 1200-1400', *A.C.* 82, 1967, 1-31

Meredith, George, *Letters*, ed. C.L. Clive, 1970

Meredith, George, *The Poetical Works*, ed. G.M. Trevelyan, 1912

Methuen-Campbell, J., *Denton Welch: Writer and Artist*, 2002

Mill, J.S., 'Walking Tour of Sussex', 1827 in *Collected Works*, vol. 27

Mill, J.S., *The Principles of Political Economy*, 1965 edn

Millward, Roy and Robinson, Adrian, *South-East England: the Channel Coastlands*, 1973

Mingay, G., 'The Agriculture of Kent' in Armstrong, A. (ed.), *The Economy of Kent 1640-1914*, 1995, 54-83

Monro, A. (ed.), *The Collected Poems of Harold Monro*, 1933

Muggeridge, M., *Chronicles of Wasted Time: the Green Stick*, 1971

Nairn, Ian and Pevsner, N., *The Buildings of England: Surrey*, 1962 edn

Nevill, R., *Old Cottage and Domestic Architecture in South-West Surrey*, 1889

Newman, John, *The Buildings of England: North East and East Kent*, 1969(a)

Newman, John, *The Buildings of England: West Kent and the Weald*, 1969(b)

Nicolson, Nigel, *Harold Nicolson's Diary and Letters, 1930-64*, 1967

Noyes, Ann, 'The Poll Tax of 1380 for Shere and Gomshall', *Surr. Hist.*, vol. 6, no. 3, 2001, 130-43

Ogley, Bob, *Biggin on the Bump*, 1990

Ogley, Bob, *Doodlebugs and Rockets*, 1992

Ogley, Bob, *Kent at War*, 1994

O'Grady, Sister M., 'Aspects of the Development of the Eastry Estate, 1350-1836', unpub.PhD thesis, National Council for Academic Awards, 1987

Owen, E. and Frost, M., *The Dover Bronze Age Boat Galley*, 2000

Owen, J.A. (ed.), *The Son of the Marshes: on Surrey Hills*, 1891; *With The Woodlanders and the Tide*, 1893; *Forest Tithes*, 1893

Paget, F.E., 'Some Records of the Ashtead Estate and of its Howard Possessors', unpub. 1873

Parfitt, K., 'Neolithic Earthen Long Barrows in east Kent: a Review', *Kent Arch. Rev.*, no. 131, 1998

Parkin, A.M., *On East Hill*, 1998

Parry, Graham, *Hollar's England: a mid-Seventeenth Century view*, 1980

Parton, A.G., 'A Note on the Open Fields of Fetcham and Bookham', *LDLHS*, vol.3, 1967, 25-6

Partridge, Frances, *Memories*, 1980

Peacock, Carlo, *Samuel Palmer: Shoreham and After*, 1968

Pearson, Sarah, 'The Archbishops' Palace at Charing in the Middle Ages', *A.C.* 121, 2001, 315-49

Perey, L., *Un Petit-Neveu du Mazarin*, 1891 edn, 494-5

Philp, Brian, *Excavations in the Darent Valley, Kent*, 1984

Philp, Brian, *The Anglo-Saxon Cemetery at Polhill. 1964-86*, Kent Archaeological Rescue Unit, 1974, 215-20

Philp, Brian, *The Discovery and Excavation of Anglo-Saxon Dover*, 2003

Piggott, Stuart, *Ruins in a Landscape*, 1976

Pitts, M. and Roberts, M., *Fairweather Eden*, 1997

Prestwich, Sir Joseph, 'On the Occurrence of Palaeolithic flint implements in the neighbourhood of Ightham', *Kent. Geol. Journ.* 45, 1869, 127-9

Prestwich, Sir Joseph, 'The Greater Antiquity of Man', *Nineteenth Century*, vol. 37, 1985, 240-56

Pye-Smith, Charlie, *National Trust News Letter*, April 1995

Quested, R.K.I., *The Isle of Thanet: A Farming Community*, Birchington, 2nd edn, 2001

Rankine, W.F., *The Mesolithic of South-East England*, 1956

Rawnsley, Canon, 'A National Benefactor – Sir Robert Hunter', *Cornhill Magazine*, Vol. xlvi, 1915, 349-60

Reynolds, P., *Farming in the Iron Age*, 1976

Rigold, S.E., 'Some Major Kentish Barns', *A.C.* 81, 1978, 1-30

Roake, M. and Whyman, John (eds), *Essays in Kentish History*, 1973

Roberts, Geoffrey, *The Woodlands of Kent*, 1999

Rose, Francis, *The Flora of Hampshire*, 1997

Rose, Francis, 'The Study of Mosses and Liverworts in the region of Juniper Hall, Dorking, Surrey', *FSC* 6, 1982, 180-94

Ruskin, John, *Modern Painters*, 1834-60

Saaller, Mary, 'The Manor of Tillingdown: the Changing Economy, of the Demesne', *Surr. Arch. Coll.* 81, 1991-2, 81-92

Salt, Henry, *The Call of the Wildflower*, 1922

Scruton, Roger, *News from Somewhere*, 2004

Shepheard, Chris and Crocker, Alan, 'Second World War Defences in Surrey' in Cotton *op. cit.*, 2004

Shere, Gomshall and Peaslake Local History Society, *Old Houses in the Parish of Shere*, 1981

Short, B.M., ' South-East England' in Thirsk, Joan (ed.), *The Agrarian History of England and Wales*, 1640-1750, vol. v(i), 1985, 418-37

Shorter, A.H., *Paper Mills and Paper Makers in England, 1475-1800*, 1957

Simond, Louis, *A Journal of a Tour and Residence in Great Britain in 1810*, 1815

Smart, W., *Economic Annals of the Nineteenth Century, 1800-10*, 1910

Smith, A., 'Regional Differences in crop production in Medieval Kent', *A.C.*, 78 1963, 147-60

Smith, R.A.L., *Canterbury Cathedral Priory*, 1943

Smythe, Frank, *The Spirit of the Hills*, 1920

Spain, R.J., 'The Loose Watermills', Part I, *A.C.* 87, 1972, 43-79; Part 2, *A.C.* 88, 1973, 159-81

Stamp, L.D., *The Land of Britain: Kent*, 1943

Stamp, L.D. and Willatts, E.C., *The Land of Britain: Surrey*, 1941

Steer, Francis (ed.), *James Dallaway: Etchings of views in the Vicarage of Leatherhead*, 1975

Stemp, David, *Three Acres and a Cow: the Life and Works of Eli Hamshire*, Cheam, 1995

Stevenson, W., *A General View of the Agriculture of the County of Surrey*, 1809

Stoyel, A.D., 'The Lost Buildings of Otford Palace', *A.C.* 100, 1985, 259-80

Street, G.E., 'On the Probability of certain churches in Kent and Surrey, being of the same Architect', *The Ecclesiologist*, 1850, 49-58

Switzer, S., *Ichnographia Rustica*, 1742 edn

Tatton-Brown, T., 'Three Great Benedictine Houses in Kent: their Buildings and Topography', *A.C.* 100, 1984, 171-88

Tatton-Brown, T., *Kent Archaeological Society Newsletter* 34, 1996

Taylor, Martin I., *St Martin's: The Cradle of English Christianity*, 1997

Thirsk, Joan, *Economic Policy and Production; the Development of a Consumer Society in early Modern England*, Ford Lecture, 1975

Thirsk, Joan, *Alternative Agriculture*, 1997

Thirsk, Joan, in Kenneth Witney (ed.), 'The Survey of the Archbishop Pecham's Manors, 1283-5', *Kent Records*, 2000, xv-xvi

Thomas, D., *London's Green Belt*, 1970

Thomas, Dennis, *Rowland Hilder Country*, 1987

Thomas, Edward, *The Happy-Go-Lucky Morgans*, 1913

Thompson, Flora, *Heatherley*, 1979

Thorne, J., *The Environs of London*, 1844

Titow, J.Z., *Winchester Yields: A study in Medieval Agriculture*, 1972

Topley, W., *The Geology of the Weald*, 1876

Trevelyan, G.M., *Clio, a Muse and other Essays*, 1932

Trotter, W.R., *The Hilltop Writers: A Writers' Colony in Surrey*, 1996

Tupper, Martin, *Proverbial Philosophy*, 1838-67

Tupper, Martin, *Stephen Langton*, 1858

Turner, D.G., 'The Later Middle Ages' in Bird, Joanna and D.G. (eds), *op.cit.*, 223-61

Urry, William, *Canterbury under the Angevin Kings*, 1967

Vardey, Edwina, 'Pre-Raphaelite links with Leatherhead and other parts, of Surrey', *LDLHS*, vol. 5, no. 5, 1992, 138-40

Vera, F.W.M., *Grazing Ecology and Forest History*, 2000

Victoria and Albert Museum, *Richard Redgrave*, 1988

Wallace, Graham, *R.A.F. Biggin Hill*, 1957

Walmsley, R. and Standring, L.C., *The Years of Ferment*, 1980

Walpole, Horace, *The Letters of Horace Walpole*, ed. Peter Cunningham, 1906

Ward, Mrs Humphry, *Robert Elsemere*, 1888

Wheeler, Helen, 'William de Shoreham', *A.C.* 108, 1990, 153-61

White, Revd Gilbert, *The Natural History and Antiquities of Selborne*, 1816 edn

Welch, Denton, *A Voice through a Cloud*, 1950

Wells, H.G., *The War of the Worlds*, 1898

Wells, Roger, 'Popular Protest and Social Crime: the evidence of criminal gangs in rural South England', *South. Hist.* 13, 1991

Whyman, J., 'Water Communications to Margate and Gravesend, as Coastal Resorts before 1840', *South. Hist.* 3, 1981

Willatts, E.C., 'Changes in Land Utilisation in the Southwest of the London Basin, 1840-1932', *Geog. Journ.*, vol. 82, no. 6, 1933

Williams-Ellis, Ammabel, *Headlong Down the Years*, 1938

Williams-Ellis, Clough, *England and the Octopus*, 1928

Williams-Ellis, Clough (ed.), *Britain and the Beast*, 1937

Williams-Ellis, Clough, *Architect Errant*, 1971

Wilton, Andrew, *Turner in his Time*, 1987

Witney, K.P., *The Jutish Forest: A study of the Weald of Kent from 450-1250*, 1976

Wood, Ruth, *Benjamin Williams Leader, R.A.*, 1998

Wooldridge, S.W. and Goldring, J.F., *The Weald*, 1953

Wooldridge, S.W., 'The Understanding of a Piece of Country', *FSC Annual Report*, 1965-6

Wooldridge, S.W. and Hutchings, G.E., *London's Countryside*, 1957

Wormald, Patrick, 'The First Code of English Law', lecture delivered at Canterbury, October 2003

Wymer, J.J., 'The Palaeolithic period' in Bird, Joanna and D.G. (eds), *op. cit.*, pp.12-26

Yates, E.M., 'Settlement Patterns', *FSC* 5, 1964, 31-8

Zarnecki, G., 'Later English Romanesque Sculpture' in *Studies in Christian Art*, ed. D.A. Rubin, 1963

Index

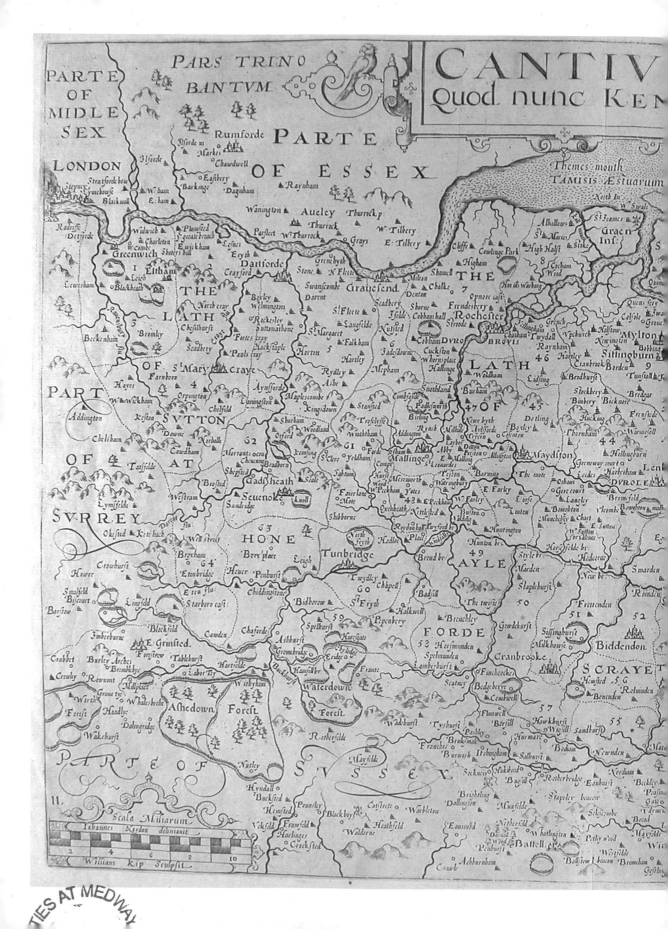